CRYSTAL MIRROR

CRYSTAL MIRROR

Volume V

Through this work, may all reach the
glorious citadel of inner peace.

Crystal Mirror is the journal of the Tibetan Nyingma Meditation Center,
2425 Hillside Avenue, Berkeley, California

Crystal mirror. v. 1–; 1971–
Emeryville, Calif., Dharma Pub.

v. ill. 26 cm. annual.

"Journal of the Tibetan Nyingma Meditation Center."
ISSN 0097-7209

1. Rñiṅ-ma-pa (Sect)–Periodicals. 2. Lamaism–Periodicals.
I. Tibetan Nyingma Meditation Center.

BQ7662.C78 294.3′923′05 75–642463 MARC–S

ISBN: 0-913546-47-x (pbk.)
Typeset in Fototronic Garamond, printed and bound by Dharma Press

"A History of the Buddhist Dharma" was composed by Tarthang Tulku, transcribed by Lawrence Gruber, technically edited by Judith Robertson and Deborah Black.

Photographs on pages 10, 15, 31, 35, 48, 49, 51, 53 (top left), 91, 119, 122–123 courtesy of John and Susan Huntington

Art on pages 2, 83, 84, 98, 99, 101, 102, 112–115, 138, 147, 148, 155, 209, 210, 212, 229, 230, 251, 259, 260, 261, 262, 266, 267, 268, 269, 270, 271, 272, 273, 274, 276, 278, 280, 282, 284, 290, 291, 292, 296, 297, 298, 299, 300, 301, 302, 303, 304, 305, 306, 307 directed by Tarthang Tulku, implemented by Rosalyn White

Art on pages 275, 277, 279, 281, 283, 285, 286 directed by Tarthang Tulku, implemented by George Omura and Rosalyn White

Frontispiece: Amitāyus, the Buddha of Infinite Life, courtesy of the Asian Art Museum of San Francisco, The Avery Brundage Collection

A Word from Tarthang Tulku

DURING THE PAST EIGHT YEARS while in America, I have met many students and professionals in various fields who have expressed an interest in pursuing the Buddhist path. Although American students seem eager to study, both students and scholars alike often tend to emphasize aspects of the teachings which, in the long run, are not of much practical use in life. Many times, there is more concern with external words and definitions than with inner meanings. Although a selective understanding of words and concepts may sometimes bring valuable insights, this form of learning seldom leads to an enlightened mind.

The teachings of the Buddha are not simply an assemblage of facts which can be obtained from books. The Buddhadharma is a dynamic tradition which finds its real meaning and value only when directly applied and integrated into one's life experience. The varied styles of expression of the Buddha's teachings are uniquely suited for different types of individuals who wish to pursue the Buddhist path. These living qualities of the teachings can be seen through the transformations Buddhism has undergone throughout the centuries–from the earliest Āgamas, to the Sūtras and Śāstras, and later to Tibetan commentaries and original treatises, as well as to the precious teachings of the bKa'-ma and gTer-ma.

The field of Buddhist studies is so expansive and the various philosophical lines are so numerous that students may not know where to begin. The emphasis of this volume of *Crystal Mirror* is on providing the student with some basic information as a kind of foundation for future studies and practice. It is offered as an introduction to those areas of Buddhist history and philosophical development which are principal factors leading to a general understanding of Tibetan Buddhism. Most of the materials presented here come from the teachings of my gurus, from various traditional texts which I consulted, and from research with my students. I hope that this volume encourages both students and academic professionals to vigorously pursue their explorations of Buddhist studies, with an openness to the vast scope of meaning which this Oral-tradition has preserved and unfolded.

So far in America, the wealth of knowledge represented by the heritage of Tibetan Buddhism and its complex and intertwining lineages of transmission has hardly been tapped. We are now fortunate to have a few translators who are beginning to uncover this treasure house of knowledge and practical insights–but this is only the beginning. There is so much more to be explored. The rNying-ma-pa in particular have preserved innumerable teachings, which directly penetrate the nature of reality by providing practical methods for living a healthy and balanced life. As we begin to discover the depth of the contributions which have been made by numerous great lamas throughout history, we cannot but begin to appreciate the beauty and richness of the rNying-ma tradition.

I believe it is in the *Sandhinirmocana-sūtra* that the Buddha made a prophecy that twenty-five hundred years after the Parinirvāṇa, the Buddhadharma would spread to the land of the red-faced people. Many of the early Tibetans placed the birth of the Buddha at a time much earlier than what is commonly accepted today; because of this difference in dating, many took this prophecy to mean that the "country of the red-faced" referred to Tibet. Actually, twenty-five hundred years after the Parinirvāṇa would place this prophecy around the end of the twentieth century, and the red-faced people could, therefore, refer to the original natives of this country, the American Indians. If we have confidence in the Buddha's prophecy, it means that the Dharma may have a successful future here in America. The openness of the American mind to Buddhist attitudes and principles makes this reading of the prophecy hopeful—yet there is so much work ahead. Right now we are only at the beginning, and it is in this spirit that the material here is presented.

If the Buddhadharma is to grow in America, thus insuring its preservation, it must be both studied and practiced within a traditional lineage. To do so, building Buddhist monasteries and communities is important, but they are only the outward face of the Buddhadharma. In order to develop the necessary foundation to sustain one's efforts on the path, a serious student needs to develop a commitment to a teacher who holds a traditional lineage. Unless these lineages are carried on, the Dharma will continue to enter America only as fragments of information which are not of much use to those who wish to actually practice the teachings. If the continuity of the lineage is broken because of the disappearance of qualified teachers, or because one's relationship with such teachers is not nurtured and maintained, the preservation of the lineage of the Oral-transmission cannot be insured. If this becomes the case, the Dharma will essentially become only an intellectual curiosity for the scholar or a 'phase' in an American student's life, in his search for spiritual fulfillment.

I would like to dedicate this volume of *Crystal Mirror* as an aid and an inspiration to those who wish to share in the rich and vast teachings of the Buddhadharma. And I would like to thank those who have contributed articles to this volume, especially to Dr. Guenther, who has provided us with a beautiful translation of Klong-chen-pa's final work.

Sarvam Mangalam,

Tarthang Tulku, Rinpoche
Head Lama of the Tibetan
Nyingma Meditation Center

CRYSTAL MIRROR

Volume V

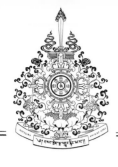

CRYSTAL MIRROR

Śākyamuni Buddha

A History of the Buddhist Dharma

Tarthang Tulku

THE MATERIAL PRESENTED in the following sections is intended to introduce the general reader to many of the facets of the philosophy and literature of the Buddhist tradition. As Buddhism developed in India, emphasis was placed on the Vinaya, Sūtras, Śāstras, Abhidharma, Prajñāpāramitā, Mādhyamika, Yogācāra, and logic. When the Dharma found new roots in Tibet, the scope of understanding the Buddha's teachings was expanded to include the teachings of the Tantras, with their emphasis on direct experience.

Though the teachings of the Enlightened Ones represent universal truth, there are many ways of interpreting the Dharma. Due to the varying levels of understanding and the cultural influences in the areas where Buddhism developed, a number of different schools arose in India, Tibet, China, Japan, and Southeast Asia. These divisions simply reflect an on-going attempt to find the most effective methods for traversing the path and arriving at the goal, as prescribed by the Buddha.

According to the methods of the Sūtras, the enlightenment path is exceedingly long and one attains realization only after countless lives devoted to arduous practice and mindful observation of the Buddha's teachings. But according to the Vajrayāna Tantras, one may attain Buddhahood in this lifetime and in this very body. Although the goal of the Sūtras and Tantras is the same, the path of the Tantras is more direct, opening to the practitioner many methods which are intended to bring swift results.

Yet, the idea and experience of Buddhahood cannot be encompassed by any set of doctrines, as its reach and range of enlightenment principles surpasses the limitations set forth by any structure. The teachings of the Tathāgatas go beyond the spacial-temporal sphere, and the collection of these teachings which have arisen in this world is a mere fraction of those which exist within the extratemporal sphere. Therefore, the limited range of an historical perspective can not account for the multi-dimensional range of 'universal Buddhahood', which occurs beyond the Life-world of Man. There are innumerable instances in the Buddhist literature in which the inspiration of a representation of the non-human sphere of pure spirituality becomes actualized in the mind of the human disciple, as in the case of revelation. Thus, the human disciple becomes the 'incarnation' (*sprul-pa*) of a higher reality.

In the case of the Ādi-buddha, Kun-tu bzang-po—the primogenitor of all Buddhas past, present, and future—this higher reality is beyond words or concepts, spaciality or temporality, and is not subject to cause and effect. In order for these enlightenment principles—the expression of this higher reality being the Dharmakāya—to be cognized by man, it must first be transferred into apprehendable symbols or patterns. These in turn form the cognizable spectra of being-made-manifest, first in the Sambhogakāya with the Five Tathāgatas, and then extending to the world of man by means of the Bodhisattvas and incarnations. Each of these Vidyādhāras, or Bearers of Pure Awareness (*ye-shes*), are bringing to the Human-tradition that particular facet of Being intelligible to the individual to whom it manifests. Just how a particular facet of Being-made-manifest is presented to an individual depends upon the level of his or her intelligence and the range of his or her experience. These various understandings of the path toward Buddhahood eventually developed into the different spiritual courses.

As Buddhism spread into Tibet, the paths and schools which had developed in India continued and flourished, at the same time that ever deeper levels of understanding the Buddhadharma unfolded. The transference of the Buddhadharma from India to Tibet was particularly auspicious for a number of reasons. Indian Buddhism in the ninth century was already showing signs of weakening and the lineage of Oral-transmission and deep meditative realization required a receptive environment in which to be preserved. So, the Indian masters like Śāntarakṣita and Vimalamitra were anxious to see the Dharma prosper in Tibet.

From the time of Śāntarakṣita and Padmasambhava, with the full support of King Khri-srong-lde'u-btsan, the Tibetans energetically carried on the study and practice of the Sūtras, Śāstras, and Tantras. The early Tibetan Vinaya provided a valuable set of guidelines and standards of self-discipline which aided in maintaining the harmony and integrity of a growing community of Dharma practitioners. The attitude of the Tibetan disciples was exemplary, for they were more than willing to dedicate their entire lives to the preservation of the Buddha's teachings. These early disciples and translators were not simply learned scholars, they were incarnations of great Bodhisattvas, endowed with the capabilities to directly perceive and communicate the inner meaning of the Buddha's teachings. In addition, these masters received assistance from scores of Paṇḍitas who had come from India to further the direct Oral-transmission of the teachings. Therefore, the translations occurring during this period are closer to the spirit of the original texts than those translations performed at a later time. The early rNying-ma masters, such as Khri-srong-lde'u-btsan, Ye-shes mTsho-rgyal, Vairocana, sKa-ba dPal-brtsegs, Cog-ro-lku'i rGyal-mtshan, Ye-shes-sde, rMa Rin-chen-mchog, Sangs-rgyas gSang-ba, and gYu-sgra sNying-po, thus played invaluable roles in the preservation and transmission of the Buddhadharma.

The short summaries presented here of some of the principal philosophical schools and their transmission lineages from India to Tibet may afford a taste of the vastness of the Buddhadharma. As a basic guideline to aid students in their future research, this volume neither compares and contrasts the differing scholarly opinions about the historical and philosophical developments of Buddhism, nor does it purport to bear a traditional or decisive point of view. This is simply an introduction to acquaint the Western reader with the basic foundation of these teachings of the Buddhadharma. There is a definite need in the future for a comprehensive investigation in these topics which would aim at greater accuracy and depth of presentation.

The Early Development of Buddhism in India

The Life of the Buddha

Within the seemingly unending process of becoming in which eternity takes on the atmosphere of time, there appears a chain of aeons or *kalpas*.* Within each *kalpa* there appear different cyclic ages or *yugas*. These begin during a time when the sentient beings live exceedingly long lives (of 80,000 years) and end when the life-span is less than ten years. In the *kalpas* preceeding our own, the appearance of Buddhas was not required, since the aversion to worldly existence was not yet great. During our present *kalpa*, which is known as the Fortunate Aeon (*bskal-pa-bzang-po*, *bhadra-kalpa*), one thousand fully accomplished Buddhas have already come into existence or are yet to appear. During this present age, marked by increased corruption, materially-dependent existences, and reduced lifespans, the Dharma can be practiced because of the imminence of old age and death. But following this age will be a period of complete degeneration, when the Buddhas will again cease to appear. That period will be characterized by five predominant features: further reduction in the lifespan, exceedingly corrupt actions, a predominance of the passions, incorrect views, and gloominess.

During this present world-cycle known as the Kali Yuga, the number of Buddhas that have already appeared or will appear is seven. Śākyamuni (Shākya-thub-pa), the historical Buddha (b. 566 B.C.), is the fourth, and Maitreya (Byams-pa), the coming Buddha, will be the fifth. These Buddhas voluntarily endure, throughout myriads of ages and numberless rebirths, whatever hardships may come in the process of helping living beings. Śākyamuni Buddha, born into this world,

---

*In the Brahman tradition, a *kalpa* is said to be 4.32×10^9 years. However, in the Buddhist tradition, the *kalpas*, though exceedingly long, are not of equal duration.

repeatedly demonstrates the practice of the Ten Pāramitās,* as a guide to the enlightenment of every individual.

The life of the Buddha includes twelve significant stages:

1. The resolve to be born in the world of man
2. The descent from Tuṣita Heaven
3. Entering the mother's womb
4. Physical birth
5. Accomplishment in worldly arts
6. A life of pleasure
7. The departure from the palace
8. Ascetic exercises
9. The conquest of Māra
10. Becoming a Buddha
11. Promulgating the teaching
12. Passing into Nirvāṇa

The resolve to be born into the world of man. Before the birth of the Buddha, a certain group of Devaputras† assumed the forms of Brahmins residing on Jambudvīpa.‡ They prophesied to the Pratyeka-buddhas that twelve years hence a Bodhisattva would be born who was endowed with the thirty-two marks of a Mahāpuruṣa (Great Man). He would become either a universal monarch or a Buddha, and would be known as Śākyamuni. The Bodhisattva, residing in Tuṣita Heaven, overhearing these words of the Brahmins, became engaged in four kinds of contemplation: that his future life would span less than one-hundred years; that Jambudvīpa was to be the continent in which he would appear; that central India was to be the country where he would be born; and that his caste was to be of the Kṣatriya (rGyal-rigs).

The descent from Tuṣita Heaven. The Bodhisattva then ascended the throne, which was bedecked with garlands of flowers and redolent with varied perfumes and burning incenses. Delivering his last sermon to the countless myriads of Bodhisattvas in Tuṣita Heaven, he

*The Ten Pāramitās (highest aims of the Bodhisattva) are: generosity, ethics and manners, patience, energy-vigor, concentration, discriminating understanding, honesty, resoluteness, compassion, and equanimity. In later times, these ten were reduced to the conventional six.

†*Devas*, or gods abiding in the pure regions

‡The Indian or Southern continent

The Dream of Queen Māyā A second century B.C. sandstone medallion from a railing post in Bharut in which the Blessed One, as an elephant, enters the sleeping queen from above.

placed his crown of precious jewels on the head of Maitreya, the coming Buddha, and made his departure for Jambudvīpa. The Bodhisattva Maitreya would now be the expounder of the Dharma to the Bodhisattvas and Devas residing in the Realm of the Thirty-three.

Entering the mother's womb. In the palace of King Śuddhodana, in the city of Kapilavāstu in northern India, there appeared eighteen miraculous signs foretelling the birth of the Buddha. During this time, when Queen Māyā was observing the Posadha fast, she had a dream that the Blessed One entered her womb through her right side, in the form of a white elephant. At that very moment, the Bodhisattva descended and the earth trembled six times as witness. Upon asking the Brahmins

The Birth of the Buddha A ninth century relief sculpture near Lumbinī, the birthplace of the Bodhisattva.

the meaning of this dream, Queen Māyā was told that a son endowed with exceptional properties was to be born to her. If he were to choose to reside in the royal palace, he would become a universal monarch, and, if he were to lead a homeless life, he would attain the state of a Buddha.

Physical birth. As the mother-to-be was strolling through the Lumbinī Garden, she reached up to the limb of a fig-tree; at that moment the Bodhisattva emerged painlessly from her right side. Immediately after his birth, the Bodhisattva took seven steps and wherever his foot touched the ground, lotuses sprouted forth. The earth became filled with innumerable jewels, flowers, and garlands, precious ornaments showered from the clouds and a resplendent light spread through all the regions of the earth. The Blessed One, born like a great physician, then announced in a clear voice that this would be his last birth.

Seven days after his birth, Queen Māyā died of a broken heart, realizing that the newly named Prince Siddhārtha (lit., "he whose aim is accomplished") was fated to lead a homeless life and take on the sorrows of the world. When the prince was still very young, a sage by the name of Asita (Nag-po), who was endowed with five supernatural faculties (*mgon-shes, abhijñā*), came to the city of Kapilavāstu and perfectly identified on the body of the Bodhisattva the thirty-two marks and eighty subsidiary characteristics of a Mahāpuruṣa. He then affirmed the previous declaration by the Brahmins that if this prince remained at home he would become a universal monarch, but if he departed to lead a homeless life, he would attain enlightenment in this world.

As the prince grew older, he followed the usual custom and joined the other youths of the Śākya clan in school. But as an example to them, he demonstrated full mastery of writing and calculation, of science and art, thus showing that he was already the receptacle of all worldly knowledge.

Accomplishment in worldly arts. King Śuddhodana, upon being reminded by the council of elders about the prophecy of the sage, ordered the nobility to find a maiden suitable for the prince to marry. He hoped that in this way the prince would so enjoy life that he would not think of retiring from the kingdom and thus bringing the Imperial Śākya lineage to an end. However, not desiring a life of sensual pleasure, the prince wrote down a list of all the virtuous qualities that would have to be met by such a wife: she must be of royalty or the daughter of a Brahmin; she must not be of the Vaiśya or Sūdra caste; and she must be possessed with virtue, truthfulness, and righteousness.

Within seven days, a number of suitable maidens were found. Among them was Gopā (Sa-'tsho-ma), who was possessed of all the qualities the prince described. To each of the maidens he offered a bouquet, but to Gopā, who arrived last, he offered a priceless ring to indicate his choice of her, as this was the custom. But before Gopā's father would relinquish his daughter to the prince, he required him to demonstrate his skill and physical prowess.

So, a tournament was held in which five-hundred youths of the

Śākya clan were assembled. At that time an elephant happened to stray into the midst of the tournament, and Devadatta, the Prince's cousin, enraged and strengthened by his envy of the prince, gave the elephant one great blow, and the beast fell dead. Then the Bodhisattva, seeing the elephant carcass, lifted it with his great toe and hurled the carcass across the seven great walls and cast it well into the outskirts of the city. Prince Siddhārtha then proceeded to outperform all the other contestants in the numerous feats of skill. Upon seeing this, the father of Gopā joyfully gave his daughter's hand in marriage to the prince.

A life of pleasure. Prince Siddhārtha, in order to act in accordance with worldly custom, crowned Gopā as the chief princess; in the company of her maidens, they led a life of pleasure. In observing these activities, several deities came before the Bodhisattva and exhorted him to remember the vow which he had made in his former life to aid all sentient beings.

Meanwhile, King Śuddhodana, who had had a dream that foretold the departure of the prince from his kingdom, provided his son with even greater pleasures–including a luxurious palace with 30,000 maidens in attendance, where no other man was allowed. But as the prince listened to the music played by the noble maidens, he heard the words of past Buddhas, hidden within the sounds: "O pure and noble hero, recall to mind your resolution for the good of the earth. This is the time; this is the moment; this is the opportunity. Issue forth from this pleasure mansion, O noble Ṛṣi."

Now, Siddhārtha was such a delicately nurtured youth that he had never been allowed to see any sign of suffering. But it happened one day that the prince ordered his charioteer to take him for a drive outside the palace walls. On the journey he observed a man suffering from old age, and the charioteer explained to him that all of us must one day grow old and suffer, due to the frailty of the body. He then saw a man stricken with an incurable disease–emaciated, weak, and with his faculties impaired. So the charioteer explained to the Prince the nature of sickness. A little later they came upon a procession bearing a corpse, and the charioteer explained to the Bodhisattva that death must eventually come to all of us. On yet another occasion the prince met a *deva* of a pure realm who assumed the appearance of a mendicant monk. This Bhikṣu, bearing an alms-bowl and clad in an ochre robe, was standing calm, quite, and self-possessed. He was leading a life of strict discipline, and embracing the spiritual path. Having been deeply affected by what he saw, the prince ordered the charioteer to swiftly return to the palace.

The departure from the palace. Although the king offered Siddhārtha every sensuous pleasure that his kingdom could supply, he was unsuccessful at keeping the Bodhisattva in his royal captivity. At that time, there appeared certain signs foretelling the Bodhisattva's inevitable departure, and the king himself was deeply distressed that the high glory of the Śākya race would soon decline. So, the prince agreed that if the king could grant him four wishes, he would stay and rule the kingdom, without entertaining another thought of leaving. The prince's first wish was that old age would never assail him and that he would retain his youthful radiance forever. His second request was that he would remain in perpetual health and that no disease would ever attack him. Thirdly, he asked that he be made immortal so that death would never haunt him. And finally, he requested that he would always be abundantly wealthy and never be subject to any misfortune.

King Śuddhodana pleaded powerlessness to grant his son any of the difficult boons he requested. Thereupon, the Bodhisattva characterized the round of life as a play, which goes on from the infinite past, deceiving, entangling, and destroying. He reflected on his life of unending pleasure in the palace, and no longer viewed it as attractive or desirable.

At that moment, King Śuddhodana, having heard that Gopā had brought forth a son, sent a messenger to announce the glad news to Prince Siddhārtha. On hearing the message, the Bodhisattva said, "An impediment and fetter (*rāhula*) has been born to me this day." When the messenger reported to the king what the prince had said, he replied, "My grandson's name will be Prince Rāhula."

Observing the life of the harem of women, the prince grew ever more conscious that his pleasure-dwelling was actually an immersion into the darkness of delusion. He was like a bird in a cage who could never fly free. Oppressed by the sorrows and tribulations of what he saw, he cast off his garments and ornaments of royalty and went forth from home, clothing himself in the ochre robe of an ascetic.

Ascetic exercises. The Bodhisattva first sought instruction from two learned sages, Ārāḍa-kālama and Udraka Rāmaputra, but he found their teaching incomplete as they did not reveal the origin of and path leading to the elimination of suffering. So he spent the next six years observing rigid ascetic practices; feeding on three grains of rice per meal and practicing the suspension of breath. During this time he was joined by five other ascetics, who looked upon him with respect and adoration. But as time passed, and he became increasingly emaciated, the thirty-two marks of a Buddha disappeared from his body, and he realized that the practice of austerities is like endeavoring to tie the air into knots—it is not possible to attain the highest aim through asceticism alone. So the former prince left the woods which were near the bank of the Nairañjanā River, and went to Uruvelā, in order to take more substantial food.

In Uruvelā, there was a young woman named Sujātā. Upon seeing the Bodhisattva sitting under a banyan-tree, she mistook him for a deity of the tree who had come to receive offerings. So, she prepared a dish of rice-milk for the Bodhisattva, and perceiving that he was a Mahāpuruṣa, she made obeisance to him. Taking the dish of rice-milk with him, he returned to the Nairañjanā River. When his ascetic companions saw that he was eating, they became disgusted at what they viewed as his self-indulgent reversion to luxury, and decided to have nothing more to do with him.

The conquest of Māra. After bathing in the Nairañjanā River, the Bodhisattva dressed himself in the garments of a Buddha and then took his noon-day meal of rice-milk. His thirty-two marks of a Mahāpuruṣa reappeared, and he vowed to take no further nourishment until the end of forty-nine days. Full of strength, and with superhuman vitality, the Bodhisattva set off toward the Bodhi tree in order to vanquish Māra. On his way, he met a grass-cutter who gave him eight handfuls of grass which would serve as a seat. Upon taking his seat on this tuft of grass underneath the Bodhi tree, he vowed that he would not arise without having first attained enlightenment, even though his body were to wither away. Thereupon, the future Buddha caused a light to issue forth from his body—a light which was seen throughout the innumerable regions of the heavens. He then sent a beam of light to penetrate the abode of Māra, the Lord of Emotionality and Illusion, announcing to him that he was ready to engage in full battle. Māra relayed the news to his army, and as the hideous horde shouted its war-cry, Māra's frightful parade came on like a flood.

Carrying swords, arrows, hatchets, and knives, they advanced against the Lion of Enlightenment. Serpents stretched out their venom-

---

Vajrasāna, beneath the Bodhi Tree This third century slab marks the place where the Bodhisattva attained enlightenment under the Bodhi tree at Bodh Gaya. The Bodhi tree, the roots and leaves of which can be seen to the left of the seat, is an ancestor of the original Bodhi tree.

ous fangs, and distorted creatures wielded firebrands. But the Bodhisattva paid no heed to the approaching torrents of wrathful forms and sensuous snares which Māra was conjuring by his magic. Unmoved by this display, the Bodhisattva became more and more deeply endowed with an all-pervading and quiescent mind. Thereupon, Māra sent forth flaming, razor-sharp missiles. But as they approached the future Buddha, they were transformed into celestial bouquets of flowers.

Once again Māra appeared, accompanied by his daughters, who manifested themselves as ravishing young maidens. But upon sight of them, the Buddha-to-be saw only manifestations of hoary-headed old women, who were bent like rafters and leaning on walking sticks. The Bodhisattva could not be seduced by any temptation that Māra could devise.

The Bodhisattva then asserted to Māra that the seat which future Buddhas had always used on the day of their complete enlightenment belonged to him. At that, Māra wished to know who was witness to that fact, and the Bodhisattva replied, "The earth goddess is my witness." As he said this, he touched the earth with his right hand, and it tremored six times. Then the earth goddess, Sthāvarā, appeared and said, "Oh Highest of Beings, you alone are the one who will achieve the highest accomplishment; no one else on this earth has achieved it before. What you have said is perfectly true." Upon hearing this, Māra and his army fled like jackals hearing the lion's roar in the forest, with their hearts full of fear and resentment, they dispersed in confusion.

Becoming a Buddha. After the Blessed One had vanquished the army of Māra during the first watch of the night, the Bodhisattva continued to sit in solitude under the Bodhi tree. During the second watch he became absorbed in the four degrees of meditation (*bsam-gtan, dhyāna*), which induce perfect mindfulness and equanimity. He then obtained the three kinds of highest knowledge, which allowed him to recall his countless past lives, the lives of all the Buddhas who had come before him, and the coming and going of endless living forms in the constant round of rebirths.

Then, during the third watch, just before sunrise, the impermanence and conditional nature of all existence unfolded before his mind. Thus, he became fearless and undismayed. His mind began to

---

The Mahābodhi Temple at Bodh Gaya The many temples and stūpas at Bodh Gaya were built at various times over many centuries. The topmost section of the main temple was constructed by Nāgārjuna.

demonstrate the perfect Buddha quality of the extinction of all craving and desire, like a fire that goes out for lack of fuel.

As dawn began to break, there was the beating of countless drums, signifying that the Buddha had attained full Enlightenment. At that moment, flowers rained from the heavens, the world grew full of light, and the earth trembled seven times. All the Buddhas of the Ten Directions made obeisance to him, as he continued to sit at the foot of the Bodhi tree.

Śākyamuni had attained the unimaginable qualities of a Buddha: he had become the manifestation of the perfectly pure absolute nature, his equaniminity in action for the benfit of himself and others showed his altruistic transcending knowledge, and he combined the utmost concern for the welfare of all sentient beings with the discriminating qualities of the enlightened mind.

For seven days the Enlightened One contemplated the meaning of his discovery. Then a great storm arose out of season, pouring forth rain, cold winds, and gloom for seven days. The Nāga King Mucilinda came out of his realm and wrapped the Blessed One's body seven times in his coils and spread his great hood out above the Buddha's head until the storm had subsided.

At the end of forty-nine days two merchants, Trapusa and Bhallika, visited the Blessed One who was residing at the root of the Rājāyatana tree. They honored him with an offering of rice cake and honey; thus the Buddha broke his forty-nine day fast.

Promulgating the teachings. Having cognized the profound truth, intelligible only to the wise, the Buddha thought it impossible to demonstrate to others the nature of his attainment. But the great Brahmā Sahampatī descended from heaven and exhorted him to expound the Dharma to those whose minds were open. So the Buddha, out of his unlimited compassion, surveyed the world with his omnipotent insight and saw the varying qualities and faculties of beings. He found many who were capable of comprehending the Dharma, so he decided to journey to the Deer Park at Ṛṣipatana in Benares and there he set the Wheel of the Dharma into motion. At this, the heavens roared; the road to Benares was draped with festoons of fine cloth, made fragrant with incense, scattered with heaps of flowers, and bedecked with necklaces of pearls. Beside the road appeared fragrant celestial streams, covered with red and white lotuses and shaded by

Dhamekh Stūpa, Sarnath This Stūpa marks the place where the Buddha first turned the Wheel of the Dharma.

mango, rose-apple, coconut, and pomegranate trees. Countless *devas* joined the Blessed One, and with great pomp and majesty, the procession grew into the thousands, including warriors on elephants, cavalry, charioteers, and infantry.

Upon approaching the river Ganges, the Buddha asked the ferryman to take him across, but as he had no fare, the ferryman refused. So the Buddha levitated into the air and passed over the river like a king of swans.

After his arrival at Benares, the Buddha collected alms, took his meal, and then proceeded to Ṛṣipatana. There he came upon his five former companions, who had left him because he had slackened in his austerities. Seeing now that he had reached the final goal, they felt ill at ease and rose up to meet him like birds whose nests are burning beneath them. The Buddha then ordained this band of five as his first disciples.

At the place where the Buddha was to set the Wheel of the Dharma into motion, there appeared one thousand seats, symbolizing the one-thousand Buddhas of this Fortunate Aeon. Each seat was made of the seven kinds of jewels, symbolizing the seven Buddhas who would appear during this world cycle. Circumambulating the seats which had belonged to the three previous Buddhas, he seated himself on the fourth. Then a light issued from his body, illuminating the 3,000 thousand worlds. The earth trembled and the deities presented him with a golden wheel of one-thousand spokes and implored him to turn the Wheel of the Dharma. With this gesture, the Blessed One proceeded to set forth his teachings which can lead all beings to liberation.

In this First Turning of the Wheel of the Dharma, the Buddha expounded his teachings of the Middle Way, declaring the Four Noble Truths and the Eight-fold Path to Enlightenment. The First Turning continued for seven years, beginning with the first sermon in Benares to his first five disciples.

The Second Turning of the Wheel of the Dharma was initiated at Vulture Peak. There the Blessed One taught such subjects as the Doctrine of Openness and the Prajñāpāramitā to five thousand monks, nuns, and laity, and to innumerable Bodhisattvas. After the Second Turning had gone on for a number of years, the Third Turning, the more subtle aspects of the Buddha's teachings, such as the nature of absolute Reality, was delivered in various places throughout India.

During his life, the Buddha visited Urubilvā, Rājagṛha, Kapilavāstu, Vaiśālī, and Kuśīnagara. It was during the Buddha's first visit to Rājagṛha that the first two great disciples of the Buddha appeared—Śāriputra and Maudgalyāyana. Ānanda, Upāli, and other principal disciples also joined him in these early days, and soon the Buddhist Saṅgha began to grow substantially.

At Rājagṛha, on an occasion when the Blessed One was out gathering alms, his former wife Gopā, saw him and had the desire of winning him back. Thus, she gave to her son, Rāhula, a special charm and told him to present it to his father. When the child came near to the place the Buddha was teaching there suddenly appeared five hundred Buddhas. But Rāhula recognized his father among them all, and gave him the charm. Śākyamuni returned the charm to his son, and he swallowed it, whereafter he could not be prevented from following the path of his father. Seeing that this was his son's last birth, the Buddha told Śāriputra to admit the child into the order, even though he was only six years old. Eventually, Gopā entered the order as a nun, and Rāhula became a foremost disciple.

Passing into Nirvāṇa. During the rainy season of his eightieth year, the Buddha contracted a fatal illness. Accepting this with self-possession, he called the venerable Ānanda, who took a seat respectfully on one side of the Blessed One. The Buddha explained to Ānanda that he had reached the sum of his days and had become like a worn-out cart. He then spoke to Ānanda on the meaning of taking refuge.

Shortly thereafter, the Buddha gave his last major lecture to his disciples, which is called the "Thirty-seven Wings of Enlightenment." Having delivered his teachings to the assembly, the Enlightened One departed in the direction of Vaiśālī. As he instructed the monks in the Three Trainings (*śīla, samādhi,* and *prajñā*), the earth trembled as a sign that he would soon pass away into final Nirvāṇa (Parinirvāṇa).

The Nirvāṇa Chitaya This Stūpa in Kuśīnagara commemorates the site of Lord Buddha's Parinirvāṇa.

The Buddha then went to Kuśīnagara and had a seat erected between two *sāla* trees. With his back to the north, he then lay down on his right side. As he was about to pass away into Nirvāṇa, he gave his last precepts to his disciplies such as his instructions on mindfulness, and the Three Marks of Existence (*anitya, anātman*, and *duḥkha*). Upon completing these last utterances, he became absorbed in four degrees of meditation, each time experiencing the peak of ecstasy and then culminating into the supreme and ineffable state of final Nirvāṇa. Immediately thereafter, the earth trembled, the stars shot from the heavens, and in the ten quarters of the sky there burst forth flames and the sounds of celestial music.

Qualities of the Buddha

The teachings that Śākyamuni transmitted were as profound and all-encompassing as was the enlightenment he attained under the Bodhi Tree. The transcending awareness and inexhaustive energy of enlightenment manifested itself in numerous qualities which distinguished his status as the Buddha—qualities that cover the full scope of human experience. Eight of the most important of these are:

1. IMMUTABILITY (*'dus ma-byas-pa-nyid, asaṃskṛttatva*) or unconditionedness. The Buddha is incapable of falling into the realm of Sāṃsaric existence, and his experience of Buddhahood has no beginning, middle, or end.

2. EFFORTLESSNESS (*lhun-gyis-grub-pa, anābhogatā*) because all dualitistic views (*spros-pa, prapañca*) and dualistic notions (*rnam-par rtog-pa, vikalpa*) have been eliminated.

3. ENLIGHTENMENT THAT IS SELF-SUSTAINING AND NOT DEPENDENT UPON OTHERS (*gzhan-gyi rkyen-gyis mngon-par rtogs-pa ma-yin-pa, aparapartyāyā-bhisaṃbodhi*). The Tathāgata, in being immutable, proceeds without effort to enlighten others from a beginningless past to an indeterminable future.

4. SELF-BORN AWARENESS (*ye-shes, jñāna*) which is able to comprehend all factors leading to Enlightenment.

5. COMPASSION (*thugs-rje, karuṇā*) that is exemplified in a Buddha's mastery of leading sentient beings toward enlightenment.

6. SUPERNORMAL POWER (*nus-pa, śakti*) which unites wisdom and compassion.

7. FULFILLMENT OF SELF-BENEFIT (*rang-gi don phun-sum-tshogs-pa, svārthasaṃpatti*), the basis of the Buddha's own Enlightenment, which is connected with the first three aspects above.

8. FULFILLMENT OF BENEFIT FOR OTHERS (*gzhan-gyi don plun-sum-tshogs-pa, parārthasaṃpatti*), the basis for setting the Wheel of the Dharma* into motion, which is connected with the second three aspects above.

The Thirty-seven Wings of Enlightenment

All of the teachings which the Buddha expounded were for the sake of leading beings out of the experience of recurring frustration into the open dimension of genuine freedom. As the practice of Buddhism developed, the Buddha's various teachings were categorized under specific topics in order to make them more accessible and memorable. But the various categories were also seen as a dynamic, interwoven pattern which precisely expressed the path to liberation. In

---

*The fathomless aspects of the Buddha's teaching, generally referred to as the Dharma, are suggested by the numerous meanings of the word *dharma* itself, which include:

1. Any element of existence, or any observable fact
2. The Buddhist Path (knowledge-in-action)
3. The experience of enlightenment
4. Any non-sensuous object of the mind
5. Any wholesome thought or action
6. Life in general, or that which gives us sustenance, supports our bodily existence, and determines our span of life
7. The teachings of the Buddha and the Bodhisattvas (viz., the Sūtras and Śāstras)
8. The ceaseless process of becoming, or the phenomenon of change-origination
9. The taking of religious vows
10. Worldly law which maintains the moral dictates of society
11. The bearer of true and incontrovertible meaning, arriving at certainty
12. That which prevents rebirth in a lower form of existence
13. That which is 'real' in terms of absolute truth
14. The true and reliable refuge
15. That which is eternal and uncreated, not subject to suffering, old age, and death, such as the *bodhi*-mind
16. The object of supreme knowledge
17. Used in the ethical sphere as merits
18. A religious denomination

his last major instructions to his disciples, called the 'Thirty-seven Wings of Enlightenment' (*Byang-chub-kyi phyogs dang mthun-pa'i chos, Bodhipākṣika-dharmāḥ*) the Buddha summarized all his major teachings into a complex pattern, showing that through their interrelationships they formed a unitary guide to a single goal.

The Four Noble Truths, the Eightfold Path, and the Three Trainings are subsumed within the thirty-seven topics (*chos, dharma*) leading towards Enlightenment (*byang-chub, bodhi*), which are divided into five sections corresponding to the Five Paths of the Bodhisattva. The Four Noble Truths and the Eightfold Noble Path, which are the principal teachings of the First Dharmacakra, are also integral teachings of the Second and Third Turnings. The actual realization and practice of the Four Noble Truths and the Eightfold Path are indications of the highest levels of spiritual attainment. Furthermore, the degree of understanding of these two facets indicates the level of attainment on the Bodhisattva Path, as set forth in the Five Stages: the Path of Accumulation (*tsogs-lam, saṃbhāra-mārga*), the Path of Application (*sbyor-lam, prayoga-mārga*), the Path of Insight (*mthong-lam, darśana-mārga*), the Path of Cultivation (*sgom-lam, bhāvana-mārga*), and the Path of Fulfillment (*mthar-phyin-pa'i-lam, niṣṭhā-mārga*).

These Five Paths can be viewed in relation to the Thirty-seven Wings of Enlightenment as a whole, as well as to the Ten Stages of the Bodhisattva, the Six Transcending Functions (*pāramitā*), and the Three Trainings: of ethics and manners (*tshul-khrims, śīla*) concentrative absorption (*ting-nge-'dzin, samādhi*) and appreciative understanding (*shes-rab, prajñā*). These Three Trainings relate to the Eightfold Noble Path in the following manner:

Right Speech Right Action Right Livelihood	Ethics and Manners
Right Effort Right Mindfulness Right Concentration	Concentrative Absorption
Right View Right Intention	Appreciative Understanding

Through the practice of these Three Trainings, we can develop the ability to perceive the world precisely, without distortion or bias, and we can begin to act in the world appropriately and fruitfully. Concentrative absorption is more than a 'technique' to enable us to calm our minds or to find some temporary sense of peace or serenity. It actually enables us to free ourselves from the desires and attachments which fetter us both emotionally and intellectually. Through the meditative stages of self-growth, we begin to see the true nature of reality, and with this, compassion for all sentient beings is born. The essence of meditative concentration is a completely focused mind (*rtse-gcig, ekāgratā*). This is a state in which the mind no longer references itself to relative values, but experiences itself as the ultimate nature of being.

The first section of the Thirty-seven Wings encompasses the Path of Accumulation, in which one practices the Four Applications of Mindfulness (*dran-pa nyer-bzhag bzhi, smṛtyupasthāna*). These consist of mindfulness of:

> the physical world (*lus, kāya, kāya-smṛty-upasthānam*) [1]*
> the world of feeling (*tshor-ba, vedanā*) [2]
> the world of the mind (*sems, citta*) [3]
> the whole of reality, or the world of meaning (*chos, dharma*) [4]

Through such mindfulness one comes to recognize all of one's experience as characterized by the Four Marks of Existence: impermanence (*mi-thag-pa, anitya*), absence of 'self' or 'ego' (*bdag-med, anātman*), unsatisfactoriness (*sdug-bsngal, duḥkha*), and absence of thingness (*stong-pa, śūnya*). Mindfulness of the physical world encompasses the ability to perceive through one's body the external world, one's own sensory apparatus, and that of others.

Mindfulness of the body (*lus, kāya*) involves impermanence, or the ceaseless flow or flux of all elements of existence (*chos, dharma*). Co-relational with the term *anātman*, the absence of any permanent substance, is the arising (*kun-'byung, samudaya*) of the body as a system followed by its passing away. Here, all thirty-two parts of the body are contemplated upon both internally and externally. Contained within the contemplation on the body are included the four elementary qualities (*khams, dhātu*), which are contained within the sphere of color-form. They are: materiality (earth, *sa, pṛthivī*), motility (air, *rlung, vāyu*), temperature (fire, *me, tejas*), and cohesion (water, *chu, ap*).

Mindfulness of the world of feeling includes the operation of those psychological processes which give the content of experience a definite value or feeling-tone: acceptance or wholesomeness (*bde-ba,*

---

*Numbers in brackets indicate aspects of the "Thirty-seven Wings of Enlightenment."

sukha), rejection or frustration (*sdug-bsngal, duḥkha*), and indifference or neutral feeling-tone (*btang-snyoms, aduḥkhamasukha*).

Mindfulness of the world of mind consists of the Six Spheres of Perception, including the Twelve Component Elements (*skye-mched, āyatana*), and the Eighteen Fields of Interaction (*khams, dhātu*).

Mindfulness of the whole of reality includes mindfulness of the motivational factors (*'du-byed, saṃskārāḥ*) with the exception of feeling.

The Path of Accumulation also consists of the Four Renunciations (*yang-dag-par spong-ba bzhi, samyakprahaṇa*) [5–8] which put an end to unwholesomeness, while fostering and strengthening wholesomeness. It also includes the Four Practices of Concentrative Absorption (*rdzu-'phrul gyi rkang-pa bzhi, ṛddhipāda*) [9–12] consisting of: strong interest (*'dun-pa, chanda*), perseverance (*brtson-pa, vīrya*), intentiveness (*sems-pa, citta*), and investigation (*dpyod-pa, mīmāṃsā*).

At the second stage, the Path of Application, consists of the Five Controlling Powers (*stops, bala*) [13–17]: confidence (*dad-pa, śraddhā*), sustained effort (*brtson-'grus, vīrya*), inspection (*dran-pa, smṛti*), concentrative absorption (*ting-nge-'dzin, dhyāna*), and appreciative descrimination (*shes-rab, prajñā*). There is then a heightening of the Five Controlling Powers [18–22] through repeated practice so that they now achieve the sovereignty of 'unshakable powers' (*dbang-po, indriya*).

The third stage, the Path of Insight, occurs upon this attainment of the Five Unshakable Powers. Here, one attains the First of the Ten Levels of the Bodhisattva, the level of the Joyous One, and one directly perceives the open dimension of being (*śūnyatā*). A tranquility arises at this point from the true awareness of the Four Noble Truths: the pervasiveness of suffering (*sdug-bsngal, duḥkha*), the cause of suffering (*kun-'byung, samudaya*), the cessation of suffering (*'gog-pa, nirodha*), and the path to liberation (*lam, mārga*). Each Truth has four aspects: acceptance of the suffering of existence, the actual awareness of this suffering, the acceptance that even the higher realms are unsatisfactory, and the awareness of that.

This third stage consists of the Seven Factors of Enlightenment [23–29] (*byang-chub-kyi yan-lag bdun, bodhyaṅga*); attentive inspection (*dran-pa, smṛti*), investigation of meanings and values (*chos rab-rnam-'byed, dharma-pravicaya*), sustained effort (*brtson-'grus, vīrya*), joy (*dga'pa, prīti*), refinement and serenity (*shin-tu sbyang-ba, praśabdhi*), concentrative absorption (*ting-nge'-dzin, samādhi*), equanimity (*btang-snyoms, upekṣā*).

The fourth stage, the Path of Cultivation, occurs upon attaining the awareness of the unsatisfactory nature of all the realms of existence. This occurs after one has attained the first gradation of Bodhisattva development, The Joyful One (*rab-tu dga'-ba, pramuditā*). There is an awareness that all the causes of misery have lost their power, and thus there can be no 'effect' of misery. Here, in the fourth division, occurs the actual practice of the Eightfold Noble Path (*'phags pa'i lam-yan-lag-brgyad, Āryamārgaṅga*) [30–37]: Right view (*yang-dag-pa'i lta-ba, samyagdṛṣti*), Right Intention (*yang-dag-pa'i rtogs-pa, samyaksaṃkalpa*), Right Speech (*yang-dag-pa'i ngag, samyagvāc*), Right Action (*yang-dag-pa'i las-kyi mtha', samyakkarmānta*), Right Livelihood (*yang-dag-pa'i 'tsho-ba, samyagājīva*), Right Effort (*yang-dag-pa'i rtsol-ba, samyagvyāyāma*), Right Mindfulness (*yang-dag-pa'i dran-pa, samyaksmṛti*), and Right Concentration (*yang-dag-pa'i ting-nge-'dzin samyaksamādhi*).

At this fourth stage one gradually progresses through the other nine of the Ten Levels of the Bodhisattva:

2. The Stainless One (*dri-ma med-pa, vimalā*)
3. The Illuminating One (*'od byed-pa, prabhākarī*)
4. The Flaming One (*'od 'phro-ba, arciṣmati*)
5. The One Difficult to Conquer (*shin-tu sbyang dka'-ba, sudurjayā*)
6. The Manifest One (*mngon-du gyur-ba, abhimukhī*)
7. The Far Going One (*ring-du song-pa, dūraṅgamā*)
8. The Unshakable One (*mi-gyo-ba, acalā*)
9. The One of Good Discrimination (*legs-pa'i blo-gros, sādhumatī*)
10. Cloud of Dharma (*chos-kyi sprin, dharmamegha*)

The Bodhisattva, on each of the ten levels, emphasizes one of the Ten Transcending Functions, although without neglecting the others. On the first level he emphasizes giving (*sbyin-pa*), on the second ethics and manners (*tshul-khrims*), on the third patience (*bzod-pa*), on the fourth vigor (*brtson-'grus*), on the fifth concentrative absorption (*ting-nge-'dzin*), on the sixth, appreciative understanding (*shes-rab*), on the seventh appropriate activity (*thabs-la mkhas-pa*), on the eighth future projection (*smon-lam*), on the ninth efficacy (*stobs*), and on the tenth pristine cognition (*ye-shes*).

The fifth and final state is the Path of Fulfillment, which is the actual experience of Buddhahood. This is the pinnacle to which all the teachings of the Buddha have been directed. Once one attains this experience, all divisions and differentiations naturally dissolve into the unity of Being.

Only a fully enlightened being would be capable of retaining and teaching the totality of the Dharma—like a single candle illuminating an entire cave. However, in order to preserve and protect the teachings and the purity of their process of transmission, the Buddha chose a number of Arhants and Bodhisattvas to carry on his life's work. The Buddhadharma in its multifaceted forms and the enlightened actions arising from these teachings are all preserved and protected by Vajrapāṇi. The teachings of Śākyamuni Buddha in particular are protected by the Bodhisattva Mañjuśrī, as well as by the deities Brahmā, Indra, and others. As is stated in the *Mañjuśrī-mūla-tantra*:

> The Master of Sages (the Tathāgata) will pass away into Nirvāṇa, and, in order to protect the Highest Doctrine, there will be one who appears in the form of Mañjuśrī; it will be he who constantly preserves the Buddhadharma.

Sixteen Arhants or Sthaviras were also entrusted by Śākyamuni Buddha with the preservation of the Buddhadharma. Each of these vowed not to pass away into Nirvāṇa, but to prolong his life so that he could continue the work of the Buddha and reveal and protect the Dharma. These sixteen Arhants possess miraculous powers which enable them to travel to various parts of the world to spread the Buddhadharma. After their duty on earth is fulfilled, they will enter into Nirvāṇa, and like the dying flame of a lamp their bodies will disappear without leaving any trace.*

---

*These sixteen Arhants are:

1. Panthaka (Lam-pa), who resides in the realm of the thirty-three
2. The Sthavira Abhedya (Mi-phyed-pa), who resides in the Himalayas
3. Kanaka (gSer-can, also Bhāradvāja), who resides in the western continent Godhanya
4. Bakula (Bhakula), who resides in the northern continent Kuru
5. Bhāradvāja, who resides in the eastern continent Videha
6. Mahākālika (Dus-ldan-chen-po), who resides in Tāmradvīpa
7. Vajrīputra (rDo-rje-mo'i-bu), who resides in Simhaladvīpa
8. Rāhula (sGra-gcan-'dzin), who resides in Priyangudvīpa
9. Srībhadra (dPal-bzang), who resides in Yamunādvīpa
10. Gopaka (sBed-byed), who resides on the mountain Bihula
11. Nāgasena (Klu-sde), who resides on the Urumunda mountain
12. Vanavasin (Nags-gnas), who resides on the Saptaparṇa mountain

The Buddha prophesized that there would be seven hierarchs (*gtad-rabs-bdun*) who would serve as guardians of the Dharma and the Vinaya lineage until the time of Nāgārjuna. Those Arhants would be Kāśyapa, Ānanda, Śānavāsika, Upagupta, Dhītika, Kṛṣṇa, and Mahāsudarṣana.* In this same prophecy the Buddha stated that one of the foremost monks who would come after him would be Aśvagupta. This monk would be a distinguished Arhant (*dus-mi-sbyor, asamaya, vimukta*) and have a large following of disciples.

It is said that the Buddha, accompanied by Ānanda (or possibly Yakśa Vajrapaṇi) traveled to Mathurā and then to Kashmir. At a later time, Aśoka, accompanied by Upagupta, went to these same regions, and at Mathurā he made a grand offering to the Stūpa of Ānanda, as recorded in the *Aśokāvandāna*. During that period, two disciples of Ānanda, Śāṇavāsa from Mathurā and the Siddha Madhyāntika, were also welcomed in the Kashmirian communities to the west.

Development of the Buddhist Saṅgha and the Three Councils

After the Parinirvāṇa of the Buddha (486 or 476 B.C.), Mahākāśyapa, one of the Buddha's closest disciples, was chosen to preside over the order of monks. Kāśyapa had been born the son of a rich Brahman in Magadha, yet at an early age he felt a distaste for the world of riches and pleasure. But complying with custom, he married a beautiful girl from Vaiśālī, who, he discovered, had an equal dislike for sensuality. So, for twelve years they lived together in complete chastity, even sleeping in separate beds. Then one evening Kāśyapa saw a large snake enter their quarters and approach the hand of his sleeping wife. Sensing imminent danger, he quickly grasped her arm, startling her from sleep. Without noticing the snake, she accused him of having impure thoughts. As a result of this incident, they both agreed that they should separate and enter the Saṅgha community. The first Saṅgha, or community of Buddhist monks, was established at the time of the ordination of the 'band of five', the ascetic companions of the Buddha who became his

13. Kṣudrapanthaka (Lam-phran), who resides on the Gṛdhrakūṭa
14. Kanakvatsa (gSer-gyi-be'u), who resides in Kashmir
15. Angirāja (Yan-lag-'byung), who resides on Mount Kailāsa
16. Ajita (Ma-pham-pa), who resides in the Crystal Wood of the sages

*The *Mūlasarvāstivādin Vinaya* adds Madhyāntika to the list.

first disciples. During the early period of his teaching the Buddha set forth rules of conduct and self-discipline which were designed to insure the health and well-being of the disciples.

The first great convocation of the Buddhist Saṅgha was held for the purpose of reciting and codifying the Buddha's teachings, in order to preserve them correctly. It was mutually decided that an assembly of five hundred Arhants would convene in Rājagṛha, where Ajātaśatru, the king of Magadha, would supply them with food and lodging, as the rainy season was upon them. Although there were considerably more than five hundred qualified masters, many were unable to join the council because they were engaged in deep meditation.

Ānanda, who had been the Buddha's personal attendant during the last twenty-five years of his life, was initially barred from admittance because he had not yet reached the state of the Arhant. But just before the Council convened, Ānanda attained Arhantship and was admitted. In these days of the early Buddhist Saṅgha, the means for preserving and handing down the teachings of the Buddha was recitation and memorization, a method which had been used in India since the earliest Vedic period. Because he had been present at almost every occasion where the Buddha had spoken, Ānanda recited the Sūtras, Upāli recounted the Vinaya rules, and Mahākāśyapa set forth the early word lists, which later developed into the Abhidharma. One of the powers which qualified one as an Arhant was the ability to remember perfectly whatever was heard. So, when these teachings of the Buddha were recited, there was unanimous agreement that they corresponded exactly to the Buddha's own words. This First Council is known by various names, including the Council at Rājagṛha, the Council of Five-hundred, the Recitation of the Vinaya, and the Vinaya-saṃgīti.

According to Nāgārjuna, a multitude of Bodhisattvas assembled at the mountain of Vimalasvābhava, south of Rājagṛha, to compile the Mahāyāna Sūtras, while the assembly of Arhants was gathered at Rājagṛha to hear the Hīnayāna Sūtras recited. The Bodhisattva Samantabhadra presided over this council; Vajrapāṇi recited the Sūtras; Maitreya, the Vinaya; and Mañjuśrī, the Abhidharma.

In its formative period, the early Saṅgha consisted of travelers (*parivrājakas*) who taught the Buddhadharma to any who wished to hear it. During the rainy season they would suspend their wandering and settle down in communities, where they eventually codified the Prātimokṣa, the monastic code of conduct consisting of approximately 250 rules which were to govern the lives of the monks. The rudiments

Rājagṛha The hills of this ancient valley were host to the First Council.

of Buddhist monastic life were thus established, and eventually, various practices emerged which served to mold the monastic community into a cohesive body. For instance, the recitation of the Prātimokṣa was performed two times each month on the day of the Upavastha, when the monks were given the opportunity to confess transgressions to the assembly. Gradually, the wandering life drew to an end and the various Saṅgha communities established themselves as distinct groups. The communities which were often geographically very separate become increasingly specialized in a particular facet or subtlety of the Doctrine. With time, the first seeds of individualism among the Saṅgha community were sown.

The Second Council at Vaiśālī occurred about one hundred years after the Parinirvāṇa. This council was held because a certain contingency of monks at Vaiśālī were accused of becoming lax in their observance of ten points of discipline. However, the only point which seems to have been transgressed is the practice of soliciting gold and silver. This Council is commonly referred to as the Council at Vaiśālī or the Recital of Seven Hundred.

The Second Council at Pāṭaliputra occurred approximately thirty-seven years after the Second Council at Vaiśālī, or about one hundred and forty years after the Parinirvāṇa. This council has a particular historical importance because it marked the initial division between what would be later distinguished as the Hīnayāna and the Mahāyāna. During this council, a monk by the name of Mahādeva voiced the observation of many practicing Buddhists at the time that, although it was commonly held that the state of the Arhant indicated a specific level of achievement, some Arhants were more spiritually accomplished than others. The majority of the monks at this council sided with Mahādeva, who represented the Mahāsaṅghika. A minority of the monks known as the Sthaviravādins ("Elders") dissented from the findings of the council and broke away, for they wished to adhere to what they considered a more orthodox view of the Vinaya code. It should be noted that both groups, the Mahāsaṅghika and the Sthaviravāda, modified their respective canons as a result of this Council at Pāṭaliputra.

Though the Sthaviravādins (Pali: Thervādins) were at the forefront of what was to become the development of the Hīnayāna, there did occur a number of diverging doctrines, classified as Hīnayāna, which were more compatible with the ideas of the Mahāyāna. The Abhayagirivāsins, a less orthodox offshoot of the Theravādins in Ceylon, is an example of such a school.

The Third Council at Pāṭaliputra, which occurred during the seventeenth year of the reign of King Aśoka, (c. 250 B.C.), was instituted by the monk Moggaliputta Tissa, who was chosen to preside over a council of one thousand monks. Both Moggaliputta Tissa and Aśoka emphasized the Sthaviravādin 'orthodox' teachings, and this partially accounts for the official rejection by the Council of the views of the Sarvāstivādin, the 'All Dharmas Exist' school. The Sarvāstivādins thus seceded from the Sthaviravādins, and many of them migrated north and west, establishing a strong center in Kashmir which flourished for a millennium. The Sarvāstivādins became dominant in the cities along the northern trade route to China, and from there they entered China, where they exerted a strong influence.

The Sthaviravādins who rejected the Sarvāstivādin thesis became known as Vibhajyavādins, or 'distinctionists'—those who distinguish between *dharmas* which 'exist' and *dharmas* which do not 'exist'. They were united as a group chiefly by their opposition to the Sarvāstivādins, and soon they broke into different groups.

It is generally agreed that during the time of the early Vinaya there were four original groups of Śrāvakas, or faithful listeners, who had directly heard the speech of the Buddha and preserved his basic teachings, such as the Four Noble Truths and the Eightfold Path. They were the Sthaviravāda, Mahāsaṅghika, Saṃmitīya, and Sarvāstivāda. Each one of these groups had its own Pratimokṣa, or code of conduct and collection of Āgamas.

The reign of King Aśoka was the most fruitful period of expansion for the early Saṅgha across all of India and Kashmir, and this expansion fostered regional particularities of the doctrine which accentuated the development of the various schools. The initial division of the Buddha's teachings into the Sthaviravāda and the Mahāsaṅghika was followed by a further division into eleven groups. Later, five other schools were formed, which, when added to the original groups of two and eleven, comprised the eighteen early schools of Buddhism.

At the time of the Buddha, King Kṛkin saw ten visions, one of which was of a whole piece of cloth being torn into eighteen pieces by different men. The Buddha explained this as signifying that although the essence of his teachings was one, like the material of the robe, the teaching itself would be divided into eighteen schools.

Although traditionally the number of original groups or associations is held to be eighteen, some early Buddhist sources list as many as twenty-four. Often, however, several different names are used to designate the same school. So, the traditional enumeration of eighteen distinct schools is essentially accurate, though there is some difference among the various traditions concerning the most common names of the groups.

According to Lama Mi-pham, the division into eighteen schools can be classified under two headings, the Mahāsaṅghikas and the Sthaviras. The Mahāsaṅghikas split into the Mahāsaṅghikas, Ekavyāvahārins, Lokottaravādins, Bahuśrutīyas, Nityavādins, Caiyakas, Pūrvaśailikas, and Uttaraśailikas. The Sthaviras divided into Haimavatas, Sarvāstivādins, Hetuvādins, Vatsīputrīyas, Dharmottaras, Bhadrayānikas, Sāṃmitiyas, Bahudeśakas, Dharmadeśakas, and Bhadravarṣikas.

The division into the four groups of Śravakas–and eventually eighteen schools–was the result of certain differences in understanding the discipline of the Vinaya, as well as disagreement on finer points of the doctrine. There were four general factors which help account for the division into the eighteen schools: (1) geographical circumstances, such as insular or mountainous isolation from external influences, or the exposure to a wide variety of ideas along the trade routes; (2) religious circumstances, such as pilgrims traveling to and from the great holy places; (3) historical influences, such as the favor or disfavor of a prince or dynasty towards a specific school, or the invasion of certain foreign tribes; (4) economic circumstances, such as famines which forced monks to leave a particular domain, or the favor shown by certain rich patrons.

There was never any violent opposition expressed between the monks of the various groups or schools. All considered themselves disciples of the Buddha and agreed upon the Blessed One's general teachings. They distinguished themselves only on secondary points of the doctrine and discipline, so that a rapport existed between members of different associations. Regardless of the affiliation of the monastery where a traveling monk would stop for the night, he was generally well-received according to the traditional practices of compassion, unobscured communication, and non-violence (*ahiṃsa*).

By the reign of the Pāla Kings (ninth to tenth centuries), only six of the eighteen schools which once flourished in India were still active. Of these only two survive today: the Mūlasarvāstivāda, which derived from the Sarvāstivāda, and Theravāda, which derived from the Sthaviravāda through the Kāśyapīya, which is sometimes equated with the Haimavata. The Mūlasarvāstivādins became the mainstay of the Vinaya practice as it migrated northward in what was to later form the Vinaya tradition of the Mahāyāna, or the Great Northern Vehicle. And the Theravādin found its way to Ceylon and to Southeast Asia, and became one of the primary Hīnayāna schools still flourishing.

The Introduction of the Dharma into Kashmir

Before he passed into Nirvāṇa, the Buddha also made the prophecy in the *Mañjuśrī-mūla-tantra* that one hundred years after the Blessed One's passing, a monk with the surname of Madhyāntika would arise to establish the Śrāvaka Piṭaka.

Sometime before the assembly of the Second Council at Vaiśālī (c. 380 B.C.), the Ārya Madhyāntika (Nyi-ma-gung-ba) went to Kashmir. There, with the help of his psychic accomplishments, he subdued the

Harwan, Kashmir This site was once an important seat of Buddhist learning in Kashmir. Nāgārjuna spent many years here.

Nāga King Auduṣṭa. Through a series of magical acts, and with the aid of the subjected Nāgas, Madhyāntika converted Kashmir into an important producer of saffron, which enabled the country to increase her wealth considerably.* Because of this act of goodwill the Dharma was readily adopted by the inhabitants of Kashmir. Madhyāntika taught the Dharma in Kashmir for at least fifteen years.

This region was soon covered with monasteries for the benefit of the growing Saṅgha and with commemorative monuments of Stūpas for the perpetuation of the memory of Śākyamuni Buddha. They consisted of a hemispherical dome fully erect on a flat roof and surrounded by a balustrade. Each was built at a place marking an important event in one of Śākyamuni's previous lives as a Bodhisattva.

After the passing of Madhyāntika, the lineage was entrusted to Śānavāsika, who journeyed to the cremation ground at Śitavana

*Another interpretation is that Madhyāntika introduced the 'saffron culture' (i.e., saffron-colored robes) which is figurative language for the Buddhist Saṅgha, thus substituting the Dharma in place of the Nāga cults predominant during this time.

(bSil-ba'i-tshal) before going to Kashmir. From Śānavāsika the lineage passed to Upagupta, who was instrumental in aiding numerous monks in their attainment of Arhantship. During this time, King Aśoka supplied the monastic communities in Kashmir with many valuable gifts.

Upon entrusting the Dharma to Ārya Dhītika, Upagupta passed into Nirvāṇa. Dhītika in turn completely maintained the Dharma and entrusted it to Kṛṣṇa, who gave it to Ārya Mahāsudarśana. From this point onwards, the Dharma spread widely in Kashmir, and the number of Saṅgha grew substantially.

The Vinaya Tradition

The Vinaya, like the Dharma itself, is concerned with the life-world of the individual—one's attitudes, mental training, and general outlook. As it evolved in the history of Buddhism, the Vinaya came to also represent the body of teachings and discipline which determines the outward lives of those who enter the religious order as monks (*bhikṣus*) or nuns (*bhikṣuṇī*).

The Vinaya is essentially a code of conduct which arose from a careful analysis of the actions in daily life that lead one to a particular goal. The Buddha acted according to this code of conduct, not only as an example to others, but also as a natural expression of his own awakening. The Sūtras expounded by the Buddha both express the possibility and nature of the goal and constitute the source of inspiration for both the analyses of the Abhidharma and the practice of the Vinaya. For both Mahāyāna and the Hīnayāna, the conduct specified by the Vinaya code is not merely a means to an end, but a manifestation of that end as an integrated achievement. The Vinaya lineage, which carries on both the living tradition of the Buddha's teachings (*lung*) and its realization (*rtogs-pa*), is essential to the preservation of the Buddhadharma, and without Vinaya the Dharma would cease to exist.

As a spiritual course, the Vinaya may be equated with the Śrāvakayāna, which is the way of those who share what they have learned rather than remaining silent, like the Pratyekabuddha. Śākyamuni Buddha often related to his disciples the simile of a traveler who found a most beautiful treasure in the jungle, and returned to tell his companions about it. What he found, however, was not something new; it had been there all the time, but the one who had buried it would not bring it out of the jungle. Like the traveler who returns with the treasure, the Śrāvakayāna as a living transmission represents the very foundation of the Buddhadharma. And this living transmission of the Śrāvakayāna is the Vinaya, which originated after Buddha Śākyamuni with Rāhula, his son. The Vinaya lineage of Rāhula was continued in the tradition of the Mūlasarvāstivādins, and survived through time as an unbroken succession, finally making its way to Tibet. The Vinaya lineage was also held by Mahākāśyapa, who presided over the First Council; his lineage found its way to Ceylon, Burma, and many of the Southeast Asian countries.

Nāgārjuna (c. 150 A.D.) also played a leading role in the development of the Vinaya, introducing a sharp discipline for his disciples. It is said that once eight thousand monks were expelled from his community when their moral purity was questioned. Vasubandhu (c. 350 A.D.) also was a leading recipient of the Vinaya Lineage of Rāhula, and Guṇaprabha, Vasubandhu's foremost disciple in the Vinaya, and the Vinayadhara Chos-kyi-bshes-gnyen composed extended commentaries on the Vinaya Sūtra. Bhāvaviveka (Bhavya, c. 550 A.D.) a spiritual successor Nāgārjuna, continued the Vinaya tradition through Śrīgupta who in turn passed it to Jñānagarbha. Śāntarakṣita (c. 750 A.D.), a disciple of Jñānagarbha, was the first one to carry the Vinaya lineage to Tibet. He was then followed by a host of Vinaya masters and translators.

The basic code of conduct for the Vinaya lineage is the Pratimokṣa. Though codified shortly after the Parinirvāṇa, its principal rules were formulated by the Buddha during his lifetime. A bi-monthly recitation of the Pratimokṣa served to keep the code fresh in the minds of the Saṅgha and also provided the opportunity for any transgressor to make known those violations that he or she had committed. In the Pāli Vinaya tradition, the Pratimokṣa rules are divided into eight sections, classified according to the seriousness of the transgression. The greatest penalty of all is expulsion from the order, and the smallest, a mild reprimand.

The code of the Hīnayāna Vinaya consists of ten fundamental rules, of which the first five are binding to laymen, while all ten form the complete collection of precepts for novices. The ten basic rules are to refrain from: (1) taking life (2) taking what is not given (3) sexual misconduct (4) lying and false speech (5) partaking of intoxicants (6) using adornments, perfumes, and unguents (7) performing as or watching an actor, juggler, or acrobat (the play of Māyā) (8) sitting on elevated and luxurious couches (9) eating at certain hours (10) possessing money, gold, silver, or precious items. In addition to these ten vows of a novice, a fully ordained monk conforms to a total of two hundred and fifty-three vows, while a nun observes three hundred and forty-eight.

The Pratimokṣa reveals such a thorough stipulation of appropriate behavior that there may seem at first to be no room left for 'personal freedom' or 'spontaneity', for it deals with nearly all aspects of one's life. However, this attention to what from the Western point of view may seem like trivia is actually a concern for maximizing essential human values. From the Buddhist point of view, each moment (*kṣaṇa*) is unique and equally important, insofar as each is an occasion for an action which will either create further karmic entanglement or lead toward liberation. Thus, such ideals as Arhantship or supreme enlightenment are realizations of what is potential during each moment of life.

Ordinary actions are often 'heedless', lacking appreciation of what is given in each moment and leading to action which is inappropriate to the succeeding situation. This in turn fosters further disorientation, so that the heedlessness is self-perpetuating. Disciplined actions, however, combat the head-long rush of entangling action, and may actually directly embody the value of each moment.

The principles outlined in the two primary philosophical traditions of the Mahāyāna, Yogācāra and Mādhyamika, find their direct application in the practice of Vinaya. For instance, Yogācāra philosophy speaks of a substratum (*ālaya-vijñana*) which preserves and resurrects every event. Heedless behavior thus remains a part of the one who does the activity, and it will later reassert itself. The Vinaya is a method of freeing oneself from actions which will lead to further frustrating and entangling experience. Mādhyamika philosophy accepts that a person's actions and experiences ordinarily occur as part of this law-like process, but it also maintains that each moment is completely open in content and thus neither bears any incriminating past history nor forces the arising of some retributory moral consequence. However, this 'open content' of each moment is difficult to perceive when one is in the midst of entangling activity. The Vinaya provides the chance for a calm and sustained attentiveness that may penetrate to the heart of each momentary presentation.

Generally, the Mahāyāna encourages its followers to actively participate in "work in the world," particularly for mature individuals who can retain their balance without the elaborate protection of the full

Vinaya refuge. However, the Mahāyāna has also preserved intact the systematic Vinaya of the Hīnayāna schools, adding further rules which are particularly Mahāyāna in scope, such as those concerned with developing Bodhicitta and practicing the Pāramitās. Mahāyāna Vinayadharas, therefore, are subject to additional and more stringent commitments than are Hīnayāna followers.

The Mahāyāna code of Vinaya consists of fifty-eight rules, of which the first ten concern themselves with the most serious offences, while the remaining forty-eight apply to the lighter transgressions. The first five of the ten serious offences coincide with the five mentioned above, while the others, as taken from the *Brahmajāla-sūtra*, are to refrain from: (6) speaking of the transgressions of those in the monastic order; (7) praising oneself and deprecating others; (8) avariciousness; (9) showing anger; and (10) speaking against the Triple Gem (Buddha, Dharma, Saṅgha). The forty-eight lighter rules are futher developments of the original ten and evidence the freer spirit of the Mahāyāna, leading one to the practice of appropriate Bodhisattva action.

The masters of the Vajrayāna must keep commitments far beyond the capacity of those practicing the two previous Yānas. The 'three vows' (*trīsaṃvara*) of the Vajrayāna include not only the vows of the full Vinaya refuge–the 253 rules of the Pratimokṣa–but also those practiced by the one following the Bodhisattva course of the Pāramitās, as well as vows of the stringent Tantric code of ethics. The *trīsaṃvara* unifies the various levels of understanding in Buddhist ethics and manners and has given rise to many important Śāstras such as Sa-skya Paṇḍita's *sDom-gsum-rab-dbye*, mNga'-ris Pang-chen's *sDom-gsum-rnam-nges*, and many others.

The Development of the Sarvāstivāda and the Abhidharma

The doctrines of the Abhidharma played a leading role in the early development of Sarvāstivādin thought. The Sarvāstivādins defined the Abhidharma as an "analysis of dharma" (*dharma-pravicaya*) and held that it presented the pure understanding (*amalā-prajñā*), as well as the primary source of the teachings. In this way, the Abhidharma was looked upon as the 'highest dharma' (*abhi* = 'above').

The Abhidharma presents experience as the total patterning of the interpenetration of 'mind' and 'mental events'. Through a proper understanding of this dynamic functioning an individual can become free from the confines of conflicting emotions or intellectual opacity. By seeing more clearly how fear, doubt, anger, desire, and other emotional states can control and fragment experience, one can learn to recognize and follow healthier life patterns.

The early community of Sarvāstivādin monks, which was centered around Mathurā, compiled its Piṭakas in Sanskrit. This body of literature later became the major inspiration for Vasubandhu's *Abhidharma-kośa*, as well as subsequent Abhidharmic exegesis in China and Tibet. This Tripiṭaka was also a major influence on the development of Mahāyāna literature. Two very important doctrines of the Mahāyāna were already being emphasized in the literature: the practice of the Six Pāramitās (transcending functions) and the ideal of the Bodhisattva. However, the practitioner was told to imitate rather than *become* the Bodhisattva, a view that arose only with the Mahāyāna.

The Mūlasarvāstivādins arose some time after the reign of King Kaniṣka II (c. 120 A.D.) and are to be distinguished from the earlier Sarvāstivādins insofar as they modified the doctrines of the latter and practiced a more stringent code of Vinaya. The Vinaya of the Sarvāstivādins arose much earlier than that of the Mūlasarvāstivādins and is composed in a mixed form of Sanskirt, whereas the Vinaya of the Mūlasarvāstivādins is in relatively pure Sanskrit.

The Chinese Sarvāstivādin Vinaya contains an additional section on the subject of Bodhisattva conduct and other matters relevant to the code of Vinaya adopted by the Mahāyāna. These additions in the Pratimokṣa can be found in the *Upālipariprcca-sūtra*, as well as at the end of the Chinese Mūlasarvāstivādin Vinaya, presumably having been added by the Chinese pilgrim and translator I-tsing (c. 690 A.D.). The Tibetan translation of the Mūlasarvāstivādin Vinaya would seem to be most accurate, as it is complete and unaltered and does not contain those additions found in the *Upālipariprcca*.

In the formation of the Sarvāstivādin school, Upagupta (c. 250 B.C.), who authored the *Netṛpada-śāstra*, played the major role. However, his scholarly excellence was valued not only by the Sarvāstivādin monks, but also later by an outgrowth of the Sarvāstivāda, the Vaibhāṣika of Mathurā, who looked upon him as a versatile teacher and gifted writer.

In the second century B.C., representatives of the Saṅgha community assembled at Puruṣapura on the suggestion of Kātyayanīputra and King Vāsiṣka. The assembly was principally attended by the

Sarvāstivādins, and presided over by the Bhadanta Vasumitra* who was assisted by Aśvaghoṣa. The purpose of the assembly was to determine which interpretations of the Dharma were correct. Of the accepted teachings, about one million *ślokas* were collected in order to compose commentaries on them. Upon completion, these accepted commentaries were carved in stone, thus insuring their preservation.

This assembly, consisting of five hundred Arhants and five hundred Bodhisattvas, was attended by Ghoṣaka and Buddhadeva. Bhadanta Dharmatrāta and Dharmaśrī, who were also members of the council, later became highly respected in Gandhāra as 'western masters' (*pāścatīyas*) of the early Sarvāstivādin school. Vasumitra (dBig-bshes), Ghoṣaka (dByangs-sgrog-author of the *Abhidharmāmṛta-śāstra*), Dharmatrāta (Chos-skyob, author of the *Pañcavastuvibhāṣa-śāstra*), and Buddhadeva (Sang-rgyas-lha) compiled the results of this great assembly into a written record of the controversy. Three huge commentaries were composed. One of these, the *Vibhāṣā* (*Abhidharma-vibhāṣā-śāstra*), was a commentary on the most important book of the Sarvāstivādin Abhidharma Piṭaka, the *Jñāna-prasthāna* by Ārya Kātyāyanīputra, who probably lived around the first or second century B.C. The *Vibhāṣā* quotes the diverging points of view raised by the differing schools and refutes them by making reference to appropriate passages in the *Jñāna-prasthāna.*

The *Vibhāṣā*, along with the *Mahāvibhāṣā*, strongly influenced the emergence of the Vaibhāṣikas (Bye-brag-smra-ba). The *Mahāvibhāṣā* (*Abhidharma-mahāvibhāṣā-śāstra*) is a huge work containing one hundred thousand *ślokas*, and is a commentary on all seven works of the Sarvāstivādin Abhidharma Piṭaka.†

---

*The title Bhadanta refers to prominent members of the Hīnayāna Buddhist hierarchy. Although they are below Arhants in spiritual excellence, they are often founders of schools, propragators of Dharma, or well-known authors. Although he held the title *bhadanta*, Vasumitra was one of the most prominent enlightened masters of his time.

†The seven works are:

1. *Jñāna-prasthāna* by Kātyāyanīputra
2. *Saṃgīti-paryāya* by Mahākauṣṭhila
3. *Prakaraṇa-pāda* by Vasumitra
4. *Vijñāna-kāya* by Devaśarman
5. *Dhātu-kāya* by Pūrna
6. *Dharma-skandha* by Śāriputra
7. *Prajñapti-śāstra* by Maudgalyāyana

Among these seven treatises, the *Dharma-skandha* and the *Saṃgīti-paryāya*, were

All of the Abhidharma teachings as delineated by the Buddha are included in the seven fundamental treatises on Abhidharma. These works were condensed into the *Mahāvibhāṣā*, which was then summarized by Vasubandu in his *Abhidharma-kośa* (*mNgon-pa mdzod*). In nine chapters the *Kośa* sets forth all the teachings of the Buddha, and has become the primary source for the Abhidharma tradition from the Hīnayāna point of view. Chapter one of the *Kośa* concerns existence (*khams, dhātu*) and contains a general classification of experience. Chapter two elucidates inherent powers (*dbang-po, indriya*) such as the senses, which are the fundamental attributes that determine our 'growth'. Chapter three presents the Buddhist cosmological vision of the world as the total environment (*'jig-rten, loka*). Chapter four deals with the relationship our actions (*las, karma*) have in determining our world of experience. Chapter five concerns the latent tendencies (*phra-rgyas, anuśaya*) and the pervasive emotional tendencies (*kun-nas-nyon-mongs, saṃkleśa*) of our experience. Chapter six sets forth the Buddhist path (*lam, mārga*) to liberation. Chapter seven presents pristine wisdom (*ye-shes, jñāna*) as a learning process. Chapter eight deals with the integration of the personality (*snyoms-'jug, samāpatti*). And chapter nine, which was written separately, is a refutation of the notion of an independently existing '*pudgala*' or personality (*gang-zag*). Important commentaries and explanatory treatises on the *Abhidharma-kośa* were written by Saṅghabhadra, Dignāga, Sthiramati, Yaśomitra, Vasumitra, and others.

The most important work on Abhidharma from a Mahāyāna point of view is the *Abhidharma-samuccaya* (*Kun-las btus-pa*) by Asaṅga, which summarizes the teachings of the Abhidharma in the light of the three Yānas.* It defines all the subjects of the Abhidharma and investigates all the elements of existence from the perspective of the Great Vehicle. It has been said that the *Abhidharma-samuccaya* is a condensation of the over one million aspects of the Abhidharma which were

---

written before the lines of thought, which later set the Sarvāstivādins apart from the other schools, had gained maturity. With the writing of the *Prajñapti-śāstra*, the doctrines of the Sarvāstivādins gained influence. Following these works came the *Vijñāna-kāya* and the *Dhātu-kāya*, and then finally the *Prakaraṇa-pāda* and the *Jñāna-prasthāna*, which represent the last stage of development of the Sarvāstivādin. In his *Abhidharma-kośa*, Vasubandhu considers the *Prakaraṇa-pāda* as important a treatise as the *Jñāna-prasthāna*, and some important classifications which he utilized in the *Kośa* were based on the *Prakaraṇa-pāda*.

*In this context, the three Yānas are the Śravakayāna, Pratyekabuddhayāna, and Bodhisattvayāna.

taught to Asaṅga by Maitreya. Asaṅga's disciple Buddhasiṃha wrote a *bhāṣya* (commentary) to the text, which further elucidated various points. Later, Sthiramati brought together Asaṅga's basic text and the *bhāṣya* to form the *Abhidharma-samuccaya-vyākhya*. The Sanskrit edition of this work remained extant in Tibet until recent times.

The development of the Abhidharma stimulated a strong literary tradition in both the Mahāyāna and the Hīnayāna. As one of the three baskets of the Tripiṭaka, its basic tenets have not only been accepted by all schools from the time of the Buddha to the present day, but have been central themes in the development of all Buddhist philosophical systems.

The Development of the Vaibhāṣika and Sautrāntika

Elements of specialization in the Dharma can be seen from very early times. At the first council after the Parinirvāṇa, Ānanda was requested to recite the Sūtras, while Upāli recited the Vinaya, and Kāśyapa the Abhidharma. The task of memorizing the different portions of the Piṭaka was entrusted to various Saṅgha associations which bore names descriptive of their particular acquisitions and which, in the course of time, grew separate from one another.

These separate groups became associated with certain doctrines which could be looked upon as unique to the group which adhered to them; the different associations eventually developed into separate schools of Buddhism. Two examples of such schools are the Vaibhāṣikas and the Sautrāntikas.

When the Buddha's teachings began to be recorded in writing, the Sūtras were written in a discursive style which made use of the simile, the metaphor, and the anecdote. The Sautrāntikas, in making a persistent effort to strictly adhere to the original discourses as primary sources (*sūtra-pramāṇika*), accepted only this body of literature as doctrinal authority. The non-discursive style, which employed a very select, precise, and impersonal terminology, became characteristic of the Abhidharma Piṭaka, which became a foundation for the Vaibhāṣika teachings.

The Vaibhāṣikas may be called 'orthodox' Sarvāstivādins who regarded with much authority the commentaries (*vibhāṣā*) on the Abhidharma. Like the Sarvāstivādins, the Vaibhāṣikas held that all elements of existence (*dharma*) exist, and that their past and future states are real. Later Vaibhāṣikas elaborated on various points which the *Mahāvibhāṣā* had left open to dispute. They honored the opinions of Bhadanta Vasumitra and held the *Udānavarga* of Dharmatrāta in high regard.

The four original compilers of the *Mahāvibhāṣā*—Vasumitra, Goṣaka, Dharmatrāta, and Buddhadeva—composed other principal works and doctrines of the Vaibhāṣikas, especially the *Trayamiśraṇa-māla* (*Lung-ni spel-ma gsum-gyi phreng-ba, The Garland of Three Mixtures*) and the *Śata-upadeśa* (*gDams-ngag brgya-pa, A Hundred Upadeśas*). Each of these important Vaibhāśika masters had one hundred thousand disciples.

The two main centers of activity for the Vaibhāṣikas were Gandhāra (the Pāścatiyas) and Kashmir. Buddhamitra, who was Vasubandu's first teacher, was an important master in Gandhāra. Skandhila, author of the *Abhidharmāvatāra*, and Saṅghabhadra were two important figures for the Kashmirian Vaibhāṣikas with whom Vasubandhu studied for some years. Saṅghabhadra contributed two major works to the Buddhist tradition: the *Samaya of Light* and the *Nyāyānusara-śāstra*. The former details the principles of the Vaibhāṣika, and the latter is principally a refutation of the *Abhidharma-kośa*.

The Kashmirian Vaibhāṣikas considered the seven Abhidharma works of the Sarvāstivādins as an organized compilation of the direct words (Āgama) of the Buddha. These works were considered to be actual lectures, delivered by him to specific groups or individuals and committed to memory by the original Arhants or Śrāvakas.

During the second century B.C. the Sautrāntika branched off from the Sarvāstivāda. The ideas which were common to the two long-lived Abhidharma traditions, the Theravāda and the Sarvāstivāda, as well as those additional lines of thought followed by the Vaibhāṣikas, were generally refuted by the Sautrāntikas, who accepted the Sūtras as the only authoritative source of the Buddha's teachings.

In the Pāli tradition of the Theravādins, the early Sautrāntikas are called the Saṃkantikas. The Sautrāntikas received this appellation due to their doctrine of the transference of the *skandha-matras* through several moments of existence. The Saṃkantikas were an off-shoot of the Kāśyapīyas (Pāli: Kassapikas), and from the Saṃkantikas the Sautrāntikas branched off.

The origin of the Sautrāntikas can be traced back to Kumāralata who appeared about one century after the Parinivāṇa and authored the *Dṛṣtantāmālā-śāstra,* the *Garland of Similes*. Kumāralata was probably a native of Taksaśīla. His major work was the *Dṛṣtantāpañkti* (*dPe'i-*

phreng-ba, Dṛṣtantamālā), which was translated into Tibetan by Dharmaśrībhadra (Tshul-khrims Yon-tan) and revised by Rin-chen-bzang-po. In addition to the *Dṛṣtantapañkti*, he composed a number of treatises which became widely circulated. His name was translated into the Chinese as Kumarālabha and is referred to by the Chinese master Hsuan-tsang (627–645) as one of the 'Four Shining Sons' (Aśvaghoṣa in the east, Āryadeva in the south, Nāgārjuna in the west, and Kumāralabha in the north).

Kumāralata wrote approximately nine hundred treatises and was one of the first to explain the teachings of the Buddha through the use of the simile. In the literature of this period, the *dṛṣtānta* (example or illustration) is set against the Sūtranta or Sūtras, for which it serves as a compliment or illustration. The name Daṛṣtāntika, ascribed to the followers of Kumāralata, was probably given to them by their opponents. Taking offense at being called Darṣṭāntikas (dPe-ston-ba) or 'exemplifiers', the later followers of the line of thought formulated by Kumāralata took the title of Sautrāntika (mDo-sde-pa). Many quotations in the *Mahāvibhāṣā* are taken from the Daṛṣtāntika, but the name Sautrāntika is mentioned only twice. This suggests that the Sautrāntika had not been fully established at the time the *Mahāvibhāṣā* was written.

Śrīlāta (Śrīlabdha, dPal-lden), who appeared sometime in the third century A.D. stands with Kumāralata as one of the original masters of the Sautrāntika, having contributed a number of original treatises to the developing Sautrāntika line of thought. He composed the *Sautrāntika-vibhāṣā* and was referred to as the 'Sthavira' by the teacher and later opponent of Vasubandhu, Saṅghabhadra.

After the time of Vasubandhu, the Sautrāntikas divided themselves into two groups; those who followed the discourses or Sūtras alone and those who followed logical investigation which was not necessarily spoken directly by the Buddha. Thus, the later Sautrāntikas differed from the earlier Sautrāntikas in their growing acceptance of the credibility of Abhidharma literature. However, they still held the view that the Sūtras were the only authoritative doctrinal source.

Early Precursors to the Mahāyāna Tradition

In the early development of the Mahāyāna doctrines, the Sarvāstivāda, as well as several of its offshoots including the Sautrāntika, Mahīśāsakas, Vātsīputrīyas, and Kāśyapīyas, played an influential role. However, the contribution of the Mahāsaṅghikas was more direct and significant.

The Mahāsaṅghikas were a proto-Mahāyāna school. Later a Stūpa was constructed by King Aśoka near Rājagṛha to mark the place where the Mahāsaṅghikas assembled their canonical texts into five baskets: Sūtra, Vinaya, Abhidharma, Saṃyukta, and Dhāraṇī. The latter two constitute supplementary baskets to the Tripiṭaka and contain Mahāyāna Sūtras. These original teachings of the Buddha which had been passed on orally from the time of the Buddha, were finally codified.

The early Mahāyāna Buddhists distinguished themselves from the followers of the Hīnayāna, who adhered closely to the original words spoken by the Buddha, primarily by their views concerning the nature of the Buddha, the ideal of the compassionate Bodhisattva, and the participation of the lay people, as well as the monks and nuns. While the Sautrāntika conception of the Buddha and Bodhisattva hardly differs from the conception of the Sthaviras, exalting the nature of the Arhant to the extent that even the Arhant's bodily constitution is considered to be absolutely pure, the Mahāsaṅghikas parallel the Mahāyāna doctrine that Buddhas and Bodhisattvas have superior capabilities that cannot be realized by the Arhant.

The Mahāsaṅghikas are also close to the Mahāyāna in that they acknowledge the existence of Nirmāṇakāya manifestations, as well as the emanations of the Sāmbhogakāya. Other early schools generally acknowledge only the Dharmakāya, in the sense of the totality of the Buddha's teaching. The *Satya-siddhi-śāstra* of Harivarman (third century A.D.) is one source that clearly states that the schools of the Mahāsaṅghika were unique in carrying forth doctrines which contained ontological theses having definite Mahāyānist tendencies.

The Mahāyāna did not in fact constitute a new set of teachings, but simply revealed a deeper level of meaning of those expounded by the Tathāgata. And in spite of doctrinal differences, all branches of the Saṅgha, whether they adhered to the views of either the Hīnayāna or Mahāyāna, respected and practiced the basic code of the Vinaya.

According to the Korean pilgrim, Houei-tch'ao, the two vehicles were being practiced conjointly at these early times in most of the Indian kingdoms. In only a few regions, such as Kapiśa, Tokharestan, Kaśgar, Karaśar, and Kuśā, did the Hīnayāna alone prevail. The regions in which only the Mahāyāna was cultivated include Khotan, Lampaka, Zabulistan, and Uḍḍiyāna, the birthplace of Padmasambhava.

Events Surrounding the Rise of Buddhism in India

The Buddhist Saṅgha, at the time of the its development, adopted much of what was in the Indian culture. The Buddha himself showed respect to the sacred places of the Brahmans and encouraged his followers to do the same. But, in believing that all men had an equal opportunity to attain enlightenment, the Buddha taught that the sacred teachings should be available to all people, not just the priestly or Brahman caste. The Blessed One spoke in the common language of the time to all who were receptive to his words, regardless of class or caste. Those who left their status in society in order to follow his teachings were no longer governed by the dictates or privileges of the traditional caste system.

The divisions into caste originated during the Vedic period, when the Āryan invaders took control of India. During this development of a new cultural tradition, India experienced great social transformations. Gradually, the early Vedic hierarchies settled into what became the four castes of Indian society. They are: the Brahman, or priestly class; the Kṣatriya, or warrior class; the Vaiśya, or agricultural class (which in later times became the merchant class); and the Śūdra, or servant class. In addition to these four, there were the 'outsiders' or *mleccha*, which included anyone outside the framework of the Indian social system. Brahmanism, which provided a philosophical foundation for the caste system, was the principal religious force present during the time of the Buddha. In spite of this, many powerful rulers, including Bimbisāra, the King of Magadha, were swayed by the Buddha's teachings.

Several years before the Buddha's Parinirvāṇa, King Bimbisāra was assassinated by his son, Ajātaśatru. Although he later became a Buddhist, Ajātaśatru continued his father's policy of expansion through military conquest. Shortly after the Buddha's passing, Ajātaśatru conquered the Vṛji Republic, the homeland of the Licchavi clan, who represented a second wave of Āryan immigration into India. Whatever their origin may have been as residents of the Himalayan foothills, they were related to the Śākya tribe and had affiliation with Nepal and Tibet from the time of gNya'-khri-btsan-po, the first king of Tibet (c. 450 B.C.) onward.

The successor to King Ajātaśatru, his son Udāyibhadra, transferred the capital of Magadha to Pāṭaliputra (modern Patnā). During this period (fourth century B.C.), the Magadhan Empire continued to

The Sāñchī Stūpa (above) ***and its Eastern Gate*** (opposite)
The various elements of this stuūpa together with its outer wall and four gates were constructed over two centuries. The gates depict birth stories and major events in the life of the Buddha.

expand and was recognized as the most powerful force in eastern India. The Buddhadharma spread towards Mathurā and the region between Magadha and the sea near Campa. Elements of the indigenous culture of the neighboring provinces were incorporated into the Buddhist canon of the local schools.

Because of the patronage by numerous influential kings like Bimbisāra (c. 542–490 B.C.) and Ajātaśatru (c. 490–458 B.C.), early Buddhism left monuments and shrines throughout its homeland. All through its history, Buddhism has provided the inspiration for the erection of great holy places. Early Buddhist art produced some of the finest examples of Indian architecture, among which is the Stūpa at Sāñchī, built around the first or second century B.C. Even more magnificent than this Stūpa at Sāñchī was the Stūpa of Amarāvatī, which, when completed at the end of the second century A.D., was adorned with carved panels portraying the life of the Buddha. From this period onward, Stūpas, which preserved the relics of the Buddha and his disciples, were erected all over India.

Buddhist paintings and sculpture adorned palaces as well as temples, and some of the frescoes and paintings of this period, such as the

The Ajantā Caves (above and opposite) These magnificent works of stone carved in the sides of the Ajantā hills are filled with innumerable relief sculptures and paintings throughout many temples and halls.

wall paintings of Ajantā, survive to this day. The collection of twenty-nine Ajantā caves, constructed between the first and seventh centuries A.D., preserve a variety of scenes from the Jātaka Tales of the Buddha's former lives, as well as scenes depicting the life of the times. The Ellorā caves, located near Ajantā, consist of approximately forty caves. Constructed between the fifth and eighth centuries, they contain Buddhist carvings and stone sculptures, some of the finest examples of Indian art.

The survival of Indian Buddhism, as well as the survival of its art, was chiefly dependent upon its patronage by kings and wealthy lay people. From the time of the Buddha onward, histories of India describe how certain kings supported Buddhism and played significant roles in its continuation. One of the most important of these rulers was King Aśoka, who, around the middle of the third century B.C., rose in power and influence.

Aśoka (Mya-ngan-med) consolidated the Mauryan empire which had been founded by his grandfather Candragupta. Greatly superior to his neighbors in military wealth and strength. Aśoka's early rule was one of warfare, culminating in the overtaking of Kalinga. Aśoka then became converted to Buddhism, and his support of Buddhism eventually led him to encourage the practice of non-violence. He strove to adorn his kingdom with the peace and harmony set forth by the teachings of the Buddha, giving up hunting, the traditional sport of kings, and serving two and a half years as a lay disciple (*upāsaka*). He thus illustrated that a king could rule in ways other than by force and bloodshed.

Aśoka supported the religious communities of the Brahmans, Jains, and Ājīvikas, as well as the Buddhists. It was his duty as emperor to remain unattached and unbiased toward any religion, although he did use Buddhism to unify his dominion. When we think of Aśoka, we may recall the time-honored inscriptions or edicts which he had placed throughout the provinces of India. At Lumbinī Grove, he had a pillar erected commemorating the birthplace of the Buddha. Written mostly in the Prakṛit dialect, similar edicts were placed on rocks, in caves, and on specially built pillars spanning from the northwest regions of Afghanistan to the Bay of Bengal, and southward nearly as far as Madras and Mysore. These edicts, which were placed throughout the entire area which Aśoka ruled, are some of the oldest forms of Indian documents. They generally described the Buddhist way of life and proper social action, emphasizing the practice of compassion and equal justice to all living beings.

Aśoka erected a temple in the village which was the birthplace of Śāriputra and which later became the site of Nālandā (Nālendra) University. He also made repairs on Śāriputra's Stūpa during one of his pilgrimages. He demonstrated the virtues of the Buddhist path in many ways, and through his royal support, Buddhism began its career as a world religion.

The Buddhadharma spread in two opposite directions from the Magadhan Empire. First it went towards the west, taking roots at Kauśāmbī, the center of the Sthaviras; then it went to Mathurā, to the northwest, and on to Kashmir. Mathurā became the center of the Sarvāstivādins, while in Kashmir the study and practice of the Mūlasarvāstivādin Vinaya blossomed and spread widely. Aśoka's influence was extended to all the neighboring kingdoms, which he encouraged to follow the teachings of the Buddhadharma. And it was Aśoka's close relative, Mahendra, who became a Buddhist monk and led the mission to Ceylon which resulted in King Devānampiya Tissa's conversion to Buddhism.

According to the Bramanical sources, Aśoka's successor, Saṃpadin, was not a Buddhist, but a Jain. Saṃpadin's successor, Śāliśūka (c. 215–202 B.C.), reestablished the cultural order set forth by Aśoka, and

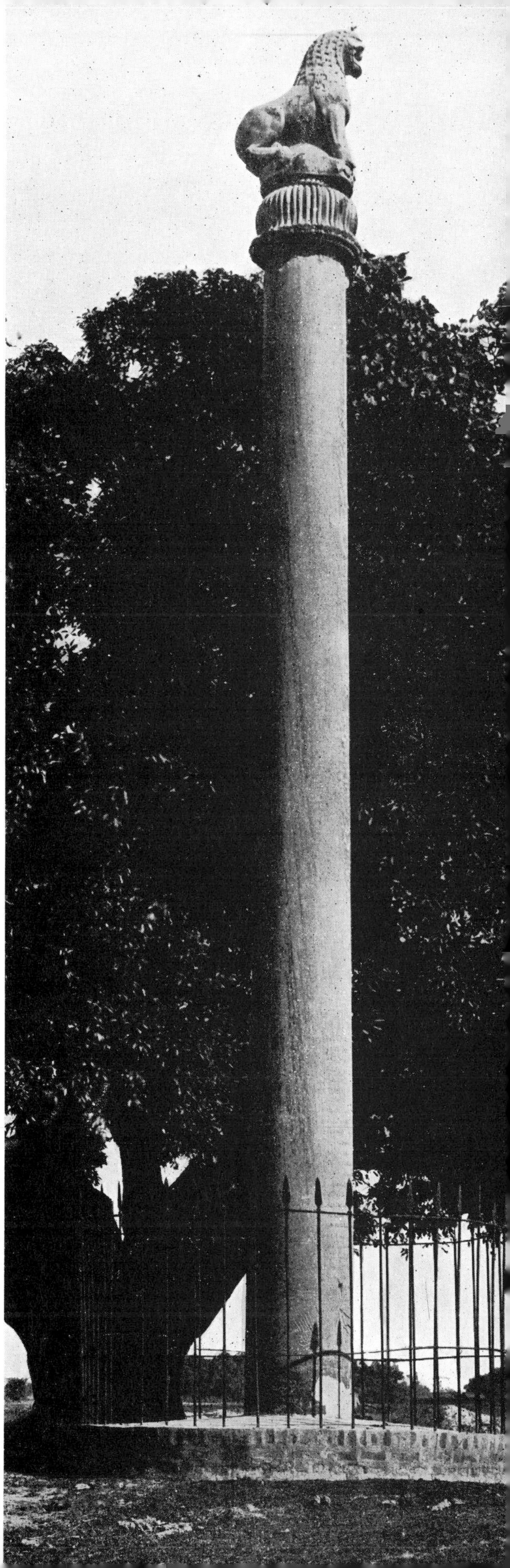

Aśokan Pillars, the Lion's Capital (above) ***from Sarnath; the Lion column*** (right) ***at Lauriya-Nandangarh***
Many such pillars were built by King Aśoka throughout India marking important places such as Lumbinī where Buddha was born and the future Nālandā where Śāriputra was born.

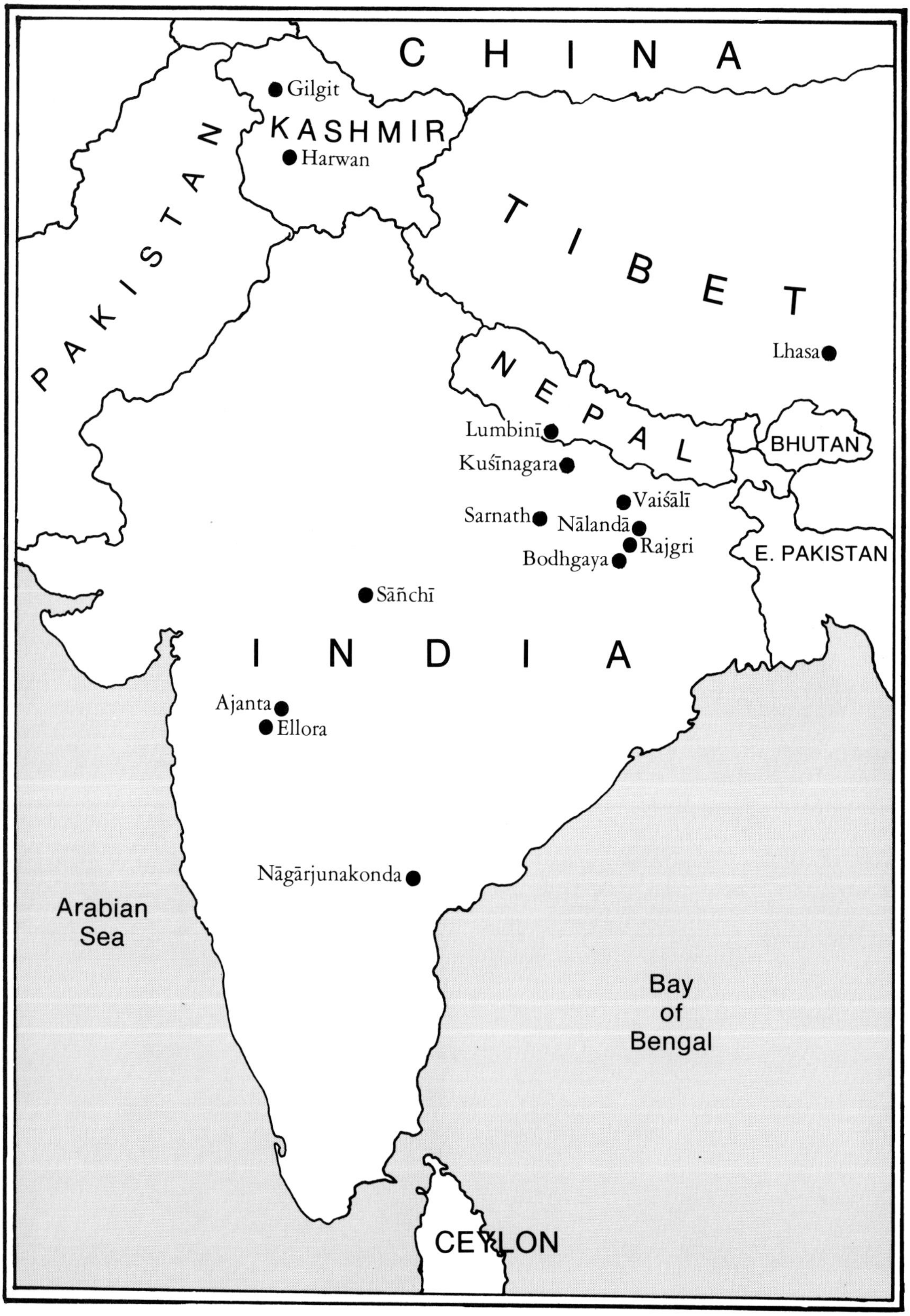
CHINA
Gilgit
KASHMIR
Harwan
PAKISTAN
TIBET
NEPAL
Lhasa
Lumbinī
Kuśīnagara
BHUTAN
Vaiśālī
Sarnath
Nālandā
Rajgri
Bodhgaya
E. PAKISTAN
Sāñchī
INDIA
Ajanta
Ellora
Nāgārjunakonda
Arabian Sea
Bay of Bengal
CEYLON

was probably a Buddhist. It seems unlikely, however, that Śāliśūka was as militarily aware as Aśoka, for it is during his reign that India's northwest frontier, the region known as Gandhāra, became dominated by Hellenistic rulers.

Almost a century before the reign of Aśoka, Alexander the Great had overthrown the Persian Empire (c. 325 B.C.), laying claim to the northwest-west sector of India. But with Alexander's departure, these militarily weak territories were easily taken hold of by King Candragupta, and hence they became part of a formidable empire which Aśoka was to inherit.

After the death of Alexander, Selencus Nicator, his successor, gained much power over the Macedonian Empire, and he attempted once again to bring the military night of the Greeks to the doors of India. It was around the year 305 B.C., that his forces came to battle, only to be defeated by Candragupta's army, which forced the Greeks to surrender a number of their newly won territories, including parts of Persia, Afghanistan, and the Punjab. From this battle, a healthy alliance was formed between the Indians and the Greeks, and Candragupta became ruler of almost the entire Indian continent.

During and shortly after the reign of Aśoka, many events were occurring to the west of India which would radically affect the peace of the Macedonian Empire. India was now entering an era during which it would suffer from recurring invasions by various forces outside its domain.*

Once the Iranian province of Parthia gained independence, the enthusiastic Parthians seized control of Persia and pushed onward until they were stopped in their tracks by the Romans in Mesopotamia (modern Iraq). India was first affected by these western invaders when a small colony of Greeks established themselves in Bactria and declared themselves independent of the Empire formed by Seleucus Nicator. This new independence must have given the rebellious Bactrian Greeks the license to invade, for they successfully took over parts of Afghanistan, up to the Hindu Kush, which was India's northwest frontier. Following this, the Bactrian Emperor, Demetrius, and his successor Demetrius II, pushed their forces in a southeasterly direction, into the Punjab. There they occupied much of the Indus valley, thus establishing Indo-Greek power in northwestern India.

---

*It should be noted that India, as we know it today, was rarely a political unity, not even during the famous Gupta Dynasty, though it may be thought of as a cultural unity.

One of the most noted emperors in Buddhist sources was King Menander, whose military might penetrated well beyond the Punjab to Pāṭaliputra, around 150 B.C. There were already indications at this time that a few of the Greek invaders supported Buddhism, and Menander was one of them. Menander became the patron of the Buddhist philosopher-monk Nāgasena. Also known as Milinda, his long dialogues with Nāgasena on the basic teachings of the Buddha were recorded in a well-known Pāli text, the *Milinda-pañhā*, the *Questions of Milinda*. In the literary sense, this text shows how the Greek form of dialogue was introduced into Indian literature.

At the death of King Menander (c. 130 B.C.), the ruling power of the Greeks in India waned, but the Greek cultural influences lived on. By the sixth century A.D., India had fully adopted the Greek sciences and had even gone beyond the Greeks in many areas of scholastic precision. It was the Indians, not the Arabs, who invented a sign for zero and developed both the decimal system and Algebra. (The Arabs later took these ideas from the Indians, and during the Dark Ages carried them to Europe, where the foundation for modern mathematics was laid).

Another result of the occupation of the northwest by the Greeks was that India became increasingly open to ideas coming from Persia and beyond. Throughout this period of its history, however, India was very much on the receiving end in the assimilation of new ideas. The Hellenistic Greeks had a substantial effect upon India in the areas of commerce and trade. They also showed the Indians how to mint coins of superb craftsmanship, and they influenced a school of religious art, known as the Gandhāran, which enhanced the Buddhist monasteries for a number of centuries.

Meanwhile, to the east of India, China was being troubled by Turkish tribes. About 175 B.C. the Yüeh-chih, later known as the Kuṣāṇas, were driven from their homes in northwestern China, and began their migrations across Central Asia. By about 100 B.C. they had driven the Śakas out of the Greek Bactrian kingdom and during the next century they established an empire which controlled the entire Indus Valley, northern and central India as far as Mathurā and Benares.

A prominent Kuṣāṇa emperor during the second century A.D., Kaniṣka, became a patron of Buddhism, and with his support the Sarvāstivādins became well-established in the regions of Mathurā and Kashmir. During this period, while the doctrines of this school were codified into the *Mahāvibhāṣā*, the Mahāyāna doctrines were spreading widely. Two distinguished scholars who appear at this time were Vasumitra and Buddhadeva. It was also at this time that the doctrines of the Elders (the Sthaviravādins, or in Pāli, the Theravādins), took root in Ceylon. From the island hermitages the Theravāda doctrine spread to Burma, Siam, and other parts of Southeast Asia, where it became the national religion.

Kaniṣka's empire extended over the western half of northern India as far as Benares and over much of the Indus basin and upper Ganges valleys, as well as Kashmir, Afghanistan, and parts of what is now Chinese Turkestan. Kaniṣika's capital was at Puruṣapura, which was the site for what was the tallest Stūpa in India, reaching more than six hundred feet. Although the Kuṣāṇa Empire was militarily ruled, it did mark a period of welcome peace and prosperity for northern India, which stimulated a rapid expansion of the Buddhist Saṅgha.

By the third century A.D., the great empires of the Kuṣāṇas had nearly disappeared. Historians indicate that this occurred because, due to the stability created by the Kuṣāṇa empire, the provincial governors managed to sever their ties with the central government and to become feudal lords. It is unclear exactly why this shift to decentralization of government took place. However, this change was at least temporarily advantageous for Buddhism, as it gave these feudal lords the ability to support the various Buddhist Saṅghas on a more individualized basis.

The rule of the Kuṣāṇas was assumed by the individual governors, most of whom consisted of the conquered Śakas, who took this opportunity in their role as 'vassal kings' to rebel against their overlords. At the same time, early in the third century A.D., a vigorous new military force in Persia, the Sāsānian Dynasty, arose and invaded Afghanistan, which at that time was under the rule of the Kuṣāṇas. Eventually, these invaders reached into the territory of Gandhāra, a trespass which contributed greatly to the downfall of the Kuṣāṇa empire. From the downfall of the Kuṣāṇa empire onwards, northern India did not become politically unified again until the rise of the Gupta Dynasty in the fourth century. The Persian rulers remained quite active in Afghanistan and Gandhāra until they were overthrown by the Turks in the seventh century.

The Later Development of Buddhism in India

The Two Most Excellent Ones and the Six Ornaments of India

Nāgārjuna and Asaṅga are traditionally known as the "Two Most Excellent Ones," while Āryadeva, Vasubandhu, Dignāga, Dharmakīrti, Guṇaprabha, and Śākyaprabha are known as the "Six Ornaments." During the development of Buddhism in India, the influence of these eight outstanding masters was unparalleled.

Nāgārjuna. Nāgārjuna (Klu-sgrub) was born in Vidarbha to a Brahman family of southern India, sometime between the first and second century A.D. His appearance was predicted by the Buddha in the *Mañjuśrī-mūla-tantra*:

> After I, the Buddha, have passed away,
> Four hundred years will elapse,
> And then a monk called Nāga will appear.
> He will be devoted to the Doctrine
> And be of great benefit to it.
> He will attain the Stage of Perfect Bliss,
> Live for six hundred years,
> And will secure the mystic knowledge
> Of the Mahāmayuri Tantra.
> He will know the subjects of the different sciences,
> And expound the Teaching of Non-substantiality.
> And after he has cast away his bodily frame,
> He will be reborn in the region of Sukhāvatī.
> And finally, he will attain Buddhahood.

There are other predictions about Nāgārjuna in the Mahāyāna Sūtras. For example, the *Laṅkāvatāra* says:

The Bodhisattva A wall painting from Ajantā.

In the southern country of Vedalys
A monk glorious and greatly renowned
Whose name is sounded Nāga
Will put an end to extreme views.
And after he has taught in this world
My teaching—that of the Great Vehicle,
Of which there is none higher—
He will secure the Stage of Perfect Bliss
And pass away into the Sukhāvatī Heaven.

When Nāgārjuna was a new-born child, an astrologer predicted that he would come to a pre-mature death. By offering feasts to the Brahman priests, the infant's life was extended to seven months, and the sooth-sayers predicted that with additional feasts, it could be extended to seven years, but absolutely no longer. His parents conducted the feasts, but at the end of the seventh year, they could no longer bear the prospect of beholding their son dead, so they sent him forth to wander with a servant. The son travelled throughout southern India until eventually he beheld the Bodhisattva Avalokiteśvara, who led him to the gates of Nālandā, the greatest Buddhist university and monastery. There he met the Brāhmaṇa Saraha (Rāhulabhadra), to whom he told his story. This teacher suggested a means for prolonging his life: reciting the *mantra* of Amitāyus, the Buddha of Long Life and Conqueror of Yāma, the Lord of Death. The boy did so, performing a special *sādhana* on the eve of his eighth birthday, and was thereby delivered from the Lord of Death. His parents were overjoyed and he was ordained by Saraha, taking the name Śrīman.

According to Ye-shes mTsho-rgyal, Padmasambhava's consort and foremost disciple, Nāgārjuna's father was a great yogi king named Balin, who was learned in medicine. The King had a son by each of his two wives. He taught all his knowledge of medicine to the son of the elder wife, but to Nāgārjuna he taught nothing. When he was about to retire, Balin announced that he would relinquish his throne to whichever son had the greater knowledge of medicine. The younger wife wept bitterly, for she knew her son had no chance. So, to make his mother happy, Nāgārjuna decided to win the contest. Going to a nearby cemetery, he met Guru Padmasambhava who was residing there, and from the Guru he learned the five basic kinds of medicine, plus the five higher kinds which were profoundly secret and studied only cursorily by the king himself. The contest between the sons took the form of a public examination, with the son of the elder wife taking the first turn. He expounded each of the five kinds of medicine

Nāgārjuna

in turn, explicitly and implicitly, and inspired the audience with awe at his all-inclusive knowledge. They said to one another: "By diligent application, the Prince has truly absorbed the wisdom of the father; just as the moon illumines the night sky, he has revealed the totality of knowledge. Of what use is it to listen to the other son who has received no teachings?"

Undaunted and full of confidence in Padmasambhava, the second son began his recital. Like the endless breakers of a vast ocean, his understanding rolled again and again over the assembly, overwhelming even King Balin with its power. After having elucidated the worldly sciences, the second son then spoke of the noble doctrines of the Buddhadharma with such great skill that Devas, Nāgas, and Ḍākinīs came to make obeisance. Now the people said, "Even though the first son is like the moon in its fullness, the second is like the sun, whose splendor is incomparable!" Abounding with such sentiment, King Balin touched his head to his son's feet, declaring him successor to the throne. But the boy had no thirst for worldly power, so instead he went to study further with Guru Padmasambhava. After this, he wrote many works on Sūtra, Mantra, and Tantra, and was known by the name Siddhi-phala, or 'Result of Realization'.

Around this same time, Dharmarāja Buddhapakṣa had a minister named Kakutsiddha, who built the great monastery of Vikramaśīla. For its dedication, Kakutsiddha arranged a lavish ceremonial feast, inviting everyone from the entire region. Two non-Buddhist beggars wandered by and asked for some morsels of food, but instead, certain of the young monks showered them with garbage, and set vicious dogs on them. The beggars became extremely angry, vowing retribution, and making plans for revenge. They decided that only one of them would continue to beg, freeing the other to engage in continuous *sūrya-siddha-sādhana*, whereby he would propitiate the sun and be empowered with its energy. After twelve years spent in a deep pit, he perfected this practice. He climbed out of the hole and scattered magic ashes all around, causing a miraculously-produced flame to emerge and engulf all the eighty-four temples of Vikramaśīla which stood nearby. All the buildings, shrines, images, and texts caught fire, nearly destroying all vestiges of the Dharma. However, on the ninth story of one of the larger temples were the Anuttara-yoga Tantras; from these texts issued forth streams of cool water which quenched the all-consuming fire. After this, the two beggars escaped in the direction of Siam, but were themselves consumed by the self-kindled flames of their own deeds. The fire was a great set-back for the Propagation of the Dharma, since more than three quarters of all the Buddhist literature was destroyed; only about one fifteenth of all the Mahāyāna works remained. For example, only one chapter of the *Laṅkāvatāra-sūtra* was left (which we regard today as its entirety) and, only thirty-eight of the one thousand chapters of the *Avataṃsaka-sūtra* survived.

The smoke from this great conflagration caused Mucilinda, the king of the Nāgas, to become very ill. His condition became increasingly desperate, and the foremost doctor in all of Jambudvīpa, Siddhi-phala, was finally summoned. The Great Doctor had little difficulty in healing Mucilinda, and as a reward, the Nāgarāja opened the treasury of the Seven Jewels, giving him the greater part of the *Prajñāpāramitā-sūtra* in one hundred thousand verses. The Nāga king had been guarding this text since Ānanda, the chief disciple of Lord Buddha, had entrusted it to him for future revelation. Later, Siddhi-phala returned to the Nāga realm for the rest of this Sūtra and for many others preserved only there. Thus, he received the name Nāgārjuna.

The significance of Nāgārjuna's name was outlined sometime later by a well-known follower, Candrakīrti, in the preface to his treatise entitled *The Clear Worded*:

> I bow before that Nāgārjuna who has rejected
> The adherence to the two extreme points of view
> Who has become born in the ocean of Dharmadhātu
> And who from compassion has expounded all the depths
> Of the Treasury of the Highest Teaching as he has known it himself.
> The fires of his Doctrine consume the fuel
> Of every contradictory, conflicting view;
> While its brilliance dispels until this very day
> The mental darkness of the entire world.
> His incomparable wisdom and words, like the weapons of the mighty,
> Secure for him sovereignty over the three spheres of existence,
> Over all the world of converts, including the gods,
> And vanquish the host of enemies–the hosts of Phenomenal Existence.

Just as the Nāgas live in the ocean, so does he live in the ocean of Dharmadhātu. Just as the Nāgas have no permanent place of abiding, neither does the Nāgārjuna hold either of the extreme views. While the Nāgas possess great treasures of jewels and gold, Nāgārjuna possesses the insurpassable Jewel of the Dharma, the Wish-Fulfilling Gem. With a single glance, like the glow of their fiery eyes, he penetrates the whole of existence. This is why he is called Nāga. Since he has subdued the sinful powers of the world and acts as guardian of the Dharma realms, he is called Ārjuna, holder of power.

Nāgārjuna began his studies at Nālandā under the guidance of Rāhulabhadra (Saraha), who was one of the Eighty-four Mahāsiddhas and a direct disciple of the Buddha's son Rāhula. Rāhulabhadra learned the Mayāyāna Sūtras and Outer Tantras principally from tutelary deities, Yi-dam, who were appointed by the Buddha to safeguard these teachings and practices. Nāgārjuna studied so extensively and became so respected that in only a short time he was made the Abbot of Nālandā University. Nālandā became so famous through the guidance of Nāgārjuna that it even eclipsed the importance of Vajrasāna (Bodh Gayā).

Although it is not completely accurate to say that Nāgārjuna was the founder of the Mādhyamika philosophy, he brought to maturity the teachings of that philosophy, which had been previously propounded by his teacher, Rāhulabhadra. Nāgārjuna composed a great number of texts, both commentaries and original works, based on the *Prajñāpāramitā-sūtras*. But Nāgārjuna's most important contribution to Buddhist philosophy was in the Mādhyamika, or Middle Path, which recognizes the logical fallacy of clinging to either facet of dualistic belief: in particular, the two extremes of nihilism and eternalism. Through the use of carefully honed logic, the Ācārya founded a dialect which can prevent any reasonable person from falling into false views. This Mādhyamika is the medicine which the Great Doctor applied to the dis-ease of sentient beings. He applied the Dharma through his knowledge of subjects ranging from logic (*nyāya*) and dialectical argumentation to magic, medicine, chemistry, alchemy, and government. Demonstrating his superior knowledge in debates with the non-Buddhists (*tīrthikas*), he caused the teachings of the Mahāyāna to shine like the sun.

The Tibetan canon lists about 180 works attributed to Nāgārjuna. Among the many diverse texts are six metaphysical treatises which later became the fundamental texts of the Mādhyamika philosophy. They are: *Śūnyatā-saptati, Prajñā-mūla, Yukti-ṣaṣtikā, Vigraha-vyāvartanī, Vaidalya-sūtra*, and *Vyavahāra-siddhi*. These texts include the subjects of logic, epistemology, sources of valid knowledge, and relative and ultimate truth (*saṃvṛti-satya* and *paramārtha-satya*). Nāgārjuna also wrote texts which served to critically evaluate the doctrines of the other Buddhist schools, such as the Sarvāstivādins.* Many of these works deal specifically with the practical side of the Doctrine, while others implement the tools of logic, thus clearing away confusion and making way for unobscured understanding (*rigs-gotra*). Nāgārjuna also wrote two important 'letters', the *Ratnāvali* and the *Suhṛllekha*, which outline the chief points of conduct for the layman. Another of his texts is the *Pratītya-samutpāda hṛdaya-śāstra*, an exposition of the Twelve-linked Chain of Interdependent Origination.†

Towards the end of his life, Nāgārjuna lived under the patronage

*These texts are: *Mūla-Mādhyamika-kārikā* (*Mādhyamika-śāstra*), *Vigraha-vyāvartanī, Ekaśloka-śāstra, Dvādaśa-mukha-śāstra, Śūnyatā-saptati, Yukti-ṣaṣtika, Bodhisattva-pātheya-śāstra, Mahāprajñāpāramitā-śāstra, Daśabhūmi-vibhāṣā-śāstra,* and *Ārya-dharmadhātu-garbha-vivaraṇa.*

†The twelve 'causes' for conditioned existence (*gleng-gzhi'i-sde, nidāna*) as set forth by the Buddha are:

1. ignorance (*ma-rig-pa, avidyā*)
2. motivation-configuration (*'du-byed, saṃskāra*)

of a King Antīvāhana. In return for the royal patronage, Nāgārjuna provided the king with an elixir of long-life. The king's son, Śaktiman, being impatient to reign, eventually realized that he would have to cut off the source of this wonder drug, and to accomplish this, would have to assasinate Nāgārjuna. Now during this time, Nāgārjuna was wont to spend his days in solitary meditation on Śrī Parvata, so he did not hear his assassin's approach, but remained seated with bowed head, deep in meditation, as Śaktiman lifted the blade high and gleaming. He did not so much as stir as the sword whistled down like a scythe. The surprise was Śaktiman's when the blade rebounded from the bared neck, as if having struck an iron column. Only then did Nāgārjuna look up and acknowledge his executioner: "You are surprised by your weapon's impotence, and afraid your purpose will be frustrated. But many life times ago, I was walking along in the forest and accidentally brushed an insect with a blade of *kuśa* grass, slicing the insect in two and killing it. Now, owing to this deed, the present situation has arisen, and though my neck is impervious to steel, it can be easily hewn with a single stalk of *kuśa* grass. May my error serve as an example of the infallibility of karma!"

As Nāgārjuna was finishing his explanation, Śaktiman's eyes searched out a piece of *kuśa* grass, and plucking it up, he easily severed the Ācārya's head, Again Śaktiman was awe-struck, as from the bloody base of the neck he heard a distant voice:

> I shall now depart for Sukhāvatī Heaven
> But afterwards I will enter this body again.

A female Yakṣa took possession of the severed head, and deposited

---

3. perception (*rnam-par shes-pa, vijñāna*)
4. name and form (*ming-gzugs, nāma-rūpa*)
5. six sensory fields (*skye-mched drug, ṣaḍāyatana*)
6. contact (*reg-pa, sparśa*)
7. feeling (*tshor-ba, vedanā*)
8. desire (*sred-pa, tṛṣṇā*)
9. ascription-organization (*len-pa, upādāna*)
10. existence (*srid-pa, bhava*)
11. birth (*skye-ba, jāti*)
12. old age and death (*rga-shi, jarāmaraṇa*)

Nāgārjuna declared that the first, eighth and ninth members represent emotionality (*nyon-mongs-pa, kleśa*); the second and tenth represent action (*las, karman*), and the remaining third, fourth, fifth, sixth seventh, eleventh, and twelfth represent misery (*sdug-bsngal, duḥkha*). The Buddha stated that one who clearly and deeply comprehends this twelve link chain (*pratītya-samutpāda*) actually penetrates the essence of the Dharma itself.

it several miles away from the rest of the corpse. However, neither part of the body decayed, but instead, year after year, as if by magnetism, they drew nearer and nearer together. Finally the head and body touched and fused, and Nāgārjuna came back to life, working for the sake of all sentient beings.

In total, Nāgārjuna worked six hundred years throughout the various regions and in various situations for the promotion of the Buddhadharma. In the course of his long life, he studied under at least five hundred learned teachers, attending carefully to their teachings and compiling their instructions; he meditated on the teachings' practical application and expounded on its import. With the splendor of the Great Doctor, few can compare, and as the Father of the Mahāyāna, he is revered as the first of the Most Excellent Ones, the most illustrious of the Charioteers of India.

Asaṅga. Together with Nāgārjuna, Asaṅga (Thogs-med) was one of the key figures in the elucidation of the Mahāyāna, and was born around 290 A.D. in Puruṣapura, the capital of Gandhāra. During his twelve-year residence at Nālandā, he brought numerous scholars—both non-Buddhist and Hīnayāna—over to the teachings of the Mahāyāna, and through his efforts, the Mahāyāna spread throughout India. Asaṅga was also a forerunner to the philosophical line known as the Cittamātra (Sems-tsam) or the Yogācāra (Vijñānavāda) tradition.

Asaṅga studied the Hīnayāna teachings as a youth, but became dissatisfied with them, as they did not help him to penetrate the meaning of the *Prajñāpāramitā-sūtras*. In an effort to deepen his understanding he began to pray to Maitreya, and for three years meditated in a cave, reciting the *Ārya-maitreya-sādhana*, but without any noticeable success. He became disheartened and decided to abandon his spiritual pursuit. Leaving the cave, he saw that the rocks near the entrance had been worn away during his three year retreat by birds brushing them daily with their wings. Similarly, he saw how dripping water had eroded even the largest of stones. This realization inspired him to continue his meditation for three more years. But still, his understanding was not complete. Once again discouraged, he left the cave in search of food and came upon an old man who was producing needles by rubbing an iron rod with a piece of cotton. Inquiring how it was possible to produce needles in this manner. Asaṅga received the reply:

> If a man possessed of moral strength
> Wishes to accomplish something

Asaṅga

> He never meets with failure,
> No matter how difficult the work may be.

He took this advice to heart, and once again resumed his practice. Yet, even after twelve years of continuous meditation, Asaṅga felt he had gained nothing. So, in total despair, he decided to abandon his quest completely. As he was leaving his retreat, he came across a dog, half-infested with maggots. Asaṅga became full of compassion for the dog, but he realized that if he removed the maggots from the dog, they would starve. Yet, if he did not, the dog would die. So he decided to remove the maggots and place them on a piece of his own flesh. But the maggots were so delicate and vulnerable that the pressure of his fingers might harm them. Thus, he resolved to remove them with his tongue. Closing his eyes, he reached out for the dog, but at that moment, she disappeared, and he beheld Maitreya, showering cascades of light in all directions.

> O my father (said Asaṅga), my unique refuge,
> I have exerted myself a hundred different ways,
> But nevertheless I saw nothing.
> Why have the rain-clouds and the might of the ocean,
> Come only now when, tormented by violent pain,
> I am no longer thirsting?

Rebuked in such manner, Ārya-Maitreya rejoined:

> Though the king of the Devas sends down rain,
> A bad seed is unable to grow!
> Though the Buddhas may appear in this world,
> He who is unworthy cannot partake of the bliss.
> From the beginning, I was here,
> But your obscurations blinded you.
> Now that Compassion has arisen,
> You have become pure and empowered to perceive me.
> To test my words, raise me on your shoulders
> For others to see—carry me across the city.

So, across the crowded bazaar of Acintya, Asaṅga carried the Bodhisattva on his shoulders, yet no one saw Maitreya. One old woman saw Asaṅga carrying a pup, and as a result, became fantastically wealthy. A poor porter saw Maitreya's toes, and attained *samādhi* and *sadharaṇa siddhi*. Asaṅga himself immediately attained the *Srotaḥ-anugataḥ-nāma-samādhi*.

Then holding Ārya-Maitreya's robe, Asaṅga went with him to Tuṣita Heaven, where he heard the Mahāyāna Doctrine expounded by the Ajītanātha. After he learned the real significance of all the Sūtras, he listened to the "Five Works of Maitreya," which are the *Mahāyāna-sūtrālaṅkāra, Madhyāntā-vibhaṅga, Dharmadharmatā-vibhaṅga, Uttara-tantra*, and *Abhisamayālaṅkāra*. As each of the five-fold teachings was being expounded, Asaṅga simultaneously attained *samādhi*. Asaṅga is said to have resided for fifty years in Tuṣita Heaven, receiving teachings from Maitreya. Although he was over ninety years old when he returned from Tuṣita, Asaṅga was possessed with the same youthful vigor that was his before he left.

When he returned to Earth, he began to expound the Dharma, but still had some difficulty completely elucidating the Teachings. Therefore, at Asaṅga's request, Maitreya descended at night, showering him with light, and recited the *Daśabhūmika-sūtra* and a commentary on it. By day, Asaṅga memorized and interpreted the text. Finally, Maitreya instructed him in the *Sūrya-prabhā-samādhi*, by which Asaṅga came to full understanding.

Working for the sake of sentient beings, he established the Dharmankūra Vihāra in Veluvana Forest. Here Asaṅga instructed eight disciples, all of whom attained freedom from re-birth; and here also, he wrote down Maitreya's Five Works, as well as several original treatises of his own, such as *Abhidharma-samuccaya* and the *Mahāyāna-saṃgraha*. In his *Abhidharma-samuccaya*, Asaṅga added a deep structural component to the picture drawn by his younger brother, Vasubandhu, in his *Abhidharma-kośa*. It is in the *Samuccaya* that Asaṅga brings to the foreground the concept of a substratum (*ālaya*) which preserves and resurrects every mental event surfacing in awareness.

Asaṅga's philosophical understanding of the many doctrines of the Buddha's teachings brought him countless students, as well as the favor of many kings. He also succeeded in convincing his younger brother, Vasubandhu, of the profundity of the Mahāyāna approach to the Dharma.

His strong moral conduct and great learning made Asaṅga highly respected by all schools. He is rightly called the foremost teacher of the Mahāyāna Doctrine, because during his life the number of Mahāyāna monks reached ten thousand.

Āryadeva. Nāgārjuna's foremost disciple and spiritual son was Āryadeva ('Phags-pa'i-lha), who continued to advance his teachings. Through his writings, Āryadeva further expounded the Mādhyamika, especially in the *Catuḥ-śataka* and *Hasta-vāla-prakaraṇa*. In other works, Āryadeva refuted the challenges of opponents, particularly the non-Buddhists, and outlined the basis of philosophical and Tantric systems.

At the time when Guru Padmasambhava was residing in a cemetery in Siṃhala (present-day Ceylon), while in deep meditation, he perceived an army destroying what was left of Vikramaśīla Monastery after the great fire. The next morning, the king's gardener found in the royal garden a gigantic lotus blossom that stayed open day and night. He sent word to the King who came to inspect the sight. In the middle of the lotus blossom King Śrī Phala beheld a young boy. When the chief priest was consulted, he predicted: "This boy is destined to defeat Maticitra, the arch-enemy of Buddhism who has taken Mahādeva as his tutelary deity. You should take this boy into your palace and raise him

Āryadeva

as your son." The child received initiation from Padmasambhava, and received the name Āryadeva. He begged Padmasambhava to grant him ordination, but was refused, since Nāgārjuna was destined to be his primary teacher.

He then entered into study, and mastered the entire Hīnayāna teachings. As a young man going on pilgrimage to India, Āryadeva travelled to Śrī Parvata, where Nāgārjuna was then staying. For quite some time he remained there, penetrating the great master's understanding of non-substantiality. At this time, Āryadeva also received the Tantric teachings and achieved magical powers.

Now, during this time there was a Brahman known as Maticitra, so named because of his devotion to his mother. Well-versed in mantra, non-Buddhist Tantra, and debate, he received direct teachings from

Mahādeva. With this power, Maticitra was able to vanquish many Buddhists in debate, forcing them to become *tīrthikas*.

Humiliated by this unconquerable opponent, the monks at Nālandā sent an invitation to Āryadeva and made many offerings to Mahākāla, that this powerful adversary might be subdued. A black crow emerged from the stone image of Mahākāla and bore this invitation to the Ācārya. The latter then realized it was time for him to travel to Nālandā.

Along the way, Āryadeva met a *tīrthika* woman who requested that he give to her one of his eyes so that she could complete some magical rites. Āryadeva complied and resumed his journey, and, using the power of supernatural travel, he arrived at the scene of the dispute. Upon arriving at Nālandā, he erected prayer flags, and encircled the entire area with magical charms. Three times Āryadeva defeated Maticitra in debate, and as Maticitra attempted to escape embracing the Buddhist Doctrine by flying into the sky, Āryadeva subdued him by means of *mantra*. Maticitra was imprisoned in a temple, and as he was reading in his room, he saw the prediction about himself in the Scriptures. Filled with great faith, he took refuge in the Triple Gem of Buddhism. The monks rejoiced at this great victory.

Later, Tārā came to Maticitra in a dream, and told him to compose many hymns to the Buddha in atonement for his past destructive actions. He did so, and became a very well known composer of beautiful *stotras* which were memorized by all.

During the reign of Candragupta, Āryadeva remained at Nālandā for quite a long time as chief professor, expounding the Dharma there, and working for the sake of all sentient beings through his dedicated study and meditation. In the course of his life, he built twenty-four monasteries, using gifts bestowed by the local deities. Each of these monasteries became a significant center for the study of the Mahāyāna. Āryadeva is said to have visited the realm of the Nāgas on seven occasions and these visits inspired him to write a number of Mahāyāna Sūtras. His scholarly contribution consists of six major works on logical disputation, epistemology, and the chief doctrines of the Mahāyāna, as well as a few works on Tantra. Tradition says that he attained the eighth Bhūmi of the Bodhisattva.

Vasubandhu. Vasubandhu (dByig-gnyen) was born to a Brahman family somewhere near Kaniṣika's capital. As a monk in a Sarvāstivādin monastery, he acquired an excellent knowledge of the literature and doctrines of this school. Under the directions of his teachers, Vasubandhu memorized the entire Tripiṭaka. He devoted himself to the study of the sacred texts and specialized in the Sarvāstivādin Abhidharma, though he was versed in Vaibhāṣika and Sautrāntika lines of thought as well. Vasubandhu is looked upon as one of India's greatest dialecticians, scholastics, and contemplatives.

At an early age Vasubandhu began studying the *Vibhāṣā* with his first teacher Buddhamitra in Gandhāra. Then, in an attempt to solve unanswered questions concerning Vaibhāṣika doctrines, he received extensive instruction in the Sautrāntika doctrines from Manoratha. Vasubandhu decided that in order to determine which of the two lines of thought was the superior he would travel to Kashmir to investigate the Vaibhāṣika teachings more fully. The Vaibhāṣika doctrines were so deeply rooted in the Kashmirian soil, that the Kasmirians had strong feelings against the Sautrāntika doctrines. Vasubandhu thus feared that the Kashmirian scholars might bar him from studying there, so he entered the country secretly, pretending to be a lunatic so that the people would be sure not to mistake him for a scholar. Posing in various, sometimes humorous, guises. Vasubandhu soon found his way to the great Vaibhāṣika study center in Kashmir. He studied there with Saṅghabhadra and spent four years (c. 342–346 A.D.) studying the *Vibhāṣā* under the master Skandhila, the author of the *Abhidharmāvatāra*, an orthodox Vaibhāṣika treatise preserved in both Tibetan and Chinese.

In the course of his studies, Vasubandhu often expressed his increasing frustration with the rigidity of the teachings. Finally, wishing to know who this brilliant yet vociferous study really was, Skandhila entered into a state of *samādhi*, by which powers he recognized Vasubandhu's true identity. This recognition worried Skandhila greatly, and he privately advised Vasubandhu to return to his native country at once, before he came to harm. Now, more convinced than ever that the Sautrāntika system displayed deeper philosophical insight than that of the Vaibhaṣika, Vasubandhu decided to return to his homeland. Upon reaching the border of Kashmir, the protective deities of the gate warned the people that a great scholar of Abhidharma, who possessed a full understanding of the teachings of the Vaibhāṣika, was about to leave the country. But the people, remembering Vasubandhu in his guise as a lunatic, did not believe it. Nevertheless, he was barred exit three times, but on his fourth attempt he was allowed to freely pass through the gate and return to his native city of Puruṣapura.

Vasubandu

After returning home, Vasubandhu supported himself by giving lectures on the Vaibhāṣika system to the general public. At the end of each lecture Vasubandhu would compose a verse or *kārikā* which summed up the day's lecture. These were engraved on copper plates which were hung around the neck of an elephant. Beating a drum, Vasubandhu would challenge anyone to refute the treatise. Within two years he had composed over six-hundred verses, which gave an extensive outline of the entire Vaibhāṣika system. These verses constitute the *Abhidharma-kośa*, which is widely accepted by the different schools even up to the present time, because of its all-encompassing scope. This great text reviews the totality of Buddhist psychology, discussing the mind and its mental events, and analysing this difficult subject into clear systems of functional relationships.

Upon completion of the *Kośa*, he sent it, along with fifty pounds of gold, to his old teachers in Kashmir. The professors of the Kashmirian school were elated that Vasubandhu had composed such a treatise on the Vaibhāṣika doctrine. Several Kashmirian Vaibhāṣikas then sent a hundred pounds of gold to Vasubandhu and asked him to write a commentary. Vasubandhu answered their request by sending them his *Abhidharmakośa-bhāṣya*, which he had already completed. This work criticizes the Vibhāṣika from the Sautrāntika viewpoint. It is one of the most outstanding works ever written on Abhidharma, but the orthodox Vaibhāṣikas were highly offended by it.

Around 350 A.D., Vasubandhu returned to Nālandā, where he heard of the fame of his brother, Asaṅga, and listened to some of his treatises. Scornful of his brother's understanding, and with a mind closed to the Mahāyāna, Vasubandhu exclaimed:

> Alas, Asaṅga, residing in the forest,
> Has practiced meditation for twelve years.
> Without having attained anything by this meditation,
> He has founded a system, so difficult and burdensome
> That it can be carried only by an elephant!

Asaṅga soon learned of this attitude, and he resolved to convert Vasubandhu to the Mahāyāna. He sent two of his students with Mahāyāna texts to recite for Vasubandhu. The evening they arrived they recited, according to their instructions, the *Akṣayamati-nirdeśa-sūtra*. At this time Vasubandhu thought that the Mahāyāna appeared to be logically well founded but that its practices were not conducive to upholding the vows, and could not lead to purification. The next morning, the students recited the *Daśabhūmika-sūtra* as had been expounded by Maitreya. From hearing these texts, Vasubandhu realized that the Mahāyāna was sound in both theory and practice, and he accepted the teachings of his brother. He was struck with great shame at having belittled the Great Doctrine, and started looking for a razor to cut off the tongue which had formed such contemptuous words towards the Mahāyāna. But Asaṅga's two students stopped him, saying, "Why cut off your tongue? Your own brother knows how to absolve you–go to the Ārya and pray to him."

Vasubandhu did so, inquiring how he could make atonement. Asaṅga, in turn, asked Maitreya and relayed the message back to Vasubandhu: "Preach the Mahāyāna doctrine extensively; prepare many commentaries on the Sūtras; and recite for a hundred thousand times, the *Uṣṇīṣavijaya-dhāraṇi*." Hearing the Mahāyāna teachings only once from Asaṅga, Vasubandhu quickly learned all of them.

Vasubandhu also was a leading recipient of the Vinaya lineage of Rāhula. He was the first to elucidate on two very important sections of the Vinaya and the Buddhadharma, known in Tibetan as *lung* and *rtogs-pa*. The *lung* (equivalent to the Sanskrit term Āgama) is the oral tradition of the Buddha's teachings as preserved through an intellectual explanation (*bshad-pa*) of the texts. The realization of the meaning which brings about the experience of true understanding is known as *rtogs-pa*, which comes about through *sādhana* (*sgrub-pa*) practice. Vasubandhu stated that the whole of the Buddha's teachings is divided up between these two, the *lung-chos* and the *rtogs-pa'i chos*. Moreover, if *lung* and *rtogs-pa* did not exist, then the Buddhadharma would not exist. *rTogs-pa* is considered to be an antidote to the *kleśas* or karmic chains, and has the beneficial result of allowing the mind to transmute all negativity into effective meditative techniques which lead to the experience of *samādhi*. Thus, *rtogs-pa*, or the realization of true meaning, is achieved through meditation (*sgrub-pa*). For the Hīnayāna, the chief focus of *rtogs-pa* is subduing the passions and negative emotions. For the Mahāyāna, the path consists of the transmutation of negative energy patterns into a healthy and balanced life.

After the passing of his brother, Vasubandhu became Abbot (Upādhyāya) of Nālandā University. During his career there, he taught some sixty thousand monks, and of these, nearly a thousand accompanied him on later travels. There also have been recorded a number of special occurrences for which he was responsible, such as the suppression of epidemics and the extinguishing of fires. His efforts towards the advancement of the Mahāyāna in Nepal were also quite successful.

When Vasubandhu was about sixty years old, he conquered the Saṃkhya philosophers who had previously defeated and humiliated his aged teacher Buddhamitra. For his victory over the Saṃkhyas in debate and for his treatise *Paramārtha-saptati*, Emperor Candragupta II awarded him three *lakhs* of gold, with which he built three monasteries for the study of both Mahāyāna and Sarvāstivāda.

Several years later, his former teacher, Saṅghabhadra, who had become a major figure in Vaibhāṣika thought, challenged Vasubandu to a debate. But because Saṅghabhadra was too aged to travel long distances, the debate never took place. Before he died, Saṅghabhadra sent his works to Vasubandhu, asking that he preserve them, which was done.

Of Vasubandhu's numerous writings, one of his chief exegetical treatises was a voluminous commentary on the *Pañcaviṃśātisahaśrīka,* which became the Mahāyāna counterpart to the Sarvāstivādin Abhi-

Dignāga

dharma. He is also known to have written a few works on logic. In all, he wrote more than fifty commentaries to both the Hīnayāna and Mahāyāna Sūtras, and eight original treatises.

Dignāga. Dignāga (Blo-gros-brtan-pa) was born into a Brahman family which resided in southern India during the second half of the fourth century. He was ordained into monkhood by Nāgadatta of the Vātsīputrīya school, which is often classified as the Pudgalavāda because they affirmed the existence of an individual substance apart from its composite elements. He diligently studed the Śrāvaka Tripiṭakas and was instructed by Nāgadatta to "seek the indescribable self which is the essence of meditation." Though he faithfully practiced meditation and critical analysis, he could not find anything similar to the 'self' described by his preceptor. In desperation, he opened all the windows by day and lit many lamps at night, looking both externally and internally for an essential self, but he still could not find one. A friend of his noticed this somewhat eccentric behavior and reported it to Nāgadatta, who called upon Dignāga for an interview.

"Why is it that you indulge in such peculiar behavior; you are disturbing others with your conduct."

"Oh Upādhyāya," replied Dignāga, "because my intellect is weak, and my insight insufficient, I am failing your instructions. Due to obscurations, I cannot see this 'indescribable self' you speak of, though I am seeking it in many ways." But Nāgadatta, feeling that Dignāga was trying to refute his Vātsīputrīya doctrine, became very angry, and expelled Dignāga from the monastery.

Dignāga wandered about for some time, and eventually came to Nālandā, where Vasubandhu was Abbot. Under his guidance, Dignāga learned the Tripiṭaka of all three Yānas. Having received the *vidyā mantra*, he attained the power to directly behold Ārya Mañjuśrī, who expounded the Dharma to him at great length. Dignāga became particularly proficient in the Vijñānavāda and Logic, which became the major fields for his contributions to Buddhist philosophy.

Retiring to a solitary place in Odvisia, he entered a cave in Bhotasela Mountain, where he attained *samādhi*. Here he wrote commentaries to the *Abhidharma-kośa* (*Abhidharma-kośa-marma-pradīpa*) and to the *Guṇāparyanta-stotra*. He also wrote over one hundred other works. In order to systematize and unite all the themes of his earlier works he resolved to compose a major compendium, the *Pramāṇa-samuccaya*. As salutation to this work, he wrote with chalk on a wall of the cave:

> Homage to him who is Logic personified,
> The Teacher, the Blessed one, the Protector,
> Who pursues the welfare of all sentient beings.
> To expound the various meanings of this Logic
> I shall herein combine
> The meanings of my previous works.

Just as he finished writing, the earth shook, thunder and lightning flashed, and the legs of all the heretical teachers in the vicinity became as stiff as wood. One of them, named Kṛṣṇamunirāja, was living nearby, and understood the signs to be marks of Dignāga's great resolve. When Dignāga left the cave to beg for alms, the *tīrthika* entered and erased the salutation. Dignāga returned, and, with surprise, inferred the intrusion.

He rewrote the salutation from memory, but the next day, when he went out for alms, again Kṛṣṇamunirāja crept into the cave and rubbed out the inscription. Dignāga returned, and again wrote out the intention, but this time, he added a message to the intruder: "If you are erasing this as a joke, you should refrain, because my purpose is very lofty. And if you erase this verse, due to envy, it will be of no use, since I have memorized it. However, if you are willing to defend yourself in debate against my theses, wait here and we will have a discussion." Again, the earth trembled, and the air was filled with ominous roaring and flashing. When Kṛṣṇamunirāja returned the next day, he read Dignāga's note, and he awaited his return. When the Ācarya came back in, the opponents staked their beliefs as prize in the contest: whoever was defeated would have to embrace the doctrine of the victor. The arguments were given on both sides, and Kṛṣṇamunirāja was defeated. Then, a second and a third time, Dignāga's logic subdued the *tīrthika*. At this the Ācarya concluded: "I have vanquished your views and they crumble into dust. Now you must take refuge in the most Noble Doctrine." Kṛṣṇamunirāja instead became enraged and caused flames to issue from his mouth, and scattered enchanted ashes around the cave, burning up all of Dignāga's belongings, and very nearly burning him. The *tīrthika* then escaped in the confusion.

Dignāga became very depressed. "I am supposed to be working for the sake of all sentient beings, but I cannot bring the Dharma to even one. It is no use to continue in this way; it would be better to give up the idea of becoming a Bodhisattva and simply realize liberation for my own benefit. So he threw the piece of chalk with which he was writing into the air, resolutely intending to enter Nirvāṇa when it touched the ground. But the chalk remained in the air. At that moment, Mañjuśrī appeared before him: "Do not give up your good intention! By associating with *tīrthikas*, incorrect ideas have arisen in your mind, but you should know that no heretic can harm your work. I will remain your spiritual friend until you attain Buddhahood; and know that in the future, this treatise will be the sovereign of the Śāstras." Speaking thus, he vanished. With his obstacles removed, Dignāga proceeded to compose the *Pramāṇa-samuccaya*, and was indeed very successful in his work. Dignāga travelled to southern India to spread the doctrine; entering into debate with various *tīrthika* rivals, he was always victorious. In fact, during his career he defeated most of the non-Buddhists, thus acquiring the fame of being the foremost logician of the time. In character, he was always self-content and never ceased observing the twelve practices of an

Dharmakīrti

accomplished yogi. He spent much time meditating in solitary forests, and despite his great fame, he had not a single servant.

Dignāga spent a number of years in Vajrāsana and established twenty-four centers of Vinaya and Abhidharma. Later, he journeyed to Kashmir, where he extensively propagated the Mahāyāna doctrine.

Dharmakīrti. Dharmakīrti (Chos-kyi-grags-pa) was born during the seventh century to a scholarly Brahman *tīrthika* in the southern kingdom of Cūḍāmaṇi. It is said that he was a contemporary of the Tibetan king Srong-btsan-sgam-po. He was exposed to the complete learning of the non-Buddhists, mastering all their various arts, sciences, and philosophies. By the time he was eighteen, he was highly regarded as an up-and-coming young scholar. Dharmakīrti, however, came upon some Buddhist scriptures, and realized the logical errors in the philosophies he had been studying. Thus, adopting the ways of a Buddhist, he was ousted by the community of non-Buddhist Paṇḍitas. He traveled north where he met Ācārya Īśvarasena who instructed him in many subjects. First Dharmakīrti analyzed and memorized all the Sūtras. Next he learned the five hundred *dhāraṇīs*. Finally, not being satisfied with this, he became desirous of penetrating the *Pramāṇa-samuccaya* of Dignāga. Īśvarasena then introduced Dharmakīrti to the great works of the Logician.

The very first time Īśvarasena expounded it, Dharmakīrti became his equal in understanding. Having questions about certain points that remained unelucidated, Dharmakīrti requested his teacher to expound the text once again. This time, Dharmakīrti understood it as Dignāga had intended, but there were still questions. Asking for a third explanation, Dharmakīrti realized the defects in Īśvarasena's understanding, and with his master's permission, enumerated these. Īśvarasena was truly delighted, for here was one of his students who equalled his own master. And so he instructed Dharmakīrti to write a commentary to the *Pramāṇa-samuccaya*, which would point out all the erroneous beliefs of Īśvarasena and all others. This work, the *Pramāṇa-varttika*, became Dharmakīrti's most important treatise. The object of this work was to meet all the criticisms and difficulties that had arisen in the field since Dignāga's pioneering work. The *Pramāṇa-varttika* is thus a reformulation of Dignāga's thinking.

Around this time, there were many *tīrthika* Paṇḍitas who excelled in the art of disputation, the foremost of these being Śaṅkarācārya.* Now the practice of the time was to make wagers on the outcome of debates; a frequent agreement would be that the vanquished would embrace the belief of the victor, and many outsiders had been converted by the great Dharma Masters in this fashion. However, the Doctrine was now starting to decline, and the virtue of the monks no longer shone resplendently. Śaṅkarācārya had challenged the Bhikṣus of various monasteries to debate, and had defeated them one by one, with the result that twenty-five Dharma centers had to be given up, and almost five hundred of the monks had to accept *tīrthika* doctrines.

When Dharmakīrti learned of this, he resolved to utterly subdue all the opponents of the Dharma. He therefore completed his studies in

*This Śaṅkarācārya is not the same as the famous founder of Advaita Vedānta who lived in the late eighth century.

the north, and returned south. Disguised as a servant, he was hired by the household of Kumāralila, who, among the *tīrthikas*, was without rival. Dharmakīrti worked very hard for his new master, performing the work of fifty or a hundred normal servants. This very much pleased Kumāralila; in gratitude, he permitted Dharmakīrti to listen to his teachings. Śrī Dharmakīrti stayed in that place only as long as it took to absorb all that he did not already know about the various non-Buddhist systems of philosophy, and then departed for the city of Kakaguha. He posted a notice on the city gate challenging all to debate. This attracted the Brahman Kanagupta and five hundred others. It took three months of debate, but Dharmakīrti defeated each of these, one by one, and converted them to Buddhism. Kumāralila became enraged when he learned of this, and vowed to vanquish this upstart student. But Dharmakīrti remained invincible, causing even this great Paṇḍita to take refuge in Lord Buddha. Then Dharmakīrti proceeded to decimate the ranks of the *tīrthika* Ācāryas, defeating the various teachers and converting them and all their students to belief in the Noble Doctrine. In the course of this, he established many Dharma centers, and caused the assembly of monks to increase greatly.

Meanwhile, Śaṅkarācārya, who had succeeded in defeating numerous followers of the Dharma, challenged the monks at Nālandā to debate. The latter wisely demurred until such time as Dharmakīrti could come up from the south and present their case. Thus, a great confrontation took place before the king and a vast assembly of spectators. Śaṅkarācārya was so confident of himself, that he vowed to jump into the river Ganges if Dharmakīrti were victorious. And, indeed, time and time again, Dharmakīrti reduced to absurdities the arguments of his opponent, until finally, the *tīrthika* had no reply left. Though Dharmakīrti tried to stop him, Śaṅkarācārya jumped into the Ganges, urging his chief disciples to carry on the debate.

Although many of the opponents were converted at this time, others fled in despondency. The disciple, Bhattācārya, continued the disputation after a recess of three years, and during this interlude, Śaṅkarācārya was re-born as Bhattācārya's son. Upon resumption of the debate, Bhattācārya could not refute Dharmakīrti's arguments, and, despite Dharmakīrti's efforts, he also jumped into the river and drowned. Again, many present were converted, while some, like the re-born Śaṅkarācārya, ran away. Later, he returned to debate again, but losing every point, again he jumped into the Ganges. Finally, toward the end of Dharmakīrti's life, when Śaṅkarācārya was again re-born, he agreed to embrace Buddhism if he were defeated. His resulting conversion thus brought an end to the series of debates.

Besides actively defending and nurturing the Buddhadharma, Dharmakīrti travelled extensively and established some fifty centers for the Dharma. He also wrote a number of important works, most of which are subsumed under the heading of the "Seven Treatises." Of these seven, the two major works besides the *Pramāṇa-varttika* are the *Nyāyabindu* and the *Pramāṇa-viniścaya*. These are primarily commentaries on the work of Dignāga, but Dharmakīrti carried the ideas further by refining and elucidating the topics of perception, inference, words, and argumentation. The four supplementary works, which concern themselves primarily with logic and disputation are: *Hetubindu, Saṃbandha-parīkṣā, Vāda-nyāya,* and *Saṃtānatara-siddhi*.

It is said that after he wrote these works, he gave copies to a number of Paṇḍitas, but only a few could understand. These few, through professional jealousy, proclaimed the inferiority of the "Seven Treatises" and tied them to the tail of a dog. But Dharmakīrti said, "That is all right, for just as dogs run about all through the town and countryside, my writings will spread in all directions."

Dharmakīrti's thought is very difficult to absorb, and even his best students had difficulty totally fathoming the subtlety of his teachings. Dharmakīrti asked Devendrabuddhi to write a commentary to the *Pramāṇa-varttika*, after he had painstakingly expounded it in all its detail. Devendrabuddhi presented the commentary for review, but Dharmakīrti washed it away with water. Devendrabuddhi rewrote it, but this time Dharmakīrti burned it. Finally, a third time, Devendrabuddhi employed the entire scope of his understanding, and Dharmakīrti accepted his thesis. But he said that the commentary explained only the literal meaning, and not the deeper implications. Realizing that in the future, no one would be able to understand his logic, Dharmakīrti wrote at the end of the *Pramāṇa-varttika*:

> Just as a river flows into the ocean,
> So will the understanding of my logic vanish with my passing.

Guṇaprabha. Guṇaprabha (Yon-tan-'od) was born in the seventh century. In his youth, he distinguished himself by his brilliance; and when he gained full maturity, he stood alone in his understanding of many facets of the Dharma.

Guṇaprabha was one of the four foremost disciples of Vasuban-

Guṇaprabha

dhu, being more learned than his Master in the Vinaya and possessing complete knowledge of all eighteen schools and the immeasurable teachings of the Buddha. A master of the Mūlasarvāstivādin Vinaya, and a later patriarch of the Mahāyāna, he was a teacher of King Harṣavardhana (c. 606–647). He lived at Mathurā in the Agrapura Monastery, where he enforced the rules of conduct among the five thousand monks residing there.

Originally, he was schooled in the study of the Mahāyāna, but before he had penetrated its profound meaning, he had the occasion to study the *Vibhāṣā-śāstras*. These texts impressed him to such an extent that he suspended his former study and devoted himself to the study of the Hīnayāna. During this time, he wrote a number of treatises

Śākyaprabha

reflecting his preference for the Hīnayāna. His compositions include: the *Vinaya-sūtra* (*'Dul-ba'i-mdo*) and its autocommentary (*vṛtti*), a commentary on the chapter on ethics and manners in the *Bodhisattva-bhūmi* (*-śila-parivarta-bhāṣya*), and the *Ekottara-karma-śataka* (*Las-brgya-rtsa-gcig*). In addition to being a monk and a scholar, as a doctor, he had great healing powers and was often flooded with gifts from the laity which he in turn distributed to the needy.

One of Guṇaprabha's primary disciples was Dharmamitra of Tukharistan, who also became a master in the Vinaya of the Mūlasarvāstivādin and wrote a commentary on the *Vinaya-sūtra.* Another disciple, Guṇamati, who attained proficiency in the Abhidharma, transmitted the Vinaya lineage through many generations of disciples until the time of Śrī Dharmapāla and Zhang-zhung rGyal-pa'i-shes-rab.

Śākyaprabha. Śākyaprabha (Śākya-'od) was born in the eighth century in western India and lived during the reign of Gopalā, the father of King Dharmapāla, who built Vikramaśīla Monastery. Śākyaprabha's teachers were Śāntiprabha and Puṇyakīrti, and his chief student was Śākyamitra. His compositions include the *Triśata-kārikā* and its commentary, the *Prabhāvatī.* Along with Guṇaprabha, Śākyaprabha was an essential link in the transmission of the Vinaya lineage.

Yogācāra: The Path of Introspection

The Yogācāra developed out of an analysis of perceptual situations refining many introspective techniques for such analysis. The adherents of the Yogācāra held to the idea that any 'commonsense' belief in an external world as existing apart from our own subjective world of experience must be rejected. For them, the entire life-world is an experience of mind–but they did not contend that everything is 'mental'. By adopting the idea of a 'pervasive substratum' (*kun-gzhi rnam-par shes-pa, ālaya-vijñāna*) capable of retaining 'traces' and 'dispositions' from past experiences, they were able to better understand and explain the operation of the interactional fields contained within mind.

Although Asaṅga and Nāgārjuna are considered the fathers of the Yogācāra and Mādhyamika schools, the ideas which formed a basis for these systems are rooted in lines of thought which emerged in the early Hīnayāna schools. For instance, the Yogācāra *ālaya-vijñāna* thesis of a substratum awareness (*kun-gzhi'i rnam-par shes-pa*), can be considered to have grown out of the Sautrāntika concept of the *mūlāntikaskandha* as the basis for all perceptual processes. The Mahāsaṅghikas had a similar concept in what they termed the *mūlavijñāna*, 'root discrimination awareness', a concept which Vasubandhu clearly elucidates in his *Mahāyāna-samparigraha-śāstra.*

The Yogācāra rejected the Sautrāntika's thesis of *svālakṣaṇa* as a unique, real object of sense perception, which was also rejected by the Mādhyamika on the basis of the Śūnyatā doctrine.

However, the Yogācārins also reject the two levels of reality proposed by the Mādhyamika, the relatively real (*kun-rdzob-bden-pa, saṃvṛti-satya*) and the ultimately real (*don-dam-bden-pa, paramārtha-satya*). Instead, they recognize three levels of reality as elucidated in the *Trisvabhava-nirdeśa.* The Three Natures (*rang-bzhin-gsum, trisvabhāna*) are: the notional-conceptual (*kun-brtags, parikalpita*), the relative (*gzhan-dbang- paratantra*), and the ideally absolute (*yongs-grub, pariniṣpanna*).

The terms Cittamātra (Sems-tsam) or Vijñānavāda are used in referring to different aspects of the Yogācāra system. While Yogācāra itself points to the practice of introspection, Cittamātra refers to the primacy of 'mind' in Yogācāra metaphysics. With the Vijñānavāda, emphasis is placed on the various strata of mind; the existence of objects external to the observer is disclaimed.

The Sūtras which primarily influenced the formation of the Yogācāra doctrine, are the *Laṅkāvatāra-sūtra*, the *Sandhinirmocana-sūtra*, the *Suvarṇaprabhāsa-sūtra*, and the *Avataṃsaka-sūtra*.

The *Laṅkāvatāra-sūtra* consists of dialogue between the Buddha and the Bodhisattva Mahāmati, at the time the Buddha was visiting Laṅkā (Ceylon). The Sūtra summarizes the basic concepts of the Mahāyāna, such as the concepts of Śūnyatā, the Tathāgata, the manifestations of the Buddha, and the Bodhisattva idea. In this Sūtra there is also an identification of the Tathāgatagarbha (Buddha-nature) with the *ālaya-vijñāna* (substratum-awareness).

The *Sandhinirmocana-sūtra* develops in some detail the main teachings of the Yogācārins concerning the Three Natures. The future advent of the Two Great Ones and the Six Ornaments is also prophesied in this Sūtra, which was very influential in Asaṅga's and Vasubandhu's development of the Yogācāra.

The *Suvarṇaprabhāsa-sūtra* explains the manifestations of the Buddha and demonstrates that even when the Buddha passes into Nirvāṇa, he does not cease to exist.

The full title of the *Avataṃsaka-sūtra* is the *Mahāvaipulya-Buddhāvataṃsaka-sūtra* (*The Great and Vast Buddha Garland Sūtra*). It consists of many parts, among them the *Gaṇḍavyūha-sūtra*, which portrays the Bodhisattva Sudhana's search for enlightenment, and the *Daśabhūmika-sūtra*, which describes the path of the Bodhisattva, and the interpenetrating nature of existence. In the *Avataṃsaka*, the teachings of the Tathāgatagarbha and the *ālaya-vijñāna* are brought together under the teachings of Cittamātra.

The *Avataṃsaka* was revealed by the Buddha upon his attainment of enlightenment and was received through Mañjuśrī, Samantabhadra, and other great Bodhisattvas known as Vidyādharas (Rigs-'dzin), or Bearers of Pure Awareness. This Sūtra was received by Nāgārjuna at the Dragon's palace, and for many years it was not written down. By the power of the *dhāraṇī*, or 'maintaining', it was safeguarded in Ḍākinī language and preserved in Tuṣita Heaven.

Although the prominent Yogācāra ideas were already being developed well before Asaṅga and Vasubandhu, as evidenced by the Sūtras just mentioned, scholars generally place the formal introduction of the Yogācāra as a philosophical system with the contributions of these two Mahāyāna masters. And the doctrines of the Yogācāra gained prominancy with the Five Doctrines of Ārya Maitreya and their commentaries by Asaṅga.

Asaṅga spent twelve years meditating on the meaning of the Mahāyāna, after which he systematized the teachings of these Sūtras into the Yogācāra. His brother, Vasubandhu, who was a prominent advocate of the Sautrāntika view before his conversion to the Mahāyāna, later wrote many important works of the Yogācāra, including commentaries on the Five Doctrines of Maitreya-Asaṅga, which are:

1. *Mahāyāna-sūtrālaṅkāra* (*mDo-sde-rgyan*)
2. *Abhisamayālaṅkāra* (*mNgon-rtogs-rgyan*)
3. *Madhyānta-vibhaṅga* (*dBus-mtha'-rnam-'byed*)
4. *Dharmadharmatā-vibhaṅga* (*Chos-dang-chos-nyid-rnam-'byed*)
5. *Uttaratantra* (*rGyud-bla-ma*)

The *Mahāyāna-sūtrālaṅkāra* contains the teachings of the Sūtras of the later period, the *Sandhinirmocana*, the *Laṅkāvatāra*, and the *Gaṇḍavyūha*, which express the Yogācāra views. The *Sutrālaṅkāra* is essentially a detailed presentation of the Bodhisattva's path towards Enlightenment. The *Abhisamayālaṅkāra* is an interpretation of the *Prajñāpāramitā-sūtras* and could be considered principally a Mādhyamika work on Śūnyatā. It does not refer to the Three Natures or to the *ālaya-vijñāna*. The *Madyānta-vibhaṅga* presents the Yogācāra view according to the teachings of the Middle Way, negating the two extremes of eternalism and nihilism. This work also elucidates the Three Natures. The *Dharmadharmatā-vibhaṅga* investigates the Three Natures as they relate to the elements of the phenomenal world and their intrinsic nature, indicating that when the reality of the elements is no longer tied down by the notional-conceptual, their nature is as Nirvāṇa. The *Uttaratantra* deals with the theory of the Tathāgatagarbha and with the absolute as an undifferentiated principle. Other works attributed to Asaṅga are the *Yogācāra-bhūmi*, the *Yogāvibhaṅga-śāstra*, and the *Vajracchedikā*. The *Yogācāra-bhūmi-śāstra* is Asaṅga's most important work. This text is both an expansion and reworking of the *Abhidharma-samuccaya* and a discussion on the stages of the Bodhisattva.

The main body of literature of the Yogācāra school consists of twenty treatises, namely: the five treatises of Maitreya-Asaṅga, the five divisions of Asaṅga's *Yogācāra-bhūmi-śāstra*, the *Abhidharma-samuccaya*, the *Mahāyāna-saṃgraha*, and the eight treatises of Vasubandhu on the Yogācāra: the *Triṃśaka-kārikā-prakaraṇa,* the *Viṃśaka-kārikā-prakaraṇa*, the *Pañcaskandha-prakaraṇa*, the *Vyākhyāyukti*, the *Karma-siddhi-prakaraṇa*, and commentaries on the *Mahāyāna-sūtrālaṅkāra*, the *Madhyānta-vibhaṅga*, and the *Daśabhūmika-śāstra*. Together, these constitute the eight *prakaraṇa* divisions. Vasubandhu's works from a Mahāyāna viewpoint include the *Saddharma-puṇḍarika*, the *Mahāparinirvāṇa-sūtra*, and the *Vajracchedikā-prajñāpāramitā*. Three other works composed by Vasubandhu which expound on the Pāramitās from the standpoint of the Yogācāra are the *Śatasāhasrikā*, the *Pancaviṁśati-sāhasrikā*, and the *Aṣṭadaśasāhasrikā*.

Sthiramati, one of Vasubandhu's foremost students, began his studies under Vasubandhu at the age of seven, and eventually became recognized as a scholar of both the Hīnayāna and Mahāyāna. He wrote brilliant commentaries on Vasubandhu's eight treatises on the Yogācāra, the most famous of which is the *Triṃśikavijñapti-bhāṣya*. He also wrote commentaries on the *Madhyānta-vibhaṅga-sūtra-bhāṣya* and the *Kāśyapaparivarta* (*Ratnakūṭa*). Sthiramati composed a commentary on the *Abhidharma-kośa* called the *Kārakānśani*, as well as a commentary on Vasubandhu's commentary to the *Kośa*, the *Abhidharmakośa-bhāṣya-ṭīkā Tattvārtha-nāma*. With Sthiramati, the mentalistic emphasis of the Yogācāra developed into a theory of perception and logic. Vimuktasena, another of Vasubandhu's disciples, was the first to synthesize the teachings of the *Prajñāpāramitā-sūtras* and the *Abhisamayālaṅkāra*. This synthesis was the precursor of the Yogācāra-Mādhyamika-Svātantrika viewpoint.

Another important text for the Yogācāra is the *Mahāyāna-śraddhotpada-śāstra*. This Śāstra goes into some detail on the *garbha* theory and contains a number of theses that are similar to the *Uttaratantra* by Maitreya-Asaṅga.

Dignāga, who is considered the father of Buddhist logic, began the second trend in Yogācāra thought by developing precise tools of logic and epistemology, such as establishing the two means of obtaining valid knowledge and reducing the five membered syllogism of medieval Indian logic to three members. He applied Yogācāra insights to the logic and epistemology of the Sautrāntikas.

Dignāga's contribution to logic is in five principal texts: the *Ālambana-parīkṣā,* the *Trikāla-parikṣā*, the *Hetu-cakra-samarthana*, the

Nyāyamukha, and his final, definitive work, the *Pramāṇa-samuccaya* and its commentary (*vṛtti*). The *Ālambana-parīkṣā* is concerned with the true nature of the *ālambana*—the epistemological object of the perceptual world. Here the Vaibhāṣika position is thoroughly analyzed and their view is proved to be untenable. Dignāga established that the *ālambana*, as it appears in a relative sense, is only a construct, and that mind alone is real. He thus reaffirmed the position of Asaṅga and Vasubandhu.

In the *Pramāṇa-samuccaya* Dignāga reorganized his earlier works and wrote a commentary to them. He wrote this work after his retirement from Nālandā University at the monastery of Achala, the site of the Ajantā caves. Dignāga's two principal opponents from the Brahmanical tradition were Kumārilabhaṭṭa and Śaṅkara, but they were unsuccessful in their opposition of his views.

The two principal commentators to Dignāga's works were Dharmapāla and Dharmakīrti. Dharmapāla (c. 671–95) is the author of a number of commentaries, including his *vyākhya* on Dignāga's *Ālambana-parīkṣā*, the *Śabdavidyāsaṃyukta-śāstra*, a commentary on the *Vidyāmātrasiddhi*, the *Nyāyadvārakarka-śāstra* (a commentary on Dignāga's *Nyāyamukha*), the *Vidyāmātrasiddhi*, the *Satasāstra-vaipulya-vyākhya*, and the *Vidyāmātrasiddhi-śāstra*. In his works, a form of mentalism that is very different from that of Asaṅga, and Vasubandhu can be seen.

Dharmakīrti (c. 600–660), the most famous successor to Dignāga, is said to have surpassed his teacher, Īśvarasena, in comprehending Dignāga's system. He composed an enlarged reworking of Dignāga's *Pramāṇa-samuccaya*, titled the *Pramāṇa-vārttika*. Along with this treatise, he authored two other works on logic, the *Nyāya-bindu* and the *Pramāṇa-viścaya*.

Dharmakīrti's outstanding works on logic stimulated a flood of commentarial literature. Devendrabuddhi, his disciple Śākyabuddhi, and mKhas-grub-rje, a disciple of bTsong-kha-pa, wrote detailed commentaries on the *Pramāṇa-vārttika*. Vinitadeva composed commentaries on the *Pramāṇa-viniścaya* and *Nyāya-bindu*.

During the time of Dharmakīrti, Buddhism's influence was already showing some signs of weakening, and the common people began to revert to the worship of the Brahmanical gods. Yet Buddhism had already begun its great northward movement where it was finding fresh roots in Tibet, Mongolia, and China. Like Dignāga, Dharmakīrti's principal successor did not arise until a generation after his death.

Dharmottara became both his successor and his principal commentator.

Dharmottara (750–810) is the founder of Dignāga's and Dharmakīrti's school of logic in Kashmir. His work is highly esteemed by the Tibetans, and he wrote commentaries on the *Pramāṇa-viniścaya* and the *Nyāya-bindu* of Dharmakīrti. Dharmottara's four minor works on logic and epistemological inquiry are available in Tibetan translation: the *Pramāṇa-parīkṣā*, the *Anya-apoha-prakaraṇa*, the *Para-loka-siddhi*, and the *Kṣaṇabhanga-siddhi*. Two commentaries to Dharmottara's *Pramāṇa-viniścaya-ṭīkā* have been preserved in the Tibetan. One was composed by the Kashmirian scholar, Jñānaśrī. The other, which was begun by Śaṅkarānanda but never completed, fills one entire volume of the *bsTan-'gyur.*

After Dharmottara the second phase of the Yogācāra line of thought, originating with Dignāga and Dharmakīrti became absorbed in the Mādhyamika-Svātantrika. But the Yogācāra tradition has wielded a very strong influence on the later development of Buddhist philosophy, particularly in the Mādhyamika, where it became a central line of thought in the Mādhyamika-Svātantrika tradition.

Prajñāpāramitā: The Heart of the Mahāyāna

The Prajñāpāramitā is an approach to absolute reality through the practice of the *pāramitās*, or six kinds of higher awareness. The vast body of literature sets forth many of the most refined elements of the Mahāyāna (Pāramitāyāna) path, particularly the nature of Śūnyatā and the *bodhicitta*. Here, enlightenment is equated with Śūnyatā, which transcends one's limited perceptions and brings one to a level of open-ended possibilities. This awakening is a gradual process of freeing the mind from its obscurations which prevent direct insight. Poetic and intellectually probing, the Prajñāpāramitā literature proclaims the entire teachings of the Buddha, from the initial embarking on the path to the final realization of one's own Buddha-nature.

The Prajñāpāramitā was first explained by the Buddha during the Second Turning of the Wheel, which occurred at Vulture Peak (near Rājagṛha), sixteen years after his enlightenment. The Buddha's disciple Mahākāśyapa recorded the Buddha's teachings on Prajñāpāramitā, and arranged for them to be kept secret for many centuries after the Parinirvāṇa. According to Nāgārjuna, the Buddha placed the written *Prajñāpāramitā-sūtras* in the custody of the Nāgas until such a time as men should be ready to receive them; Nāgārjuna later collected these

Vulture Peak A modern stūpa rests atop the hill where Lord Buddha expounded the Prajñāpāramitā.

Sūtras from the Palace of the Nāgas for King Amarāvati. The Prajñāpāramitā tradition also has an oral transmission.

Pāramitā (*pha-rol-tu phyin-pa*) means "to go to the other shore" and refers to the means of transcending limitations. The term *pāramitā* is not to be found in the early Buddhist texts; probably one of the first in which this word may be found is the *Mahāvastu*, a famous account of the life of the Buddha.

Development of the Prajñāpāramitā in India mainly occurred between the years 100 and 900 A.D.; and by the fourth century, the Prajñāpāramitā was personified as a deity of the Buddhist pantheon. The Prajñāpāramitā as a spiritual course is more commonly referred to as the Pāramitāyāna, which distinguishes it from the Śrāvakayāna and Pratyekabuddhayāna by its emphasis on the development of compassion and the practice of the Six Pāramitās: generosity (*sbyin-pa, dāna*), ethics and manners (*tshul-khrims, śīla*), patience (*bzod-pa, kṣānti*), vigor (*brtson-'grus, vīrya*), meditation (*bsam-gtan, dhyāna*), and discriminating understanding (*shes-rab, prajñā*). The Mahāyāna maintains that through these practices one can reach a state of liberation which surpasses the Hīnayāna goal of the Arhant.

The *Prajñāpāramitā-sūtras* emphasize the non-dual nature of reality and repeatedly negate all aspects of both existence and non-existence. It was this Mahāyāna doctrine of Śūnyatā which the followers of the Hīnayāna found frightening and could not accept, and which became the very foundation for the philosophy of the Mādhyamika. Originally, all the Prajñāpāramitā texts were contained under this single title, but as the proliferation of Sūtras bearing this name continued, distinctions among them were made as to their length.*

---

*The Eight Thousand Line *Aṣṭasāhasrikā-prajñāpāramitā-sūtra* is regarded as the earliest and most basic text of the Prajñāpāramitā literature. According to Tāranātha it had been placed in the dwelling of Candragupta, King of Orissa, by the Bodhisattva Mañjuśrī, who disguised himself as a monk. There are many editors and commentaries of this often-studied Sūtra. The longer Sūtras were expansions of the same basic themes with increasing repetition in the longer versions. The *Diamond* and the *Heart Sūtras* appeared later; they summarized the material presented and extracted the essence of the teachings.

The Twenty-five Thousand Line *Prajñāpāramitā-sūtra*, the *Pañcaviṃsatisāhasrikā*, has been lost in the original. However, an excellent Tibetan translation of it (*Shes-rab-kyi pha-rol-tu phyin-pa stong-phrag-nyi-shu-lnga-pa*) was made by the scholar Ye-shes-sde. It has a number of commentaries which were translated by Kumārajīva in China and Śāntibhadra and Tshul-khrims-rgyal-ba in Tibet. One of the better known commentaries is the *Abhisamayālaṅkara-nāma-prajñāpāramitā-upadeśa-śāstra*, known in Tibetan as the *Shes-rab-kyi pha-rol-tu phyin-pa'i man-ngag-gi bstan-bcos mngon-par rtogs-pa'i rgyan ces-bya-ba'i tshig*, translated by Go-mi-'chi-med and Blo-ldan-shes-rab (1059–1109).

The Sanskrit edition of the Eighteen Thousand Line *Prajñāpāramitā-sūtra* has not survived but there exists a translation of its eighty-seven chapters (*Shes-rab-kyi pha-rol-tu phyin-pa khri-brgyad-stong-pa*) by Ye-shes-sde. The Ten Thousand Line Sūtra, the *Daśasāhasrikā-prajñāpāramitā-sūtra* is also lost. A Tibetan translation (*Shes-rab-kyi pha-rol-tu phyin-pa khri-ba-stong-pa*) was made by Jinamitra, Prajñāvarman, and Ye-shes-sde. Rin-chen bzang-po, sKa-ba dPal-brtsegs, and Śīlendrabodhi were also among the translators of these texts.

The Seven Hundred Line Sūtra, the *Saptaśatikā-prajñāpāramitā-sūtra* (*'Phags-pa shes-rab-kyi pha-rol-tu phyin-pa bdun-brgya-pa*) was translated by Surendrabodhi and Ye-shes-sde. Commentaries on this work were written by Vimalamitra and Kamalaśīla. The Five Hundred Line Sūtra, the *Pañcasatikā-prajñāpāramitā-sūtra* (*Shes-rab-kyi pha-rol-tu phyin-pa lnga-brgya-pa*) is lost in the original but translations of it were made by Śīlendrabodhi, Jinamitra, and Ye-shes-sde.

The *Abhisamayālaṅkāra* (*mNgon-rtogs-rgyan*) by Maitreya-Asaṅga forms a basic summary of the *Prajñāpāramitā-sūtras* as a path toward Buddhahood. It is one of the five works Asaṅga composed through the inspiration (*byin-rlabs*) of Maitreya. The text contains eight main sections and seventy sub-sections. Each of the eight sections deals with a specific aspect of the Buddhist path, and taken together they form a practical guide to liberation.

The first three sections explicate the three forms of intuitive understanding. The first section outlines the three foundations of knowledge: hearing the Teachings, contemplating what has been heard, and making this a lived experience. The second section encourages one to acquire the knowledge gained on the Four Paths (the paths of accumulation, of application, of insight, and of meditation) and to realize that there is no abiding essence in external objects. The third section points to the non-existence of an eternal essence abiding in the self. Through the openness generated by these understandings, the Bodhisattva becomes free to work for the Enlightenment of all beings.

The fourth section deals with the realization of the three topics previously described. The fifth is the accumulation and refinement of this process. The sixth is the instantaneous realization of the three

---

The Three Hundred Line Sūtra, the *Vajracchedikā* or *Diamond Sūtra* (*Shes-rab-kyi pha-rol-tu phyin-pa rdo-rje gcod-pa*) was translated by Śīlendrabodhi and Ye-shes-sde. Excellent Tibetan translations of its commentaries by Asaṅga (i.e., the *Shes-rab-kyi pha-rol-tu phyin-pa rdo-rje gcod-pa bshad sbyor-gyi tshig-le'ur byas-pa, Prajñāpāramitāyaḥ kārikāsaptati*) and subcommentaries by Vasubandhu were made by Kamalaśīla and Ye-shes-rgyal-mtshan.

The Fifty Line *Prajñāpāramitā-aradhaśatikā* (*'Phags-pa bcom-ldan-'das ma shes-rab-kyi pha-rol-tu phyin-pa lnga-bcu-pa*) is lost in the Sanskrit original but is available in Tibetan translation.

One of the most treasured Sūtras of the entire Mahāyāna, the *Heart Sūtra*, or *Prajñāpāramitā-hṛdaya-sūtra* (*bCom-ldan-'das-ma shes-rab-kyi pha-rol-tu phyin-pa'i snying-po*) found its way to China by way of the great translator, Kumārajīva (c. 400), who made available the first Chinese edition of this work. Tibetan commentaries of the *Heart Sūtra* have been written by Vimalamitra, Jñānamitra, Vajrapāṇi, Kamalaśīla, Vairocana, and Atīśa. The Sūtra consists of a dialogue between Avalokiteśvara and Śāriputra, in which the Bodhisattva explains the heart of the Doctrine. The entire meaning of Prajñāpāramitā is shown to be contained in the mantra, GATE GATE PĀRAGATE PĀRASAṂGATE BODHI SVĀHĀ!

The One Hundred Thousand Line *Prajñāpāramitā-sūtra* (*Śatasāhasrikā-prajñāpāramitā-sūtra, Shes-rab-kyi pha-rol-tu phyin-pa stong-phrag-brgya-pa*) has at least seven commentaries which were translated into Tibetan by Surendrabodhi, Ye-shes-sde, and others.

topics. The seventh section describes the result of practicing these four methods just mentioned. And the eighth and final section concerns the results of reaching the goal: Buddhahood.*

The Prajñāpāramitā literature has played a significant role in the development of Buddhist thought in Tibet. The *Prajñāpāramitā-sūtras* alone comprise over twenty volumes of the Tibetan Buddhist canon (*bKa'-gyur*).

Mādhyamika: The Open Dimension

The blossoming of the Mahāyāna began early in the second century A.D. shortly after the Buddhist Council at Puruṣapura. During this time, Buddhism was flourishing. There appeared innumerable masters from all parts of India who displayed an unusual faculty for teaching the doctrines of the Mahāyāna; many of these had the ability to directly receive the Dharma from the principal Bodhisattvas who serve as both protectors and transmitters of the Dharma from the realm of transcendent meaning. Maitreya (Byams-pa), who disseminated Śāstra texts or commentaries to such human masters as Nāgārjuna, Asaṅga, and Vasubandhu, is often considered the 'originator' of the Mahāyāna school. Other Bodhisattvas who transmitted or protected the Mahāyāna texts include Mañjuśrī (Mañjughoṣa, 'Jam-dbyangs),

---

*There are over thirty commentaries on the *Abhisamayālaṅkāra*. The Indian commentators include Surendrabodhi, Jinamitra, Vimuktisena, Ratnākaraśānti, Haribhadra (Seng-ge-bzang-po), Prajñākarmati, Dharmamitra, Dharmakīrtiśrī, Kumaraśrībhadra, Buddhaśrījñāna, and Ratnakīrti. Vimalamitra (Dri-med-pa'i bShes-gnyen) and Kamalaśīla also translated several works and wrote commentaries. The Tibetan commentators and translators include sKa-ba dPal-brtsegs, Cog-ro-klu'i rGyal-mtshan, Nam-mkha'i sNying-po, Ye-shes-sde, Shakya-'od, Bu-ston Rin-chen-grub, Dar-ma-rin-chen, Dīpaṁkaraśrījñāna (Mar-me-mdzad Ye-shes, Atīśa) Rin-chen-bzang-po, bKra-shis rGyal-mtshan, Tshul-khrims-rgyal-ba, Grubs-byams-pa'i-dpal, Chings Yon-tan-'bar, bTsong-kha-pa, Chos-kyi rGyal-mtshan, Ye-shes rgyal-mtshan, Rong-ston Sha-kya'i-rgyal-mtshan dGe-'dun-grub-pa, Ngag-dbang Blo-bzang-rgya-mtsho, mKhas-grub bStan-pa-dar-ba, dByangs-can dGa'-ba'i-blo-gros, and 'Jam-dpal rGya-mtsho.

In later times, lucid and precise commentaries were composed on particularly difficult aspects of the *Abhisamayālaṅkara* by the rNying-ma lamas Mi-pham, dPal-sprul Rinpoche, and sPo-ba Sprul-sku (mDo-snags-bstan-pa'i-nyi-ma), as well as many later lamas of the bSar-ma-pa tradition.

Avalokiteśvara (sPyan-ras-gzigs), Vajrapāṇi (Phyag-na rdo-rje), Samantabhadra (not to be confused with the Ādi-buddha), Guhyapati (gSang-ba'i bDag-po), Kṣitigarbha (Sa-'i sNying-po), Sarvanirvāṇaviṣkambhī (sGrib-pa rNam-par-sel), and Ākāśagarbha (Nam-mkha' sNying-po).

In addition to the presence of these uniquely endowed teachers, there appeared five hundred learned masters, including the Mahābhaṭṭāraka Avitarka, Vigatarāgadvaja, Divyākaragupta, Rāhulamitra, Jñānatala, and the Mahā-upāsaka Saṅgatala.

The Brahman Kuika invited many of the Ācāryas to the West, and King Lakṣāśva, who worked extensively to support the Dharma, ordered the erection of five hundred temples to be built on the summit of mount Abhu for these masters. The King selected five hundred of his most intelligent and devout followers to be ordained and had them engage in the study of the Mahāyāna. A great number of these Mahāyāna followers became brilliantly versed in the Sūtras, attained the faculty of prescience (*mngon-par shes-pa, abhijnana*) and the capacity of displaying miraculous accomplishments (*rdzu-'phrul, ṛddhi*) to their disciples. Subsequently, King Lakṣāśva secured many Mahāyāna Sūtras which he placed at the site of the future Nālandā University, so that eventually, Nālandā became celebrated for its innumerable Mahāyāna texts. From the heavenly spheres, the Nāga worlds, the realm of the Gandharvas and the Rākṣasas—but particularly from the world of the Nāgas—a multitude of Mahāyāna Sūtras began appearing.*

Sadaprarudita found one of the *Prajñāpāramitā-sūtras* in the center of a tower in the town of Gandhavati in Gandhāra. The text, which had been placed there by the Bodhisattva Dharmodgata, was written with melted beryl on sheets of gold, and sealed with seven seals. It was enclosed in a box resting on a "litiere" enhanced with seven jewels.

At the time King Candrapāla ascended the throne, the Ācārya Rāhulabhadra (Saraha) was ordained at Nālandā by the Bhaṭṭāraka

*These Sūtras included the *Ratnakūṭa* (*Ārya-ratnakūṭa-dharma-paryāya-śata-sāhasrikā, 'Phags-pa-dkon-mchog-brtsegs-pa-chos-kyi-rnam-grangs-'bum*), the *Sannipāta-sāhasrikā* (*'Kus-pa-stong-yod-pa*), the *Avataṃsaka* (*Ārya-avataṃsaka-dharmaparyāya-śata-sāhasrikā, 'Phags-pa-phal bo-che-chos-kyi-rnam-grangs-'bum*) the *Laṅkāvatāra* (*Ārya-laṅkāvatāra-pañcaviṃśati-sāhasrikā, 'Phags-pa-lankara-gshegs-pa-nyi-khri-lnga-stong-pa*), the *Gaṇḍavyūha* (*Gaṇḍavyūha-dvādaśa-sāhasrikā, rGyan-stug-po-stong-phrag-bcu-gnyis-pa*), and the *Dharma-sañcaya-gāthā-dvādaśa-sāhasrikā* (*Chos-yang-dag-par-sdud-pa-stong-phrag-bcu-gnyis*).

Kṛṣṇa. After mastering the teachings of the Hīnayāna, Rāhulabhadra received instructions in the doctrines of Mahāyāna from Ācārya Avitarka. His principle teachers, however, were the tutelary deities such as the Bodhisattva Guhyapati, who extensively instructed him in the Sūtras and Tantras. Rāhulabhadra, along with Kamalagarbha, Ghanasa, and others, then began to teach the doctrines of the Mādhyamika. The formulation and systematization of the Mādhyamika philosophy was the work of Nāgārjuna and Āryadeva, and its development in India witnessed brilliance in every phase of its development, spanning from the second to the eleventh century.

Nāgārjuna, the student of Rāhulabhadra, brought to maturity the Mādhyamika philosophy with the aid of his great teacher. Both Bodhisattvas brought into focus the elements of Mādhyamika dominant in the *Prajñāpāramitā-sūtras,* and under Nāgārjuna's leadership, Nālandā flourished and soon surpassed the beauty of Bodh Gayā, the principal seat of the followers of the Hīnayāna.

Nāgārjuna's philosophy became known as the Mādhyamika or the doctrine of the Middle Way (Mādhyama-pratipad), as initially discoursed by the Buddha. These doctrines teach that the highest truth is realized by the avoidance of the extremes of either luxury or asceticism, eternalism or nihilism.

As an expression of this doctrine in daily conduct Nāgārjuna instituted a very strict Vinaya code in Nālandā. But many Śrāvakas and Sthaviras claimed that his teachings were different than the teachings of the Buddha, for Nāgārjuna followed the Mahāyāna Sūtras which the orthodox Śrāvakas did not accept.

The teachings of the Middle Way developed the doctrine of Śūnyatā, for they avoided the two extremes. Through the work of Nāgārjuna, the Mādhyamika became the systematized form of the Śūnyatā doctrine as presented in the treatises of the Prajñāpāramitā.

Both the philosophy of the *Prajñāpāramitā-sūtras* and the doctrine of Śūnyatā as expounded by Nāgārjuna present the premise that 'existence' (*bhāva*) is devoid of a reality of its own. Throughout his philosophical treatises, Nāgārjuna draws upon the ten similes found in the *Prajñāpāramitā-sūtras* to illustrate Śūnyatā. These similes liken existence to a dream, a vision, or a reflection on the water. Although the Yogācāra criticized aspects of the Mādhyamika conception of Śūnyatā, it was strongly influenced by the doctrine itself.

According to tradition, in addition to the voluminous *Prajñāpāramitā-sūtras*, Nāgārjuna had access to nearly a hundred other Mahāyāna texts.* Of the six main treatises of Nāgārjuna, the *Mūla-mādhyamika-kārikas* became the primary text of the Mādhyamika. So important was this root text from the fourth century onward, numerous followers of this tradition have written commentaries on it.†

Nāgārjuna's *Vigraha-vyāvartanī* is a refutation of possible objections that could be raised against the Śūnyatā dialectic. Nāgārjuna directs his argument against the Abhidharmikas and demonstrates Śūnyatā as the central theme of the Mahāyāna Sūtras. Both the *Vigraha-vyāvartanī* and the *Vaidalya* are works using the 'logic of the four alternatives' (tetralemma = *catuṣkoṭi*) their central subject is a critical study of the Nyāya school of Indian philosophy. The *Śūnyatā-sapatī* is, on the whole, a summary of the *Mūla-mādhyamaka-kārikās*, while the *Dvadaśadvāra-śāstra* is essentially a compendium of the *Śūnyatā-saptatī* and the *Mūla-mādhyamika*. The *Yukti-ṣaṣtika* differs from the other principal works of Nāgārjuna in its emphasis on the primacy of mind.

Āryadeva, Nāgārjuna's foremost disciple, continued Nāgārjuna's criticism of the Abhidharma tradition. He also strongly argued against the non-Buddhist schools of the Saṃkhya and Vaiśeṣika, as evidenced in his chief work, the *Catuḥ-śataka*. Āryadeva's other main works include the *Akṣara-śatakam* (*The Hundred Letters*), the *Hasta-vāla-prakaraṇa* (*The Hand Treatise*), the *Cittaviśuddhi-prakaraṇa*, and the *Jñānasāra-samuccaya*.

Nāgārjuna's *Mādhyamika-śāstra* and *Dvadaśa-śāstra* and Āryadeva's *Catuḥ-śataka* are the three treatises which Kumārajiva (344–413 A.D.) took to China and on which the Chinese Mādhyamika school, the *San-Lun*, is based. Kumārajiva translated these texts into Chinese between the years 401 and 409. Although Kumārajiva's native city of Kuchā was a primary center for the Sarvāstivāda school, rather than the Mahāyāna, he is principally responsible for the transmission of the

---

*Both Nāgārjuna and Āryadeva, in the formulation of the Mādhyamika doctrine, were influenced by the *Aṣṭasāhasrikā*, the *Saddharma-puṇḍarīka*, the *Lalitavistara*, the *Laṅkāvatāra*, the *Gaṇḍavyūha*, the *Tathāgataguhyaka*, the *Samādhirāja*, the *Suvarṇa-prabhāsa*, and the *Daśabhūmika* Sūtras. Nāgārjuna himself composed a number of expositions which are of major import to Mahāyāna Buddhist philosophy. His principal texts include the *Mūla-mādhyamaka-kārikas* (*Prajñā-mūla*), the *Śūnyatā-saptatī*, the *Yukti-ṣaṣtikā*, the *Vigraha-vyāvartanī*, the *Vyavahāra-siddhi*, and the *Dvadaśadvāra-śāstra*.

†These include: Asaṅga (310–90), Piṅgala (fourth century), Kumārajīva (344–413), Buddhapālita (c. 400–450), Guṇamati (420–500), Saṅgharakṣita (fifth century), Bhāvaviveka (500–570), Sthiramati (510–570), Dharmapāla (530–561), Candrakīrti (600–650), Śāntideva (c. 700), and Jñānaprabha (eighth century).

Bhāvaviveka

Mādhyamika from India to China. Kumārajiva was also important in the propagation of the Mahāyāna in Kuchā. By the seventh century, more than a hundred titles were attributed to Kumārajiva as translator. He showed a particularly excellent faculty of mind for translating and advancing the Prajñāpāramitā and Śūnyavādin doctrines in China. His biography of Nāgārjuna is a primary source for the life of this master of the Mādhyamika.

Around the fifth century a doctrinal split occurred within the Mādhyamika which gave rise to two separate lines of thought. Buddhapālita (470–540) became the main proponent for the Prāsaṅgika (Thal-'gyur-pa) school, which holds that the true method of Nāgārjuna's and Āryadeva's philosophy is to reduce to absurdity the arguments of the opponent without ever taking a position oneself. The

Candrakīrti

Prāsaṅgika, whose doctrines are derived from Nāgārjuna's original treatise (*kārikā*) on the Mādhyamika, hold five works by Nāgārjuna as its doctrinal authority: the *Mūla-mādhyamika*, the *Yukti-ṣaṣtika*, the *Śūnyatā-saptatī*, the *Vigraha-vyāvartanī*, and the *Vaidalya*.

Bhāvaviveka, a contemporary of Buddhapālita and the founder of the Svātantrika (Rang-rgyud-pa) school of Mādhyamika, argued strongly against the Prāsaṅgika's use of refutation without counter-argument as being simply a dependence on the position or arguments of others. Bhāvaviveka adopted methods of logic from Dignāga and utilized these in setting forth proofs of the Mādhyamika doctrine. He wrote the *Karatalaratna*, in which he attempts to establish the basic Mādhyamika standpoint by syllogistic arguments. Other works by Bhāvaviveka include the *Tarkajvālā*, the *Mādhyamakāratha-Saṅgraha*, the *Prajñāpradīpa* (a commentary on the *Mūla-mādhyamika-kārikā*) the *Madhyamaka-āvatāra-pradīpa*, the *Madhyamaka-pratītya-samutpāda*, and the *Madhyamaka-hṛdaya*. Due to his assertation that external objects conventionally exist by means of their own natures, Bhāvaviveka was later looked upon as the primary exponent of what became known as the Sautrāntika-Mādhyamika-Svātantrika school.

Although Buddhapālita represented the Prāsaṅgika and Bhāvaviveka the Svātantrika, their works are very similar in content and impact. They were writing about the same experience and goal simply from different points of view. Therefore, from the viewpoint of a higher reality, within the meditative experience itself, both schools are in perfect agreement.

During the early seventh century Candrakīrti arose as the chief exponent of the Prāsaṅgika school. Reaffirming the standpoint of Buddhapālita, Candrakīrti refuted not only the Svātantrika position but that of the Vijñānavāda and the Sautrāntika as well. His principal work is the *Prasannapadā*, a commentary on the *Mūla-mādhyamaka-kārikās*. Other works by Candrakīrti include the *Mādhyamakāvatāra* and commentaries on Nāgārjuna's *Śūnyatā-saptatī* and *Yukti-ṣaṣtika*. He also wrote two smaller manuals, the *Mādhyamaka-prajñāvatāra* and the *Pañcaskandha*.

Śāntideva (c. 685–763) is another important follower of the Prāsaṅgika method of Buddhapālita and Candrakīrti, and his *Śikṣā-samuccaya* and *Bodhicaryāvatāra* are two of the most popular works in the entire Mahāyāna literature. The *Śikṣa*, a compendium of the major Mahāyāna doctrines, especially those of the Mādhyamika, relies heavily on quotations from the Sūtras, many of which are now lost in the original. Both this work and the *Bodhicaryāvatāra* are practice oriented texts which encourage the cultivation of the Bodhisattva path.

When Śāntideva was studying at Nālandā, the other monks required him to teach before the great assembly, thinking that they would thus embarrass him due to his apparent lack of understanding of the Dharma. But his great knowledge was made manifest as he began to recite the *Bodhicaryāvatāra*. When he came to the ninth chapter on the Perfection of Discriminating Awareness, he rose into the sky until he became invisible. After completing the recitation from beyond the clouds, he once again appeared. The works of Śāntideva were thereafter of great importance in the development of Mahāyāna in India, and they have been extensively studied by all schools in Tibet since Buddhism was introduced there.

Śāntideva

In the eighth century there developed a strong mentalistic phenomenalistic trend in Mādhyamika, with Śāntarakṣita and his pupil Kamalaśīla as its adherents. Both figures extensively studied the works of Dignāga and Dharmakīrti and wrote brilliant expositions on their philosophical trends. Although they fundamentally held the Mādhyamika-Svātantrika line of thought, Yogācāra aspects become increasingly apparent in their works. They provided an important synthesis of thought in both India and Tibet between the Yogācāra and the Svātantrika, and are thus identified as two of the principal proponents of the Yogācāra-Mādhyamika-Svātantrika (rNal-'byor-spyod-pa'i-dbu-ma rang-rgyud-pa) in Tibet. Thus both Śāntarakṣita and Kamalaśīla followed the Mādhyamika-Svātantrika line of Bhāvaviveka, but added to it their comprehensive understanding of the *Pramāṇa-vārttika* and other of Dharmakīrti's works.

Kamalaśīla

Kamalaśīla, born about 710, was author of a number of works on logic (*nyāya*), and, like his teacher, Śāntarakṣita, also wrote treatises on Tantra. Most of these compositions were completed during his professorship at Nālandā. Unfortunately, none of these works have been preserved in the original Sanskrit, though all are extant in Tibetan translations.*

Another of Śāntarakṣita's students, Haribhadra, continued the

*In addition to his commentary (*pañjikā*) to the *Tattvasaṅgraha*, Kamalaśīla's works include: the *Mādhyamakālaṅkārapañjikā*, the *Nyāyabindu purvapakṣe-samkṣipta*, the *Āryasapataśaṭīkā-prajñāpāramitā-ṭīkā*, the *Āryavajracchedikā-prajñāpāramitā-ṭīkā*, *Āryasapataśaṭīkā-prajñāpāramitā-hṛdayanāma-ṭīkā*, the *Ḍākinīvajra-guhyagīta-nama-marmopadeśa*, and the *Mahāmudropadeśa-vajraguhyagīti*.

Yogācāra-Mādhyamika-Svātantrika line of thought, but he placed particular emphasis on the study of the Prajñāpāramitā. He wrote an important commentary on the Eight Thousand Line *Prajñāpāramitā-sūtra*, the *Aṣṭasāhasrika-vṛhattika*, and was a leading scholar on the *Abhisamayālaṅkāra*. His student Buddhajñānapāda became the Vajrācārya at Vikramaśīla Monastery. Haribhadra taught the *Prajñāpāramitā-sūtra*, the *Guhyasamāja*, and other Tantras extensively. In the rNyingma tradition, he is considered one of the early lineage holders of the Sems-sde class of the rDzogs-chen, as well as continuing the line of the Yogācāra-Mādhyamika-Svātantrika.

Also during this period, Prajñākaragupta became a prominent figure in a trend of Mahāyāna Buddhism which subordinated the subject of logic to the purpose of establishing a firm basis for new metaphysical principles concerning the conception of Buddhahood and the Buddha-nature. He is noted for his use of the *drang-don* (*neyārtha*) approach of 'indirect' meaning in which he incorporates much stylistic ornamentation to elucidate his thesis. Prajñākaragupta's principal work is the *Prāmaṇa-varttika-bhāṣya*, in which he interprets Dharmakīrti's *Prāmaṇa-vārttika* from the standpoint of the Mādhyamika-Prāsaṅgika line of thought stemming from Buddhapālita and Candrakīrti. Prajñākaragupta reiterates the point made by Candrakīrti that absolute reality cannot be cognized by logical methods exclusively. Although Śāntarakṣita and Kamalaśīla are Yogācāra-Mādhyamika-Svātantrikas, they hold a similar position.

In the eleventh century, Jñānaśrīmitra (c. 980–1030) and Ratnakīrti continued the line of thought presented by Prajñākaragupta. The primary works of Jñānaśrīmitra include the *Apoḥa-prakaraṇa*, the *Vyapticarcā, Kāryakāraṇabhāvasiddhi*, and the *Kṣaṇabhangādhyaya*, which consists of four parts: the *pakṣadharmā-dhikāra*, the *anvayādhikāra*, the *vyatirekādhikāra*, and the *ahetuka-vināśādhikāra*. In these texts, Jñānaśrīmitra elucidates the doctrines of Dharmakīrti and Prajñākaragupta, who were receiving heavy criticism by the Bramanical logicians of that period. Ratnakīrti, a student of Jñānaśrīmitra continued his work and presented the views of his teacher in more concise terms.* As one of the last major figures in India to follow the Yogācāra-Mādhyamika-Svātantrika line, Ratnakīrti's disciple Ratnā-

---

*Ratnakīrti's treatises include the *Citrādvaitaprakāśavāda*, the *Iśvarasādhanadūṣaṇa*, the *Kṣaṇabhaṅga-siddhi* (*Anvayamika*), the *Santānāntaradūṣaṇa*, the *Sthirasiddhidūṣaṇa*, the *Apohasiddhi* and the *Vyāptinirṇaya*.

karaśānti wrote two important texts, the *Antarvyāptisamarthana* and the *Vijñaptimatratāsiddhi*, both of which are available in Tibetan translation.*

The Three Dharmacakras and the Implicit and Definitive Meanings of the Buddha's Teachings

The entire body of the Buddha's teachings are traditionally known as the Three Dharmacakras, which refer to the Blessed One's act of setting into motion the Wheel of the Dharma on three occasions, or in three divisions, each occuring for a number of years. The division into the Three Turnings also refers to the degree of profundity and level of philosophical precision of the Sūtras.

The First Dharmacaka, which contained the issues central to the Abhidharma, generally revealed the teachings of the Hīnayāna, or the vehicle (Yāna) of the Śrāvakas. Yet there are teachings of the other Yānas also included in this first period. The Second and Third Dharmacakras are considered Mahāyāna, the Second containing the issues central to both the Prajñāpāramitā and Mādhyamika doctrines. The Third Dharmacakra introduces the concepts of Tathāgatagarbha (*de-gzhin gshegs-pa'i snyings-po*) and *ālaya-vijñāna* (*kun-gzhi'i rnam-shes*), as well as a threefold division of reality which distinguishes between:

1. the notional-conceptual (*kun-brtags-parikalpita*)
2. the relative (*gzhan-dbang, paratantra*)
3. the ideally absolute (*yongs-grub, pariniṣpanna*)

In general, when a Sūtra introduces this threefold division, it belongs to the commentarial literature of the Third Turning. These teachings are considered teachings of the Yogācāra doctrines.

The different Yānas, and hence the teachings of the Three Dharmacakras, are individually tailored to the differing needs of individuals wishing to pursue a spiritual course. Each discipline of study and practice, that of the Vinaya, the Śrāvakas, the Pratyekabuddhas, the Sixteen Arhants, the Sūtras, and Śāstras, Abhidharma, Prajñāpāramitā, Yogācāra, Mādhyamika, and so on, emphasizes a different aspect or

---

*Ratnākaraśānti also wrote a number of Prajñāpāramitā texts, such as the *Prajñāpāramitāupadeśa,* the *Prajñāpāramitā-bhāvanā-upadeśa,* the *Abhisamayālaṅkāra-pañjika*, the *Abhisamayālaṅkāra-vṛtti*, the *Sarottamā*, and the *Śuddhamatī*.

approach to the Buddha's teachings, depending on whether they take on a provisional meaning or a direct and definitive meaning.

As he taught, the Buddha would sometimes use conventional language, incorporating the more popular viewpoints of his day, so that he could be readily understood by the average person. At other times he spoke specifically about topics which were more difficult to comprehend. For example, the Buddha explained that desire exists because of certain conditions, yet there is no *one* or abiding self which desires. These distinctions generally led to two levels of statements: one which was made in more popular terms, and one that was made in more exacting language.

Statements made in more popular terms may have provisional meanings which either do not express, or express only indirectly, the real meaning. Often an evaluation has to be made of the extent to which a statement is to be interpreted literally or the extent to which the meaning is implied. For example, if we hear the statement, "Skyflowers are above time," we can be almost certain that we cannot understand the statement simply through its apparent meaning, because 'time' cannot exist in a spacial relationship which the preposition 'above' implies. Therefore, this statement is either nonsense or it is pointing to a deeper implication.

In addition to this provisional or conventional meaning, statements can also have a definite, direct, or 'real' meaning through the use of definitive statements which lend themselves towards deeper implications. Inherent in such statements is the compatibility of the literal interpretation with the actual intent of a given expression.

The spirit of a given teaching is not the letter, or the words themselves, but the meaning. If the meaning is implicit or indeterminate, and hence must be assumed, it is a *drang-don* teaching. A Sūtra of this category of indeterminate meaning might contain a passage as follows: "The master of the Dharma assures himself of five advantages through his teachings—great merit, admiration by fellow men, beauty, fame, and final arrival in Nirvāṇa." Although such a statement is easy to understand, its implicit meaning is less clear. If this were a Sūtra of the *nges-don* division of definitive meaning, it might be rendered as follows: "Among the omniscient ones (Sarvajña), the Buddha is foremost; among all texts, the Buddhist Sūtras are foremost; and among all beings (*sattva*), the Bhikṣus are foremost. Through generosity (*dāna*) one gains merit (*puṇya*). Moral conduct (*śīla*) enables one to be reborn among the Devas, etc."

A passage from the Tibetan version of the *Laṅkāvatāra-sūtra* illustrates the importance of clearly perceiving the distinction between the provisional and the definitive meanings of the Buddha's teachings:

> It is not necessary to act like those who look at a finger, Mahāmati. It is as if one were to point something out to somebody with his finger and the latter obstinately looked only at the fingertip. In the same way, Oh Mahāmati, like veritable babies, common foolish ones remain attached to this fingertip which one calls literal interpretation, and they would die being thus attached to the fingertip which one calls the 'letter'. Because they have neglected the meaning intended by the fingertip, which one calls literal interpretation, they are not able to penetrate to the Absolute (truth).

Thus, early masters of Buddhism placed the two levels of statement found in the early Sūtras into these two categories: the provisional (*drang-don, neyārtha*) and 'real' or definitive (*nges-don, nītārtha*). Those Sūtras which fall into the category of provisional meaning (*drang-don*) may be taken to be generalizations of a given doctrine or doctrines. Such texts are usually easier to understand and are often intended for persons who are insufficiently prepared to receive more philosophical teachings. Texts of an explicit and definitive meaning are more difficult to grasp because they are generally written with more philosophical precision and draw upon more exacting terminology.

Throughout the centuries, Buddhist masters have had differing approaches in determining the distinction between *drang-don* and *nges-don*. The Buddha undoubtedly foresaw that later followers of the Buddhdharma would have difficulty in choosing between the *drang-don* and *nges-don* divisions of meaning. Therefore, he stated a prophecy in the *Mañjuśrī-mūla-tantra* that Asaṅga would be the one to establish the criteria for the distinction between *drang-don* and *nges-don*. Although there are a number of logically valid ways of making the distinction, the majority of scholars favor Asaṅga's method of determination which puts an emphasis on meaning rather than mere categorization of texts.

However, attempting to follow the criteria set forth by Asaṅga, the newer schools of the Mahāyāna began pointing out that those texts written in earlier times are almost exclusively of the *drang-don* division—their meanings needed to be drawn out. A text such as the *Sandhinirmocana-sūtra* of the Yogācāra (Cittamātra) trend and of the Third Turning, is exclusvely a *nges-don* text, because it renders clarity through the use of definitive statements. In the title, the term *sandhi* refers to a 'connection' or a 'bridge', which indicates the process of making explicit what the Buddha intended or implicitly had in mind in his teachings. In fact, all the texts of the Third Turning are generally held to be *nges-don*. The Second Dharmacakra, according to this system, has components of both *drang-don* and *nges-don*.

This division arose partially as a result of the transition from the Prajñāpāramitā to the Mādhyamika. The texts falling under these two headings are considered to be commentaries on the Second Dharmacakra, which emphasizes the Śūnyatā doctrine, one of the central issues of both the Prajñāpāramitā and Mādhyamika. However, this transition from the Prajñāpāramitā to the Mādhyamika also represented a shift from the *drang-don* to the *nges-don* divisions, which serves to explain why it was maintained that the Second Turning had components of both divisions of meaning. Some Yogācāras, however, who mainly followed the teachings of the Third Dharmacakra, put both the First and Second Turnings in the *drang-don* division.

A single method of categorizing the Dharmacakras was not followed by all schools. Even the two divisions of the Mādhyamika, the Svātantrikas and the Prāsaṅgikas—in the process of setting their doctrines into precise philosophical terms—had different ways of interpreting the various divisions within the Dharma.

According to the proponents of the Prāsaṅgika-Mādhyamika, the Second Dharmacakra—which contains the teachings of Śūnyata—is of the direct meaning (*nges-don*), whereas the First and Third Turnings are considered to contain the teachings of the assumed meaning (*drang-don*). The Prāsaṅgikas rejected the interpretations of the Yogācāra (teachings of the Third Turning)—and hence, also those of the Yogācāra-Svātantrika-Mādhyamika. Many of the Svātantrika, on the other hand, accepted the Third Turning, the Yogācāra Teachings, as *nges-don*.

The controversy between the Prāsaṅgika and Svātantrika Mādyamikas centered around the interpretation of the Tathāgatagarbha, particularly, as set forth in the *Uttaratantra* (Third Turning). The Prāsaṅgika strongly considered these teachings as being *drang-don*, while others completely accepted them as *nges-don*.

The *drang-don* approach of provisional meaning and the *nges-don* approach of definitive meaning should not, however, be considered as mutually exclusive, for the one follows the other like a bridge in the direct course leading towards the experience of enlightenment. It is in this sense that the *drang-don* approach lays the foundation for the *nges-don*.

All too often religious or spiritual language ends up in dogma which hems the individual in, forcing him to accept that which is static, as opposed to that which is suggestive. It is for this reason that Dharma texts have used both approaches delineated above.

Unfortunately, however, a 'blanket' systematization of the Three Dharmacakras in terms of their assumed or real content of meaning is too often an oversimplified or a philosophically biased approach. For instance, although the First Dharmacakra was placed exclusively in the *drang-don* division, within the First Turning are contained Sūtras that are in the *nges-don* division. Some Jo-nang-pa, dGe-lugs-pa and Sa-skya-pa lamas, such as Kun-mkhyen Dol-po-pa, bTsong-kha-pa, and others, attempted to provide standardized definitions of the contents and doctrinal emphasis for the Three Dharmackras which resulted in rather static interpretations.

The rNying-ma lama Mi-pham ('Jam-dbyangs rNam-gyal rgya-mtsho, 1846–1912) followed Asaṅga's distinctions between the two divisions of meaning. Rather than grouping the texts of the various Dharmacakras into *drang-don* and *nges-don* divisions, and then accepting some and rejecting others according to these divisions, Lama Mi-pham emphasized the interconnection between the teachings of the Three Dharmacakras. In doing so, he pointed out the interplay of such terms as 'openness' (*stong-pa-nyid, śūnyatā*) and 'radiance' (*'od-gsal-ba, prabhāsvarā*), 'open-ended facticity' (*ngo-bo*) and 'presentational immediacy' (*rang-bzhin*). *Stong-pa-nyid* and *ngo-bo* are emphasized in the Second Dharmacakra, whereas *'od-gsal-ba* and *rang-bzhin* play a more active role in the Third Dharmacakra. In actuality, both standpoints are talking about the same level of reality, but in two different ways, which is the meaning of 'interpenetration' (*zung-'jug, yuganaddha*). Basically, the Third Dharmacakra concerns itself with the nature of absolute reality as it is an experience of radiance (*'od-gsal-ba*). From this standpoint, Śūnyatā is not looked upon as 'nothingness' or 'emptiness' which would be a negation of existence, but as an open and pure radiance, a kind of luster. Śūnya (*stong-pa*) is thus viewed as being ever-present in an utter freedom from concretizations and determinate characteristics. This description is also accompanied by the term *ngo-bo*, which refers to the pure fact or facticity of the experience, its counterpart being *rang-bzhin*, the presentational immediacy of the experience.

Without the dynamic interplay of *stong-pa-nyid* and *'od-gsal-ba*, or *ngo-bo* and *rang-bzhin*, these two approaches could become doctrines leading to the extremes of nihilism or eternalism. It is the very function of 'interpenetration' which keeps this from occurring. Together they function like the sun and its radiance—you cannot have the one at the exclusion of the other.

This idea of interpenetration (coincidence) is intimately related with the Tantras, which developed principally out of the commentarial literature surrounding the Third Promulgation, that emphasizes the experiential approach. The *Uttaratantra*, one of Ārya Maitreya's Five Doctrines, is placed with the Third Dharmacakra because it explains the application of the various philosophical principles previously set forth and it serves as a bridge between the Sūtras and the Tantras. The ten so-called *Tathāgatagarbha-sūtras* thus belong to the Third Dharmacakra and are of the *nges-don* division.*

The twelfth century lama, 'Bri-gung-skyob-pa (Rin-chen dPal, 1143–1218) who originated the 'Bri-gung school and who was considered to be an emanation of Nāgārjuna, contributed greatly to a clarification of the distinction between the various topics of the Three Dharmacakras and their division into the two categories of assumed and definite meaning.

The more unified approach of looking at the various Yānas within the Buddhist path, as propounded by Lama Mi-pham, has also been emphasized by mNga'-ris Paṇḍita. sPo-ba sPrul-sku (mDo-sngas-bstan-pa'i Nyi-ma, b. 1900) also wrote a stylistically beautiful discourse on the Three Dharmacakras and their relation to the two divisions of provisional and definite meaning, based upon Lama Mi-pham's previous work. All of these lamas, however, support Asaṅga's original distinctions, and, in the rNying-ma tradition alone, hundred of pages of explication have been written about this highly technical subject.

The Eighty-four Mahāsiddhas

During the eighth through the twelfth centuries, the Buddhist tradition in India centered around the monastic settlements, which by this time had become primarily academically oriented. In contrast to

*The ten *Tathāgatagarbha Sūtras* are: *Tathāgatagarbha-sūtra*, *Dhāraṇīśvararājaparipṛcchā* (*Tathāgatamahākaruṇā-nirdeśa-sūtra*), *Mahāparinirvāṇa-sūtra*, *Ārya-aṅgulimālīya-sūtra*, *Jñānalokālaṃkāra-sūtra*, *Śrī-mālā-devi-siṃhanāda-sūtra*, *Anūnatvāpūrṇatvanirdeśa-parivarta*, *Mahābherīharaka-sūtra*, *Avikalparapraveśa-dhāraṇī*, and *Saṅdhinirmocana-sūtra*.

this predominant scholasticism, the Mahāsiddha tradition re-emphasized the importance of realization through direct experience of the Buddha's teaching. It is out of the Indian Mahāsiddha tradition that the teachings of the Vajrayāna, and particularly those of Mahāmudrā arose and were brought to Tibet, where they took firm root and blossomed.

In the context of Indian religious culture, the term *siddhi* has the specialized meaning of 'powers', more specifically extra-normal powers arising naturally as a by-product of meditation and yogic practice. Within Indian Buddhism, *siddhi* means 'accomplishment', and a Siddha is a 'holder of *siddhi*'; Mahāsiddha is thus a 'great-holder of *siddhi*' or a highly accomplished one. The Buddhist distinguish different types of *siddhi*. The first type could be termed worldly *siddhi*, the super-normal faculties such as the ability to fly or to control the elements. Such accomplishments are said to be obtainable through other methods besides those outlined by the Buddhist tradition. However, within the Buddhist context these *siddhi* were never taken as ends in themselves, but merely as incidental abilities resulting from increased awareness. Such powers, it was warned, may be more of a hindrance than a help, as they can divert the practitioner's attention from the goal of enlightenment. Although the path of worldly *siddhi* is sometimes regarded as an aspect of the Path of Accumulation, if the practitioner's motives are not pure and he accomplishes *siddhi* out of a desire for personal power rather than the wish to benefit all sentient beings, he may fall into an enmeshing trap of egotism. To avoid such diversion, the practitioner is urged to first strive to attain the superior *siddhi*, and then the trans-worldly *siddhi* which is Buddhahood. This *siddhi* is obtainable only by following the Dharma.

Traditionally, as Buddhism developed in India, there were recognized Eighty-four Madhāsiddhas, who, through the power of their efforts in following the path of the Vajrayāna, attained enlightenment in a single lifetime. These eighty-four Siddhas came from all backgrounds and social positions; many belonged to the lower caste, and thus worked in rather menial positions. Adopting the path of the Tantric yogin, they often disregarded conventions of the orthodox Saṅgha resorting at times to outrageous behavior as an expression of a spontaneity that is all-encompassing. The ranks of the Mahāsiddhas include Catrapa the beggar, Kantali the tailor, Acinta the woodseller, Pacari the baker, Ṭeṅgipa the rice husker, and Minapa the fisherman who, having been swallowed by a large fish, meditated in its belly for twelve years.

The Mahāsiddhas were often taught by celestial Bodhisattvas or Ḍākinīs, who, understanding that all activity can be an expression of Buddha-nature and that any situation is an opportunity to cultivate an enlightened mind, offered instructions uniquely suited to the individual needs of the aspirant. Spontaneity and freedom thus became an expression of their meditative insight, and such qualities typify the accounts of many of the Eighty-four Mahāsiddhas.

Camaripa, the cobbler, was instructed to sew the leather of the reaction patterns and conceptual activity with the cords of the eight worldly concerns (gain and loss, pleasure and pain, praise and blame, and fame and disgrace) on the board of friendliness and compassion, using the guru's instructions as the drill to produce the wonderful shoe of the Dharmakāya.

Kotali, the mountain man, received special instructions on cultivating the Six Pāramitās by hoeing the mountain of the mind.

Kamaripa, the smith, received instructions in *rtsa-rlung-yoga*. He was told to visualize perceptual activity as the smith, to light the fire of knowledge with conceptions as the coal, to use the right and left flow-patterns (*rtsa*) as the bellows and the central flow pattern as the anvil, and then to hammer into usable forms the iron of the Three Poisons (cupidity-attachment, aversion-hatred, and bewilderment-errancy).

Ajohi, whose name means 'lazy man', was given practices he could do lying down. He often resided in cemeteries, which were utilized by many Siddhas for increasing their realization of impermanence.

Nāropa, like many of the Mahāsiddhas, had to undergo severe hardships under the hand of his guru, Tilopa, who had attained enlightenment through his practice of pressing oil from sesame seeds.

Kacipa, who suffered from a tumor on his neck, was instructed by Nāgārjuna to imbibe pain as the path and to meditate on the growth as the Developing Stage of the path. Through his practice the growth grew larger, and as he became discouraged, he was further instructed to meditate on all existants as being contained in the tumor, as the practice of the Fulfillment Stage. In this manner, he obtained enlightenment and his tumor disappeared.

The guru, embodying enlightened understanding, realizes that the individual's greatest attachment or fear may actually be transformed into an asset to his own freedom. King Kanhava, who was attached to beauty, was instructed to blend into one the 'unattached mind' and the luster of the jewels on his bracelet. Vinapa, who loved nothing more

Samantabhadra
Ṭeṅgipa
Lilapa
Kokalipa
Mīnapa
Vinapa
Shantipa
Gorakṣa
Pacari
Koṭali
Tantipa
Khadgap
Camaripa
Vajradhara
Thaganapa
Karṇaripa
Dhombipa
Nāropa
Kalapa
Bhadrapa
Khandipa
Ajokipa
Śalipa

Vajrasattva
Ghandapa
Jālandhari
Rahula
Telipa
Virūpa
Dharmapa
Paṅkaja
Dhokaripa
Medhina
Jogipa
Gorura
Caluki
dGa-'rab-rdo-rje
Kambala
Kaṅkanapa
Lucika
Mahipa
Acinta
Dharmapa
Kucipa
Nalina
Laksmīnkarā

rDo-rje-snying-po
Jayānanda
Naguna
Capari
Campaka
Maṇibhadrā
Kumaripa
Caurāngi
Kanakhalā
Makhalā
Kalakala
Śrī Siṃha
Kantali
Dhahuli
Nāgabodhi
Sarvabhakṣa
Putali
Kirava
Samudra
Kapalapa
Panaha
Vyalipa
Anaṅga

Amitābha
Lūyipa
Darika
Kamaparipa
Indrabhūti
Mekopa
Saraha
Bhikṣana
Tilopa
Ḍombipa
Shavaripa
Kanhapa
Catrapa
Nyi-ma-'od-zer
Bandhepa
Tandhepa
Udheli
Kaṅkaripa
Sakara
Nāgārjuna
Kukkuripa
Babhahi
Bhusuku

than playing the *vīṇā*, was told to give up the idea of separate tones and to combine sound and its perceptual components into one. Similarly, Gorura, the bird-catcher, learned to join the songs of birds and their individual notes into one, and then to abandon even the notion of sound. The Siddha Shalipa overcame his fear of wolves by meditating on all sounds as being identical with the howl of the wolf. The Brahman Bhadrapa overcame his resistance to eating pork and drinking wine, while meditating in a cemetery. Lūyipa received his name due to his diet of fish-entrails which he assumed after a Ḍākinī had aided him in freeing his mind from pride in social status and clean food.

Kukuripa attained the worldly *siddhi* and grew attached to dwelling in the Heaven of the Thirty-three. However, having become moved by compassion, he returned to help a dog that he had left in his cave. When he arrived, he found that the dog was actually a Ḍākinī who granted him the highest *siddhi*.

Perhaps the most well-known of the Mahāsiddhas was the arrow-maker, Saraha, who was born the son of a Ḍākinī. He lived as a Brahman by day and a Tantric practitioner by night. Accused of the un-Brahman-like activity of drunkenness, he proved his freedom from ordinary worldly restraints by drinking molten copper! Impressed with his abilities, the king, the queen, and the people requested his teaching. He responded with the "Three Cycles of Dohā"–the 'King Dohā', the 'Queen Dohā', and the 'People Dohā'.

Later Saraha resided in a solitary place with a fifteen year old girl. One day he requested that she prepare some radishes for him. She returned with radishes in buffalo yogurt, only to find Saraha sunk deep in meditation, where he remained for twelve years. Arising from meditation, he asked for his radishes. After being told by the girl that, after twelve years, the radishes no longer existed, he told her that he would go then to the mountains to meditate. As he was leaving, the girl said to him: "A solitary body does not mean solitude . . . the best solitude is that of the mind free from names and concepts. . . . In twelve years of meditation you did not get rid of the idea of radishes. . . ." Saraha realized that this was true, and, abandoning his attachment to names and concepts, he gained supreme *siddhi*.

In addition to adding new life to Buddhist culture through an emphasis on the spontaneous practice of meditation, the Mahāsiddhas played an important role in the development and propagation of Vajrayāna Buddhism. In many of the biographies, we are told that on meeting the guru, the Siddha is given empowerment into the Tantras, most often the Anuttara-yoga Tantras of the Guhyasamāja, Hevajra, or Cakrasaṃvara. The Eighty-four Mahāsiddhas are credited with having compiled many Tantric Sādhanas which are found in the Tibetan canon.

Although the Mahāsiddhas were often outlandish and iconoclastic individuals, they were above all highly accomplished yogis who, through the diligent practice of a wide range of meditative techniques suitable to their particular natures, demonstrated that Buddhahood in one's lifetime is indeed possible.

Events Surrounding the Flourishing and Decline of Buddhism in India

About 320 A.D., the Gupta Dynasty was established in India as a result of the marriage of Candragupta, a local ruler in Magadha, with a daughter of the ancient Licchavi aristocracy. Earlier, the Licchavi Clan had become part of the independent Vṛji Republic. This was also the period of the great Buddhist masters Asaṅga and Vasubandhu, who, it is likely, lived long enough to see Pāṭaliputra rise again to become a great center of political unification. This unification occurred through the efforts of Candragupta's successor, Samudragupta (c. 335–376). Samudragupta reinstated a central government for northern India and ceased to permit the feudal lords and Śaka vassals to maintain a purely independent status.

The period of Gupta supremacy provided the conditions which enabled Indian culture to rise to its highest peak of achievement; it was a time of great peace and prosperity for India. Travelers were seldom attacked by bandits and Indian society in general was ethically and religiously at its peak. During this time many sacrificial forms and rituals as outlined in the Vedas were restored and the worship of the Bramanical pantheon was revived. Buddhism during this period was also greatly flourishing.

Towards the end of the fifth century, the Hephthalites or "White Huns," Indo-european tribes from Central Asia, began to cause the Gupta Dynasty great alarm. And by the beginning of the seventh century, they were seriously threatening many of the established Buddhist institutions. A Hephthalite by the name of Mihirakula destroyed single-handedly several Buddhist monasteries and executed a number of monks. While this was occurring in the northwest, Saśaṅka, described as a fanatical Śaivite king of Bengal, attempted to destroy the Bodhi Tree at Gayā.

But the invasion of the barbaric Huns was not the principal factor leading to the fall of the Gupta Dynasty. Perhaps the more essential factors in the fate of the Guptas were the internal dissension of the royal family and the revolts of the provincial governors or feudal lords.

The Chinese Buddhist pilgrim Hsüan-tsang, who traveled throughout northwestern India between the years of 630 and 643, observed that the influence of Buddhism was showing definite signs of weakening. Some of the great monasteries were already in ruins and a number of places of pilgrimage were not well frequented. However, he also noted that both the spirit of Buddhism and the lineages of the Buddha were still strong. There were prosperous monasteries, such as Nālandā, which, under the patronage of the kings of the Pāla Dynasty, remained principal centers for Buddhist learning until the Muslim invasion around the eleventh century.

With the downfall of the Guptas in the sixth century, came Harṣa's reign. This was a career of conquest and successful military leadership, resulting in the seizure of most of northern India, although Kashmir, western Punjab, Nepal, and a few other areas remained independent. Harṣa-vardhana (Silāditya) demonstrated much tolerance and respect for Buddhism and the Buddhist Saṅgha. Although he also supported Brahmanical religious establishments, later in life, he showed a distinct partiality to Buddhism, and even outlawed the slaughter of animals. In one of his commentaries, Guṇaprabha, the great Vinaya master of Mathurā, mentions that he had been the teacher of Harṣa.

Harṣa erected thousands of Buddhist Stūpas on the banks of the Ganges, and founded a number of monasteries at the sacred places of the Buddhists. On the west bank of the Ganges he built a large monastery and a one-hundred foot high tower in which he placed a golden image of Śākyamuni Buddha. Every morning a small golden image of the Buddha was carried in splendid procession from the royal palace to the tower. After the procession was over, the king offered to the image of the Buddha innumerable silken garments, decorated with precious gems. This solemn ceremony was repeated every day. About a month after the monastery was built, it suddenly caught fire. As Harṣa was observing the scene from the top of a Stūpa, a fanatic would-be assassin with knife in hand rushed towards him. After seizing the man and delivering him to his magistrates, the king ordered him to be interrogated. He confessed that he had been bribed by certain Brahmans who were infuriated at the excessive favor shown by the king towards the Buddhists. After capturing the instigators of the plot,

King Harṣa banished five hundred Brahmans to the frontiers of India. This episode illustrates the tension that existed among members of the ruling class during this period of India's history. Buddhism and Brahmanism were at odds for their very survival.

After meeting with the Chinese pilgrim Hsüan-tsang, Harṣa sent an envoy to the Chinese emperor T'ai-tsung in order to initiate greater cultural and religious exchanges between India and China. The Chinese emperor responded by sending three delegations to India, the last of which left China in 646. By the time the delegation arrived, Harṣavardhana had died, and the king did not appear to have left any heir to his throne. A militant usurper by the name of Aruṇāśva (Ārjuna) ordered Harṣa's troops to forceably drive out the incoming Chinese delegation. After a few members of the envoy were killed, the rest fled to Tibet.

Upon hearing of Aruṇāśva's treachery, the Tibetan King Srong-btsan-sgam-po ordered the powerful Tibetan army into India. Assisted by the Chinese, they besieged the Indian stronghold at Kānya-kubja and rendered Aruṇāśya powerless. Thus, for a time India had to pay 'tribute'

Vikramaśīla For many centuries this university was a renowned center of Buddhist scholarship.

Nālandā University This famous center of learning near the banks of the Ganges, only a small portion of which is shown above, played a crucial role in the development and maintenance of the Buddhist philosophical tradition over a millenium.

to China. During this military expedition, Srong-btsan-sgam-po temporarily occupied and had complete control of nearly every province of northern India. Because of the sheer strength and magnitude of his forces, the conquest was made without bloodshed; the Indian forces were defeated by fear alone. Through this carefully executed maneuver, Srong-btsan-sgam-po's army successfully removed numerous Buddha relics before they could be damaged or destroyed by the forces in India attempting to eradicate Buddhism.

Buddhism's last phase of royal patronage in India was under the Pāla kings of Bengal and Bihar. This was a period which emerged at the end of the eighth century, and lasted four centuries. Essentially the entire Pāla Dynasty supported the Buddhist Saṅgha, and the monasteries at Bodh Gayā, Nālandā, and Vikramaśīla became active once again. During this period Buddhism also became officially recognized in Tibet.

Dharmapāla (c. 770–810), undoubtedly the greatest king of Bengal, ruled for more than thirty-two years. He founded many Budhist monasteries, but his greatest achievement was the founding of the Vikramaśīla University, which soon almost rivaled Nālandā. Dharmapāla's successor was Devapāla (c. 810–850) who remodeled the Vihāra of Odantapurī—which had been built by Dharmapāla's father, Gopāla (d. 780). The Vinaya master Śākyaprabha was born during the time of Gopāla's reign, and it was during this period that the Bodhisattva Śāntarakṣita journeyed to Tibet. Impressed with the architectural beauty of the Odantapurī Monastery, Śāntarakṣita modeled the first monastery in Tibet at bSam-yas after that magnificent Vihāra.

During the reigns of King Dharmapāla and his successor, Devapāla, a number of Buddhist logicians, scholars, Vinayadhāras, and master of the Prajñāpāramitā gained fame throughout India. One of these was Dharmapāla's teacher Haribhadra; other learned masters who lived during the reign of King Dharmapāla were Buddhajñānapāda, Rāhulabhadra, Buddhaguhya, Buddhaśānti, and the master Kamalaśīla.

The reign of the seven principal Pāla rulers survived in Bengal up to the time of Atīśa (982–1054), who was a principal teacher at Vikramaśīla. In fact, the Pāla Dynasty of Buddhist kings was centered at Vikramaśīla. Both Odantapurī and Vikramaśīla were still quite active teaching institutions during the time of Nāropa (1016–1100) and his disciple Dombi-pā. But after the demise of the Pāla Dynasty, Vikramaśīla and Odantapurī Monasteries were converted partially into fortresses in which a number of soldiers were stationed. Eventually, the Turks sacked these two principal Vihāras, burning them to the ground and massacring a number of ordained monks. These invaders later built a fort from the ruins of Odantapurī.

From the ninth century onwards, India was in the midst of a turbulent sea of social change, but the demise of Buddhism in India was probably not due to persecution as such, but to the development of a new form of devotional Hinduism, which made a vigorous emotional appeal to the common person. India at this time was a great melting pot of religious ideologies. The persistent tendency of Hinduism is to assimilate, and the Hindus incorporated many of the teachings of the Buddha into their own beliefs and practices. The Buddha was eventually included within the Hindu pantheon and is still regarded by more orthodox Hindus as one of the ten incarnations of Viṣṇu.

The extinction of Buddhism in India was also brought about by its refusal to become incorporated within the caste system, by its loss of royal patronage, and by the influence of two strong proponents

The Main Temple at Nālandā Literally thousands of Buddha images have been found in the vicinity of this extraordinary university.

of the new Hindu religion—Kumārilabhaṭṭa (c. 700) and Śaṅkara (c. 788–820). Śaṅkara, one of the great Hindu philosophers, was very much an independent thinker. His philosopical views tended to go against the developing forms of devotional Hinduism, and through his repeated debates with the Buddhists, he was forced to move in the direction of Buddhist philosophy. As a result of his contact with the Buddhists, many of his doctrinal principles came very close to the basic Buddhist premises. As Śaṅkara's influence within the Hindu community grew, Buddhism was absorbed into Indian culture and lost its significance as an independent system.

During the seventh century, Islam was arising in the Middle East,

but it was too absorbed in westward expansion and in conflict with the Byzantine Empire of Constantinople to look eastward beyond Iran. Early in the eighth century, however, the recently conquered and aggressive Turks began to move into and overshadow many areas of traditional Indian civilization. The Kashmirian king Lalitāditya (c. 724–760) was able to protect his domain against these incoming forces of Islam, but the movement was gaining strength.

Early in the eleventh century, India was experiencing economic difficulties due to famine and constant invasions by 'outsiders' (*kla-klo, mleccha*). The Buddhist Saṅgha was forced to leave many of the places where they had settled—a trend which seems to have played an important role in the expansion of Buddhism outside of India. For example, the Mūlasarvāstivādins, who had settled in the northwest, found it necessary to move out of India and form new communities in the west and to the south. They soon formed nearly the whole of the Buddhist community in Java and Sumatra, and flourished in Tibet as well.

With the invasion of the Turks in the eleventh century, many of the Mahāyāna and Mantrayāna practitioners from the regions of Magadha fled to the countries of eastern India for refuge. There they built temples and established innumerable Dharma centers, with the help of such Dharma kings as Śobhajāta and Siṃhajaṭi. Over thirty thousand monks were affected by this migration of Buddhism.

Because the Vinaya is the mainstay of the Buddhadharma, the reduction in number of Vinayadharas in India weakened the Saṅgha to the extent that Buddhism survived only within the academic institutions such as Nālandā, Vikramaśīla, Vajrāsana (Bodh Gayā), and Odantapurī. Although Nālandā University was probably the last to be destroyed by the invading forces, the living spirit of Buddhism was no longer present during the final days of this institution; in the end, Buddhism was only another department of study among the Hinduistic departments.

Between 1001 and 1027 the Muhammadan Sultan Mahmud raided India on seventeen occasions. During this series of attacks, numerous royal palaces and Buddhist and Hindu temples were looted and desecrated. The Muslim intention was to convert the unbelievers, Buddhists and Hindus alike, to the 'One God' of the Islamic faith. Those who would not conform to the creed of the Muslims were put to the sword for the sake of Islam. The amount of wholesale killing and destroying that these invading forces performed was so extensive that the Tibetan historian, Tāranātha, equated these 'savages' with the forces of Māra, the Lord of Destruction.

In Bengal, the previous Pāla Dynasty was taken over by the Senas, who were strong supporters of orthodox Hinduism and showed definite signs of anti-Buddhist sentiment. While in India, the lesser Hindu kings, militarily conservative and generally incapable of forming any effective cooperative alliances, were eventually overpowered by the continuing raids of the Muslim invaders. However, with the death of Mahmud in 1030, India was spared from further invasion for nearly fifty years.

A principal Buddhist figure during this time was Abhayākaragupta ('Jigs-med 'Byung-gnas-sbas-pa, d. 1125), a recognized master of the Mahāyāna and Guhya-Mantrayāna. Revered in Tibet as an incarnation of Amitābha, he wrote a number of significant works including the *Munimatālaṃkāra*, a text which attempted to alleviated the logical difficulties that occurred in the different interpretations of certain points of the Doctrine which were held by proponents of differing Saṅgha communities. He also authored the *Vajrāvali* (*rDo-rje phreng-ba*), a work which was integrated into the system of Ye-shes-zhabs (Jñānapāda) that developed out of the practice of the *Guhyasamāja*, a root tantric text in the Mahāyoga lineages in Tibet. Both Abhayākaragupta and Ratnākaraśānti (Śānti-pa) are regarded as distinguished Vinaya masters, as well as chief synthesizers and systematizers of the Mādhyamika and Mantrayāna—probably the last significant Buddhist development in India.

By the twelfth century, the Buddhist Saṅgha was confined to the territory of Bihār. In 1194, the Muslims moved eastward and down the Ganges. Benares was captured by a powerful general of Muhammad, and in 1199, Bihār was taken. The Buddhist monks were slaughtered, Nālandā and the other Buddhist monasteries of Bihār were sacked, and their libraries turned to ashes. The temples were destroyed and mosques were erected in their places. With the destruction of a great number of Indian universities, much of the cultural heritage of India perished forever.

Those who survived the massacre fled to the mountains of Nepal and Tibet; many of these refugees found lasting refuge at bSam-yas Monastery. The monks and Paṇḍitas who were left in India were too few to preserve the Buddhist Sanskrit texts that managed to survive the humidity, heat, mealworms, and of course, the torches of the military hordes who continued to loot, pillage, and destroy for many decades. By the end of the thirteenth century, the time of the Venetian traveller, Marco Polo, Buddhism was completely gone from its motherland.

The Development of Buddhism in Tibet

The Ancestral and Dynastic Origins of the Tibetan Civilization

In the history of ancient Tibet, cosmology, myth, and history combine to form a unified view of man. To discuss any one of these aspects without considering its relationship with the other two would prove ineffective and misleading. But traditional Tibetan viewpoints, which provide the heritage with a unique cohesiveness, are often ignored in favor of a more analytical approach to Tibetan history. Yet, by not carefully considering the oral tradition and the living spirit of a people, one may misinterpret or confuse occurrences which cannot be fully understood apart from their religious or spiritual significance.

A prevalent misunderstanding is that Tibet had no noticeable form of civilization until its adoption of a centralized government during the reign of Srong-btsan-sgam-po, in the seventh century A.D. This misunderstanding is due, in part, to the reliance, by many scholars of Tibetan history, on Chinese sources which have been known to be colored by the ideological struggles between Taoism and Buddhism which were taking place in China at that time. During various periods, certain Chinese emperors would suppress or support Buddhism, depending upon which had the greater political leverage. China generally considered herself ruler not only of the Chinese, but of groups of people in bordering regions, all of whom she looked upon as uncivilized.

Chinese accounts of Tibet during the three hundred year period of the T'ang Dynasty (618–907 A.D.) include the works of I-tsing, who recorded brief biographies of numerous Chinese pilgrims who went abroad between the reigns of T'ai-tsung and Empress Wu Tse-t'ien in the seventh century.

However, in light of the highly sophisticated civilization that arose with the advent of Buddhism in Tibet, beginning with the reign of Srong-btsan-sgam-po, it is apparent that a well-developed culture was

Padmasambhava This image at bSam-yas was blessed by Padmasambhava himself.

present in Tibet long before the reign of the Buddhist kings. And the Tibetan Empire itself, in this early period, was a politically autonomous power whose lands extended well over one thousand miles, including such areas a Ladakh, Gu-ge, Kashmir, parts of Burma, Chinese Turkestan, Bengal, Sikkim, Bhutan, and Gyal-mo-rong.

To get a clear picture of early Tibetan history, one must look at the origin of the Tibetan land, people, and royal dynasties through the light of the early Tibetan chronicles. According to these, the ancient land of Bod (Tibet)–before the advent of man–was filled with *mi-ma-yin*, or the 'non-human ones'. The term designates spirits, apparitions, and demons in general–all of whom possessed malignant natures.

The Tibetan chronicles also sketch the world as a drama of creation, beginning with the 'essence of the five primary senses', a kind of primordial and undifferentiated potential. Out of this potential was formed a particular kind of being, which we can call the macrocosm, serving as a convenient label for anything that holds up or supports the notion of existence.

The ancient Tibetan equivalent for the macrocosm was the 'cosmic egg' (*sgo-nga chen-po gcig*), and what was identified as the microcosm was the 'origin egg' (*dung-ti sgo-nga*). This origin egg was the primeval source from which succeeding generations of Tibetans derived their origin. The first generation of Tibetans came about simply by the breaking of the cosmic egg, which gave rise to six principal tribes (*Bod-mi'u gdung-drug*). Each of these was said to have differentiated into three sub-ordinate tribes, making a total of eighteen tribes or clans (*Rus-chen bco-brgyad*). In this mythological conception, the 'origin egg' is the archetype of all creative human activity and preceeds the notion of dualism by representing the cosmos in its totality. The breaking of the egg symbolizes a fundamental split and the introduction of what may be called a 'cosmological dualism', which gives rise to the differentiation into light and dark, good and evil, masculinity and femininity, and so on.

The origin egg was further divided into three principal constituents: the yolk, the white, and the shell. These stood for inner, middle, and outer sections, giving rise to the idea of the three strata or realms of existence: the upper world (*gnam*) as heaven; the middle world (*bar*) as the habitat of man; and the lower world, the earth (*sa*), as the habitat of demons.

Other traditional sources, revered by the Bon-po, present a different account of the 'origin egg', beginning with the 'inert potential of the elements' and proceeding directly to the sphere of the microcosm.

Here, the dualistic structure of existence is brought about by means of a mutual co-arising of two origin eggs, one white and the other black. Emerging from the white egg was the beneficent being (*phan-byed*) symbolizing goodness, light, and everything with positive existence (*yod*). The black egg yielded the malificent being (*gnod-byed*) symbolizing evil, darkness, negativity, and malevolent demons.

From the point of view of human existence, the origin egg and its three elements are seen as the structure of a world horizon permeated with the qualities of Tibet's unique geography. When the origin egg was broken, the white of the egg became the white origin lake, fragments of the shell formed the glacier mountains, and the yolk developed into the six families.

The ideas of the origin egg as the primal substance of creation, and the cosmic egg as that which is prior to creation, come very close to the view of the origination held by the Greek philosopher Anaximander of Milesia (c. 600 B.C.), who proposed a conception of Being in terms of an indeterminate infinite which comes prior to the determinate primary element, making the clear distinction between the macrocosm and the microcosm.

In the early Tibetan chronicles there are also various views of the creation and origin of the Tibetan people and of the Tibetan kings. Before the advent of the Bon, it was believed that one's relatives or ancestors continued to exist after death in the realm of the dead—the underworld. As members of this realm, the ancestral spirits were roaming manifestations from the tombs of the dead. This belief in the power of the defunct ancestry led to a doctrine of animism, and to the introduction of malignant spirits that menaced the people—causing sickness, famine, earthquakes, floods, and other disasters.

With the appearance of gNya'-khri-btsan-po, the first king of Tibet (c. 410 B.C.), the sphere of the *lha*, or gods, was linked with the earth, in the form of the royal dynastic kings. There were five divisions of these kings, representing a progressive descent from the 'divine' to the 'worldly' realms. The five divisions of twenty-eight kings ended with lHa-tho-tho-ri gNyan-btsan. There also existed a 'spirit rope' used by these kings which bound earth to the heaven realm. It is said that the eighth king of the royal succession—the first member of the second grouping, Gri-gdum-btsan-po—was slain by an evil minister, causing the spirit rope to be cut forever. Gri-gdum-btsan-po's successor, the ninth king of Tibet, whose name was Bya-khri-btsan-po, marked the beginning of the religion of Bon, whose legendary founder was gShen-rabs of the region of Zhang-zhung.

The Bon-po's view of existence considered that the boundaries between the heavens, the intermediate world, and the lower world of the demons–between men and gods and between men and the dead–could be broached by the shaman priests. This resulted in the establishment of special funeral rites and the worship of the celestial *lha*. The shamans could close the doors of tombs and thus cut the ties man had with the world of the dead; while by opening the door to the *lha*, the door to the light radiating from the celestial spheres was metaphorically opened. The significance of this radical shift was that it totally changed the position of man, of the living, in the cosmic sense, and provided him with an entirely new view of himself and his relation with the life-world.

The Bon-po priests also assisted the royalty both by providing a protective function and by exercising their sacred power to help unite the kingdom, which at that time was more or less a confederation of family-clans. Up to the time of lHa-tho-tho-ri gNyan-btsan (c. 300 A.D.), the integral power of the ancient Tibetan monarchy consisted of the king (*btsan-po*), the head shaman (*gshen-gnyan*), and the minister. The king was believed to be the son of the *lha* and was the continually reborn essence of the divine ancestor. He ascended the throne as the consecutive link of the ancestral principle of reincarnation. This procedure of succession also applied to the shaman and the minister, so that a new trinity of power was installed at the accession of each king.

From the formal emergence of the Bon onward, the royal dynastic kings from the region of Yar-lung continued to serve the essential function of intermediator between heaven and earth.

The Bon-po explanation for the appearance of gNya'-khri-btsan-po, 'the first ruler of men', places him as a descendant from the gNam-gyi-khri-btsun, the place of heaven, who exercised the power of his sacred kingship over the Kingdom of Bod. The chronicles recount that he descended from the heavens to the peak of Mount lHa-ri Gyang-tho. He looked around and saw the great beauty of the snow mountain of Yar-lha-sham-po–a beauty like the moonstone in the embrace of the full moon. Twelve herdsmen saw him, and asked him from whence he had come, and he pointed towards the heavens. As they had no king, they raised him upon their shoulders, accepting him as their king destined from heaven.

The introduction of Buddhism in Tibet provided a connection between the origins of gNya'-khri-btsan-po and the royal lines of India. The various traditional accounts which generally agree with each other on the origin of gNya'-khri-btsan-po may be summarized as follows:

A son was born to dMag-brgya-pa, the King of the Śākya clan of

lHa-tho-tho-ri

the Licchavis. He had eyes which closed from below, turquoise eyebrows, teeth like a row of conch shells, and fingers webbed like the King of Geese. Fearing that these signs portended great evil, the parents put the child in a copper box and floated it away on the river Ganges. The child was rescued by a farmer, and when, years later, he was told about his past, he fled North and was later made ruler of Bod. (The signs such as webbed fingers and teeth like shells, which were attributed to gNya-khri-btsan-po, are the signs of a Cakravartin, indicating a great king).

An older Tibetan account connects gNya'-khri-btsan-po with Ajātaśatru. King Ajātaśatru made war with another king who was trying to eradicate the Śākya clan. A youth of the Śākyas, who possessed the signs of a Cakravartin, took flight to the glacier mountains of Bod, and became known as gNya-khri-btsan-po, the first King of Tibet.

The Tibetan dynasty thus became a branch of the Indian dynasty, and the introduction of Buddhism provided the king with a further means for the consolidation of his rule by placing the throne on a more spiritually potent foundation. By connecting gNya-khri-btsan-po with the famous Indian dynasties of the Śākyas or Licchavis, there was introduced into Tibet a tradition of direct descent from the Buddha. Furthermore, the Licchavi clan was so highly regarded, that inscriptions which later praised King Srong-btsan-sgam-po, the virtual founder of the Tibetan Empire, always mentioned that he was a descendant of the Licchavi clan.

With the introduction of Buddhism into Tibet, the Tibetan's views concerning their ancestral roots, as well as the ancestral roots of the Tibetan Dynastic Kings, radically shifted. According to Buddhist tradition, the Tibetan people arose from the union of an Ape-Bodhisattva, an incarnation of Avalokiteśvara, and a rock-demoness. As the story is related, the demoness grew enamoured of the monkey who was meditating in a cave, and threatened to kill herself if he did not comply with her desires. The monkey, not wishing to either break his meditation or cause harm to the demoness, asked Avalokiteśvara and Tārā for advice. The deities told him to marry the demoness, and out of this union came six offspring, each signifying one of the six realms of existence: hell beings, hungry ghosts, animals, men, jealous deities, and gods. Gradually, the monkey transformed into mankind. This origin myth is essentially a theory of evolution, inasmuch as it maintains that the different forms of life developed gradually from a common ancestry. This Tibetan explanation of the origin of man is found in the *Ma-ni-bka'-'bum*, one of the earliest Tibetan records, which was compiled during the time of Srong-btsan-sgam-po.

When Buddhism entered Tibet, the Buddhist explanation of the origin of the Tibetan civilization became so fully accepted that the early beliefs of the origin egg were essentially forgotten. The transition to the newer beliefs may account for some of the confusion that exists between the origins of the Tibetan ancestry and the origins of the dynastic heritage. For instance, the belief that the ancient land of Bod was once submerged in a great lake is, by itself, an outgrowth of the earlier creation myths. But to pass over this description as pure myth would ignore the fact that it is in close accord with recent geological findings. The Tibetan description speaks of an origin lake, obviously of great dimension, surrounded by mountains. The lake subsequently receeds over time, giving rise to civilization.

Geologists have recently deduced that the Himalayan range and the country of Tibet were formed between forty and sixty million years ago through the collision between the continents of India and Eurasia.* During this period, the Indus and Tsang-po valleys in southern Tibet existed as an ocean basin. Geologists presume that the two continents came into contact initially as peninsulas whose 'zone of contact' eventually grew until the ocean basin between the continents was swallowed up. During this interim, a great salt lake must have formed. In the course of collision between the continents, geologists futher indicate that a huge amount of material was displaced, some of which accounts for the formation of the Himalayas.

The great salt lake, that is presumed to have been formed out of the collision, and the aquatic zone between the peninsulas can be equated with the origin lake described in the Tibetan sources. An observer located at the center of this aquatic zone might very likely view himself as resting on a lake surrounded by a circular mountainous region, which presumably could be covered entirely with glacial formation having the appearance of the whiteness of a huge shell. Such a comparison of this geological and mythic 'evidence' may be somewhat presumptuous. However, it does tend to illustrate how mythic development evolved out of symbols provided by nature, and how these symbols can just as easily stand for physical realities as for metaphorical expressions of mythic perception. It is true however, that the ocean basin existed at least fifty million years ago, and not during the time that Śākyamuni Buddha walked the earth, as was commonly believed. Such an error undoubtedly came about with the tendency to mix together the origins of the two distinct cultural heritages (Bon and Buddhist) and the two theories of the Tibetan ancestral roots (the one for the civilization and the one for the dynastic kings). The former follows an evolutionary course, considering the origins of human civilization and viewing the world as an integral cosmos of aeonic duration; the latter has definite historical (or legendary) roots extending back in time to particular historical events which provide necessary links between different cultural traditions.

In light of the ease with which new origins for their ancestry were adopted in response to religious or cultural changes, the Tibetan's unusual degree of religious tolerance and flexibility is apparent. The advent of Buddhism actually brought an end to the principal religious and cosmological conceptions of the early Tibetans, which were at the very roots of their ancestry.

---

*Molner, Peter and Tapponnier, Paul; "The Collision Between India and Eurasia." *Scientific American*, April, 1977. pp. 30–41.

TIBET
AND
THE SURROUNDING REGIONS
Compiled from the latest information
Scales.
69 Miles - 1 Degree
104.3 Versts - 1 Degree
Natural Scale 1: 3 800 000
Explanation of Tibetan and Mongolian Names.
Bulak . . Spring   Gompa . . . . Monastery   Muren . . River
Tso . . . . . Lake   Dzong . . . . Fort   Nor . . . . Lake
Chu . . . . River   Kul . . . . Lake   Tagh Mountains
Davan . . Pass   Kurghan Enclosure Fort   Ula Mountains
Gol . . . Stream   La . . . . Pass   Ussu . . . River
Mazar . . . . . Tomb, Shrine   Oghil . . . Shepherd's Station
C. Camp   L. Lake   P. Pass   R. River   W. Well   Railways
CHINESE TURKISTAN
TARIM BASIN
TAKLA MAKAN
DESERT
UNEXPLORED
TIBET
KACHI
HOR PROVINCE
DOKTHOL PROVINCE
UTSANG
NEPAL
Central Altyn Tagh
Arka Tagh
Aksai Chin
Ling-zi Thang
Cherchen
Khotan
Yarkand
Kashgar
Lob Nor
Leh
Almora
Bareilly
Khatmandu
Dhwlagiri
Mt. Everest
Tsangpo or Brahmaputra R.
Indus
80
82
84
86
88
90
78
40
38
36
32
30
28

92
94
96
98
100
102
40
38
36
34
32
28
KUM-TAGH SANDS
Saitu or Sachu
(Sha chau)
An-si-chau
Yu-min-hsien
Po-lisien-tsi Mts
Khara Ula
SU CHAU
KAN-CHAU
ALA-SHAN
Humboldt Range
Ritter Range
SIRTIN DISTRICT
Sirtin Plain
Tsaidamin Ula
HAJJAR DISTRICT
KOKO NOR
South Koko Nor Range
Si-ning
Tamirtin Ula
BANAKHASUM
Tolai Ula
Shuga
Mt Marco Polo
West Koko-shili Range
East Koko-shili Range
Amnen Kor
Tsaring Nor
Amne Machin Range
TIBET
NAGCHUKHA
AMDO
NAGRA
LHASA
Yamdrok Tso
PO-YUL
PO-MED
ZYUL-TED
LO-TAWA
LO-NAKPO
Chiamdo
Batang
Litang
Darchendo
Atun-tse
YUN-NAN
ASSAM
BURMA
BRAHMAPUTRA R.
Sadiya
Dibrugarh
Tezpur
Lakhimpur
92
94
96
98
100

The Vinaya Lineage in Tibet

There are three Vinaya lineages which successfully developed in Tibet: the sMad Vinaya which came to Tibet through Śāntarakṣita, the sTod Vinaya which was established in western Tibet in the eleventh century, and the Kha-che Vinaya which came from Kashmir. Together they carry the philosophical tradition of the Mūlasarvāstivādins, a later branch of the Śrāvakayāna. All three lineages are the living transmission of the Vinaya originating with the Buddha's son Rāhula.

By the time of the Third Council at Pāṭaliputra, the Saṅgha was divided into eighteen groups. However, even though there was some disagreement among the Saṅgha in matters of philosophy, logic and rhetoric, the Vinaya lineage of Rāhula survived through time as an unbroken succession until Śāntarakṣita brought it to Tibet in the eighth century. The Indian Ācārya Jinamitra, the Tibetan Cog-ro-klu'i rGyal-mtshan, and many others translated various sections of the Vinaya Piṭaka. What was preserved by these early translators was a complete and unaltered translation of the Mūlasarvāstivādin Vinaya which the Mahāyānists in India, China and Tibet had all seen fit to preserve and practice in its original form.

In the seventh century, Srong-btsan-sgam-po was recognized as the first Dharma King of Tibet. In order to make the Buddhist texts from India available to the Tibetans, he commissioned the scholar 'Thon-mi Sambhoṭa to devise a Tibetan alphabet suitable for the translation of the incoming Buddhist works. As most of Central Asia was under Tibetan domination during this period, the Sūtras and Śāstras came into Tibet from China and Nepal, as well as from India. With his royal patronage of the Buddhadharma, Srong-btsan-sgam-po prepared his country for the flowering of Buddhism in Tibet, which would come a century later. Of his innumerable achievements, the King instituted a general code of conduct which served to prepare his subjects for the practice of the Vinaya.

Following the suggestions of his two wives, Princess Bri-btsun (Ṭhi-tsun) of Nepal and Princess Ong-co of China, King Srong-btsan-sgam-po adapted the Vinaya texts provided by 'Thon-mi Sambhoṭa to the social mores of the Tibetan people. With the translation of the *Pan-gong-phyag-rgya-pa*, this gifted translator and linguist provided Tibet with its first text on the subject of conduct and ethics and manners. Impressed with the sensibility of the Buddhist rules of conduct, the

Srong-btsan-sgam-po

king instituted a legal code of sixteen moral virtues. These sixteen rules may be described as follows:

1. Those who kill, steal, or commit adultery will be fined, otherwise punished, or banished from the country.
2. Take refuge in the Buddha, Dharma, and Saṅgha.
3. Carry on the social tradition of respecting your parents and the elders of the community.
4. Practice non-violence, live without hostility and resentment, and respect those who bring out the wholesomeness in themselves and others.
5. Show genuine friendliness to all, especially relatives and friends, and encourage them when they are in need of support.

'Thon-mi Sambhoṭa

6. Be as helpful to your fellow citizens as you would have them be to you.
7. Be unassuming and straightforward in your speech by being honest and not evasive.
8. Follow the healthy influences of others, especially those who are learned, wise, or who are the respected leaders of the community.
9. Practice conservation of material wealth and moderation in consumption of food and drink.
10. Do not use harsh, violent, bitter, or deceptive language to your friends.
11. Pay debts to others in due time.
12. Be straightforward in all financial agreements, and do not cheat others through counterfeiting, deception, or trickery.

Khri-srong-lde'u-btsan

13. Practice emotional balance and do not be envious of those who have attained what you desire.
14. Do not cultivate hostile or dangerous people, especially those who seek to upset the community.
15. Words that are spoken should be preceded with reflection—be sparing of words and speak with a genuine concern for others.
16. Do not gossip about the mistakes of others or interfere with the personal affairs of others unless asked for help.

The second great Dharma King of Tibet, Khri-srong-lde'u-btsan (c. 760) was determined to put Buddhism on a firm foothold. He thus invited the Bodhisattva Śāntarakṣita to Tibet to teach the Dharma. Upon his arrival, Śāntarakṣita was beset with insurmountable obstacles

Śāntarakṣita

in the form of wrathful demons who created floods and earthquakes and who in general launched an all-out attack on the incoming religion, for the Bon-po shamanistic priests knew that the new religion of Buddhism was a major threat to the indigenous religion of Bon. Śāntarakṣita, knowing that he himself could not control these demons, suggested to the King that he invite the renowned master Padmasambhava to Tibet. Padmasambhava, having been born in the ancient country of Uḍḍiyāna, and having traveled throughout all parts of the known world, was presently residing in India. He had great knowledge of the shamanistic practices of the time, and thus was well equipped to subdue the demons which were obstructing the development of Buddhism in Tibet.

Upon arrival in Tibet, Padmasambhava began to clear the way for the firm establishment of the Buddhadharma. King Khri-srong-

Padmasambhava

lde'u-btsan, Śāntarakṣita, and Padmasambhava then proceeded to establish the bSam-yas Monastery, which was built in the shape of a *maṇḍala* following the model of the Odantapurī Monastery in India. bSam-yas became the first institution of Buddhist learning in Tibet; in later times, it was open to all the schools of Tibetan Buddhism, and during the tenth century it served as a place of refuge for many Indian Paṇḍitas who were troubled by the gradual decline of Buddhism in India. Upon consecration of the bSam-yas temple by Padmasambhava, the King made plans for the arrival of scores of translators from India, Nepal, Kashmir, and even China—who would assemble the first comprehensive corpus of Doctrine in the native tongue of the Tibetans. The first to arrive were such masters as Vimalamitra, Śāntigarbha, Dharmakīrti (the Second), and other members of the renowned 108

bSam-yas Monastery

Mahāpaṇḍitas. For this early period, the Vinaya was the root and mainstay of the Buddhadharma. Śāntarakṣita ordained the first seven monks: rBa-gsal-snang, Vairocana, Ngan-lam rGyal-ba-mchog-dbyangs, Nam-mkha'i sNying-po, rMa Rin-chen-mchog, 'Khon Klu'i-dbang-po-bsrung-ba, and La-gsum rGyal-ba-byang-chub. Subsequently, these monks helped the Indian masters with the work of translation, and later an additional three hundred novices were ordained. To announce the success and rapid spread of the Saṅgha, King Khri-srong-lde'u-btsan had innumerable pillars erected which contained inscriptions proclaiming the institution of a new religious order for the land of Tibet.

A second significant wave of newcomers arrived guided by sKa-ba dPal-brtsegs, who brought with him one hundred translators, and Cog-ro-klu'i rGyal-mtshan, who headed nearly one-thousand apprentice translators. Both masters were of the twenty-five original disciples of Guru Padmasambhava. At the outset, the fundamental Āgamas and Mahāyāna Sūtras and Śāstras were translated in order to lay a firm foundation for the establishment of a viable code of Vinaya derived from the newly translated Vinaya texts, as well as to develop a system of standardization for translation.

Yer-ba Hermitage
The early meditation centers were built as residences for the Indian paṇḍitas and their Tibetan disciples in the valleys around Lhasa.

Along with the written word of the Vinaya came the Oral-transmission and the beginning of the Mantrayāna tradition in Tibet. In the course of time, King Khri-srong-lde'u-tsan established twelve meditation centers—the three most noted being mChims-phu, Yer-ba, and dPal Chu-bo-ri—for the transmission of the teachings of the Mantrayāna. Padmasambhava had many of these Mantrayāna teachings hidden, to be discovered and utilized at a later time. The twenty-five great Siddhas who came from the meditative centers of mChims-phu, were responsible for hiding these (*sa-gter*, buried treasure) in various locations. As Guru Rinpoche had already converted the demonic forces to the role of Dharmapālas, protectors of the Dharma, there were many suitable locations on mountains, or in crevasses, caves, and canyons, where these treasures (gTer-ma) would be safely protected. The Great Guru imparted to these twenty-five Siddhas instructions granting them the ability to be reborn at the time and location most auspicious to insure that the texts be recovered. Consequently, these Siddhas took rebirth as 108 masterful gTer-stons and teachers of the esoteric Tantras.

Khri-srong-lde'u-btsan's three sons, Mu-ne-btsan-po, Mu-rug-btsan-po, and Mu-tig-btsan-po, also did much to propagate the Dharma.

Ral-pa-can

Mu-ne-btsan-po attempted to equalize the wealth of the people. This unsuccessful attempt illustrated that it was the individual's own motivation that determined his social status. Mu-tig-btsan-po (804–17), also known as Sad-na-legs, was responsible for the restoration of the temple at Lhasa which had been built by Srong-btsan-sgam-po at the request of his Nepalese wife. Also during his reign, the early translator sKa-ba dPal-brtsegs, assisted by Nam-mkha'i sNying-po and others, compiled a catalogue (*dkar-chags*) of the Sūtras and Śāstras translated during the time of King Khri-srong-lde'u-btsan. The translator 'Khon Klu'i-dbang-po and other early scholars completed this index which then became known as the *dKar-chag-ldan-dkar-ma*. During a later time, under the reign of King Ral-pa-can (817–36), the first son of Mu-tig-btsan-po, a new catalogue was compiled. It was a résumé done on special commission by Indian and Tibetan scholars engaged in editing and unifying the already existing translations. Because of the new grammars which King Ral-pa-can instituted, certain changes in the usage of language were needed. In this later catalogue (which is no longer extant) it was observed that the later editors often took the credit as translators, although these texts had been translated during Khri-srong-lde'u-btsan's time. These early translators, many of which were direct disciples of Padmasambhava, were supported by the royalty and devoted their entire lives and all their energies towards the translation of Dharma texts. Their translations, although often grammatically imperfect, had more depth and meaning than the translations of the later periods.

During his reign Ral-pa-can gave the edict that every seven households of lay people would carry the responsibility of supporting one monk. Through his influence, over one hundred temples and Dharma centers were constructed, enabling many monks to engage in advanced meditative practices in a conducive environment. In formal assembly, Ral-pa-can also showed his respect for the monks by seating the two monastic orders of the time—the Red Saṅgha and the White Saṅgha—on the dias to the left and to the right of his throne. He put new life into the promulgation of the Sūtras, and particularly the Vinaya, by inviting a number of Indian Paṇḍitas to the newly constructed study centers to teach the Tibetan monks and lay disciples.

Some of the Dharma texts which had been translated during the periods preceding Ral-pa-can's reign, from India, Kashmir (Kha-che), Za-hor, and other lands were open to conflicting interpretations. Ral-pa-can therefore invited the Indian scholars and translators Dānaśīla, Jinamitra, Surendrabodhi and Śīlendrabodhi to Tibet to work with the Tibetan teachers and translators Ratnarakṣita, Dharmatāśīla, and Jñānasena in the standardization of the more difficult terms. Together, these masters edited the existing texts.

The three most honored kings of Tibet—Srong-btsan-sgam-po, Khri-srong-lde'u-tsan, and Ral-pa-can—all shared in the common concern for the propagation of the Vinaya. Each king represented a significant phase of Dharma activity, and this period is known as the "Twelve and a Half Happy Generations."

Up until the year of the enthronement of Glang Dar-ma (901 A.D.), the Vinaya lineage as begun in Tibet by Khri-srong-lde'u-btsan, Śāntarakṣita, and Padmasambhava was very successful, receiving full support by the royal line. Glang Dar-ma, however, opposed Buddhism, and began the wholesale slaughter and expulsion of the Buddhist monks who would not renounce their vows. So, the Vinaya lineage, as well as the other lineages of transmission, were forced to go underground.

At the time of the suppression of the Doctrine by Glang-Dar-ma, three monks from the monastery of dPal-Chu-bo-ri were abiding in meditation. These three, who later became known as the 'Three Men from Khams', were sMar Shākya-mu-ne of To-lung, gYo dGe-'byung of Pho-thong-pa, and Rab-gsal of gTsang. They had been ordained by Cog-ro-klu'i rGyal-mtshan and others of the first seven monks of Tibet, and were holders of the complete Mūlasarvāstivādin Vinaya. Hearing of a monk arriving on foot from the direction of Lhasa, they approached him, asking him the news. Upon finding out that the Doctrine was being completely destroyed, they quickly loaded the necessary books of the Vinaya ('Dul-ba) and Abhidharma (mNgon-pa) onto a mule, and hiding by day and traveling by night, they fled to Western Tibet (sTod-phyogs) to the province of mNga'-ris. Unable to remain there, they continued on their flight to Gar-log and on to the country of Hor (Eastern Mongolia) by a lesser traveled northern route. They had the intention of introducing the Doctrine into this land of a different race and language, but the obstacles were too great. and so, gathering the necessary supplies, they proceeded on to southern A-mdo (mDo-smad).

At A-mdo they met an individual who would play a prominent role in the subsequent propagation of the Doctrine. Upon meeting the three fugitive monks, he requested ordination, but they told him that would be impossible, for a minimum of five monks was required to perform the ordination ceremony. However, seeing that he was a man of virtue and devotion, one of them handed him a text of the Vinaya and said, "Read this! If you believe in what it has to say we will seriously consider arranging for your ordination." He read the Vinaya text and, shedding tears, became full of conviction. Seeing this, the three monks made him a novice and gave him the religious name of dGe-ba-rab-gsal. Later on, owing to his sublime mind, he became known as La-chen dGongs-pa-rab-gsal ("He with sublime thoughts"). The monks then instructed him to seek out two more monks so that the proper number would be present. Searching for additional members of an ordination committee, dGong-pa-rab-gsal encountered dPal-gyi-rdo-rje, the monk who had gone to Lhasa and had assassinated Glang Dar-ma. dPal-gyi-rdo-rje was asked to join the committee, but he told them that since he had killed the king he could not be included in the number required. But he gave dGong-pa-rab-gsal his blessing, and then continued on to his

La-chen dGongs-pa Rab-gsal

beloved mountains where he spent the remainder of his life in solitude. La-chen again set out in search of others, and upon meeting two Hva-shang Chinese monks, Ke-lbang and Gyi-phan, the conclave of five monks was finally assembled and conferred full initiation upon him.

After his ordination, La-chen studied the Vinaya with the Master Go-rong-seng-ge for fifteen years. For the teachings of the Prajñā-pāramitā, he studied with the venerable Ka-ba 'Od-mchog. And for the Sems-sde, or 'Mind Section' of the rDzogs-pa-chen-po, he studied with gYu-sgra sNying-po. The conclave of five monks meanwhile remained with La-chen dGongs-pa-rab-gsal. In his forty ninth year (940), La-chen went to the vicinity of Mount Dan-tug, on the bank of the rMa-chu River near Lake Ko-ko-nor in A-mdo, where he stayed until his death in 975.

Ten men who became important to the Vinaya lineage came to

dPal-gyi rDo-rje

La-chen requesting ordination. Known as the "Ten Men of dbUs and gTsang," they were Klag-pa-dam-pa Klu-mes-tshul-khrims, Shes-rab-'brin Ye-shes-yon-tan, Rag-shi Tshul-khrims-'byung-gnas, rBa Tshul-khrims-blo-gros, and Ye-shes-blo—all from the province of dbUs; and Rab-kha-pa Lo-ston, rDo-rje-dbang-phyug, Shes-rab-seng-ge, and the two brothers 'Od-brgyad-sbung-nyis and U-pa-de-dkar-pa—from the province of gTsang. After they received initiation under the leadership of Grum Ye-shes-rgyal-mtshan, they left, wishing to spread the Vinaya lineage. Klu-mes, however, decided to remain with his teacher, the learned Grum Ye-shes-rgyal-mtshan, a disciple of La-chen, in order to study the more advanced Vinaya texts.

A year later, Klu-mes, along with five other monks, proceeded to central Tibet. Klu-mes, who carried the sMad Vinaya Lineage, proved to be a very significant figure for the preservation of the Vinaya. Under his direction, Vinaya centers were established in many locations, which enabled numerous monks to become ordained. In order to increase the number of monastic communities, Klu-mes had a number of temples built throughout eastern Tibet. His principal disciples became known as the 'Four Pillars' (*ka-ba-bzhi*), the 'Eight Beams' (*gdung-brgyud*), the 'Thirty-two Rafters' (*lcham-sum-bchu-rtsa-gnyis*), and innumerable 'Planks' (*dral-ma*). This lineage extended like a great parasol over the entire province of Khams.

Because Lhasa had been a place of great learning in former times, an entourage consisting of Klu-mes, Lo-ston rDo-rje-dbang-phyug, and their immediate disciples proceeded to the great city. Finding that Lhasa had not recovered from the massacre by Glang Dar-ma, they took residence in bSam-yes Monastery which was nearly deserted. From there they gradually restored the Saṅgha.

The "Ten Men of dbUs and gTsang" enabled the Vinaya to be spread to many distant localities. The monks, or Vinayadharas, often went on long journeys outside Tibet, to Mongolia, Turkestan, and even parts of what is now lower Russia (*rGya-sen*). However, because of language difficulties and strikingly different cultures, the monks were generally unsuccessful in spreading the lineage to these more remote areas.

During the interim of Buddhist suppression, the Siddha gNubs-chen Sangs-rgyas Ye-shes protected many of the Sūtras and esoteric Tantras which he had collected during his travels throughout the Himalayas. This Siddha had perfected the potent exorcisms which he had learned from Padmasambhava and he had become a master at propitiating the 'Protectors of the Dharma' (Dharmapālas). By utilizing these practices the temples of Lhasa, bSam-yas, and other monasteries escaped destruction, although for a number of decades there was little open expression of the Doctrine in the Central Provinces.

With the advice and blessing of gNub-chen Sangs-rgyas Ye-shes, a rNying-ma White Saṅgha holder, some of the lay Tantrics, who led the life of householders and dwelt in mountain glens, continued to practice religion privately, and hid many of the Sūtras and Śāstras which had been translated up until the time of King Ral-pa-can. Because of this foresightedness, future generations of disciples, scholars, and saints benefited greatly by this ancient heritage. In later times, the monks from Khams were most heartened to see that the majority of the early translations had been preserved.

About this time distinctions in the Vinaya lineages began to emerge. In East Tibet was the sMad Vinaya Lineage; in the West there appeared the sTod Vinaya Lineage; and at a later period came the Kha-che Vinaya Lineage from Kashmir.

Lama Ye-shes-'od of mNga'-ris, formerly King Tsen-po-khore of the Lineage of Religious King (*chos-rgyal*), out of an intense concern for the preservation of the Dharma, relinquished his kingship to his nephew and took on the appellation of Lama Ye-shes-'od. He then invited Śrī Dharmapāla, a Paṇḍita from eastern India to Tibet for the purpose of promulgating the Vinaya teachings. Many commentaries on the Prātimokṣa and Vinaya Sūtras were composed at this time.

The 'meditative lineage' (*sgrub-pa'i brgyud*), which arose in Tibet from Ye-shes-'od, was one of the two principle Indian lineages of the sTod Vinaya, along with the 'lineage of teaching' (*bshad-pa'i brgyud*). Out of the intense efforts of these Vinayadharas, the restoration of the Vinaya Lineage in West Tibet occurred before similar restorations in the central provinces of dbUs and gTsang, and was most fruitful. In later times, this lineage was known as *Phala rnam-gsum*. As prophesied in the *Mañjuśrī-mūla-tantra*, Ye-shes'od also built Tho-ling Monastery.

Under the auspices of La-ma Ye-shes-'od, Lo-chen Rin-chen-bzang-po (958–1055) went to India to study with the learned masters of the time. In India he received the Vinaya as well as the Bodhisattva lineages, and upon returning to Tibet he began translating the important texts. The great Indian Ācārya Atīśa (Dīpaṃkara Śrījñāna, dPal Mar-me-mdzad-ye-shes, 982–1054), known also as Jo-bo-rje, came to Tibet on the invitation of Byang-chub-'od, a nephew of Ye-shes-'od. Upon meeting the rNying-ma lama Rin-chen-bzang-po, Atīśa was very impressed with his knowledge, saying that if he had known there were such scholars in Tibet, he would not have had to make the journey.

Other noteworthy holders of the Vinaya Lineage during this period were rNgog Lo-tsā-ba Blo-ldan-shes-rab, 'Bre-shes-rab-bar, Phag-mo-grub-pa, and bCom-ldan-rig-ral, as well as the master sGam-po-pa (1079–1153), who is recognized to be an emanation of Padmasambhava, and the luminary 'Bri-khung-skyob-pa Rin-chen dPal (1143–1218), who is considered an emanation of Nāgārjuna.

A number of Tibetans went to India at this time to acquire texts and teachings. One of the most famous of these was Mar-pa, the teacher of Mi-la-ras-pa and the student of the Siddha Nāropa. Each of the four major schools of Buddhism in Tibet–rNying-ma-pa, Sa-skya-pa, bKa'-brgyud-pa, and dGe-lugs-pa–can be considered to have their roots in this period. The eight original schools of Tibetan Buddhism were: rNying-ma-pa, bKa'-gdams-pa, Lam-'bras-pa, bKa'-brgyud-pa, Shangs-pa (whose originator was the Siddha Khung-po), Zhi-byed-pa (arising from Dam-pa Sangs-rgyas and incorporating the gCod, which originated with his consort, Ma-gcig-lab-kyi-sgron-ma), sByor-drug-pa, and O-rgyan-bsnyen-sgrub-pa. However, the Vinaya lineages are not necessarily traced through these schools, but through three principal lineages: the sMad Vinaya, the sTod Vinaya, and the Kha-che Vinaya.

During the initial spread of the Dharma, the Kha-che Vinaya had developed in Tibet into four significant transmissions, two in the central distinct of gTsang, and two from the central district of dbUs. These lineages, however, did not remain strong. The Kha-che lineage entered Tibet again with the Great Paṇḍita of Kashmir, Śākyaśrībhadra (Kha-che Pang-chen, 1126–1225) who received his Vinaya ordination and training from the lineage of several important teachers including Śrī Dharmapāla and Zhang-zhung rGyal-ba'i-shes-rab (a disciple of Prajñā-pāla who was also a disciple of Śrī Dharmāpala in the lineage coming from Guṇamati, the disciple of Guṇaprabha).

When Kha-che Pang-chen arrived at bSam-yas Monastery (1204), he discovered the Sanskrit text of the *gSang-ba snying-po*, which had been translated by Vimalamitra, gNyags Jñānakumāra, and rMa Rin-chen-mchog. From Samanta Śrījñāna, Kha-che Pang-chen received the *Śrāmaṇerakārikā*, and translated it into Tibetan. He then journeyed to Tho-ling Monastery, taking with him a very authoritative edition of the *Śrāmaṇera-varṣāgra-pṛcchā*, a sort of expanded catechism for young monks. At Tho-ling, he translated this work while consulting the original edition belonging to Dharmapāla. After spending ten very active years in Tibet, he returned to Kashmir in 1214.

The Kha-che lineage further spread through the efforts of three disciples of Kha-che Pang-chen. These were dPal Lo-tsā-ba Chos-kyi-bzang-po and Chag-dgra-bcom, both of whom were ordained by Kha-che pan-chen, and Khro-phu Lo-tsā-ba Byams-pa-dpal, who had come to Tibet with Kha-che and had acted as his interpreter. When the Great Paṇḍita returned to Kashmir, Khro-phu stayed in Tibet, although he escorted Kha-che as far as mNga'ris. The Mahāpaṇḍita, upon leaving Tibet, gave him gold to continue his translation work.

Among the significant texts for the Vinaya lineage of this period was the *Bhikṣuvarṣāgrapṛccā* (*dGe-slong-gi dang-po'i lo-dri-ba*), translated by Atīśa, the *Bhikṣukārikā* (*Vinayakārikā*), an important Nepalese text translated by the monk Prajñākīrti and his assistant Jayākara, and the

Lo-chen Dharma Śrī

Śrāmaṇera Śikṣāpada-sūtra (*dGe-tshul bslab-pa'i gzhi-mdo*), translated about this time by the monk gZon-nu-mchog at Tho-ling Monastery.

Other noteworthy Vinayadharas were Shangs-pa Jo-stan and Seng-ge Zil-gnon, who wrote commentaries on the *kārikās* given to them by Kha-che Pang-chen. Sa-skya Paṇḍita Kun-dga' rGyal-mtshan (1182–1252), the fourth Sa-skya master, received this lineage, as did a few masters of the Kar-ma-pa line. The dGe-lugs-pa scholar, Bu-ston, received the lineage from his teacher bSod-nams-mgon-po who was the chief disciple of Seng-ge Zil-gnon. rJe Rin-po-che (bTsong-kha-pa) also inherited this lineage when he received ordination from the Abbot Blo-gsal-ba.

The sMad Lineage continued to be strong up to and through the time of the blossoming of the gSar-ma traditions. Lo-chen Dharma Śrī practiced and spread the teachings of the sMad, and these continued to be followed in the rNying-ma monastic college of sMin-grol-gling, which was founded and which was also attended by Lo-chen Dharma Śrī's brother, the great scholar and contemplative O-rgyan gTer-bdag-gling-pa. Both brothers, under the patronage of the Fifth Dalai Lama, were highly instrumental in the preservation of the Vinaya, Sūtra, and bKa'-ma in this area of Tibet. However, for the rNying-ma sMad Vinaya lineage, Lo-chen Dharma Śrī is the most significant propagator.

The rNying-ma tradition of Vinaya reached its pinnacle in the eighteenth century with the monastic reformer rDzogs-chen rGyal-sras gZhan-phan-mtha'-yas (b. 1740), who served for a number of years as Abbot of rDzogs-chen Monastery, and composed several important works, including the *Phung-lnga'i-rab-dbye* and the *sDom-byang-rgyas-bshad.* gZhan-phan-mtha'-yas stressed the importance of strict observance of the Vinaya rules externally, while practicing the higher esoteric teachings internally. In his comparatively short life he brought about a thorough revitalization of rNying-ma-pa monastic scholasticism. gZhan-phan-mtha'-yas and his disciple lineage became closely aligned with dGe-mang, a retreat in the rDza-chu-kha area belonging to rDzogs-chen Monastery. It was here that such reforms continued to prosper, and they soon spread throughout Khams.

The rNying-ma Lama, mKhan-po Ngag-dga' (mKhan-po Ngag-dbang-dpal-bzang, 1879–1941) carried on the dGe-mang movement which involved the development of the principles of monastic discipline and solid scholasticism into a strong theory of social commitment for the monk, beyond the performance of special rituals or ceremonies. Unfortunately, this movement was cut short by communist occupation of Tibet in 1959. However, the twenty-five hundred year old lineage of Vinaya which this movement represents—stemming from the Buddha's son Rāhula—exists to this day in Nepal, Bhutan, India, Japan, and other countries.

The Abhidharma Tradition in Tibet

The Abhidharma tradition has been a vital factor in the unfolding of Tibetan Buddhism throughout its history. Most of the primary works of the Abhidharma were translated into Tibetan between 790 and 840 A.D., during the reigns of Kings Khri-srong-lde'u-btsan and Ral-pa-can. The seven fundamental treatises of the Abhidharma were translated at this time by Jinamitra, sKa-ba dPal-brtsegs, and others. The *Jñāna-prasthāna* by Kātyāyanīputra, was considered the basic text and the six others were considered its 'six feet'. The only one of these seven texts still extant in Tibetan is the *Prajñapti-śāstra* (*gDags-pa'i bstan-bcos*) by Maudgalyāyana, which was translated and explained by Jinamitra and sKa-ba dPal-brtsegs. The *Mahāvibhāṣā*, although it now exists only in its Chinese version, apparently was translated into Tibetan during this early period. The text is listed in an index which sKa-ba dPal-brtsegs and Cog-ro-klu'i rGyal-mtshan compiled, and it is quoted by many later lamas, such as Klong-chen-rab-'byams-pa; but in later years it seems to have been lost.*

Asaṅga's *Abhidharma-samuccaya*, known as the "Higher Exposition," and Vasubandhu's *Abhidharma-kośa*, known as the "Lower Exposition," were also among the first texts to be translated. Jinamitra, sKa-ba dPal-brtsegs, and Cog-ro-klu'i rGyal-mtshan translated and taught both of these works as well as Vasubandhu's auto-commentary to the *Kośa*.

The Abhidharma lineage in Tibet branched from these early translator's three disciples, sNa-nam Zla-ba'i-rdo-rje, lHa-lung dPal-gyi-rdo-rje, and dBas Ye-shes-rgyal. dBas Ye-shes-rgyal was invited to go to Khams where he taught Grub-rgyal-ba'i-ye-shes, from whom the lineage spread throughout dbUs and gTsang.

Among dBas Ye-shes-rgyal's other disciples were Grub-mchog-gi-ye-shes and Rwa Khri-bzang-'bar. The latter passed the teachings to Brang-ti-dar-ma, who taught the *Abhidharma-samuccaya* to Rog Chos-kyi-brtson-'grus, who in turn spread these teachings throughout Central Tibet. He had many disciples, one of whom wrote a large com-

---

*The information presented here about the Vinaya, Abhidharma, Mādhyamika, and Prajñāpāramitā traditions in Tibet is based on Kong-sprul's *Shes-bya-kun-khyab*. The full title of this work may be roughly rendered "The Encompassment of All Knowledge, a Śāstra which Well Explains the Precepts of the Three Trainings, a Treasury of Precious Scripture, Compiled from the Approaches Followed by each of the Vehicles." This is one of the greatest works which grew out of the nineteenth century Eclectic Movement (Ris-med) of Eastern Tibet, centered at sDe-dge. Also known as *The Treasury of Knowledge* (*Shes-bya-mdzod*), this work was composed at the request of 'Jam-dbyangs mKhyen-brtse'i-dbang-po (1820–1892), who prophesized that it would be one of the 'Five Treasures' Kong-sprul Rinpoche would give to the world. He also urged Kong-sprul to write a commentary on the root text (*kārikā*), and his significant work, completed in 1864, demonstrates that just as the Hīnayāna and Mahāyāna lead naturally to the Vajrayāna, the methods of the Vajrayāna reached their epitome with the Atiyoga theory and practices of the rNying-ma rDzogs-chen system.

Ye-shes-sde

mentary on the *Abhidharma-samuccaya.* This lineage went on down to Kun-mkhyen Dharma-kara and 'Gos Lo-tsā-ba (1392–1481), after which time the *Abhidharma-samuccaya* was emphasized more strongly than the *Abhidharma-kośa.* Although the primary teachings of the Abhidharma lineage after this time dealt with the "Higher Exposition," the *Kośa* lineage continued as a vital source of the Abhidharma lineage itself. Numerous Tibetan commentaries were composed on the *Kośa,* including *mDzod 'grel mngon pa'i rgyan* by mChims-'jam-dbyangs from sNar Thang Monastery.

At the time of King Ral-pa-can, Jinamitra and Śīlendrabodhi (both of whom were direct disciples of Pūrṇavardhana, who was a disciple of Sthiramati), together with Ye-shes-sde, translated and wrote a commentary on the *Abhidharma-samuccaya* (*Kun-las btus-pa*), called the *Kun-las btus-pa'i bshad-pa.* By collating this commentary with the

Kun-las btus-pa, Nyi-ma-rgyal-mtshan dPal-bzang-po created a work called the *Kun-las btus-pa'i btus-pa bshad-pa* which was translated by Jinamitra, Śīlendrabodhi, and Ye-shes-sde.

Important Tibetan commentaries written on the *Samuccaya* include the *Chos-mngon-pa kun-las-btus-pa'i-rnam bshad nyi-ma'i 'od-zer* by Bu-ston and the *rNam-pa bshad legs-par bshad-pa'i chos-mngon rgya-mtsho'i-snying-po* by rGyal-tshab. The great rNying-ma teacher Mi-pham-rgya-mtsho (1846–1912) also wrote the commentary the *mNgon-pa kun-btus-kyi rnam-grangs sna-tshogs bshad-pa ldeb.*

From Ye-shes-sde the transmission went to Nagādhvajra. After Bu-ston's time (1290–1364) it went without interruption to Chos-kyi-dpal-ba, bTsong-kha-pa, and others.

At the time of Ye-she-'od, two Paṇḍitas, Smṛti Jñāna who was a disciple of Nāropa, and Sūkṣmadīrgha were invited to Tibet by the Nepalese Padmaruci. Their translator died, leaving them to make their way alone around Tibet, and as a result, Smṛti Jñāna became a shepherd in Ta-nag. Subsequently, Kal-se-tshab bSod-nams-rgyal-mtshan invited him to Man-lung, where he studied with him. Smṛti Jñāna then went to Khams where he established a school for the study of the Abhidharma; having learned Tibetan, he translated his own works including the *Cutuḥpīṭha-ṭīkā*. He then went to Li-chu-gser-khab where he composed the *Vācanamukha*. While in Khams, Smṛti Jñāna wrote a commentary on the *Abhidharma-kośa*. Many disciples gathered around him, and established a strong tradition of the "Lower Exposition."

gYas Chen-po-shes-rab-grags, along with several others who followed this lineage, spread these teachings throughout provinces of dbUs, gTsang, and Khams. Brang-ti-dar-ma sNying-po, who was instructed to teach both "Higher" and "Lower" Expositions, was a key figure in the wide propagation of the teachings. Also important were Brang-ti's disciple Rog Chos-kyi-brtson-'grus and Ko-bo Ye-shes-byung-gnas, whose disciple was 'Phan mKon-mchog-rdo-rje, and his disciple Tho Gar-nam-lde, also known as Tho Kun-dga'-rdo-rje. This lineage was then carried on by mChims brTson-seng, who composed the first Tibetan *ṭīkā*, and then by mChims Nam-mkha'-grags and bSam-gtan-bzang-po. It was passed to bChom-ldan-rig-ral, who obtained funds from the ruler of the Yuan Dynasty for the purpose of compiling a canonical collection which was stored at sNar-thang. It was this collection upon which Bu-ston based his history of Buddhism (*Chos-'byung*). Red-mda'-pa also helped to maintain the lineage. These scholars composed *ṭīkās* on the commentaries and distributed them widely.

These lineages of the Abhidharma tradition have been both a foundation and a blossoming for the philosophical developments of all schools of Tibetan Buddhism. The Abhidharma teachings are studied and practiced to this day as a primary source for understanding one's mind and experience as a basis for liberation.

The Spread of Prajñāpāramitā in Tibet

The ideas of the Prajñāpāramitā (Phar-phyin) were formally introduced into Tibet by Śāntarakṣita and Kamalaśīla (c. 750). In India at this time the *Prajñāpāramitā-sūtras* were receiving the highest acclaim, especially through the efforts of King Dharmapāla, who propagated the Doctrine so extensively that there were thirty-five centers for the study of Prajñāpāramitā alone. As King Dharmapāla and King Khri-srong-lde'u-btsan were contemporaries, the spread of the Prajñāpāramitā was also most successful in Tibet.

Under the sponsorship of Dharmapāla, Haribhadra (Seng-ge-bzang-po), who was one of the foremost scholars in India of that time, wrote two famous commentaries on the *Prajñāpāramitā-sūtra*, the *Sputārtha* and the *Abhisamayālaṅkāra-loka*, as well as numerous other commentaries. He had listened to the exposition of the Mādhyamika works from Ācārya Śāntarakṣīta and had received teachings from Vairocanabhadra on the *Prajñāpāramitā-sūtra*, as well as the *Abhisamayālaṅkāra-śāstra-upadeṣa*. He was also a great scholar in the Abhidharma. In Tibet, Haribhadra is regarded as the principal source for the interpretation of the *Abhisamayālaṅkāra*, the basic text on the Prajñāpāramitā. This text is essentially an elucidation of the various meanings of *pārāmitā* as both the source and the goal of the Buddhist path.

The spread of the Prajñāpāramitā lineage in Tibet occurred during two distinctive periods. The earlier period began with rLangs Khams-pa, who went to India and returned with the One Hundred Thousand Line *Prajñāpāramitā-sūtra*, which he then translated. Kamalaśīla, a renowned commentator on the *Prajñāpāramitā-sūtra*, assisted the Tibetan king Khri-srong-lde'u-btsan with oral explanations of the translated texts which the king had received. The king, because of his great devotion to the Mahāyāna, wrote the text down in a mixture of goat's milk and his own blood. This was known as the 'Red Notes' (*Reg-zik dmar-po*) which, after its completion, was put into a Stūpa at Lhasa.

The scholars dBas Mañjuśrī and Nyang Indravaro also went to India, returning with numerous original manuscripts and translated texts. A spiritual son of the king wrote these down in a mixture of goat's milk, lapis lazuli, and other precious minerals. These were known as the 'Blue Notes (*Reg-zik sngon-po*). A few sections of these works were found to be incomplete, so Vairocana edited them, completed the missing sections, and wrote them out in his own hand. They were later catalogued and placed in mChims-phu Monastery where they remained for many centuries.

The principal period of translation of Prajñāpāramitā texts occurred between the years 790 and 840. The Tibetan scholar Ye-shes-sde, the Indian Paṇḍitas Jinamitra, Surendrabodhi, and Śīlendrabodhi, along with two disciples of Padmasambhava, sKa-ba dPal-brtsegs and Cog-ro-klu'i rGyal-mtshan translated about sixteen different *Prajñāpāramitā-sūtras* and issued corrections on the texts. At this time, the commentary of Daṃṣṭrāsena was also translated.

During this period of extensive translation, both the lineages of experience and of explanation in the Prajñāpāramitā increased with great vigor in Tibet, having been stimulated by the many Indo-Tibetan cross currents. Buddhism in Nālandā at that time was still flourishing, and many of the Buddhist doctrines centering around Nālandā were finding new roots in Bengal and elsewhere in the Pāla Empire. The scholars of this period preserved the living heritage of the texts by fostering an oral transmission of the teachings through a long tradition of interpreters and commentators, going back to such masters as Vimuktasena and Haribhadra.

During the eclipse of Buddhism in Tibet from around 840 to 950 when Buddhism was undergoing persecution in the central provinces by the usurper Glang Dar-ma, the Saṅgha was forced to go underground or flee to the remote regions. Following this period, the Mahāpaṇḍita Rin-chen-bzang-po (958–1055) initiated what is known as the later spread of the Dharma (*phyi-dar*) and the doctrines of the Prajñāpāramitā once again blossomed. He went to India to study one of the fundamental texts for the development of Prajñāpāramitā in Tibet, the *Abhisamayālaṅkāra*, and its multitude of commentaries. Rin-chen-bzang-po was assisted by Paṇḍita Guṇamitra, who had studied with Buddhajñāna, a disciple of Haribhadra.

Another prominant figure of this period was Atīśa (Dīpaṃkara Śrījñāna), who had numerous Prajñāpāramitā teachers, including Jñānaśrīmati and the younger Kusali. Atīśa worked on many translations of the *Prajñāpāramitā-sūtra* with his students who included Khu-chen lHa-ldings-pa and 'Brom-ston-rGyal-ba'i. Atīśa and Rin-chen-bzang-po translated the *rTogs-dka' snang-ba* and made many new translations of the Eight Thousand Line and Twenty-five Thousand Line *Prajñāpāramitā*, the *Abhisamayālaṅkāra-loka* of Haribhadra, and other texts. Atīśa handed down the tradition of the Lineage of Explanation, which became known as the 'Khams method'.

As prophesied in the *Mañjuśrī-mūla-tantra*, rNgog Lo-tsā-ba Blo-ldan-shes-rab (who lived after Rin-chen-bzang-po), having heard the teachings of Paṇḍita bsTan-bskyong on the Prajñāpāramitā, went to Nepal and revised the terms for *samādhi* in the One Hundred Thousand Line *Prajñāpāramitā-sūtra* at the monastic library of Pham-thing. He also revised and retranslated the *Abhisamayālaṅkāra* root text and commentaries. In so doing, he finalized their internal meanings and widely propagated the Lineage of Explanation.

The Oral-transmission Lineage then continued with the teacher 'Bre Shes-rab-'bar, who assembled the lineage of the four elder disciples of rNgog Lo-tsā-ba, as well as the lineages of Atīśa, Rin-chen-bzang-po, and rNgog himself. These he united with the Khams lineage from the period of the early spread of the Doctrine. The Lineage of teachings was continued by the numerous disciples of 'Bre, but in particular by Byang-chub-ye-shes of Ar, who taught until a very old age at gNam-rtse-ldan (near Rwa-sgreng), mChim-phu, and various other monasteries. During his later years, he composed many expositions on the *Prajñāpāramitā-sūtras* and their commentaries, including numerous expositions on the *Abhisamayālaṅkāra* and its commentary (*ṭīkā*).

The traditional Tibetan interpretation of the *Prajñāpāramitā-sūtras* is mainly based on the exegeses of 'Bre and Ar. The prominent Lama, gZhon-nu Tshul-khrims (known as sKar-chun-ring-mo) who studied under Ar, wrote numerous commentaries on the *Abhisamayālaṅkāra* and its commentaries. Bu-ston (Rin-chen-grub-pa)and 'Gos Lo-tsā-ba (gZhon-nu-dpal, 1392–1481), author of the *Blue Annals* (*Deb-ther sngon-po*) were in this lineage. Bu-ston's closest disciple, Lo-tsā-ba Rin-chen-rnam-rgyal, discoursed to gYag Mi-pham Chos-kyi-bla-ma, who made commentaries on the large, medium, and short *Prajñāpāramitā-sūtras*. Through his teaching, the Prajñāpāramitā lineage was brought to gYag, which is located in the rMa-chen-spom-ra area of A-mdo. His chief disciple was Rong-ston-chen-po Shes-bya-kun-gzigs (1367–1449), a Sa-skya lama. These lineages continued into this century and were spread widely. The other important lineage for the Prajñāpāramitā extends from Phya-pa Chos-kyi-seng-ge (d. 1169), who had studied with the disciple of rNgog Lo-tsā-ba, Gro-lung-pa Blo-gros-'byung-gnas.

The Prajñāpāramitā tradition in Tibet has produced numerous commentaries explaining from the point of view of practical application many difficult points contained in the Sūtras. The *Abhismayālaṅkāra* was the fundamental texts for the study of Prajñāpāramitā in Tibet, where there were at least ten different schools of Prajñāpāramitā, each with its own particular manuals for study (*yig-cha*). The Prajñāpāramitā usually represents the second branch of study in which all learning is accomplished by heart.*

These are just a small sampling of the lineages of Prajñāpāramitā commentarial literature in Tibet. A discussion of the full growth and development of the Prajñāpāramitā would require an exceedingly vast and complex presentation.

The Mādhyamika Tradition in Tibet

Throughout the history of Buddhism, there has been a tradition of critical analysis between philosophical schools, with each school refuting the other's standpoints in order to establish the highest and purest of the Buddha's teachings. Out of this healthy tradition of criticism, certain syncretic trends developed, creating a very strong philosophical tradition.

In Tibetan Buddhism the two most influential philosophical systems have been the Yogācāra-Mādhyamika-Svātantrika and the Prāsaṅgika-Mādhyamika. Most Tibetans favor the Prāsaṅgika line; but the Svātantrika line is also highly respected, and many great masters of both India and Tibet have been very much influenced by the Yogācāra-Mādhyamika-Svātantrika. The basic text for this tradition is the *Mādhyamakālaṅkāra* (*dbU-ma rgyan*) by Śāntarakṣita. Candrakīrti's and Śāntideva's works are the basic texts for the Prāsaṅgikas. Each of the four schools in Tibet explicate their tenets from their own particular standpoints.

---

*The traditional order for the study of Buddhist philosophy in Tibet was: Logic and general topics (*tshad-ma* and *bsdus-grva*), lasting five to six years; Prajñāpāramitā (Phar-phyin), four years, Mādhyamika (dbUs-ma), two years, and Vinaya ('Dul-ba), ten years. In actual practice, these subjects were taught for significantly shorter periods of time (typically six months to a year) and then repeated at a later time, allowing the student to raise his level of understanding with repeated exposure.

Śāntarakṣita was born about 700 A.D. to a royal family in Za-hor (Bengal) in the small village of Sābhār during the reign of Gopāla, the first king of the Pāla Dynasty. He became one of the most renowned scholars at Nālandā University, and later went to Tibet during King Khri-srong-lde'u-btsan's reign to propagate the Dharma. Although he is considered a Yogācāra-Mādhyamika-Svātantrika, he was interested in preserving all aspects of the Dharma, and his efforts in firmly establishing all the important lineages were extremely fruitful.

Śāntarakṣita's major literary contribution, the *Tattvasaṅgraha*, which he composed before his first journey to Tibet, is a logical refutation of the philosophical systems and conceptions current in India from the Yogācāra-Mādhyamika-Svātantrika viewpoint.* In his *Mādhyamikālaṅkāra* Śāntarakṣita clearly analyzes existents by a subtle logic of experience, and proves by the use of syllogism that all the particular existents (*chos, dharma*) have no actuality, no essence (*rang-bzhin*)—that they are like reflections on a mirror, like a presence devoid of any 'thing-ness'.

During the early period of translation of Buddhist texts into Tibetan (eighth century), Cog-ro-klu'i rGyal-mtshan and Paṇḍita Jñānagarba translated the *Mūla-mādhyamika-kārikā* of Nāgārjuna and the *Prajñā-pradīpa* (*Shes-rab sgron-me*) of Bhāvaviveka, thus introducing many of the doctrines of the Yogācāra-Mādhyamika-Svātantrika school. Very few Prāsaṅgika texts were translated in the early period, as opposed to several texts of the Svātantrikas by Bhāvaviveka, Śāntarakṣita, and Kamalaśīla, as well as numerous texts by Nāgārjuna and Āryadeva. At that time the division between Svātantrika and Prāsaṅgika had not been specifically introduced. As a result, Ye-shes-sde, in his *lTa-ba-khyad-par*, divided the Mādhyamikas into two, the Sautrāntrika-Mādhyamikas and the Yogācāra-Mādhyamikas. The great rNying-ma master of Mādhyamika and rDzogs-chen, Rong-zom Chos-kyi bzang-po (eleventh century), was one of the few early masters who understood the distinction among the Mādhyamika of Svātantrika and Prā-

*In addition to the *Tattvasaṅgraha*, which was translated into Tibetan by the Kashmirian Paṇḍita Guṇākara Śrī Bhadra, a contemporary to the Kashmirian King Lalitāditya (693–729), there are several other works by Śāntarakṣita: the *Vipañcitārthā-ṭīkā* (on *Vādanyāya*), the *Mādhyamakālaṅkāra-kārikā* and *Vṛtti*, the *Vajravidāraṇī-nāmadhāraṇīṭīkā*, the *Sarvatathāgata-pūrva-praṇidhāna-viśeṣa-vistara-sūtrāntopadeśa*, the *Saptatathāgata-pūrva-praṇidhāna-viśeṣa-vistara-kalpavacanavidhi*, the *Saptathatā-gata-praṇidhāna-viśeṣa-vistara-nāmasūtrantāvacana*, the *Vajradhara-saṅgīta-bhagavata-stotraṭīkā*, the *Aṣṭatathāgata-stotra*, and the *Hevajradbhava-kurukullāyāh-pañca mahopadeśa*.

saṅgika. The terms Rang-rgyud-pa (Svātantrika) and Thal-'gyur-pa (Prāsaṅgika) only come in about the time of Bu-ston (1290–1364).

During the eleventh century, rNgog Lo-tsā-ba (1008–1064) studied with the Kashmirian, Sajjana, who taught him the *Mahāyāna-sūtralaṅkāra*, the two *Vibhaṅgas*, and the *Uttaratantra* of Maitreya-Asaṅga. Sajjana himself had helped translate the *Uttaratantra* and *Uttaratantra-vyākyā*. rNgog also taught the *Prajñāpradīpa* of Bhāvaviveka, and through him the Svātantrika became widespread, with the lineage centering at gSang-phu Monastery south of Lhasa. His student, Gra-ba mNgon-shes, taught bTsan Kha-bo-che (b. 1021) the *Uttaratantra* (*rGyud-bla-ma*) and other works, while Cang-ra-ba and others continued this teaching, which gradually began to accept the view of a consciousness beyond duality, non-referential and self-illuminating, as the impetus of Buddhahood. This is the insight contained in the dbU-ma Chen-po, the Great Mādhyamika, which contains definitive meaning surpassing the viewpoint of the Yogācāra. Its teachers include gTsang-nag-pa, Padmasambhava, Klong-chen-pa, Jo-nang Dol-po-pa-shes-rab rGyal-mtshan (1292–1361), sMin-grol-gling Lo-chen Dharma Śrī (1654–1717), and his brother, the great master gTer-bdag-gling-pa (1646–1714).

The Fifth Abbot at gSang-phu Monastery had eight students who were known as the "Eight Great Lions." Two of these followed the line of Candrakīrti (Prāsaṅgika), while the rest followed the Yogācāra-Mādhyamika-Svāntantrika approach of Kamalaśīla. These followers of the Svātantrika, along with many rNying-ma study centers, continued to propagate the Yogācāra-Mādhyamika-Svātantrika line, which is still being followed to this day, although it has not come down as a continuous line of explanation.

The Prāsaṅgika line of Mādhyamika developed through Pa-tshab Lo-tsā-ba. From his primary disciples, known as the "Four Sons of Pa-tshab," came many of the followers of the Prāsaṅgika in Tibet, this line continues to the present day.

The rNying-ma lama Mi-pham 'Jam-byangs rNam-rgyal-rgya-mtsho (1846–1912) studied Śāntarakṣita's *Mādhyamakālaṅkāra* and Śāntideva's *Bodhicaryāvatāra* from dPal-sprul Rinpoche. Lama Mi-pham intensively researched the different positions within the Mādhyamika, and even studied at dGe-lugs-pa monasteries, learning the dGe-lugs-pa scholastic tradition of the Prāsaṅgika. Although he himself was a Prāsaṅgika, he differed from their positions. He set forth his difference of position in his commentaries to the ninth chapter of the

Bodhicaryāvatāra and to the *Mādhyamakālaṅkāra*. As he indicates in these works, the primary difference between the Yogācāra-Svātantrika and the Prāsaṅgika is in the way they understood the Two Truths, the relative or conventional truth (*kun-rdzob-bden-pa, saṃvṛti-satya*) and the absolute truth (*don-dam-bden-pa, paramārtha-satya*). The Yogācāra-Mādhyamika-Svātantrikas, in establishing the Two Truths as separate, accept the Yogācāra view of conventional reality, as well as the Mādhyamika view of absolute reality.

According to Mi-pham, the Svātantrikas initially set up this distinction between the Two Truths—using the point of view of the ultimate truth—in order to be able to truly examine the relative truth. In their use of a logic of the syllogistic form, they, in a sense, leave an anchor in the field of conventional thought in order to show that all entities of reality are devoid of an essence (*niḥsvabhāva*).

The Yogācāra-Svātantrikas distinguish two kinds of Ultimate Truth—an ultimate reality that cannot be expressed in words (*rnam-grangs-min-pa'i-don-dam*, the realization of the meditative experience), and the Ultimate Reality that can be expressed in words (*rnam-grangs-pa'i-don-dam*, which comes in the phase after the realization of the Ultimate Truth of the meditation). The Prāsaṅgika do not accept that this distinction. The Prāsaṅgikas emphasize the indivisibility (*zung-'jug*) of the Two Truths and looks at Ultimate Truth from the viewpoint of the goal, rather than the path.

According to Mi-pham, Śāntarakṣita's *Mādhyamakālaṅkāra* contains the Prāsaṅgika view from within the meditative experience, but approaches this view from a logic showing the separation of the Two Truths. Śāntarakṣita exphasizes the emptiness of all things, thus refuting the contention that entities exist in truth—this being a first step to the Śūnyatā experience of meditation, which cannot be talked about. The Yogācāra-Mādhyamika-Svātantrika position of Śāntarakṣita serves as a bridge which crosses over to the Prāsaṅgika. In order to completely understand the Prāsaṅgika approach, one must enter by the way of the Yogācāra-Mādhyamika standpoint, which allows one to utilize the conventional framework in order to experience the ultimate.

In his works Lama Mi-pham points out that the intent of the Yogācāra-Mādhyamika-Svātantrika and the Prāsaṅgika-Mādhyamika are the same; it is just their emphasis which differs. Both these traditions have long extensive lineages which continue to the present day.

Vajrasattva

The Vajrayāna Lineages in Tibet

The Spiritual Courses of the Buddhist Tradition

In his Sūtras, the Buddha proclaimed that the various ways or methods of enlightenment can be divided and subdivided endlessly. It is a habitual function of the mind to make distinctions and divisions, and to create doctrines and more doctrines. For practical purposes, individuals with different frames of reference need different spiritual courses (Yāna) that are appropriate for their individual natures. In early times, during or shortly after the time of the Buddha, enlightenment could be attained often by simply listening to the words (bKa'-ma, Āgama) of the Buddha or his successors, thinking or reflecting on what had been heard, and making it a lived experience. During the early years of the Buddhist Saṅgha, in addition to the Enlightened Ones, Bodhisattvas, and Arhants, there existed four classes of followers:

monks (*dge-slong, bhikṣu*)
nuns (*dge-slong-ma, bhikṣuṇī*)
laymen (*dge-bsnyen, upāsaka*)
laywomen (*dge-bsnyen-ma, upāsikā*)

The *upāsakas* and *upāsikās* were those who listened intently to what the Buddha had to say and followed his advice and counsel. While retaining their secular occupations, these laymen and women honored the Vinaya code of ethics and renounced the five cardinal transgressions: murder, theft, sexual misconduct, lying, and drunkenness.

In later times, in order to account for the variability and uniqueness of the human personality, the followers of the Mahāyāna divided the Buddhist Saṅgha into:

The Faithful Listeners (Nyan-thos, Śrāvaka)
The Self-styled Buddhas (Rang-sangs-rgyas, Pratyekabuddha)
The Bodhisattva (Byang-chub-sems-dpa')
The Saṅgha Followers

The last consisting of:

Monks (*dge-slong, bhikṣu*)
Nuns (*dge-slong-ma, bhikṣuṇī*)
Novice Monks (*dge-tshul, śrāmaṇera*)
Novice Nuns (*dge-tshul-ma, śrāmaṇerikā*)

In the course of time, as the ways of the world became more complex and the inclination towards rampant materialism increased–giving rise to more distractions and allurements–the Path towards Buddhahood became more difficult. This led to the need for practicing the more esoteric or internal teachings of the Buddha.

Throughout the course of time, the various teachings of the Tathāgatas were classified in different ways which generally indicated progressive stages of development along the spiritual path. Such divisions include Hīnayāna, Mahāyāna, Bodhisattvayāna, Mantrayāna, and Vajrayāna. However, the most basic division of the graded teachings of the Buddhas are referred to as the Three Yānas.

The Three Yānas. The first Yāna, the Hīnayāna refers to the first two divisions of the Buddhist Saṅgha: the Śrāvakas, or Faithful Listeners, who have been indispensible in the preservation and propagation of the Buddha's Sūtras; and the Pratyekabuddhas, or self-enlightened Buddhas, who are individuals of exceedingly self-reliant natures who have become living examples of how to pursue the path of self-development. The Hīnayāna tradition generally accepts only those lines of transmission which stem directly from the historical Buddha Śākyamuni.

The paths of Śrāvakayāna and Pratyekabuddhayāna emphasize analytical methods of meditation as the primary means for putting an end to the roots of suffering–desire, confusion, and hatred. The Śrāvaka is one who hears, understands, and communicates to others the teachings of the Buddha and who seeks purification (*viśuddhi*) through strenous training involving the Three Trainings of 'ethics and manners' (*śīla*), 'meditative development' (*samādhi*), and 'appreciative discrimination' (*prajñā*). The Pratyekabuddha is one who does not verbally communicate his understanding to others, and certain persons have attained the state of a Pratyekabuddha without having heard the teachings of the Enlightened One. These two divisions also may relate to stages in an individual's growth typified by a more individualistically oriented approach.

The second major Yāna, the Mahāyāna, brings to light the more socially oriented approach which is the Bodhisattvayāna, a path followed by those whose primary concern is for the welfare of others. Compassion is the principal quality of the Bodhisattva, who is a person that has accepted the responsibility of leading all beings out of the recurring cycle of frustration. The Pāramitāyāna, which is encompassed within the Mahāyāna, involves the practice of the Six Pāramitās and the scaling of the Ten Spiritual Levels (*sa, bhūmi*) by means of the Five Paths (*lam, mārga*).

The third major vehicle is the Vajrayāna, which is specifically concerned with the practice of yoga, as the most practical approach towards the union of appropriate action (*upāya*) and appreciative discrimination (*prajñā*). Within this context, the Mantrayāna, which utilizes a more hidden or secret approach towards spiritual transformation, can be seen as an extension of the path set forth in the Pāramitāyāna. The great rNying-ma lama 'Jigs-med-gling-pa explained that, in the Vajrayāna, the Mantrayāna and the Pāramitāyāna are fused into a union of cause and effect. The language of the Pāramitāyāna, however, is more 'categorizing', involving judgmental faculties, while that of the Mantrayāna is more 'embodying', involving feelings and lived experience. The teachings and practices of the Mantrayāna favor an intimate approach which is appropriate only for certain types of people. As its name reveals, the Mantrayāna involves the use of the *mantra*, which is an outgrowth of *dhāraṇī*, as well as the *maṇḍala*. In its practical application, the *mantra* may be thought of as the 'protection of the mind', and its use aims at purification and the burning away of accumulated karma. The deep meditative realization of the Inner Mantrayāna contains teachings and practices which resemble many of the applications of the Atiyoga doctrines, as held specifically by the rNying-ma-pa. The doctrines and practices of the Vajrayāna are derived not only from the Sūtras, but from the sphere of the absolute, the Dharmakāya, which is the origin of all Buddhas. The Bodhisattva Vajrasattva is the central figure of the Vajrayāna path, and it is he who is the symbol for the unity of the Sphere of Pure Spirituality, the Dharmakāya, with the instrumental or Rūpakāya, consisting of the Sambhogakāya and Nirmāṇakāya.

The development of the Vajrayāna was a direct response by

enlightened and compassionate masters to the needs of the Saṅgha as both the internal and external obstacles to spiritual growth became more pronounced. Numberless precepts and practical instructions, enough to bear comparison with the sky, were brought to the Human-tradition—although only a fraction were brought to our world (Jambudvīpa, the Indian or Southern continent), for the majority of these enlightenment principles were taken to other spheres or world systems.

It is through Vajrapāṇi that the Tantras, which include both the practices and the literature of the Vajrayāna, were disseminated to the Human tradition. Tantra refers primarily to one's individual growth and only secondarily to the body of literature which deals with this developmental process. Thus, we have the distinctions between *don-gyi rgyud,* Tantra as the spiritual development of man, and *tshig-gi rgyud,* Tantra as literature.

The Tantras are divided by the rNying-ma-pa into the Outer Tantras (*phyi-rgyud*) and the Inner Tantras (*nang-rgyud*). The Outer Tantras are practiced by all the schools of Tibetan Buddhism—rNying-ma-pa and bSar-ma-pa. The Inner Tantras, or more specifically, the Three Perfectly Internal Tantras (*nang-rgyud-sde-gsum*), are the essence of rNying-ma teachings and are practiced by the rNying-ma-pa alone.

The Nine Yānas. The rNying-ma-pa have divided the various Yānas or teachings of the Tathāgatas into nine categories: The External Teachings, consisting of the Śrāvakayāna, Pratyekabuddhayāna, and Bodhisattvayāna; The Outer Tantras, the Kriyā-, Caryā, and Yogatantras; and the Three Perfectly Internal Tantras constituting the Mahāyoga, Anuyoga, and Atiyoga.

The first three Yānas—Śrāvakayāna, Pratyekabuddhayāna, and Bodhisattvayāna—find their origin with the Nirmāṇakāya transmission stemming from Śākyamuni Buddha and his disciples. Because of their leading roles throughout the history of Buddhism, disciples of these three traditions have been called the Three Sons of the Buddha. The second three Yānas—Kriyā-, Caryā-, and Yoga-tantras—originated with Vajrasattva, Mañjuśrī, and Avalokiteśvara, and constitute a Sambhōgakāya transmission. The last three Yānas—Mahāyoga, Anuyoga, and Atiyoga—find their origin in the Dharmakāya with the Ādi-buddha Kun-tu-bzang-po.

While the Mahāyāna tradition recognizes ten *bhūmi* or levels of Bodhisattva development, in the rNying-ma system, there are a total of sixteen *bhūmi.* The Pāramitāyāna represents the tenth *bhūmi,* while the eleventh, which is known as *lam-rgyud,* consists of the Mantrayāna practices and realizations leading to direct enlightenment, as outlined in the Anuttarayoga-tantra. The twelfth stage is realized with the practice of the Mahāyoga; the thirteenth in the Anuyoga; and the fourteenth through sixteenth in the Sems-sde, Klong-sde, and Man-ngag-sde divisions of Atiyoga (rDzogs-pa-chen-po).

The process of spiritual maturation which occurs as one progresses through the Nine Yānas can be subsumed under four headings: *gzhi-rgyud, lam-rgyud, 'bras-bu rgyud,* and *thabs-rgyud.* The first, *gzhi-rgyud,* refers to the foundation, which rests upon Absolute Being and is symbolized by the Primordial Buddha, Kun-tu-bzang-po who is absolutely pure from a beginning that is beginningless (*gdod-ma'i ka-dag chen-po*) and which was present before the split into Saṃsāra and Nirvāṇa occurred. The term *gzhi* also refers to 'view' (*lta-ba*) and consists of three factors: 'facticity' (*ngo-bo*), 'actuality' (*rang-bzhin*), and 'responsiveness' (*thugs-rje*). *gZhi-rgyud* is also inherent in the word *gzhi* or *garbha* which refers to a potentiality that cannot be immediately seen because it is obscured by incidental stains (*nyong-mongs, kleśa*). The second, *lam-rgyud,* is that which cleans up the *kleśas* through the accumulation of merit (*puṇyasaṃbhāra*) and knowledge (*jñānasaṃbhāra*) which serve as antidotes to the mind's proclivity to wishfulness and emotivity as well as that of obscuration by notions about the knowable. More generally, *lam-rgyud* refers to the entire body of the Mahāyāna tradition, including the philosophical tenets of the Mādhyamika, Yogācāra (Vijñānavāda) and Cittamātra, and the deep religious practices of the Mantrayāna. The third, *'bras-bu rgyud,* refers to the eleventh stage, after the first ten stages (*bhūmi*) have been scaled and the Bodhisattva achieves the status of a Fully Enlightened One. The fourth, *thabs-rgyud,* indicates 'activity', but not as activity that is heedless or misdirected but supremely focused into working for the benefit of others without preconceived ideas or notions. Such compassionate activity promotes the swift enlightenment of others, which is immanent because it is self-originated knowledge. Activity refers to the act of living in the world fully and completely as a healthy human being. This does not bar imaginative activity, as the process of visualization is tantamount to success in the practices of the Tantras. *Thabs-rgyud* also refers to the actions possessed by a person who has proven himself as a responsible holder of the lineage and thus prevents it from becoming imbued with an individual's predispositions and biases.

Lineage. The thread, the link, or the uninterrupted continuity of living exemplars and teachings, which have been handed down to this day, constitutes what is termed a lineage. The foundation of the living lineages have provided a seemingly inexhaustible basis for examination and application, and it is through them that the various paths within the Buddhist tradition remain dynamic and vital vehicles for spiritual growth.

The basis of the lineage is first, the so-called 'outer lineage' of teachings, which originated with the appearance in this world of the historical Buddha, who manifested as the fruition of the potential that exists in all of us. This potential, the so-called 'inner lineage', means that the seed of enlightenment, or the Tathāgatagarbha (Buddha-nature) embraces and permeates all sentient beings as cream permeates fresh milk. The union of this outer and inner lineage is the continuity, down through history, of a long line of spiritual teachers, or living exemplars, who have recognized and actualized this Buddha-nature within themselves and who have either directly transmitted or pointed out this intrinsic nature to others, who, in turn, have successfully achieved an identical realization.

The Outer Tantras. The three Outer divisions of the Vajrayāna of Tantrayāna were transmitted from Vārāṇasī, Ri-bo-rkyang-cen, and Dur khrad-me-ru-'bab. These three Tantras, as practiced by all schools of Tibetan Buddhism, may be briefly summarized as follows:

The Kriyā-tantra (Bya-pa'i-rgyud) emphasizes external development leading towards purification through the observance of ritual actions of body and speech. The divine power (*lha*)—the supreme essence of Buddhahood—is the embodiment of pristine awareness (*ye-shes*) and confers temporal and lasting benefits like a donor to his beneficiaries. In more psychological terms, an individual identifies himself as a servant to the divine power with the conviction that such patterning of behavior will eventually lead one to realize the origin of that power. Ultimately speaking, one's developing viewpoint, meditative activity, and conduct bring forth the lasting realization that the supreme nature of Buddhahood may be realized by the individual. Following the methods laid down by the Kriyā-tantra, realization is attained over a period of sixteen human lifetimes.

The Caryā-tantra (sPyod-pa'i-rgyud) places equal emphasis on external ritual purity and internal meditative development (*sgom, bhāvana*). The basis of realization is the view of oneself as of equal status with the divine power, like a friend or brother. In these practices, meditative activity involves the creative visualization of the embodiment of pristine awareness so that beliefs in the distinction between the enlightened patterns of action and those of oneself dissolve. It is in this manner that an individual's actions become significant within the realm of the truly transcendent to the extent that the level of Vajradhara (rDo-rje-'dzin-pa) is attained within a period of seven lifetimes.

The Yoga-tantra (rNal-'byor-pa'i-rgyud) consists of two parts, the Outer Yoga-tantra and the Inner unsurpassable spiritual course, otherwise known as the Anuttarayoga-tantra. With the Outer Yoga-tantra (Upā-yoga), ritual purity and other observances found in the former Tantras are only aids to the realization of the path. The primary concern of these teachings is inward contemplation and introspection to directly perceive, in the atmosphere of meditative settledness, the functioning of the mind. Here, realization is attained through the contemplation of non-duality which comes about by the fusion of the individual committed to the service of the divine power with the power itself, as an embodiment of primordial awareness. The act of meditation on non-duality comes about through the dedicated practice of the Four Seals (*phyag-rgya bzhi*): Mahāmudrā, Dharmamudrā, Samayamudrā, and Karmamudrā. Through the practice of the Outer Yoga-tantra, the five psychophysical constituents (*skandha*), the five senses, and the five emotional reaction patterns are transformed into the five Buddha action patterns representing the five kinds of pristine awareness. This occurs within a period of three human lives.

During the early spread (*snga-dar*) of the Dharma, the Kriyā- and Caryā-tantras were propagated by the Ācārya Buddhaguhya (sLob-dpon Sangs-rgyas gSang-ba). The Tantras of these classes include the *Ārya-Subāhuparipṛccha-nāma-tantra* (*dPung-bzangs*), the *Sarvamaṇḍalasāmānya vidhīnām guhyatantra* (*gSang-ba spyi-rgyud*), the *Dhyānottara-paṭalakrama* (*bSam-gtan phyi-ma*) and their related commentaries. During the later spread (*phyi-dar*) a vast number of translations of the Kriyā-, Caryā-, and Yoga-tantras was instituted by Lo-chen Rin-chen-bzang-po (958–1055) and his successors. The various Tantric traditions that were preserved in China and are presently practiced in Japan are based primarily upon these three divisions of Outer Tantras. Chinese Buddhism was briefly exposed to the Inner Tantras as late as the time of Srong-btsan sgam-po (c. 600 A.D.), but they did not prosper in China or Japan.

The Mahāmudrā. The Mahāmudrā (Phyag-rgya-chen-po) is an extension of those practices outlined in the Prajñāpāramitā which emphasize inner realization. In the Vajrayāna tradition, the origin of

rDo-rje-'chang

the Mahāmudrā lies in the *Samādhirāja-sūtra*, which elucidates the ultimate meaning of the Prajñāpāramitā. Such figures as Advayavajra, Saraha, Nāropa, and Mi-la-ras-pa (Milarepa) were foremost early masters of the Mahāmudrā, which is closely aligned with the Siddha tradition. The highest realization of the Mahāmudrā is the experience of the indivisible unity of the 'vastness' of the Developing Stage and the 'profoundness' of the Fulfillment Stage. This realization is experienced as the most supreme form of pristine awareness, and, through the integration of the Two Truths, the palace of rDo-rje-'chang, the symbol of the absolute self-sameness of Being, is reached.

The Anuttara-yoga. Because of its special applications in the rNying-ma tradition, the Inner Yoga-tantra or Anuttara-yoga-tantra (Bla-na-med-pa'i rnal-'byor) overlaps the two categories of Outer and

Inner Tantras. It contains both the Tantra of meaning which is to be explained, and the Tantra of words which explains it. The principal text of the division, the rNying-ma Tantra *Guhyasamāja* is included under the former heading and refers to the aspects of body, speech, and mind of the Buddha which are considered 'hidden' or *guhya*, because they were not revealed to the assembly (*samāja*) of the Śrāvakas, Pratyekabuddhas, and the general followers of the Mahāyāna.

The *Guhyasamāja* is also known as the System of Sangs-rgyas Ye-shes-zhabs. This Tantra was formally introduced to Tibet around the eleventh century during the later spread of the Dharma by Lo-chen Rin-chen-bzang-po. During this time, however, Paṇḍita Smṛti was extensively teaching the lineage of explanation of Sangs-rgyas Ye-shes in Khams and other localities in East Tibet.

The history of the *Guhyasamāja* in Tibet thus actually begins with Sangs-rgyas Ye-shes-zhabs, who, after studying the Prajñāpāramitā treatises with Haribhadra, the chief commentator to the *Abhisamayālaṅkarā*, composed the *Sañcaya-gātha-pañjikā* on the *Prajñāpāramitā-sañcaya-gāthā*. Sangs-rgyas Ye-shes then journeyed to the country of Uḍḍiyāna in search of the Mantrayāna. After being greeted by an assembly of Ḍākinīs, he studied the Kriyā- and Yoga-tantras with Ācārya Lalitavajra (sGeg-pa rDo-rje) and the Anuttara-yoga-tantra from the Yoginī Gu-ne-ru (Guṇeru), and received initiation (*dbang-tshig, samaya*) from her.

In a dream, Sangs-rgyas Ye-shes was told to go to the Northern Gate of Uḍḍiyāna to meet the Mahā-Lakṣmī; he immediately went there and studied with the Yoginī for several months. He then proceeded to a forest near Jālandhara and studied the Yoga-tantras (Upāya-tantra) and related subjects for nine years with the Ācārya bSrung-ba'i-zhabs (Rakṣitapāda), a spiritual descendent of Nāgārjuna. After that, he traveled to another forest to the north of Bodh Gayā, which was inhabited by many wild animals. Meditating upon this forest as the wilderness of Saṃsāra, he resided there for six months. By the conclusion of his stay, he had gained insight into the essence of all the elements of existence (*dharmatā*).

Sangs-rgyas Ye-shes then met 'Jam-dpal bShes-gnyen (Mañjuśrīmitra) who recognized his accomplishment in spiritual practices. Transforming himself into the Maṇḍala of Mañjughoṣa, 'Jam-dpal bShes-gnyen asked him whether he had greater confidence in the teacher or in the Maṇḍala. When he replied that his confidence was in the Maṇḍala, it vanished and 'Jam-dpal bShes-gnyen appeared. Sangs-rgyas Ye-shes then requested instructions from the teacher, who in turn bestowed upon him the oral instructions (*zhal-lung*). Thus, directly apprehending the ultimate essence of Śūnyatā, Sangs-rgyas Ye-shes became a yogin possessed of an immeasurable purity of mind. His teacher then permitted him to compose fourteen treatises on the *Guhyasamāja* commentaries, which are called the *Chos-bcu-bzhi.**

Sangs-rgyas Ye-shes trained eighteen outstanding disciples. Among them was Vitapāda (sMan-zhabs), who composed an important commentary on the *zhal-lung* (the *Sukusuma-nāma-dvidramatattva-bhāvanamukhāgamavṛtti*). The learned Tibetan masters, Sangs-rgyas gSang-ba (Buddhaguhya) and Sangs-rgyas Zhi-ba (Buddhaśānta), who were immediate disciples of Sangs-rgyas Ye-shes, were also direct lineage holders. Sangs-rgyas Ye-shes spent his later years in Vajrāsana, where he built a temple.

The Paṇḍita Śūnyaśrī and gNyan Lo-tsā-ba were also members of this lineage. The translator gNyos-'byung-po went to India to study the *Guhyasamāja* under the Ācārya Balin, who is a spiritual son of 'Jam-dpal bShes-gnyen and Sangs-rgyas Ye-shes's lineage. Ācārya Balin was the spiritual teacher of King Dharmapāla. From here, the transmission of the *Guhyasamāja* teachings and practices spread throughout East Tibet and the central provinces.

The Inner Tantras. The Inner Tantras (*nang-rgyud-sde-gsum*) constitute the most secret oral transmission of the masters from India and elsewhere. Together they are known as the "Tantra Arriving at a Wholesome Communication with Being" (*rNal-'byor-pa'i-rgyud*), which is the most widely disseminated body of Tantras among the rNying-ma-pa. Its three divisions are:

1. The Mahāyoga (rGyud-mahayoga'i-theg-pa)

---

*These fourteen works which are found in the *bsTan-'gyur* are as follows: The three Kun-tu-bzang-po, i.e., *Kun-tu-bzang-po* (*Samantabhadra-nāma-sādhana*), *Kun-tu-bzang-mo* (*Caturaṅgasādhana-samantabhadrī-nāma*), and the *Kun-tu-bzang-po'i don-bsdus-pa* (*Śrī Herukasādhana*); *sByin-bsreg-gnyis-kyi cho-ga; gTor-ma mi-nub-pa'i sgron-ma; Tshogs-kyi 'khor-lo'i cho-ga; Rin-po-che 'bar-pa* (*Śrī Guhyasamājatantrarāja-ṭīkā candra-prabhā-nāma, rGyud-kyi rnam-bshad*); *dKyil-'khor-gyi cho-ga shlo-ka bzhi-brgya-lnga-bchu-pa* (*Śrī Guhyasamāja-maṇḍalavidhināma*); *rTsa-ba'i ye-shes-chen-po; Tshings-su bcad-pa'i mdzod; Muktitilakanāma* (*Grol-ba'i thig-le zhes-bya-ba*); *Ātmasādhana-avatāra-nāma; Byang-chub sems-kyi thig-le; dPal bkra-shis-kyi rnam-par bshad-pa chen-po; bZhi-pa-la 'Jug-pa thabs-dang-bcas-pa;* and the *Chu-sbyin dbang-po'i sgrub-pa'i thabs-gsum* (*Bhaṭṭāraka-Ārya-jaṃbhala-jalendra-sādhana, Guhya-jaṃbhala-sādhana* and the *Vistara-jaṃbhala-sādhana*).

2. The Anuyoga (Lung-anuyoga'i-theg-pa)
3. The Atiyoga (Man-ngag-rdzogs-pa-chen-po).

The Mahāyoga may also be related to the foundation or basis (*gzhi, bhūmi*), the Anuyoga, the path or method (*lam, mārga*), and the Atiyoga, the fruit or result (*'bras-bu, phala*).

The two principal types of transmission as recognized by the rNying-ma-pa, are the bKa'-ma and the gTer-ma. The bKa'-ma represents the continuous transmission of the teachings of the Buddha, unbounded by time or space. The gTer-ma represents the continuing transmission of particular texts, practices, and realizations which are rediscovered after having been concealed for a period of time.

bKa'-ma and gTer-ma share certain similarities as they both contain the precious body of internal teachings, particularly the highly experientially oriented Atiyoga transmissions which enjoyed tremendous development and application in Tibet. Both bKa'-ma and gTer-ma are unique as their existence does not depend upon the Vinaya or Mahāyāna lineages. Even if the entire body of doctrines and practices which constitute the Buddhadharma became non-existent, the transmission of the esoteric enlightenment principles could continue by way of the bKa'-ma and gTer-ma for the sake of the fortunate ones who sincerely wish to become enlightened.

The rNying-ma-pa also recognize two basic divisions for their tradition, the Transmission Tradition (*rgyud-sde*) and the Tradition of Meditative Realization (*sgrub-sde*). Related to these are nine distinctive lineages that correspond to a unique cosmological framework. The first three of the nine, which are considered the major lineages, correspond to the three transmissions of the Transmission Tradition (*rgyud-sde*), which constitute the bKa'-ma transmission of canonic teaching texts. These three transmissions are:

1. The lineage of Buddha-overall-intentionality (*rgyal-ba dgongs-brgyud*), which is represented by the Ādi-buddha, Kun-tu-bzang-po, who resides in Akaniṣṭha Heaven and symbolizes the Dharmakāya.

2. The Lineage of the Bearers of Pure Awareness (*Rig-'dzin-brda-brgyud*), which constitutes the teaching of the Atiyoga (rDzogs-chen) among both men and the higher Bodhisattvas. It is a symbolic lineage (*brda*) and cannot be taught by means of ordinary language. Corresponding to the Sambhogakāya, it has both a human and non-human transmission, with the Human-tradition beginning with dGa'-rab rDo-rje and Śrī-Siṃha.

3. The Lineage of the Oral-transmission, or the 'Mouth-to-ear Lineage' (*gang-zag-snyan-brgyud*), which King Indrabodhi of Za-hor (*rGyal-po-rā-dza*) first received from the Five Tathāgatas, or Buddha Affinities. The Bodhisattva rDo-rje-sems-dpa' (Vajrasattva) is also uniquely connected with this lineage.

In addition to these three major lineages, there are six minor lineages, which are more practice-oriented. These exist to the present day:

4. The Ḍākinī Lineage (*mkha'-'gro-gtad-rgya'i-brgyud-pa*), in which the Ḍākinīs assist the gTer-ma masters in uncovering and deciphering precious hidden texts.

5. The Bodhisattva Lineage (*smon-lam-las-'phros-brgyud-pa*), symbolized by the Bodhisattva Mañjuśrī, the most excellent prototype of compassion.

6. Whispered Oral-teachings Lineage (*shog-ser-tshigs-gi-brgyud-pa*), in which highly guarded instructions are transmitted by the Ḍākinīs (*mkha'-'gro-ma*) and spiritual guides (*bla-ma*) to their human disciples.

7. Visionary Lineage (*dag-snang-gi-brgyud-pa*), which is exemplified by the intense meditative visions 'Jigs-med-gling-pa had while he experienced the presence of Klong-chen-pa, or which 'Jam-dbyangs-mkhyen-brtse'i-dbang-po had of Vimalamitra.

8. Recollection Lineage (*rjes-dran-gi-brgyud-pa*), which implements a sophisticated symbolic language formulated by scholarly Siddhas.

9. gTer-ma Lineage (*yang-gter-gi-brgyud-pa*), or the lineage of buried treasure texts.

While the Transmission Tradition (*rgyud-sde*) is the more theoretical or philosophical side of the division of the Inner Tantras, the Tradition of Meditative Realization (*sgrub-sde*) preserves the practical instructions for meditation and spiritual development. The Tradition of Meditative Realization contains the Eight Heruka Sādhanas of Padmasambhava, which became the foundation for the gTer-ma tradition in Tibet, as well as the sNying-thig teachings which Klong-chen-rab-'byams-pa summarized in his *sNying-thig ya-bzhi*.

The three Inner Tantras, which are practiced only by the rNying-ma-pa represent a further stage towards the various gradations of 'inwardness' as outlined in the Anuttarayoga-tantra, and are based upon several root Tantric texts, the foremost of which are: the *Hevajra*, the *Cakrasaṃvara*, the *Guhyasamāja*, and the *Kālacakra*. Of these, the most widely disseminated is the *Guhyasamāja*.

While some schools of philosophy distinguish between Two Truths, the conventional (*kun-rdzob*) and the ultimate (*don-dam*), the Mahāyoga presents a third truth, and teaches how to become enlightened in this very lifetime. All the emotions are used as vehicles to sustain and heighten awareness and each situation presents its potentiality, becoming transformed into the deities of the *maṇḍala*. Emotive energies, as described in the Abhidharma, become transformed so that they find exemplary realization in the manifestations of deities within the meditative *maṇḍala*. Each of the Meditation Buddhas (Yi-dam) is represented by specific sounds, colors, and images, and each manifests the body, speech, and mind of the Nirmāṇakāya, Sambhōgakāya, and Dharmakāya. Through the internal practice of Sādhana, rituals, *mudrās*, and *mantras*, the mind becomes a mirror-like *maṇḍala*.

While Mahāyoga may be said to be essentially concerned with a visionary experience, the Anuyoga emphasizes the feeling tones of this vision. In Anuyoga teachings, all thought and form is directly experienced to be of the nature of Śūnyatā and is identified with Kun-tu-bzang-mo (Samantabhadrī), the female embodiment of the Dharmakāya. Appearance itself is identified with Kun-tu-bzang-po (Samantabhadra), the male primogenitor. The interpenetration of these two (*zung-'jug*)—from which all things are derived, yet without cause and effect—signifies their inseparability. By gradually traversing the Five Bodhisattva Paths in Anuyoga, one reaches the citadel of Buddhahood.

Atiyoga is an expression of a perfect harmony between 'appearance' and 'openness' (*śūnya*). It is a complete view whereby the goal becomes the path. Atiyoga dispenses with visualized images and with manipulation of internal energy focal points. It is concerned with direct realization of the intrinsic nature of the mind, which has been immaculately pure and free from beginningless time. All experience is perfectly reflected on the pure surface of mind, because mind is unoriginated and unoriginating. This self-existent pristine awareness which recognizes the utter perfection of all experience is the very quintessence of the Vajrayāna Path.

Of the Three Inner Tantras, the Atiyoga, or rDzogs-chen, contains the most practical instructions, as Atiyoga can be realized in any activity which is performed. Atiyoga does not depend upon the relevancy of time and the prospect of endless rebirths. Through Atiyoga, enlightenment can be achieved in a single lifetime, and it is the most fruitful of all Buddhist paths.

The term rDzogs-chen (rDzogs-pa-chen-po) means 'full', 'complete', 'not in any way deficient'. This term was coined around 500 A.D. when these ideas were already prominent in India and along the silk routes to China. Klong-chen-rab-'byams-pa expanded the meaning for rDzogs-chen to indicate that it is the 'all-complete' or 'all-perfect' doctrine.

The Atiyoga teachings came from the area of the Dhanakośa Lake in the western country of Uḍḍiyāna. The basic text of the Atiyoga system is called the *sNying-thig ya-bzhi*, and the basic philosophical background of this system rests on the doctrine of the Mādhyamika as developed by the Indian Paṇḍitas, Nāgārjuna and Āryadeva. The master 'Jam-dpal bShes-gnyen received the rDzogs-chen transmission from the first representative of the Human-tradition, dGa'-rab rDo-rje, in a golden box. He then divided its six million four hundred thousand verses into three sections, known as the *rDzogs-pa chen-po sde-gsum*:

1. Mind Section (Sems-sde), which relates to the firmness of mind (*sems-gnas-rnams-la sems-sde*).
2. Section on the Unending Experience of Being (Klong-sde), which relates to effortlessness (*bya-bral-rnams-la klong-sde*).
3. Guidance Section (Man-ngag-gi-sde), which relates to the most important essence (*gnad-gtso bo-la man-ngag-sde*). This section, which encompasses the teachings of the sNying-thig, the most profoundly deep instructions in all of Buddhism, is subdivided into two sections:
   a. The transmission of what is heard (*snyan-brgyud*), consisting of:
      i. 'mouth to ear Tantra' (*rnar-rgyud*)
      ii. 'explanatory Tantra' (*bshad-rgyud*)
   b. The transmission of what is explained (*bshad-brgyud*)

Śrī Siṃha, the disciple of 'Jam-dpal bShes-gnyen, journeyed to Vajrāsana (rDo-rje-gdan) and uncovered the Guidance Section of the rDzogs-chen, which his teacher had hidden there. He divided the section into four parts:

1. 'exoteric cycle' (*phyi-skor*)
2. 'esoteric cycle' (*nang-skor*)
3. 'secret cycle' (*gsang-skor*)
4. 'most inner secret cycle' (*gsang-ba bla-na-med-pa skor*)

The sNying-thig teachings ('Quintessential Instructions') are classified into two aspects: the first spiritual instructions came in succession from Guru Rinpoche, Padmasambhava, and are called the *sLob-dpon-chen-po-pad-ma'i-bka'-srol-snying-thig*; and the second spiritual discourses originated with Vimalamitra and are known as the *Bi-ma'i-bka'-srol-snying-thig*. In the fourteenth century Kun-mkhyen Klong-chen-rab-'byams-pa, one of the greatest of all rNying-ma masters, compiled and systematized the sNying-thig teachings in his *Klong-chen-snying-thig*.

The bKa'-ma Tradition

The bKa'-ma tradition is the continuous transmission of teachings, texts, practices, Sādhanas, and realizations that have passed from teacher to student in an unbroken succession since the time of the Buddha. bKa' literally means the Buddha's Word. It is the Ādi-Buddha, Kun-tu-bzang-po (Samantabhadra), who teaches the bKa'-ma, which are essentially timeless and yet appear in all times and in all the ten directions. The Ādi-buddha radiates as a five-fold light emanating from the very meaningfulness of Being (*chos-nyid*) and is representative of a *maṇḍala* ever-present in all modes of space and time. This is the tradition of the Buddha-intentionality; the teachings derived from this transmission are allegorically represented by the Buddha Kun-bzang Che-mchog Heruka. Thus, the Ādi-buddha, through Che-mchog Heruka, entrusts the Buddha-word, or bKa'-ma, to the Vidyādhara of the intermediate sphere of the Sambhōgakāya, Rig-'dzin rDo-rje-chos-rab, who in turn entrusts the bKa'-ma to the Ḍākinī (mKha'-'gro-ma) Las-kyi-dbang-mo-che for safe keeping. This transmission also is given to Vajrasattva, who imparts it to the Human-tradition.

The bKa'-ma tradition may be subdivided into three sections, known as the *mDo-sgyu-sems-gsum*:

1. sGyu consists of the eighteen Tantric cycles of the Mahāyoga, with the *Guhya-mūla-garbha-tantra* as its root text.
2. mDo includes the Anuyoga practices and realizations and has five sections, each of which is related to one of the five Sūtras of the Anuyoga. Its root text is the *'Dus-pa'i-mdo*.
3. Sems encompasses all three subdivisions of the Atiyoga (rDzogs-pa-chen-po), and deals with the Openness of Being.

Kun-tu-bzang-po

*The Transmission of the Atiyoga bKa'-ma up to Vimalamitra and Padmasambhava**

Vajrasattva (rDo-rje-sems-dpa') is the spiritual intermediary who transmitted the bKa'-ma, which originated in the Dharmakāya, to the first of the Human-tradition, dGa'-rab rDo-rje. Being an emanation of

*The *Deb-ther-sngon-po* (*Blue Annals*) by 'Gos Lo-tsā-ba gZhon-nu-dpal (1392–1481) has been a valuable source for tracing the early rNying-ma lineages of direct transmission which are presented in the following sections. Also, the siddha O-rgyan-pa reported in his writings that he discovered a multitude of original early rNying-ma works and translations at the Bi-har-ri Monastery in Nepal. Many of these works are not in the bKa'-gyur or not apparently known to 'Gos Lo-tsā-ba.

rDo-rje-chos-rab

the Nirmāṇakāya (*sPrul-sku*), dGa'-rab rDo-rje was a Bearer of Pure Awareness (Rig-'dzin, Vidyādhara). On three occasions he had a vision of rDo-rje-sems-dpa', listened to his teachings, and fully understood their meaning. In bKra-shis-khrigs-sgo in China, dGa'-rab rDo-rje passed on the doctrine he had received to 'Jam-dpal bShes-gnyen, who in turn taught Śrī Siṃha. Śrī Siṃha instructed Vimalamitra in the cremation ground bSil-ba'i-tshal (Śītavana), and in bKra-shis-khrigs-gso he instructed the Ācārya Jñānasūtra (Ye-shes-mdo), who in turn imparted the transmission to Vimalamitra. Padmasambhava received the Oral-transmission from 'Jam-dpal bShes-gnyen through 'Jam-dpal the Younger, as well as directly from dGa'-rab rDo-rje in the form of meditative visions. This first Oral-explanation lineage is called "Transmission of that Doctrine which leads to the Final Goal of the Atiyoga" (*rDzogs-chen mthar-thig-gi chos-kyi-brgyud-pa*).

Las-kyi-dbang-mo-che

dGa'-rab rDo-rje. dGa'-rab rDo-rje (b. 55 A.D.), was born in the country of Uḍḍiyāna, near Dhanakośa Lake. The rulers of that region were King Uparāja and Queen sNang-ba-gsal-ba'i 'Od-ldan-ma, whose royal residence was a large temple called bDe-byed-brtsegs-pa, surrounded by one thousand six hundred and eight smaller temples. Their second daughter, Sudharmā, grew up into a beautiful and virtuous young woman. She and her five hundred handmaidens, all of whom were virgins, renounced the worldly life and took full monastic vows. Then Sudharmā, together with her maids, retreated to an island where they meditated on the Yoga-tantra (rNal-'byor-gyi-rgyud).

In the year of the Wood-Female-Ox, shortly after dawn on the eighth lunar day of the first summer month, while taking a bath near the lake, Sudharmā had a wonderful meditative vision. In this vision she

Vajrasattva

perceived a brilliant light coming from an easterly direction, emanating from the origin of all Buddhas. Out of this light emerged the sun and moon; the sun entered her body through the top of her head while the moon came into her body through her lower extremities. Suddenly, Vajrapāṇi manifested before her as a beautiful Vajra-bird–a great swan of golden hue. Descending upon the lake with four other swans, they showered themselves with the crystalline water. Then the four swans took flight, but the Vajra-bird remained. Showing no sign of fear, he came up to Sudharmā and touched his beak to her heart cakra three times. As soon as he did this, a bright light appeared and dissolved into her body, and Sudharmā beheld the three-fold world as perfect and clear. The swan then took flight. Sudharmā was astonished at what had happened but had no idea of the significance of the event.

dGa'-rab-rDo-rje

When she returned to her maids, she told them of the vision; when her father learned of the incident, he was both amazed and happy because he felt that it must be a sign marking the birth of an enlightened master. The king then told his nobility to keep watch over her, insuring her safety.

Meanwhile, the princess' heart cakra transformed into a vajra gem and a vajra light came forth from her body and manifested as a beautiful infant. Because Sudharmā was a virgin, she was greatly disturbed, fearful that the whole kingdom would regard the child as a phantom. Her maids reminded Sudharmā of her visionary experience and told her that the baby must surely be a gift of the enlightened ones; nevertheless, she was full of shame and fear, and placed the child out of view in a dust heap. After three days she went out to look at the child, and found that his body was healthy and radiant. Thereupon, beautiful music filled the air, flowers came raining down from the heavens, and rainbow lights filled the skies. Seeing this, the Bhikṣuṇī cast away all her doubts and fears, and, realizing the infant must be an incarnation (*sprul-sku*), she took him to her chambers, and bathed him, while many Ḍākinīs appeared and gave offerings to this child who had come from the heavens. The infant possessed many signs of a great man: his right hand held a vajra, and his left, a walking stick embedded with precious gems. The Brahman soothsayers predicted that the infant would be a great incarnated one who would put forth the most excellent of teachings.

Shortly after the child was born, Vajrapāṇi appeared to him and instantaneously initiated him into all the esoteric Tantras, which he grew up to perfectly comprehend. After this initiation, many Dharmapālas surrounded him, taking an oath that they would remain with him throughout his life. As he was an emanation of rDo-rje-sems-dpa', the Vidyādhara who is the holder of the knowledge of all Buddhas, the child was to become a great master of the Atiyoga (rDzogs-chen), endowed with the capacity for protecting the Dharma and instructing others in it with the utmost precision.

When he had reached the age of seven, he asked his mother several times for permission to dispute with the learned Paṇḍitas, but each time she refused. One day soon after, King Uparāja had as guests five hundred learned Paṇḍitas. Plagued by his constant entreaties, the princess finally consented to allow the child to talk with the Paṇḍitas at the palace. The youth stepped in front of the assembly, and the debate began. Putting forth arguments from the viewpoint of the goal or final attainment (*'bras-bu*), he severely defeated all five hundred masters, who had all taken the viewpoint of the starting point (*gzhi*). After defeating them in every form of disputation, he began to instruct them on the subject matter of the Atiyoga, the All-complete Doctrine of the rDzogs-chen, which he had fully cognized since birth. Astonished at this knowledge, the entire assembly of scholars surrounded the child and fell to their knees, referring to him as Prajñābhadra, "the one whose being is appreciative understanding." They all agreed that he was the incarnation of a great teacher.

The king was so pleased with the boy and experienced such extraordinary joy in his presence that he named him dGa'-rab rDo-rje, "Joyous Vajra." Because his mother had once thrown him in the dust heap, he was also known as Ro-langs-bde-ba, "he who rose joyous from the dust."

Later, dGa'-rab rDo-rje journeyed north to mountain ranges and solitudes where Preta appeared in hordes. There on a mountain called "Where the Sun Rises" he lived and meditated for thirty-two years. During this time, rDo-rje-sems-dpa' appeared to him enveloped in a brilliant light. Initiating him as a perfectly endowed *sprul-sku* (tulku), he then bestowed on him both the texts and complete oral instructions of the six million four hundred thousand rDzogs-chen verses.

At one time when he was living in the mountain ranges, the earth trembled seven times. A non-Buddhist priest accused dGa'-rab rDo-rje of causing the quakes by "injuring the belief of the Brahmans." The Brahman king of the region then proceeded to charge dGa'-rab rDo-rje with committing a crime, and neighboring herdsmen joined the king's vassals in search of him. When they arrived at his meditation cave they heard a deep and powerful sound coming from its entrance; he appeared before them in rays of light and no one could lay their hands on him. Because of this, the Brahman king and his entire entourage were converted to the Buddhadharma.

dGa'-rab rDo-rje was endowed with numerous unusual powers, such as the ability to walk unhindered through rocks, stone, and swift running water. He appeared before many people enveloped in light, inspiring them with great faith and devotion. dGa'-rab rDo-rje attracted a great number of disciples, and many of these received special empowerments (*dbang-bskur*).

Accompanied by a spiritual daughter of Rāhula who was psychically endowed, dGa'-rab rDo-rje proceeded to a cemetery near the grove at Śītavana (bSil-ba'i-tsal) in Magadha (India). There he delivered the instantaneous transmission, which transforms the mind of the student into that of the teacher, to numerous Ḍākinīs who assumed the form of both humans and apparitions. To all these disciples he uttered the teachings of the *rDzogs-chen rDo-rje-sems-dpa'*, explaining its subtle meaning; thus, by means of his intuitive capacity (*rtogs-pa*), he transmitted the Atiyoga, the All-perfect Doctrine. His disciples, who included learned scholars and knowledge-bearing Ḍākinīs, put the teachings into writing; together with dGa'-rab rDo-rje they compiled an index (*dkar-chags*) of the six-million four hundred thousand Atiyoga verses.

'Jam-dpal bShes-gnyen. During that time, in a village just west of Vajrāsana (rDo-rje-gdan) there lived a very learned Brahman by the name of sNying-po Grub-pa, who was a master of Sanskrit, linguistics,

'Jam-dpal bShes-gnyen

philosophy, logic, and art. Because of his comprehensive knowledge of the sacred writings he was also called 'Jam-dpal bShes-gnyen (Mañjuśrīmitra). One day he was visited by the bodily apparition of Bodhisattva Mañjuśrī, who advised him to go to the cremation ground at Śītavana where he would find an enlightened teacher that would explain to him the direct course to Buddhahood.

'Jam-dpal bShes-gnyen then studied with dGa'-rab rDo-rje for seventy-five years and received innumerable instructions in the Dharma, including the whole of the rDzogs-chen Atiyoga system, which was directly transmitted to him from the mind of rDo-rje-sems-dpa' by way of the voice of his teacher. After passing all the lineages of the teachings to 'Jam-dpal bShes-gnyen, dGa'-rab rDo-rje's body became the nature of light and disappeared. At the commemoration ceremony after his passing, dGa'-rab rDo-rje appeared at the fountain of the River Tan-tig, surrounded by light and numerous spiritual emanations. He then handed 'Jam-dpal bShes-gnyen a golden box which contained all of the six million four-hundred thousand Atiyoga verses. 'Jam-dpal divided these into the three sections of the Atiyoga. As there was no one prepared to receive his explanations concerning the main body of the first section, he hid the texts underneath a rock east of Bodh Gayā and sealed them with a double vajra. He then went to the cremation ground of So-sa'i-gling, where for nine hundred years he stayed absorbed in meditation.

Śrī Siṃha. In the year 289 A.D. in the country known as 'the black expanse' (Western China, or Khotan), Śrī Siṃha was born to a wise and virtuous householder. At the age of fifteen, he went to the Bodhi-tree temple where he studied literature, astrology, grammar, logic, and religion with the master Haribhadra for three years, after which time he became a recognized scholar.

One night, in the locality of gSer-gling, Avalokiteśvara appeared to him and instructed him to go to the cremation ground of So-sa'i-gling in India. Before following the Bodhisattva's advice, Śrī Siṃha believed that he should first undergo preliminary studies in Tantra. So he journeyed to 'the five mountain peaks' (Ri-bo-rtse-lnga) in China, a famous place of pilgrimage dedicated to Mañjuśrī, where he studied the exoteric and esoteric Tantra with the teacher Bhelakirti (Bi-le-le-ti) for seven years. He became a monk, and practiced according to the Vinaya methods for three years at Yar-tha in China.

At further requests by the Lord of Compassion, he finally set out for India in search of 'Jam-dpal bShes-gnyen. Because of his spiritual power (*siddhi*) he encountered no hardship in his travels, and safely arrived at the cremation ground So-sa'i-gling, where he was accepted as a student. 'Jam-dpal bShes-gnyen gave him instructions and exposition on the more difficult areas of study for twenty-five years until, assured of his student's success, he dissolved into a mass of light. 'Jam-dpal then appeared to Śrī Siṃha in a vision, giving him final instructions, and presenting him with a box inlaid with jewels that contained the 'Six meditation experiences' (*sgom-nyams-drug-pa*). Upon reading these texts, Śrī Siṃha immediately realized the same intrinsic awareness as 'Jam-dpal bShes-gnyen. One hundred and twenty-five years after his death, sLob-dpon 'Jam-dpal bShes-gnyen was miraculously reborn, without physical parents, in gSer-gyi brGyan-pa'i-gling, a western region

Śrī Siṃha

of India. This incarnation, 'Jam-dpal bShes-gnyen the Younger, instructed Padmasambhava, the Lotus-born, in all the exoteric and esoteric Tantra (*sngags-phyi-dang-nang*). He also taught Āryadeva the Atiyoga (rDzogs-chen) doctrine, whereupon the latter renounced the world and achieved the rainbow body.

After his teacher's passing, Śrī Siṃha went to Vajrāsana and uncovered the Atiyoga (rDzogs-chen) Tantra concerning the Guidance Section (Man-ngag-gi-sde) which 'Jam-dpal bShes-gnyen (the elder) had hidden there. Śrī Siṃha divided the whole section of Instructions into four parts: the 'exoteric cycle' (*phyi-skor*), the 'esoteric cycle' (*nang-skor*), the 'secret cycle' (*gsang-skor*), and the 'most inner secret cycle' (*gsang-ba bla-na-med-pa skor*). He took the first three cycles and hid them in the garret floor of the temple Byang-chub-zhing.

According to the prophecy of the Ḍākinī, he concealed the fourth part, the most inner secret cycle, in a column of the temple bKra-shis-khrigs-sgo and also placed them in his heart, only to be revealed to Ḍākas, Ḍākinīs, and other givers of spiritual afflatus. Śrī Siṃha then went to the cremation ground called bSil-byed, where certain non-human beings honored him. He taught them the Dharma and stayed there in meditation.

Śrī Siṃha is an important link in the rise of the lineage holders of the higher rNying-ma Tantras. He conferred his Oral-transmission on Vairocana, who was often a co-author with him. The bsTan-'gyur contains about twenty-five works either composed or co-translated by Śrī Siṃha. His works reveal a solid understanding of the earlier Indian philosophical schools of the Vaibhāṣikas, Sautrāntikas, Mādhyamikas, and the Mantrayāna. The noticeable absence of the Yogācāra, however, indicated that Yogācāra ideas were not brought to maturity during his lifetime.

The three progenitors of this lineage, dGa'-rab rDo-rje, 'Jam-dpal bShes-gnyen, and Śrī Siṃha, all attained rainbow bodies and disappeared without leaving a trace. These enlightened masters have achieved an internal stability and a sensitivity to others such that their role as teacher or 'spiritual guide' (*bla-ma*) is the exemplification of the highest sense of Bodhisattva action that man can achieve. Countless thousands of lineage-holders throughout the centuries have totally comprehended the teachings and methods stemming from these spiritual masters. The streamlined methods they taught, otherwise known as the Atiyoga (rDzogs-chen), have the ability to direct one to the citadel of Buddhahood in a single lifetime.

Ye-shes-mdo. After receiving empowerments from Śrī Siṃha, Ye-shes-mdo meditated on the Atiyoga teachings for sixteen years. Thereafter, he traveled to various cemeteries and even to other realms. When Ye-shes-mdo was teaching in Khotan at the invitation of King dPal-byin, he beheld Śrī Siṃha sitting in mid-air, encircled by a halo of light. At this moment of his teacher's passing, Ye-shes-mdo received from the sky the book *gZer-bu bdun-pa*, which contained the last teachings of Śrī Siṃha, as well as the seven essential teachings of the rDzogs-pa-chen-po. Following the instructions given there, Ye-shes-mdo recovered the Secret Instructions of the sNying-thig (*sNying-thig gsang-ba'i ngag*) from the column of the temple of bKra-shis-khri-sgo; he then journeyed to the cremation ground Bha-shing, where he found

Ye-shes-mdo

numerous other rDzogs-chen doctrines. He then preached the secret instructions of the sNying-thig to worldly and transworldly beings. Remaining in the cremation ground for many years, he received numerous other teachings from Śrī Siṃha through visions.

Ten years after conferring the rDzogs-chen empowerments on Vimalamitra, Ye-shes-mdo, due to his spiritual purity, attained a rainbow body; enveloped by a brilliant light, he passed away at the age of one hundred and thirteen without leaving a trace.

Vimalamitra. Mahāpaṇḍita Vimalamitra was born in western India and he began his studies in the Hīnayāna and Mahāyāna at a very early age. Having become a scholar in the Sarvāstivādin Vinaya, he then studied the numerous Sūtras and Śāstras with the five hundred Paṇḍitas

Vimalamitra

who resided at Bodh Gayā (rDo-rje-gdan). He acquired great respect for the writings of Vasubandhu and other early masters. After fully mastering the Three Baskets (Tripiṭaka), he began his studies in the Vajrayāna under the Ācārya Buddhaguhya (Sangs-rgyas gSang-ba).

Vimalamitra then journeyed to China where he studied for nine years with Śrī Siṃha, receiving the inner, outer, and secret cycles of the Oral-transmission (*snyan-brgyud*) of the Atiyoga. Upon returning to India he transmitted these teachings to Ye-shes-mdo (Jñānasūtra), and with great enthusiasm, these two great masters returned to China, where, as predicted by the Ḍākinīs, they found Śrī Siṃha in the cremation ground bSil-byed. During the following twelve years Śrī Siṃha conferred upon them further teachings of the Oral-transmission of the inner, outer, and secret cycles. In the course of time Śrī Siṃha transmitted to Ye-shes-mdo the most inner secret teachings of the Atiyoga as well. Thus, Ye-shes-mdo learned all the esoteric instructions and initiations of the Atiyoga (rDzogs-chen), and his mind was completely transformed into the nature of these profound instructions.

When Vimalamitra was over one hundred years old, he journeyed to the Bha-shing cemetery to receive teachings from Ye-shes-mdo, as prophesized by a Ḍākinī. Bowing his head in obeisance to the master, immeasurable rays of light came forth from his forehead. Ye-shes-mdo then conferred the three exoteric and esoteric empowerments upon Vimalamitra which he had received from Śrī Siṃha. At that moment the seed syllable AH appeared in white on the tip of Vimalamitra's nose. Thus, Ye-shes-mdo imparted to him the most profound teachings of the Atiyoga system, the 'Heart-drop Instructions' (sNying-thig-gi gdam-pa).

Following the passing of his master, Vimalamitra proceeded eastward to the town Kāmarūpa (Ka-ma-ru), which King Siṃhabhadra Seng-ge bZang-po ruled, and stayed in the temple there for twenty years as a court chaplain. Afterwards, he went to the city of Bhiryal (Bhir-ya-la) where he became a monk and was patronized by King Dharmapāla. Next, he traveled north to the burial ground Rab-tu-snang-byed (Pramāsa) where he practiced the teachings and taught the Dharma to the non-human beings who resided there. He also practiced the 'Quintessential Instruction', the supremely subtle teachings leading to perfect attainment. During the seven year period of his residency, he made three copies of the texts which had been given to him by the Ḍākinīs. He then hid one copy on the 'Island in the ocean where the golden land is scattered' (rGya-mtsho gser-gyi bye-ma-gdal-ba'i bling) in the western sector of the country of Uḍḍiyāna. The second copy he hid under a rock at gSer-gling in Kashmir, and the last copy was hidden in the Rab-tu-snang-byed cremation ground as an aid to the Ḍākinīs. There Vimalamitra practiced the highest teachings of the Tantras, and by means of repeated oral instruction, enlightened numerous beings who dwelled there.

Following this, Vimalamitra traveled to Uḍḍiyāna where he instructed King Indrabodhi the Middle for many years. While he was teaching there, King Khri-srong-lde'u-btsan instructed sKa-ba dPal-brtsegs, Cog-ro-klu'i rGyal-mtshan, rMa Rin-chen-mchog, and others to travel to India and invite Vimalamitra to spread the Dharma in Tibet. After having presented Vimalamitra with seven precious golden images and a large quantity of gold dust, the envoys made their request.

Though King Indrabodhi was opposed to his leaving, Vimalamitra set out for Tibet accompanied by his attendant, the Ācārya Kṣitigarbha (Sa'i-snying-po), the Tibetan lo-tsā-bas, and a caravan of sacred texts.

That very night the people of India dreamt that the sun, moon, flowers, trees, and all the crops were leaning toward Tibet. All of nature seemed disturbed, and even the astrologers calculated inauspicious omens. King Indrabodhi then realized that he had relinquished a most precious jewel to the Tibetans, and he hastily sent swift-footed messengers to Tibet with instructions to place warning signs in all the valleys and crossroads of Tibet to proclaim that the Tibetan translators had carried out of India pernicious magical formulas which would lead the entire kingdom of Tibet to ruin.

In spite of such obstacles, when Vimalamitra arrived at bSam-yas Monastery, Khri-srong-lde'u-btsan and his subjects received him most warmly. In the meantime, however, some of the king's ministers who had become jealous, took notice of the rumors; loudly questioning Vimalamitra's credibility, they claimed that he was worthy of renown only as a black magician. The King was overcome with doubt and grief and the translators became depressed and disappointed, but on the morning of the third day, Vimalamitra put all their doubts to rest. In the central section of bSam-yas, where Vimalamitra was meditating, there was enshrined a clay image of the master sPa-gor Vairocana, who had been banished to East Tibet. After Vimalamitra uttered a powerful *mantra*, the clay image turned into a heap of dust. At first, the ministers believed that this gesture only confirmed their suspicions, but Vimalamitra placed his hand over the broken pieces of clay and again restored it into a very handsome image of Vairocana, from which streams of light emanated, pervading the entire inner sanctuary of bSam-yas.

Thereupon, Khri-srong-lde'u-btsan built upon a tall pillar a turquoise studded throne inlaid with gold; and from this seat of honor, Vimalamitra proceeded to explain the Sūtras, Tantras, and their commentaries. Through Vimalamitra's collaboration with Tibetan scholars, many other outer, inner, and secret treatises of the Vajrayāna were translated. He was aided by gNyags Jñānakumāra, sKa-ba dPal-brtsegs, Cog-ro-klu'i rGyal-msthan, Yu-sgra-sNying-po, and rMa Rin-chen-mchog, to whom he transmitted the Mahāyoga teachings of the *Guhya-mūla-garbha-tantra*. All of these translators became major influences in laying the foundation for the early preservation and transmission of rNying-ma texts and oral teachings. They were not ordinary scholars but incarnate Bodhisattvas who demonstrated unusual abilities to directly translate the essential meanings of the texts.

Vimalamitra, together with these scholars, translated the Sūtras (mDo) in the light of the Tantric interpretation, the *rDo-rje-sems-dpa' sgyu-'phrul-dra-ba*, the *dPal-yang-dag* the *Vajra-kila-rdo-rje-phur-pa*, and various texts on the rDzogs-pa-chen-po. The Tibetan bKa'-'gyur contains over eighty works by Vimalamitra, ten of which he authored, and the others he translated. In addition, the *rNying-ma'i rgyud-'bum* contains forty-two works directly attributed to Vimalamitra.

Vimalamitra lived in Tibet for thirteen years, and during that time he worked in close collaboration with the principal disciples of Padmasambhava. Through meditative visions, Vimalamitra met dGa'-rab rDo-rje seven times, and received from him the direct transmission of the Atiyoga (rDzogs-chen) lineage. Master of both the Sūtras and the Mantrayāna, Vimalamitra secretly taught the precepts of the Man-ngag-snying-thig to King Khri-srong-lde'u-btsan and to Nyang Ting-'dzin-bzang-po, his two foremost disciples. Because of his rare and comprehensive understanding of the entire corpus of the Buddhist tradition, and because of his desire to preserve the deepest meditative practices, Vimalamitra wrote four original works in the Tibetan language and secretly hid them near bSam-yas in the 'red-rock cave' at mChims-phu.

He later retired to a mountain retreat in China known as Ri-bo-rtse-lnga ("mountain with five pointed peaks"), where he passed away at an age of well over two hundred years. Vimalamitra promised that as long as the Buddhadharma prevailed, he would reincarnate in Tibet each century in order to revive the Doctrine of the 'Quintessential Instructions'. Of his many manifestations, Klong-chen-rab-'byams-pa in the fourteenth century and 'Jigs-med-gling-pa in the eighteenth century, are his two most important emanations. Numerous lamas since the time of Vimalamitra have attained rainbow bodies through practicing his teachings.

Direct Transmission. These direct realization lineages of the Tantras were secretly and orally handed down from teacher to disciple. The Tantras were never openly displayed or discussed in public, but were reserved for those select few who had the necessary intellectual and psychological prerequisites. The special *mantras*, visualizations, and inner esoteric instructions were thus carefully guarded by the masters from India, Nepal, China, Burma, and elsewhere. In addition, as the most precious of the teachings were transmitted to the most excellent human disciples from the transcendent spheres—which possessed a particularly pure spiritual World-horizon (Longs-sku, Sambhogakāya) or the founding stratum of Meaning itself (Chos-sku, Dharmakāya)—their contents were regarded with the utmost respect. The disciples of these teachings realized that an open and casual market-place approach could easily result in misappropriation of the precepts.

In later times, teachers such as Marpa Lo-tsā-ba, who received some of the Indian lineages under the Siddha Nāropa, returned to Tibet and practiced the teachings secretly, imparting the most esoteric teachings only to his closest disciple, Milarepa. Even though Marpa is said to have given Milarepa the advanced methods leading to realization, Milarepa did not fully perfect them until he practiced them on his own. In a similar manner, Kar-ma Pang-chen Sa-skya Śrī, the reincarnation of a disciple of dGa'-rab rDo-rje, received the Vajrakīla Sādhana from Padmasambhava and became an enlightened Siddha, but his contemporaries did not recognize his attainment. In such cases as with Dam-pa Sangs-rgyas and Buddhaguhya, it was not common knowledge that they had received the teachings until they became enlightened—so well had they quietly traversed the difficult path to enlightenment according to the instructions they were given. Still others, such as the master Rang-'byung rDo-rje (the third Karma-pa), student of the rNying-ma-pa master Rig-'dzin Ku-ma-rā-dza, received the oral precepts while deep in meditation. In this particular instance, he visually perceived Vimalamitra through the psychic aperture (*mdzod-spu, ūrṇa-kośa*) in the center of his forehead, and thereafter perfectly comprehended the vast teachings of the Atiyoga (rDzogs-chen). Similarly, while Śrī Siṃha obtained many of the esoteric teachings from 'Jam-dpal bShes-gnyen orally, he also received a direct transmission from dGa'-rab rDo-rje by means of psychic and visionary methods. Through this transmission, Śrī Siṃha thus acquired the *lde-mig* or 'cipher key' to the esoteric precepts (Man-ngag-gi-sde).

The Transmission of the Mahāyoga and the Lineage of the Guhya-mūla-garbha-tantra

Mahāyoga (rGyud-mahayoga'i-theg-pa) refers to Being-as-such, which is manifested through the Buddha's very lifestyle and which is ever-present and in all things. This sense of totality, comprising the whole of Being, is represented by the Ādi-buddha Kun-tu-bzang-po. The Ādi-buddha, being completely pure creativity and capable of becoming anything and everything, has the nature of being incessant. At the same time, the Ādi-buddha embodies the unchanging great bliss which cannot be encompassed by any concept, thus demonstrating the nature of being invariable. Being the primordial representative of the Dharmakāya (*chos-sku*), the Ādi-buddha is the origin of the Lineage of Buddha-overall-intentionality (*rgyal-ba dgongs-brgyud*) and resides in Akaniṣṭha, the most supreme and non-material heaven. The Ādi-buddha as a symbol for that which is in a state of utter perfection remains as a totality pattern representing every undulation of being-made-manifest. In being the origin of the Maṇḍala of 'existence' (*sku*) and 'awareness' (*ye-shes*), the Ādi-buddha is also the primogenitor of the Dharmadhātu (*chos-kyi-dbyings*). It is the Dharmakāya, with the Ādi-buddha as the source of the all and everything, yet being no thing-in-itself, that is spontaneously present as the Maṇḍala of the Sambhōgakāya, which is the five Buddha Families (*rgyal-tshab-rigs-lnga*) appearing as a five-fold light.

Thus, the transmission of the Mahāyoga originates in the Sphere of Ultimate Being, the Dharmakāya. From there it is transmitted by Kun-tu-bzang-po to the five affinity patterns, or Buddha families who reside in the five heavenly spheres of the Sambhogakāya. This manifestation pattern forms the Maṇḍala of the Rūpakāya extending to the five heavenly realms: sTug-po-bkod-pa, in the Center; mNgon-dga', in the East; Rin-po-ches-brgyan-pa in the South; bDe-ba-can, in the West; and Las-rab-grub-pa, in the North. From these divine abodes, arise the five principal Buddhas, as well as all the Buddhas who teach in the six realms. In the center of the Maṇḍala resides Vairocana Buddha (sometimes Vajrasattva), and from here the transmission extends to the three higher Bodhisattvas (*rigs-gsum-drva-ma-lnga*), who are primogenitors of the three lineages of Vidyādharas (Rig-'dzin): Avalokiteśvara (sPyan-ras-gzigs) who imparts the transmission to the Nāgas; Mañjuśrī ('Jam-dpal-dbyangs), who imparts the transmission to the Devas and Asuras of the heaven realms; and Vajrapāṇi (Phyag-na rDo-rje), who imparts the transmission to the world of man through the instrumentality of the Nirmāṇakāya manifestations (*sPrul-sku*).

Vajrasattva, the spiritual intermediator (*zung-'jug*) between the Dharmakāya and Sambhōgakāya, transmitted the basis for the Mahāyoga, consisting of eighteen Mahāyoga Tantras, to Vajrapāṇi. Vajrapāṇi, in turn, was the Vidyādhara who transmitted this body of

Indrabodhi

teaching to the Human-tradition, beginning with King Indrabodhi (Indrabhūti) the Elder, also known as King rGyal-po-rā-dza.

The Eighteen Mahāyoga Tantras. Outlined below are the five principal classifications of the Mahāyoga Tantras:

I. *rTsa-ba-rgyud sde-lnga'i nang-tshan*: The five basic Mahāyoga Tantras which are concerned with the five aspects of Buddhahood

A. *Sang-rgyas mnyam-sbyor* (*Sku'i-rgyud dpal sangs-rgyas thams-cad mnyam-par-sbyor-ba*). The Tantra dealing with 'existence' (*sku, kāya*) [1]

B. *gSung thig-le* (*gSung-gi-rgyud zla-gsang thig-le*). The Tantra dealing with 'communication' (*gsung, vāk*) [2]

C. *gSang-ba 'dus-pa* (*Thugs-kyi-rgyud gsang-ba 'dus-pa*). The Tantra dealing with 'noeticness' or 'spirituality' (*thugs, citta*) [3]
D. *dPal-mchog-dang-po* (*Yon-tan-gyi-rgyud dpal-mchog-dang-po*). The Tantra dealing with 'excellent capabilities' (*yon-tan, guṇa*) [4]
E. *Kar-ma ma-le* (*'Phrin-las-kyi-rgyud kar-ma ma-le*). The Tantra dealing with 'activity' or 'performance' (*'phrin-las, karma*) [5]

II. *Rol-pa'i-rgyud-sde-lnga*: The five Tantras which are additions to the Section of Meditative Realization (*sgrub-sde*)
A. (*sKu-*) *gShin-rje skor.* [6] In two divisions:
1. *Kha-thun nag-po'i skor*
2. *gNub-lugs gshin-rje ru-mtshan dmar-po*
B. (*gSung-*) *rTa-mchog rol-pa'i skor* [7]
C. (*Thugs-*) *He-ru-ka rol-pa'i skor* [8]
D. (*Yon-tan-*) *bDud-rtsi rol-pa'i skor* [9]
E. (*'Phrin-las-*) *Phur-pa rol-pa'i skor.* [10] In two divisions:
1. *Rog-lugs* (following the lineage of Rog Shes-rab-'od)
2. *Rong-zom lugs* (following the lineage of Rong-zom)

III. *Spyod-pa'i yan-lag-tu 'gro-ba'i rgyud-sde-lnga* [11–15]: The five Tantras which are additions to the Caryā-yoga (*spyod-pa*). These Tantras deal principally with man's life-world as animated in his being-with others and in the observance and rituals he performs. These Tantras are not included in the bKa'-ma texts and are only to be found in the *rNying-ma'i rgyud-bum*.

IV. *Ma-tshang kaḥ-skong-gi rgyud-sde-gnyis-kyi skor* [16–17]: Two later Tantras (*phyi-ma'i-rgyud*) which contain supplements. These also are not found in the bKa'-ma collection and are to be found in the *rNying-ma'i rgyud-bum*.

V. (*sPyi-rgyud-*) *sGyu-'phrul drva-ba'i skor* [18]. *The Guhya-mūla-garbha-tantra,* (*sGyu-'phrul gsang-ba snying-bo*). This is the root text of the entire Mahāyoga group, and is the most important text for this division.

The *Guhya-mūla-garbha-tantra* has inspired numerous commentaries, including Padmasambhava's *Garland of Views* (*Man-ngag lta-ba'i phreng-ba*), an important commentary by King Indrabodhi, and Vimalamitra's *rDo-rje-sems-dpa' sgyu-'phrul dra-ba gsang-ba snying-po de-kho-na nyid nges-pa'i rgyud-kyi rgyal-po chen-po.* G-yung-ston rDo-rje dPal-bzang, one of the most important rNying-ma masters, wrote a commentary, the *dPal gsang-ba snying-po'i rgyud don-gsal byed me-long*, and Rong-zom Chos-kyi-bzang-po composed two important texts on this Tantra. Both O-rgyan gTer-bdag-gling-pa and his brother Lo-chen Dharma Śrī also wrote major commentaries on the text, as did the Ācārya Nyi-ma Nyi-'od-seng-ge, of the lineage of Vairocana. The omniscient master, Klong-chen-pa wrote three voluminous commentaries contained in the *Mun-sel skor-gsum*: *sPyi-don yid-kyi mun-sel, gZhung-don phyogs-bcu'i mun-sel*, and *bsDus-don ma-rig mun-sel*. Of these, the second is the most lucid interpretation and has remained unsurpassed to this day. Lama Mi-pham then wrote a beautiful commentary to Klong-chen-pa's *gZhung-don phyogs-bcu'i mun-sel.*

The eighteen Mahāyoga Tantras, arising from the totality-field of being (*chos-dbying*), are without origin or cause; they are the transmission of the spontaneously present arising from the extratemporal sphere and finding its way to the first human recipient, King Indrabodhi the Elder. According to the tradition of the Tantras, King Indrabodhi came into the world twenty-eight years after the Buddha's Parinirvāṇa and received the esoteric transmission of the sGyu-'phrul by way of the root Tantric text of the Mahāyoga, the *Guhya-mūla-garbha-tantra*, from the Bodhisattva Vajrapāṇi. Like all Tantras of this transmission, the *Guhya-mūla-garbha-tantra* emphasizes appropriate action (*thabs*) and the Developing Stage (*bskyed-rim*).

The transmission of the sGyu-'phrul occurred through seven successive dreams or visions provided by Vajrapāṇi to King Indrabodhi. At first, Indrabodhi did not understand the text of the *Guhya-mūla-garbha-tantra*, so he went to the Siddha Ku-ku-rā-dza, who understood the text but could not entirely explain its meaning. Ku-ku-rā-dza therefore instructed the king to meditate on Vajrasattva, which he did so earnestly that a vision of the Bodhisattva was perfectly realized in his mind. Thoroughly understanding the text, Indrabodhi became enlightened. The king then imparted the entire body of teachings to Ku-ku-rā-dza, who attained the same realization as Indrabodhi.

Ku-ku-rā-dza then studied the one hundred thousand chapters of the Mahāyoga Tantras, completely comprehending their meanings. During this time, as Vajrasattva psychically tutored him over a period of seven months, Ku-ku-rā-dza intensely practiced the rDo-rje-sems-dpa' Sādhanas. Upon mastering these instructions from Vajrasattva,

Ku-ku-rā-dza

Ku-ku-rā-dza beheld a vision of Vajrapāṇi in which he imparted to him all the instructions concerning the nature of all Dharmas and all teachings.

Ku-ku-rā-dza then retired to the forest where he lived among wild animals, neither being frightened by the most ferocious of them nor arousing fear in even the most timid of the creatures. During the day, he would manifest as master of yoga, and at night, he would appear in various localities throughout the world to teach the Mahāyoga Tantras. In the course of his twelve intensive years of teaching, one hundred thousand of his students achieved enlightenement.

Ku-ku-rā-dza, one of the eighty-four Mahāsiddhas, is the foremost of the five disciples of King Indrabodhi the Elder. The other four disciples are: Li-tsā-bi 'Phrin-las-'brag-pa (dGe-bsnyen Li-tsā-ba Dri-med-grags), Śatraputri, Nāgaputri, and Guhyaputri. Each of these disciples went to a different locality to spread the teachings of the Mahāyoga.

Ku-ku-rā-dza passed the lineage stemming from King Indrabodhi the Elder to Indrabodhi the Middle, and ten thousand of his disciples became enlightened. Then Indrabodhi the Middle imparted the teachings to Siṃha Rā-dza, and one thousand of his disciples attained enlightenment. From Siṃha Rā-dza the lineage was transmitted to Upā Rā-dza, and one hundred of his disciples became enlightened. Upa Rā-dza then taught the princess Gom-ma-devī, and five hundred of her disciples became instantaneously enlightened. This line of transmission then spread to the realms of the Devas, Yakṣas, Nāgas, Rudras, and Man.

After Princess Gom-ma-devī became enlightened, she instructed the highly respected scholar Lalitavajra, (sGeg-pa rDo-rje), who had been teaching at Nālandā for over ten years. He attained *siddhi* and became endowed with psychic abilities—by clearly apprehending the lucient nature of mind, he directly contacted Avalokiteśvara (sPyan-ras-gzigs), the Bodhisattva of Compassion, and Tārā (sGrol-ma), the redemptress. Upon becoming highly learned in the Mahāyoga Tantras, he traveled to parts of Uḍḍiyāna and Kapilavāstu to promulgate the esoteric transmission, and as a result of his accomplishments, the Mahāyoga teachings and practices spread widely in those areas. Later, he received the appellation, sNa-tshogs rDo-rje, because he could disguise himself by manifesting in many forms, such as elephants, horses, children, cows, and peacocks. Lalitavajra wrote a number of expositions and commentaries which are available in their Tibetan translation.

Lalitavajra, himself, never journeyed to Tibet, but transmitted the Mahāyoga lineage to his three major disciples, Vimalamitra, Padmasambhava, and Buddhaguhya, who later journeyed to Tibet and became the principal transmitters of the Mahāyoga in that country. Each of these three enlightened masters contributed his own translation of the *Guhya-mūla-garbha-tantra* to the Tibetan lineage. The three translations which were done at various times differed only slightly in wording.

Padmasambhava, Buddhaguhya, and other masters received the esoteric transmission of the Tantras from the human (e.g., Indrabodhi) or non-human (e.g., Vajrapāṇi) Vidyādharas either directly from the primogenitors of the lineage or indirectly through a lineage of successive masters. The former is known as the Shorter Lineage and may be exemplified by Padmasambhava directly receiving the Mahāyoga transmission from Vajrasattva, and by Buddhaguhya receiving it from Indra-

Lalitavajra

bodhi the Elder. The significance of the Shorter Lineage is very close to the meaning of *rgyal-ba dgongs-brgyud* (*rgyal-ba'i-dgongs-pa'i-rgyud-pa*, Buddha-overall-intentionality) as its method of transmission is beyond explanation or words. The Longer Lineage is exemplified by these masters receiving the lineage through a series of human masters.*

*The chart which appears in the appendix on pg. 327 is not intended to suggest a static order of transmission. The lineages are so interpenetrating that any particular representation of a spiritual lineage simply depends upon which individual masters and teachings are emphasized. A lineage founded upon a particular mode of instruction or Tantric Cycle may follow a genealogy centered around localities, ranging from mountain retreats to a favorite hamlet to large monastic institutions. For example, when specific meditative practices, esoteric empowerments, or Sādhanas are the key to the development of spiritual insight, quiet retreat centers may be most suitable as the center of transmission. The lineages of the Ancient Tantras evolved within varying circumstances as an ongoing quest for life's meaning (*chos*).

According to the traditional view, the Tantric Cycle of the sGyu-'phrul, representing the principal lineage of the Mahāyoga, originated chiefly with Buddhaguhya (Sangs-rgyas gSang-ba) who journeyed to Tibet and resided on the heavenly Mount Kailāsa, which towers over the rim of the turquoise circle of Lake Manasarowar. Having received the Mahāyoga lineage from Lalitavajra, he was the holder of the root text of the sGu-'phrul, the *Guhya-mūla-garbha-tantra.*

Following the principal line of the bKa'-ma transmission, Buddhaguhya was the direct disciple of Sangs-rgyas Ye-shes-zhabs (Buddhajñānapāda); following the line of the Mahāyoga transmission, he received the Longer Lineage of the sGyu-'phrul from Lalitavajra and the Shorter Lineage from King Indrabodhi. The great sLob-dpon Vimalamitra was foremost among Buddhaguhya's five hundred disciples. Vimalamitra also received the esoteric Mahāyoga from Lalitavajra, as well as directly from Mañjuśrī. Vimalamitra then taught the sGyu-'phrul cycle to rMa Rin-chen-mchog, and together they translated the entire text of the *Guhya-mūla-garbha-tantra.* This line of transmission passed through gTsug-ru Rin-chen-gzhon-nu and Gye-re mChog-skyong, who imparted it to Dar-rje dPal-gyi-grags-pa and Zhang rGyal-ba'i-yon-tan. From Zhang onwards, the lineage became known as the bKa' mChims phu-bas, or the 'Lineage of Precepts' (Man-ngag-brgyud). Vimalamitra and rMa Rin-chen-mchog were both prime translators of those texts related to the mDo and Sems divisions of the bKa'-ma transmission.

The lineage of Dar-rje dPal-gyi-grags-pa spread through the central districts of dbUs and gTsang, as well as Khams. Among the followers of the lineage of Dar-rje, two schools are known to have existed: the 'School of dbUs' (*dbUs-lugs-pa*) and the 'School of Khams' (*Khams-lugs-pa*). In Khams, the spiritual descendents of rMa Rin-chen-mchog specialized in the practice of the Vajrakīla Sādhana and transmitted it to Kaḥ-'dam-pa bDe-gshegs, who founded Kaḥ-thog Monastery in 1159 A.D., which was the first major rNying-ma monastery constructed during the later spread.

The Master Vairocana. Vairocana (rNam-par sNags-mdzad) was born of the sPa-gor clan in the fertile valley of sNye-mo Bye-mkhas (sNye-mo rGyal-byed tshal) which lies between rGyal-rtse (Gyantse) and Lha-sa. One of Padmasambhava's three most important disciples, he was also one of the original seven monks (*sad-mi*) ordained by Śāntarakṣita. He received the principal lineage of the Mahāyoga from Buddhaguhya and the esoteric transmission from his teacher Śrī Siṃha.

Vairocana

Vairocana had been sent by Khri-srong-lde'u-btsan to India, where he travelled from place to place receiving the pinnacle of Buddhist teachings from over three hundred prominant masters, scholars, and translators. While in India, he gained a wide reputation as a brilliant young scholar by demonstrating his proficiency in discourse and practice. When the Indian Paṇḍitas realized that he would soon return to Tibet, they felt great compassion for the Tibetans, whom they knew had not fully received the teachings of the Dharma. So they secretly bestowed on Vairocana all the precious root Tantras of the Sems-sde and Klong-sde classes of the Atiyoga rDzogs-chen teachings. Only a few copies of these early Tantras were available, but even these were privately removed from their concealed locations at Bodh Gayā and the surrounding regions, and were given to Vairocana. By the tenth century, these root Tantras were very rare in India, where both the texts and

rGyal-ba-mChog-dbyangs

Oral-transmission were diminishing; they were only to be found at bSam-yas Monastery and the surrounding regions.

During his travels, Vairocana visited many remote areas including Chang-thang, Mongolia, Khotan, and China. Through his innumerable experiences with over twenty-five gifted masters from these regions where Buddhism had spread, Vairocana became the direct recipient of the teachings of the Sūtrayāna, Pāramitāyāna, and Vajrayāna. Upon his return to Tibet, he transmitted what he had learned to the scholars in the court of King Khri-srong-lde'u-btsan; and the most precious and powerful of these teachings he privately imparted to the king and to a few of his most intellectually gifted and trusted nobility.

Vairocana's teachings, however, caused disharmony in the king's court. Some of the nobility were members of an underground nation-

Nam-mkha'i sNying-po

alistic party that had been opposed, from the very beginning, to the introduction of Buddhism into the country. Although not all of these men were ardent followers of Bon, they tended to side with the Bon, not only because it contained the early beliefs and legendary history of Tibet, but also because these men were rapidly losing their ministerial powers as a result of the incoming Dharma. Furthermore, individual jealousies arose among certain members of the nobility and these became directed toward Vairocana.

Damaging rumors about the nature of Vairocana's teachings were circulated from the Indian side by those who were jealous that Vairocana had been given such highly guarded doctrines. A number of counterfeit letters and messages were sent to the court to convince the royalty that Vairocana was not teaching genuine Buddhism and that the

Nam-mkha'i 'Jigs-med

texts and oral instructions which he was importing were apocryphal and contained mystic formulas which could bring much harm to the country.

At this time, Khri-srong-lde'u-btsan had five wives: 'Chims-bza' lHa-mo-btsan, mKhar-chen-bza' mTsho-rgyal, 'Bro-bza' Byang-chub-sgron, Pho-yong-bza' rGyal-mo-btsan, and Tshe-spong-bza' rMa-rgyal mTsho-skar-ma. Tshe-spong-bza', a fervent supporter of Bon, had been infatuated with Vairocana even before his journey to India. Vairocana discouraged her attentions, but one day, she would not leave him alone; she even tried to detain him in a room by locking the door—but, Vairocana managed to escape from her. Spitefully, she accused him of making improper advances. As a result of the malicious slander, the king decided to provide a refuge for the Master in his private chambers.

Cog-ro-klu'i rGyal-mtshan

When he was no longer seen in public, rumors began to spread that even the king had doubts about Vairocana's authenticity and had thus banished Vairocana to East Tibet in accordance with the demands of the nobility. For a while the nobility remained content; however, because of the queen's failure in seducing Vairocana, she began spreading rumors that he was being protected in the chambers of the king, and the king was accused of trickery and of fostering a split in the nobility. A contingency of ministers even secretly plotted to seal Vairocana in a copper casket and cast him into the river. Finally, Khri-srong-lde'u-btsan was pressured into banishing Vairocana, but by this time the Master had slipped away toward East Tibet.

After some time had passed, Khri-srong-lde'u-btsan began to seek out another spiritual guide to his court, who would be acceptable to the

gYu-sgra sNying-po

nobility. At the suggestion of a high priest of the palace, Nyang (Myang) Ting-'dzin-bzang-po, who had the faculty of prescience, the king sent sKa-ba dPal-brtsegs and Cog-ro-klu'i rGyal-mtshan to India to invite Vimalamitra to teach the quintessence of the Buddhadharma to the royal court.

When Vimalamitra arrived in Tibet, Khri-srong-lde'u-btsan was amazed to hear teachings from him that were similar to those delivered by Vairocana. And, when the king showed him the texts which Vairocana had asked the king to secretly safeguard, Vimalamitra affirmed that the texts were not only genuine, but were rare and valuable. Thus, all the doubts which the king had begun to have about Vairocana and his doctrines were put to rest. Meanwhile, Vimalamitra began his teaching appointment with lectures on Vinaya and basic Buddhism, thus

Pal-gyi-senge

remaining conservative and conventional in his teachings so as to restore the nobility's confidence in the Indian Tantric masters.

By this time, Vairocana had passed through Khams in East Tibet and had founded the hermitage at Tsha-ba-rong in the territory of rGyal-rong, on the borders of the Chin-ch'uan region of Szechwan. There he continued the spiritual lineage of Guru Padmasambhava, and received doctrines from followers of the Buddhist lineages which had developed in these regions. Throughout his innumerable travels, Vairocana mastered over three hundred dialects.

While he was in rGyal-rong, Vairocana taught the Inner Tantras to a few disciples, the brightest and most accomplished of whom was rGyal-mo gYu-sgra sNying-po. After instructing gYu-sgra in Sanskrit and the esoteric Tantras, Vairocana asked him to travel to bSam-yas

rMa Rin-chen-mchog

Monastery in central Tibet in order to confirm a report by a wayfarer that only the practice of the Vinaya and study of the Sūtras were being taught there; that the higher Doctrines were not even being discussed.

So in the tattered clothes of a mendicant, gYu-sgra sNying-po reached bSam-yas and found Vimalamitra teaching in the spacious Three-pinnacled Temple. When queried by those near-by, he mumbled three significant Sanskrit words, which startled his questioners, causing them to wonder if this ragged man could be a real scholar. Remaining at the rear of the hall and disdainfully propping his chin on his walking stick, he listened intently to Vimalamitra for some time, gYu-sgra then called out, asking Vimalamitra why he was teaching the Hīnayāna approach, which was not the direct course to full enlightenment.

Vimalamitra pretended not to hear the question but closed his

Sog-po dPal-gyi-ye-shes

class early and asked one of his pupils to seek out the man who had shouted from the rear of the temple. gYu-sgra was found in a public house, drinking *chang* in the company of a merchant, and was invited to come talk with Vimalamitra. When asked who his teacher was, gYu-sgra replied that his teacher was Vairocana of the sPa-gor clan and that he had come from rGyal-rong. Then he asked Vimalamitra why he was teaching inferior doctrines to those with superior minds. Vimalamitra thus realized that gYu-sgra had knowledge of the Tantras, so he sent a messenger to Khri-srong-lde'u-btsan informing him of the meeting.

Vimalamitra, up to that time, had been presenting Khri-srong-lde'u-btsan with a review of the teachings given to the king at an earlier time by Vairocana. Once the king realized this, he saw that despite all the disruption in the court, it had been a mistake to send Vairocana

Rig-'dzin Padma 'phrin-las

away. Therefore, he asked gYu-sgra to return to Vairocana and implore him on behalf of the king to return to his court and continue his teachings. In due time Vairocana returned, and together with the mystic queen Ye-shes mTsho-rgyal, Khri-srong-lde'u-btsan, and Vimalamitra, he spread the exoteric and esoteric doctrines throughout the region.

During his later career, Vairocana taught the expositions on the sGyu-'phrul cycle which he had translated to gNyags Jñānakumāra, who, being a highly acclaimed translator himself, went over the text with Vairocana and rMa Rin-chen-mchog, revising and improving the translation, gNyag Jñānakumāra's chief disciple, Sog-po dPal-gyi-ye-shes, was also a foremost disciple of Vairocana.

gNubs-chen Sangs-rgyas Ye-shes, who lived at the time of King

mNga'-ris Pang-chen

Ral-pa-can (817–836), transmitted these teachings to five principal disciples: So Ye-shes dBang-phyug, who specialized in philosophy; sPa-gor Blong-chen 'Phags-pa, who was a master in the system according to the *'Grel-ṭīkā*; Ngan Yon-tan-mchog, who learned the method of obstructing bleeding; Gru Legs-pa'i-sgron-ma, who learned the system in poetic verses; and Yon-tan rGya-mtsho, his most important spiritual son, to whom he taught the secret and profound precepts until the disciple possessed complete understanding of all the systems of meditation. Yon-tan rGya-mtsho had two principal spiritual sons, Ye-shes rGya-mtsho and mNga'-ris Pang-chen Padma-dbang-gi-rgyal-po.

Nyang Shes-rab-mchog was a disciple of both Yon-tan rGya-mtsho and his spiritual son, Ye-shes rGya-mtsho. He was learned in the

rJe-btsun Seng-ge-dbang-phyug

theory and application of the three classes of the Atiyoga (rDzogs-chen), Sems-sde, Klong-sde, and Man-ngag-gi-sde, and built the Vihāra (gTsug-lag-khang) of gShongs at Ngag. While practicing meditation on the rock of Ha'o-rgol, he had a vision of the Vajrakīla Maṇḍala, and there are many stories about his acquisition of psychic powers (*siddhi*), such as the ability to split a rock with a *vajra*. Nyang Shes-rab-mchog taught Nyang Ye-shes-'byung-gnas of Chos-lung his knowledge of the three classes of the Atiyoga (rDzogs-chen). Most of their followers are called the 'School of Rong', or the 'School of Nyang', after their family names.

Thereafter, Nyang Ye-shes-'byung-gnas taught the venerable master, Zur-po-che the Elder (Zur-chen-pa), who excelled in the practice of the Vajrakīla Sādhana. Together with Zur-chung-pa and sGro-sbug-pa,

Zur-po-che

these important masters are known as the Three Zur (Zur-rnam-pa-gsum).

Zur-po-che. lHa-rje Zur-po-che Shākya-'byung-gnas (b. 954) had numerous teachers. He studied the sGyu-'phrul with Nyang Ye-shes-'byung-gnas of Chos-lung and obtained the bDud-rtsi (one of the eight rNying-ma propitiatory Tantras) from rJe Shākya-mchog of dGe-rong. From gNyan-nag dBang-grags of Yul-gsar, he obtained the secret initiation (*gsang-dbang*) and other inner practices, and from Thod-dkar Nam-mkha'-sde he received the mDo class of rNying-ma Tantras. 'Bre Khro-chung-pa of Upper Nyang instructed him in the Two Truths (*ka-dag* and *lhun-grub*) and the *Lam-rim chen-mo* (a rNying-ma text). In addition, he obtained initiation into the Yang-dag (a rNying-ma pro-

lDang-ma lHun-rgyal

pitiatory Tantra) from Rog Shākya-'byung-gnas of bSam-yas-mChims-phu, as well as much instruction from this famed 'Brog-mi translator.

Zur-chen-pa's major contribution was to classify the Tantras, grouping together the texts with their commentaries, the Tantras with their corresponding Sādhanas, and the Sādhanas with their ritual manuals. He then lectured on these philosophies and meditative practices to large assemblies of disciples, and eventually he established the Vihāra of Ug-pa-lung (the Canyon of Owls). Nearby, he built an elaborate Maṇḍala, erecting the images of the eight deities symbolizing the Eight rNying-ma Heruka Sādhanas (bKa'-brgyad). Thereafter, he received the name Ug-pa-lung-pa.

Once, while traveling up into the mountains, Ug-pa-lung-pa captured a Nāga, who was dwelling in the rock of 'Og-gdong, and

QUEST BOOK SHOP

717 BROADWAY EAST

SEATTLE, WASHINGTON 98102

323-4281

Customer's Order No. ______ Date 10-6 1982

Name ______

Address ______

SOLD BY	CASH	C.O.D.	CHARGE	ON ACCT.	MDSE. RETD.	PAID OUT	
wp							

QUAN.	DESCRIPTION	PRICE	AMOUNT	
	Crystal Mirror III		5	95
	Crystal Mirror II		12	95
			18	90
		tx	1	23
	TOTAL		20	13

501-A ALL claims and returned goods MUST be accompanied by this bill

68346 Rec'd by ______

Flatpakit ® Moore Business Forms, Inc.

Zur-chung-pa

placed it in a jar which he sealed with a piece of leather. Thereafter, the Nāga acted as his attendant and gathered wine from all quarters. During the building and consecration of the Ug-pa-lung Monastery, wine was served to all from this one jar, without exhausting its contents. In addition, Ug-pa-lung-pa borrowed cattle from the villagers and killed them during the consecration ceremony (*sha-ston*), but at the end of the day, he returned alive all the cattle he had borrowed.*

*Before the rise of Buddhism in Tibet, it was customary for animals to be killed to appease the wrath of evil spirits or non-humans (*mi-ma-yin*), who were believed to be the cause of plagues and natural disasters such as earthquakes and floods. After subduing these malignant apparitions by means of the Heruka Sādhanas, Padmasambhava abolished the system of animal sacrifice for which he substituted barley cake offerings called *gtor-ma*.

Kaḥ-'dam-pa-bde-shegs

Zur-chung-pa. Shortly before he passed away, Ug-pa-lung-pa met an elderly beggar monk, accompanied by his son, a young novice monk. When they arrived at the monastery, Zur-po-che asked them their family name. Upon hearing that it was Zur, Zur-po-che instructed the father to leave the young novice in his care and promised to foster the boy, to whom he gave the name Zur-chung-pa, or 'Little Zur'. Later, he became known as Zur-chung Shes-rab-grags-pa (1014–1074).

Under the care of Zur-po-che, Zur-chung-pa's knowledge excelled, for by following his master's wish in every detail, he became capable of benefiting all living beings. Zur-chung-pa attained the ability to raise himself into the air as high as a full-grown palm tree when he walked; when he chanted *mantras*, his voice could be heard echoing throughout the valleys. Whatever he needed always came to him—once when he was tormented by heat while walking in the desert, he was offered wine; when climbing to the summit of a desert mountain, he was offered food. Even at a young age, he could sit in meditation, unmoved and unshakeable as a mountain.

Thus, as a vase is filled to overflowing, Zur-chung-pa came to possess all wisdom. He mastered the Vajrasattva Sādhana of meditation and *mudra* and received a vision of Vajrasattva, through which he understood the nature of all perceptual objects (*snang-bzang-bar-gyi, kṛstnāyatana*) to be of the nature of Vajrasattva. Zur-chung-pa gained the faculty of abiding in the effortless meditation of the Atiyoga (rDzogs-chen); he was matchless in debate, for his mind was not attached to any particular thought. He attracted, by his mere presence, hundreds of devoted followers. In his sixty-first year, having perfected the Atiyoga teachings, Zur-chung-pa passed away.

sGro-sbug-pa. In the same year (1074) that Zur-chung-pa passed away, lHa-rje sGro-sbug-pa was born. In his youth he studied the Dharma, but as his responsibilities increased, he no longer had the time to continue his formal studies. So, he invited learned teachers to his home and thus mastered the Tantras, such as the sGyu-'phrul cycle of the Mahāyoga, the Anuyoga, and the Sems-sde or Mind Section of the Atiyoga, together with their respective precepts, methods of propitiation and ritual, and numerous empowerments. He also studied the system of the Atiyoga with Glan Shākya-byang-chub, and with lHa-rje Sangs-pa Nag-po studied the Tantra and the precepts of the 'later' lineage (*phyi-rgyud*) of the Atiyoga.

lHa-rje sGro-sbug-pa, a manifestation of Vajrapāṇi (the guardian of all the Tantras [Guhya-pati]), was one of the most important links in the propagation of the entire bKa'-ma transmission. He journeyed to the northern region to spread the doctrine of the Tantras to numerous assemblies of disciples, including over one thousand *kalyāṇa-mitra* (spiritual friends) who were already upholders of various philosophical traditions. All these mastered the teachings and spread the Tantras far and wide.

Before his passing, sGro-sbug-pa invited a few of his disciples to the summit of a hill where they performed a ritual offering feast. Then lHa-rje instructed them, "Do not feel sad in my absence, for I shall pass into the realm of the Vidyādharas (Bearers of Pure Awareness) without

sGro-sbug-pa

leaving my physical body behind." Then, after singing a spiritual song (*do-ha*), he raised himself into the air, and finally disappeared in the sky. His followers implored him to return, which he did, but reprimanded them for their dependency on his physical presence. One year later (1134) he passed away.

lHa-rje rJe-ston-gya-nag. Among the disciples of lHa-rje sGro-sbug-pa, the most excellent was lHa-rje rJe-ston-rgya-nag. His grandfather built the Vihāra of sKyi-mkhar, and his elder brothers were sent to study at the philosophical college in upper Nyang (Myang). lHa-rje rGya-nag used to bring them provisions, and while doing so listened to the exposition of the Doctrine. He understood all the teachings after hearing them just one time; studying in this manner for nine years he learned the Prajñāpāramitā, Abhidharma, Nyāya and Pramāṇa, and the Mādhyamika. After that he studied the Tantras with lHa-rje sGro-sbug-pa, remaining with him for eleven years. sGro-sbug-pa bestowed on him all the secret precepts and detailed notes on their branches, and implanted in him effective methods of practice.

lHa-rje lHa-khang-pa. lHa-rje lHa-khang-pa (1094–1149), another disciple of sGro-sbug-pa, was attended by sTon-shāk and Zhig-po, both natives of dbUs, along with about thirty other students of sGro-sbug-pa. Between the ages of twenty-one and thirty, he mastered all the Abhidharma and the texts and Sādhanas of the Mantrayāna, together with their precepts—although he emphasized the Vajrakīla Cycle. He heard the system of the Atiyoga (rDzogs-chen) according to the Khams tradition from Dam-pa sBor-mang and from a Yoginī by the name of Jo-mo Myang-mo. Afterwards, he continued his studies under sGro-sbug-pa until he was forty-one, when sGro-sbug-pa passed away. From that time until he passed away at the age of fifty-six, he labored for the benefit of others.

Zhig-po of dbUs. Zhig-po of dbUs, after living the life of a householder in the valley of Yar-klung, studied under both sGro-sbug-pa and lHa-rje rGya-nag-pa, from whom he learned the three applications of the Developing Stage and Fulfillment Stage as implemented in the Atiyoga (*bskyed-rdzogs*): *bskyed-rim, rdzogs-rim,* and *rdzogs-chen.* He then decided to journey to Nepal, but one night while on the road, it occurred to him that although he possessed considerable knowledge of the Dharma, he had no precepts by which to practice this understanding. Thus, he returned to his teacher, who bestowed on him the precepts of the Precious Oral-tradition (*snyan-brgyud*). Zhig-po then left again for Nepal, and proceeded toward the mountains to practice meditation. He developed the power of passing unhindered through soil, mountains, and rocks. Continuing his meditation, all of a sudden he understood the words of the Doctrines of all the vehicles (*thegs-pa, yāna*) without the omission of a single word. This great master of yoga was endowed with many such outstanding achievements, and furthered numerous disciples in wisdom and virtuous deeds. He passed away at the age of seventy in the year 1195.

Zhig-po bDud-rtsi. The spiritual son of lHa-rje lHa-khang-pa and Zhig-po of dbUs, was the Tulku, Zhig-po bDud-rtsi. At his birth in 1149 at the hermitage of lHa-gdong, a rainbow descended upon him. His father, Sangs-rgyas Dags-chung, a well-known master of the Mahāyoga, died when Zhig-po was two, but before he died, he prophesied that his son would become responsible for the welfare of all living beings. When Zhig-po was thirteen, he gave away all his clothes to a wretched beggar, and at sixteen he took up residence with his uncle, Dam-pa Se-brag-pa, who had been a student of lHa-rje lHa-khang-pa. From his uncle, he heard the exposition of the Atiyoga according to the method of Rong. Zhig-po then studied with another of Se-brag-pa's teachers, Yon-tan-bzungs of sKyil-mkhar-lha-khang Monastery, who was the cousin of rGya-nag-pa and who succeeded him as Abbot of sKyil-mkhar-lha-khang. Zhig-po stayed with Yon-tan-gzungs and mastered the twenty-four great Tantras of the Mind Section (Sems-sde) of the Atiyoga, and followed this system in all his studies and meditation practices.

At thirty Zhig-po left his teacher and assumed the leadership of the hermitages of Se-sbrag, Chos-ldings, and others. His fortune increased; his mind shone like the sky and his compassion like the sun and moon, and he was surrounded by a multitude of disciples. Not once did he break his devotion to his teacher, for as he used to say, "Whenever I left the presence of my teacher, I was unable to take leave without placing his foot on my head." He gave generous offerings of religious and worldly gifts and presented to his teacher seventeen copies of Sūtras, such as the three *Prajñāpāramitās* (*rGyas-'bring-rnam-gsum*), and others embossed in gold. As his generosity and insight increased, so did his mind become liberated. Having found methods of concentration based on the teachings of the Atiyoga, he became able to pass unhindered through mountains and rocks. Other stories tell of his faculty of prescience, his vanishing into a boulder while residing at the monastery of Da-lung of gZad-phu, and his passing unhindered through a mud wall on the Srin-po-ri River.

Zhig-po bDud-rtsi also visited the districts nestled between the snow-capped peaks to the north; he performed numberless deeds for the benefit of the Dharma, assisting with donations of materials used in the building of temples and healing the sick. He assisted the great Tripiṭaka masters, learned in the Sūtras and Tantras; he became the fulfillment of all the needs of numerous persons from India, China, Nepal, and other countries, who had gathered round him. In this way, he was similar to the Wish-fulfilling Gem (Cintāmaṇi).

Zhig-po bDud-rtsi passed away at the Monastery of rGya-ra Gadlogs of gSang-phu in the year 1199. During the funeral rites, the earth tremored and a lotus flower appeared in the sacred water placed before his body, radiating rainbow light for three days.

rTa-ston Jo-yes. Among Zhig-po's disciples, the one who obtained the essence of his knowledge was rTa-ston Jo-yes (1163–1230). His father, rTa-ston Jo-'bum, had received teachings as a youth, and had possessed trustworthy attendants and extensive landed property. One of Jo-'bum's principal teachers was Phag-mo-grub-pa. Feeling sadness for the ways of the world, he sought out the doctrines of the Old Tantras and especially became learned in the basic text of the Atiyoga (rDzogs-chen), together with its oral precepts.

From his father and others rTa-ston Jo-yes received initiations into the Saṃvara system, sGyu-'phrul, the basic text of the sKor method of the Atiyoga, the method of the Mahāmudrā system (Phyag-rgya chen-mo), the Hevajra system, the 'Path and Fruit' (Lam-'bras), and the three cycles of Zhi-byed. He studied under astute teachers who imparted to him precious doctrines, rites of propitiation, and methods of meditative contemplation. At the age of twenty-four, he left lower Ngams-shod, and, upon hearing the cycle of Vajrakīla, he practiced vigorous meditation.

At the age of twenty-five, rTa-ston Jo-yes met Zhig-po bDud-rtsi and stayed with the master for eleven years without parting from him for even a day. Recounting the effect his teacher had upon him, he once said, "Though the Dharmkāya was present in me, I had not recognized it. From eternity the nature of illusion is inconceivable. By reason of the awakening of my former deeds and through accumulated merit, I had the opportunity of meeting a perfect teacher, and of studying a little of the profound Tantric teachings. All my doubts concerning the nature of the Mind were removed in the presence of Zhig-po, who bestowed on me profound precepts handed down through four Spiritual Lineages, and which reflected the essence of the mind of this precious and matchless teacher."*

Throughout all his life he felt deep devotion towards his teacher, and never grew tired of serving him and his monastery. He was endowed with great compassion, and without thinking about his personal benefit, he labored continually for the welfare of beings. In whatever he did, he was a king of yogins (*rtogs-ldan*), never sepa-

---

*George N. Roerich, *The Blue Annals*, I., p. 145f. (Delhi: Motilal Banarsidass, 1976).

rate from the direct perception of the Ultimate Essence (*chos-nyid-kyi rtogs-pa*).

Upon the death of his teacher, rTa-ston Jo-yes renounced his worldly possessions. On four occasions he held religious assemblies in honor of Zhig-po bDud-rtsi; he recorded all the precepts and advice of his teacher, which greatly benefitted later followers. Altogether there were thirteen teachers under whom he studied. Among them were six mūla-gurus (*rtsa-ba'i bla-ma*), and among these, three were of particular benefit to him, but the greatest and matchless one was Zhig-po Rin-po-che.

rTa-ston Jo-yes desired to behold the Dharma with the same clarity as his teacher Zhig-po, so he decided to practice his teachings in a country of forests and mountain valleys, unseen and unheard of by men. However, while he was engaged in casting a copper image of Avalokiteśvara in a foundry at Zung-mkhar, a yogic insight was born in him, and he suddenly obtained the extraordinary perception that all objective constituents belong to the sphere of the Absolute (*chos-nyid, dharmatā*). From that time onward, he visited remote kingdoms and labored extensively for the welfare of all beings, until he passed away at the age of sixty-eight.

gYung-ston-pa. Another significant line of the sGyu-'phrul arose with two disciples of the master sGro-sbug-pa, namely gTsang-pa Byi-ston and sGong-dri-ngas-pa Nye-ston Chos-kyi-seng-ge, who in turn passed the lineage on to gTsang-nag 'Od-'bar, Mes-ston-mgon-po, Bla-ma Sro, Zur Byams-pa-seng-ge, and then conjointly to 'Jam-dbyangs bSam-grub-rdo-rje (1295–1376) and gYung-ston-pa (1284–1365).

At an early age gYung-ston-pa (gYung-ston rDo-rje-dpal) was recognized for his brilliant mind, and each year his understanding of the Tantras grew substantially. After mastering the *Abhidharma-samuccaya* (*mNgon-pa kun-las btus-pa*), he studied the cycle of Yamantaka (gShin-rje) and the method of *yantra* (*'khrul-khor*). As a result of this, his psychic abilities magnified. While gYung-ston-pa was still in his youth, the emperor of China summoned him in order to produce rain for the drought-stricken villagers. Upon arriving in China, gYung-ston-pa prayed to the Triple Gem and rain began to fall. The emperor was greatly pleased and gave him many valuable gifts. Returning to Tibet, he offered all the gifts which he received to his teacher and monastic community. Several renowed teachers subsequently bestowed many precepts and doctrines upon him. Two of his principal teachers at this

gYung-ston-pa

time were Rang-'byung rDo-rje (1284–1339), who was an important rNying-ma gTer-ston, and Bu-ston Rin-po-che (Bu-ston Rin-chen-grub-pa, 1290–1364) the learned scholar of the bKa'-gdams-pa. After gaining much insight into the Kālacakra and rDzogs-pa-chen-po, gYung-ston-pa traveled widely, transmitting the Dharma for the benefit of others. During his travels, he performed many wondrous acts, and often delineated the difference between the path to Buddhahood as described in the Sūtras and that described in the Tantras.

The Spiritual Line of gYung-ston-pa. After the time of gYung-ston-pa, the lineages of the Mahāyāna became very complex, with multitudinous branches and arteries. To trace all the various branches is beyond the scope of this brief summary of the major rNying-ma lineages. However, a few other major followers of the sGyu-'phrul particularly stand out during the period preceding Klong-chen-rab-'byams-pa (1308–1363) and 'Gos lo-tsā-ba gZhon-nu-dpal (1392–1481).

The principal disciple of the master gYung-ston-pa was gYag-ston-pang-chen rDo-rje-dpal, whose student was 'Jam-dbyangs bSam-grub rDo-rje (1295–1376). Sam-grub rDo-rje also received instruction from Zur Byams-pa-seng-ge and became outstanding in his knowledge of the sGyu-'phrul. He was taught by many of the masters of the direct lineage of Ug-pa-lung-pa, or the lineage following the Master Zur-chen-pa. He then concentrated his study on the sNying-thig teachings of the Atiyoga (rDzogs-chen). Because of his highly refined mental development and meditative concentration, he gained the faculty of visiting Buddha-realms. On his deathbed, he said to his foremost disciple that he was going to Sukhāvatī Heaven (bDe-ba-can, the Western paradise of Amitābha Buddha) and the disciple would join him there when he passed away, also at the age of eighty-two.

The receiver of this prophecy was Shangs-pa Kun-mkhyen, to whom Sam-grub rDo-rje imparted all of his major lineages and teachings. This disciple was also known as Sangs-rgyas Rin-chen rGyal-mtshan dPal-bzang-po (1350–1431). At the age of six, Sangs-rgyas Rin-chen memorized the entire text of the commentary to the *Guhya-mūla-garbha-tantra*. But when he came into the presence of a high lama, he forgot it. He again memorized the Tantra when he was eight. A year later, after studying ritual ceremony, his intrinsic understanding of the Dharma blossomed, and he began to act as a teacher and bestow empowerments.

Sangs-rgyas Rin-chen then requested his father that he be allowed to study the Tantras of the gSar-ma class, but his father asked him, as he was the only son, to first marry and have children before taking monastic vows. So, he married at the age of twenty-four and his wife bore him six sons and two daughters. As he spent many years rearing his family, he was not able to be ordained until he was fifty-six. In his later life he wrote many commentaries to the Tantras, composed ritual texts, and taught others the methods of empowerment, including the *Yamantaka, Yang-bdag*, and *Vajrakīla* empowerments. Sangs-rgyas Rin-chen could recite by memory over forty texts of the Mahāyoga. For many years his principal teachers were Myang-nag mDo-po, a disciple of sGro-sbug-pa, and Myang's disciple, lHa-rje mNga'-seng-ge. Sangs-rgyas Rin-chen's chief disciple was the illustrious Chos-kyi-seng-ge.

Chos-kyi-seng-ge. Also known as rNgog-thog-pa, Chos-kyi-seng-ge became very learned and attained spiritual realization. Once when

Rig-'dzin Kumarāja

he visited the Mongolian Emperor Se-chen (Qubilai), the emperor behaved towards him in such a tyrannical manner that he ordered him to be sealed inside a Stūpa. At the end of a year when the door of the Stūpa was opened, they found Chos-kyi-seng-ge inside, transformed into an image of Vajrakīla (rDo-rje Phur-bu). This caused such amazement that the emperor bestowed on him large gifts of costly silks and other precious materials.

Chos-kyi-seng-ge also received the spiritual lineage of Guru Padmasambhava and his consort Ye-shes-mTsho-rgyal through a succession of twelve intermediate masters.* This lineage, passing through Chos-

*This succession includes: 'Bre A-tsar Sa-le, Lang-lab Byang-chub rDo-rje, sNa-nam Tshul-khrims-shes-rab, Khyung-po 'Chal-chen, Chal-chung, Blo-gros rGyal-mtshan, Ya-'brog-pa Gu-rub-yang-dag, 'Gos-ston Byang-'bar, Khyung-po-seng-ge, Khyung-po-khro-bo, and gNyal-ston-grags.

Rog Shes-rab-'od

kyi-seng-ge, continued its line of transmission through a succession of more than eight masters, whereupon it spread throughout the central provinces and East Tibet.

sMan-lung Shākya-'od, whose secret name was Mi-bskyod rDo-rje, studied the sGyu-'phrul and the Anuyoga (mDo) systems under Chos-kyi-seng-ge. He composed numerous texts and summaries, propagated the doctrine in Khams, and had a large following.

'Gos lo-tsā-ba gZhon-nu-dpal (1392–1481) received this spiritual lineage through the two masters, Zhang-mkhar-ba bSod-nams-bzang-po, and his disciple, the Ācārya bDag-nyid-chen-po bKra-shis-rgya-mtsho.

Rog Shes-rab-'od. The life of Rog Shes-rab-'od, another prominent figure in both the Mahāyoga (sGyu-'phrul) and the Anuyoga (mDo) lineages, exemplifies how magnificently interwoven the lineages of the Ancient Tantras became during the period of the later spread (*phyi-dar*). He received the sGyu-'phrul and mDo systems according to the method of So, Zur, and sKyo. His teachers in these systems are innumerable, many coming from the lineage of Zhig-po. He was also the receiver of countless precepts and esoteric instructions contained within the numerous spiritual transmissions under the gCod and Zhi-byed systems. Both of these systems contain lineages that weave in and out of the major esoteric lineages of the rNying-ma-pa.

Recognized by his contemporaries as a great scholar, Rog Shes-rab-'od composed an abridgement of the basic text of the 'Path and Fruit' (Lam-'bras) doctrine of the Mahāyoga system and a few important commentaries on the *Guhya-mūla-garbha-tantra* related texts. His expositions greatly facilitated the teachings of the Tantras and brought about a better understanding of their various empowerments. His spiritual line became known as the Lineage of Rog.

Klong-chen-rab-'byams-pa. The omniscient master, Klong-chen-rab-'byams-pa (b. 1308) studied the Mahāyoga (sGyu-'phrul) and Anuyoga (mDo) systems from the lineage of Rog at the hamlet of Dan-bag near the great Monastery of 'Bras-spungs near Lha-sa. His father was a member of the direct line of the lineage of Rog. Klong-chen-pa also received the *Guhya-mūla-garbha-tantra* from the lineage of the most learned Rong-zom Mahāpaṇḍita. Klong-chen-pa composed two works on these systems, the *sPyi'i Khog-dbub-pa*, and the *rGyud-kyi-rnam-bshad* (known as the *Klong-chen-pa'i gSang-snying 'grel-pa*), basing their orientation on the precepts of the sNying-thig system.

Also in the fourteenth century, Zhang-btsun Lo-tsā-ba discovered the original manuscript of the *Guhya-mūla-garbha-tantra* in Padmasambhava's own handwriting at bSam-yas Monastery. After it was shown to Sa-skya Paṇḍita and Bu-ston Rin-po-che, the adherents of the New Tantrism increased their respect for the Mahāyoga transmission.

The Later Mahāyoga Transmission. Ten distinctive Mahāyoga lineages unfolded out of the rich soil of the Ancient Ones cultivated by the masters Padmasambhava, Vimalamitra, and Vairocana. The root lineages which pass through these three masters strengthened and multiplied with the great pillars known as So, Zur, gNubs, gNyags, rMa, and Rong: So Ye-shes dBang-phyug, Zur Shākya-'byung-nas, gNubs-chen Sangs-rgyas Ye-shes, gNyags Jñānakumāra, rMa Rin-chen-mchog, and Ron-zom Chos-kyi-bzang-po.

The Mahāyoga is also distinguished by three significant stages of transmission, known as the bKa' mChims-phu-ma, because they found their common origin at mChims-phu retreat center, which was located in a mountainous canyon several miles from bSam-yas Monastery. These three important stages of transmission were kindled by the masters gNyags Jñānakumāra (gNyags dZana-kumara), gNubs-chen Sangs-rgyas Ye-shes, and Zur-po-che Shākya-'byung-gnas.

One of the principal preservers of the Mahāyoga texts, commentaries, and spiritual lineages in the more recent times was Kaḥ-thog Siddha. The recipient of a long line of distinguished masters of the Mahāyoga, he obtained full mastery of the over one hundred texts and commentaries of the Mahāyoga, some of which were written by Klong-chen-rab-'byams-pa.

Kaḥ-thog Siddha Chos-kyi-rgya-mtsho was a disciple of the First 'Jam-dbyangs-mKhyen-brtse'i-dbang-po (b. 1819) and a teacher to his incarnation, mKhyen-brtse'i-chos-kyi-blo-gros (the Second 'Jam-dbyangs-mKhyen-brtse'i-dbang-po, b. 1896). Kaḥ-thog Siddha was very essential to the transmission of rNying-ma lineages. Approximately eighty different disciple lineages pass through him, most of which were received by the Second 'Jam-dbyangs mKhyen-brtse'i-dbang-po.

Through the Mahāyoga lineage of Kaḥ-'dam-pa bDe-gshegs, over the course of several centuries some one hundred thousand followers of the Mahāyoga achieved the miraculous rainbow body (*'ja'-lus*), a phenomena which stands as a testimony to their enlightenment. This mystical occurrence, in which the bodily substance of the luminary is transformed into multi-hued light, has been observed to this day. For the practitioner of the Inner Tantras, particularly the Atiyoga sNying-thig, the moment of physical death is the climax of life. It is at this moment when the mind, totally liberated and free, experiences a horizon of beauty containing an infinite wealth of possibilities in what lies beyond.

The Lineage of the Anuyoga

The lineage of the mDo, or the Anuyoga (Lung-anuyoga'i-theg-pa), was propagated by Vajrapāṇi on the summit of mount Malaya to an assembly of Vidyādharas (Rig-'dzin). After this, the Anuyoga was transmitted from mouth-to-ear among the Bodhisattvas of the earth. Through the blessings of Vajrapāṇi, King rGyal-po-rā-dza had seven visions which initiated him into the meaning of the sacred texts of the

Anuyoga. Altogether, there are five principal Anuyoga texts, the most important are the two root texts, the *Mūla-tantra Kun-'dus rig-pa'i mdo* and the *bShad-rgyud mDo-dgongs-pa 'dus-pa*. The Vidyādhara, dGe-bsnyen Li-tsā-bi Dri-med-grags, after initiating the king into the essential teachings of the doctrine, fully explained its meaning orally. The king then preached this doctrine to his son Indrabodhi the Younger and, through a succession of several teachers, the texts eventually were transmitted to Dharmabodhi (Bodhidharma), and to Vasudhara. Eventually, they found their way to the territory of Bru-sha (Turkestan), where they were honored by the Abbot Ru-che bTsan-skyes.

The succession of teachers stemming from Indrabodhi begins with Ku-ku-rā-dza, who also received the lineage from the master through Na-ga-pu-tri and Ga-ya-su-tri. Ku-ku-rā-dza in turn gave the lineage to Ro-langs-bde-ba (Vetālakṣema), whose incarnation was the Nirmāṇakāya manifestation, dGa'-rab rDo-rje. After teaching a high spiritual attainment (*siddhi*), Ro-lang-bde-ba edited the *rNal-'byor-rig-pa'i-nyi-ma* which teaches the profound path of the Buddha's Sūtras (*mdo'i-zab-lam*). His two disciples were Vajrahāsta (rDo-rje-bzhad-pa) and Prabhahasti (Pra-ba-ha-sti), king of Za-hor. After Prabhahasti received an empowerment (*dbang-bskur*) from his teacher at the banks of the River Sindhu, he entered the monastic order, receiving the name Shākya-'od. Of his students, Shākya-'od the younger, Shākya-bshes-gnyen, and Shākya-seng-ge are the most noteworthy. Shākya-bshes-gnyen, who attained a vast knowledge of the Tantras, composed a commentary on the *'Dus-pa'i-mdo*, which is also called the *Ko-sa-la'i-rgyan* because it came from the country of Kosala.

Dhanarakṣita learned the Sūtras from his teacher, Shākya-bshes-gnyen, and taught them to Hūṃkara (rDo-rje Hum-mdzad in the Diamond-cavern of Padmasambhava. Dhanarakṣita then wrote one hundred and seven commentaries to the *Mūla-tantra* (*rTsa-rgyud*) as well as the *rNal-'byor-pa'i sgron-ma* and other texts. After receiving instructions from Ga-ga-si-dhi in the cavern of the Asuras on the border between India and Persia, Hūṃkara became a Vidyādhara. Sustaining himself by practicing a technique called 'taking the essential juices' (*bcud-len*); he eventually became invisible.

Hūṃkara's two primary disciples were Sthiramati and Sukhaprasanna (bDe-ba-gsal-mdzad). Sukhaprasanna wrote a number of works, including the *mDo'i yig-sna bco-brgyad-dang rnal-'byor-gyi rim-pa theg-chen sgron-ma*. He had four principal disciples to whom he imparted the teachings: Dharmabodhi of Magadha who became a master of the Sūtras (mDo'i-mkhan-po) and composed *mDo'i-dob-bsdu-ba, Shes-rab sgron-ma*, and *bKol-mdo*; Dharmarājapāla, who became the Abbot (*mKhan-po*) of Nālandā University and received the oral explanation of the Tantras from bDe-ba-gsal-mdzad; Vasudhara, the king of Nepal who also received teachings from Dharmarakṣita; and gTsug-lag-dpal-dge. bDe-ba-gsal-mdzad imparted to these four disciples, the three aspects of the tradition: the Initiation (*dbang-bka'*), the Explanation (*bshad-bka'*), and the Guidance (*man-ngag-bka'*).

The Upādhayāya from Bru-sha, Ru-she bTsan-skyes, invited Dhanarakṣita to translate the *mDo-dgnogs-pa 'dus-pa'i mdo*. However, he was unable to complete his translation, and, returning to Nepal, entreated Vasudhara and Dharmabodhi to travel to Bru-sha to translate this work under the sponsorship of the Upādhyāya.*

gNubs-chen Sangs-rgyas Ye-shes, who wrote a commentary on this work, was unsurpassed in spreading the Anuyoga throughout Tibet. He received the lineage of mDo principally from Dharmabodhi, Vasudhara, and Ru-she bTsan-skyes. Of his many writings, the one that stands foremost is his instruction concerning the Atiyoga which is called the *bSam-gtan-mig-sgron*. The principal disciples of gNubs-chen Sangs-rgyas Ye-shes were sPa-gor Blon-chen-'phags-pa, Gru Legs-pa'i-sgron-ma, Ngan Yon-tan-mchog, So Ye-shes dBang-phyug, and Khu-lung-pa Yon-tan rGya-mtsho. Yon-tan rGya-mtsho was the most noted of gNubs-chen's disciples, and transmitted the lineage to his son Ye-shes rGya-mtsho.

This lineage has continued down to such notables as the Three Zur (*Zur-rnam-pa-gsum*), Mar-pa Lo-tsā-ba (1012–1096), Chos-kyi-seng-ge, and the brilliant O-rgyan gTer-bdag-gling-pa ('Gyur-med rDo-rje). This line of transmission has merged in many places with the Lineage of the *Guhya-mūla-garbha-tantra* (Mahāyoga).

One particular lineage which is now rare, existed during the time of gNubs-chen Sangs-rgyas Ye-shes who received it from Padmasambhava through the transmission of the bKa' mChims-phu-ma. This lineage textually bases itself on the commentary gNubs-chen wrote on the *bShad-rgyud mDo-dgongs-pa 'dus-pa* dictated to him by Padmasambhava. This is a very essential practice-oriented text for the Anuyoga. During the long interim between gNubs-chen, and Kaḥ-thog Kaḥ-

*Upādhāyas are teachers instituted within the Saṅgha to guide new monks in manners and decorum.

dam-pa bDe-gshegs, the lineage of this practice-oriented instruction cannot be traced.

Kaḥ-thog Siddha recovered this text in the nineteenth century in an extraordinary way. He was able to prefectly reconstruct this important commentary through his intent contemplation on a statue of sNubs-chen Sangs-rgyas Ye-shes which contained the precious bodily relics of the master. It is said that the statue, having become mystically animated, transmitted, from mouth to ear, the entire contents of the text to Kaḥ-thog Siddha, who then wrote it down. mKhan-chen Legs-bshad-'byor-ldan received this lineage of explanation from Kaḥ-thog Siddha and passed it on to mKhan-po Thub-dga' of dPal-sprul Rinpoche's lineage. He in turn imparted it to his niece, lHan-du-tsha-po who transmitted it to Zhe-chen Kong-sprul (Padma-dri-med-legs-pa'i-blo-gros, b. 1901).

gNubs-chen Sangs-rgyas Ye-shes. gNubs-chen Sangs-rgyas Ye-shes is an essential link in the preservation of the rNying-ma lineages of Oral-transmission and explanation of the esoteric treatises. Essentially, the entire transmission of bKa'-ma pass through him or his family-clan members. gNubs-chen Sangs-rgyas Ye-shes not only was an important disciple of Padmasambhava, but learned numerous teachings and practices from Guru Rinpoche's mystic consort, Ye-shes mTsho-rgyal, who lived with gNubs-chen's family-clan for a few years during Glang Dar-ma's reign of suppression. gNubs-chen is said to have lived for a period covering nearly three generations, perhaps one hundred and ten years.

During the reign of King Ral-pa-can, there were two types of Saṅgha—the Red Saṅgha and the White Saṅgha. The Red Saṅgha were fully ordained monks who wore red robes in formal assemblies; while the White Saṅgha were generally yogis or householders who wore white robes in formal assembly and often had long hair. Most of the disciples of Padmasambhava were members of the family-clan lineage of the White Saṅgha. For the rNying-ma-pa, it was not essential to become a monk and take the full Vinaya refuge, for they realized that spiritual excellence and exemplary compassion can be practiced in the milieu of everyday society and are not restricted to the cloistered halls of a monastery.

Because of Ral-pa-can's generous support of the Buddhist community, and because the king felt it would be beneficial to the people if the power of the throne were subsumed under the auspices of religious

gNubs-chen Sangs-rgyas Ye-shes

authority, the Dharma became the mandate for social action. However, his malicious half-brother, Glang Dar-ma, so dispised the king's support of the Saṅgha that he had Ral-pa-can assassinated. Glang Dar-ma then secured power by playing up to the Bon-po priests and shamans, who from ancient times, accepted the role of religious vassals to the king. In this way, Glang Dar-ma reestablished for a time the ancient hierarchy of king, priest, and shaman in its tripartite ruling body. This malevolent usurper then demonstrated his hatred and resentment towards Buddhism and the monastic community; whenever he came upon a Buddhist statue, he commanded it to speak, and if it failed to do so, he ordered a nose or finger to be removed. These partially defaced statues existed for many centuries in the vicinity of central Lhasa, artifacts of this dark period in the history of the Dharma in Tibet. Glang Dar-ma ordered the execution of any monk, or member of the Red Saṅgha, who refused to conform to his edicts, However, he usually did not harm the White Saṅgha, for he identified them as householders, not monks.

But on one occasion Glang Dar-ma journeyed well beyond the outskirts of the city to seek out gNubs-chen Sangs-rgyas Ye-shes, who was the head of a distinguished group of White Saṅgha. The king wished to investigate certain rumors that a very large and thriving Saṅgha community was preserving the sacred texts and Oral-transmission of the Dharma. Upon the king's arrival at the retreat center, gNubs-chen approached him without hesitation, and pointing in the direction of the king, out burst a flash of lightening from the tip of his finger. Immediately there appeared a huge scorpion the size of a yak. This display of magic so frightened the king that he promised not to make any further trouble for gNubs-chen's lay-community. Glang Dar-ma then instituted an edict that no one was to torment or harm the community of gNubs.

During this period, a major number of the early translations of texts were saved by gNubs-chen Sangs-rgyas Ye-shes and his followers. This outstanding Siddha, scholar, and translator of the esoteric doctrines stemming from Padmasambhava marks the end of the early spread of the Dharma in Tibet. It was the successive generations of gNubs-chen's family-clan lineage of Siddhas, yogis, scholars, contemplatives, and lay followers who preserved the oral transmission and texts during the nearly half a century haitus of Buddhist suppression in Tibet.

Rong-zom Mahāpaṇḍita. Rong-zom Chos-kyi-bzang-po (1012–1088) was the recipient of numerous secret instructions, including the secret precepts of Padmasambhava transmitted through the spiritual lineage of sNa-nam rDo-rje-bdud-'joms and mKhar-chen dPal-gyi-dbang-phyug (disciples of Padmasambhava), and their disciples who taught the precepts to Rong-zom's father, Rong-ban Rin-chen-tshul-krims. Rong-zom also received the teachings of the lineage which originated with Vairocana, beginning with rGyal-mo gYu-sgra sNying-po and continuing in the line of: Bla-chen-po dGongs-pa-gsal, Grum-shing-gla-can, sNubs dPa'-brtan, Ya-zi Bon-ston, and finally to Rong-zom Chos-kyi-bzang-po. This is one of the Lineages of the 'Mind Section' (Sems-sde) of the Atiyoga teachings.

Rong-zom, who was born during the time of Zur-chung-pa (1014–1074) in the same valley of Khungs-rong on the border of lower gTsang, was an incarnation of a learned scholar named Ācārya Smṛti-

Rong-zom Chos-kyi-bzang-po

jñānakīrti who had come to Khams some years before, composed several treatises on grammar, and translated several Tantras and numerous Tantric commentaries. Some regarded Rong-zom as an emanation of the Buddha, others, of Mañjuśrī. Atīśa met Rong-zom shortly after arriving in Tibet, and saw in his features the manifestation of his Indian guru, Nag-po-pa. Rong-zom Chos-kyi-bzang-po was considered by all a master and scholar of unparalleled depth and insight.

It is said that, while playing with other children, he would often recite by heart the teachings of his guru, 'Gar-ston Tshul-khrims-bzang-po, after having heard them only once. In his childhood, he was attracted to every learned teacher he met, and he learned to converse in several dialects. He studied all branches of knowledge and learned the contents of each text at a single reading. In this manner, he mastered the

Rang-'byung rDo-rje

Sūtras, Śāstras, and Tantras, being able to quote difficult texts without omitting a word. Well-versed in treatises on logic, medicine, poetry, the worldly and spiritual sciences, Sanskrit, and the science of linguistics, he also established a system of suitable Tibetan translations of many technical terms that occurred in the scholastic literature.

In his own writings, Rong-zom never contradicted the sacred texts, reason, or the explanations given him by his teachers, and he was considered irrefutable by other famous scholars of his time. A compassionate and effective teacher, Rong-zom guided many students in the methods and practices of the Vajrayāna and effected in them the subtle discoveries that lead to realization of the Mantrayāna path. Thus, it was said, anyone who followed his guidance would surely be led to the most supreme teachings.

Many lo-tsā-bas and scholars attended Rong-zom's classes and considered him to be a true luminary. Once, while reading the text of the *sGyu-'phrul gsang-ba snying-po* (*Guhya-mūla-garbha-tantra*) the root text of the Mahāyoga, Rong-zom said: "If we had the Sanskrit text to consult, this passage should be read thus. . . . But since none is available, we are helpless." Go-rub Lo-tsā-ba sGe-slong Chos-kyi-shes-rab remembered these words, and later acquired the Sanskrit text. Upon studying it, he discovered that the text perfectly agreed with the interpretations of the master Rong-zom. Mar-pa Lo-tsā-ba Chos-kyi dBang-phyug (1012–1096) was also a prominent student of Rong-zom.

In fulfillment of his teacher's wishes, Rong-zom composed three texts containing the secret precepts of his spiritual preceptors. He also composed various treatises, including the "Precepts on the Theory and Meditative Practice of the All-Perfect Doctrine" (*rDzogs-pa-chen-po'i lta-sgom man-ngag*), several commentaries on the outer Tantras, and translations of new Indian Tantric texts.

During this period there was a doctrinal debate which was attended by scholars from the four districts of Tibet. Many of these teachers held the opinion that it was improper for persons born in Tibet to compose treatises. But after they had carefully examined Rong-zom's "An Introduction to the System of the Mahāyoga," and had debated the subject matter with him, they became amazed at his erudition and natural intelligence and listened intently to his expositions of the precepts.

Rong-zom received another Atiyoga lineage through a Siddha named A-ro Ye-shes-byung-gnas, who possessed the secret precepts of the seventh link in the chain of the Indian lineage, as well as the precepts of the seventh link of the Chinese lineage of Hwa-shang. This Siddha passed this system on to Cog-ro Zangs-dkar-mdzod-khur and to Ya-zi Bon-ston; these two in turn taught it to Rong-zom. Taken together, this lineage is called the "Lineage of the All-perfect Doctrine (*rDzogs-chen*) according to the Khams method."

Rong-zom also received teachings from the lineage of Vimalamitra, who taught the secret precepts to Nyang Ting-nge-dzin bzang-po, as well as to rMa Rin-chen-mchog and gNyags Jñānakumāra. These two transmitted them through Khu Byang-chub-'od and Khyung-po dByig-'od to Rong-zom Chos-kyi-bzang-po. Thus, three hundred years after the arrival of Guru Rinpoche in Tibet, all the rNying-ma lineages, traditions, and influences again merged in Rong-zom Chos-kyi-bzang-po, and from him flowed the quintessence of the Three Inner Tantras (*nang-rgyud-sde-gsum*) according to the Khams Tradition.

The Mind Section (Sems-sde) of the Atiyoga

The Mind Section (Sems-sde) of the Atiyoga teachings deals with the realization of the true nature of the mind. Sems-sde has eighteen different Tantras, initiations, Sādhanas, and stages of realization through practice. Five precepts of this section originated with Vimalamitra and thirteen with Vairocana. Vairocana is thus the central figure in this transmission, as well as in the transmission of the 'Unending Experience of Being' (Klong-sde). These teachings were prominent among the Zur lineage (Zur-lugs-pa) as transmitted through a successive lineage stemming from Padmasambhava's disciples. Some of these teachings also come from India through direct transmissions between teacher and disciple.

In order to receive the transmission of the Atiyoga (rDzogs-chen) from Śrī Siṃha, Vairocana was sent by King Khri-srong-lde'u-btsan to Śrī Siṃha's home in the sandlewood forest near Dhanakośa Lake in Uḍḍiyāna. After displaying his various psychic powers to the Yoginī who was guarding Śrī Siṃha's nine-storied pagoda, Vairocana was granted admittance. Presenting numerous gifts, he begged to be instructed in the Higher Tantras; Śrī Siṃha, after due consideration, agreed to explain the him the secret, sealed, and profound aspects of the doctrine. But, because the king of that region had forbidden the spread of such teachings at the threat of death, Śrī Siṃha suggested that Vairocana study the accepted philosophical doctrines with the other Paṇḍitas during the day and study Atiyoga secretly with him at night. Śrī Siṃha wrote the Atiyoga teachings with goat's milk onto a white cloth; he then instructed Vairocana to hold these invisible letters over smoke in order to make them visible. In this way, the teachings were passed on, and yet their secrecy continued to be guarded.

In addition to these eighteen Instructions, Śrī Siṃha transmitted to Vairocana the Section of the Unending Experience of Being (Klong-sde), in the three traditional manners: 'black', 'white', and 'multicolored' (*dkar, nag, khra*). Śrī Siṃha also taught him the Guidance Section (Man-ngag-gi-sde), as well as the initiations (*dbang-bskur*) and instructions (*man-ngag*) in the sixty Tantra Sections (*rgyud-sde*). After Vairocana perfectly mastered all these doctrines, Śrī Siṃha taught him the three ways that instruction is to be sought, the four ways it is to be transmitted, and the four ways it is not to be transmitted.

Later, in a meditative vision, Vairocana received instructions from dGa'-rab rDo-rje, the first human transmitter of the Atiyoga teachings. Directly perceiving these teachings (via the Shorter Lineage), Vairocana attained Nirvāṇa. Then, practicing the art of meditative speed running (*rkang-mgyogs*), he returned to Tibet, where he strictly adhered to the guidance of his teachers.

After instructing King Khri-srong-lde'u-btsan in the Atiyoga, Vairocana taught the Sems-sde on three occasions in Khams. First he transmitted it to rGyal-mo gYu-sgra sNying-po, who belonged to the monastery rGyal-rong Brag-la-mgon, in the meditative retreat of the Natha on the rock of rGyal-mo-rong; then he taught it to gSang-ston Ye-shes-bla-ma at the hermitage of sTag-rtse-mkhar of Tsha-ba-rong. He then transmitted the teachings to the medicant Sangs-rgyas-mgon-po at the settlement of Brag-dmar-rdzong of sTong-khung-rong. At a later time, having gone to dbUs in central Tibet, he taught it to the Tibetan queen from Khotan, Li-bza' Shes-rab-sgron-ma. He also translated the *Sems-sde snga-gyur*.

gNyags Jñānakumāra, who was born to sTa-sgra-lha-snang of gNyags in Yar-klungs Valley and to Sru-gza' sGron-ma-skyid, studied with Vairocana and gYu-sgra sNying-po on five occasions. He also studied the 'later' transmission with Vimalamitra. Thus, the four great streams of the highest doctrine came together: the stream of the extensive explanation of basic texts together with an abridged commentary; the stream of the precepts of Oral-instructions together with primary notes; the stream of Blessing and Empowerment together with the Exposition of Method and Guidance; and the stream of Practice and Abstinent Method together with the *mantras* which Protect the Sacred Precepts. gNyags Jñānakumāra taught the instructions to Sog-po dPal-gyi-ye-shes and numerous disciples, and from Sog-po the transmission passed to gNubs-chen Sangs-rgyas Ye-shes through the lineage of *Zur*, and then to sGro-sbug-pa.

The Section of the Unending Experience of Being (Klong-gi-sde) of the Atiyoga

Each of the four divisions of the Klong-sde section of the Atiyoga teachings develops meditative awareness so that whatever is reflected in the clarity and vastness of the mind becomes radiant. All the Tantras, teachings, Sādhanas, and practices of this section are internally experienced as a natural and self-created movement towards the higher reality of Being.

Among the texts belonging to the Section of the Unending

gNyags Jñānakumāra

Experience of Being (Klong-sde) is the *rDo-rje-sems-dpa' nam-mkha'i mtha'-dang-mnyam-pa'i rgyud chen-po*, which contains nine 'spheres' (*klong*) of subject matter. These nine spheres are (1) the Sphere of the Doctrine (lTa-ba'i klong); (2) the Sphere of Practice (sPyod-pa'i klong); (3) the Sphere of the Maṇḍala (dKyil-'khor-gyi-klong); (4) the Sphere of Empowerment (dBang-gi klong); (5) the Sphere of the Vow (Dam-tshig-gi klong); (6) the Sphere of Meditation (sGrub-pa'i klong); (7) the Sphere of Action (Phrin-las-kyi klong); (8) the Sphere of the Path and Stages (Sa-lam-gyi klong); and (9) the Sphere of the Result ('Bras-bu'i klong).

The Klong-sde teachings originated with Vairocana, who bestowed the precepts of *rDo-rje zam-pa* ("The Teaching of the Diamond Bridge") on sPangs Mi-pham-mgon-po according to various lineages,

sPangs Mi-pham

including that of Ye-shes gSang-ba. Though sPangs Mi-pham-mgon-po did not practice meditation as a youth, when he was an old man he began to vigorously practice with the aid of a meditative cord and chin support which kept his ailing body erect. Following his teacher's advice, he perceived the meaning of non-origination and lived for over a hundred years.

sPangs Mi-pham's chief disciple was the monk Ngan-lam Byang-chub rGyal-mtshan, who at age sixty-seven, received instructions from him. Ngan-lam's principal disciple was Za-ngam Rin-chen-dbyig, a native of upper A-mdo, who remained with him on the Wa-seng-ge ('Fox and Lion') Rock. The lineage then passed to Chos-kyi-khu-'gyur gSal-ba'i-mchog of Yar-klungs, who obtained instructions from Za-ngam as a monk of fifty-seven.

These three masters all passed away in the same year on the rock of Wa-seng-ge, their bodies vanishing like mist or a rainbow (*'ja'-lus*). Ngam-lam Byang-chub rGyal-mtshan was one hundred and seventy two; Za-ngam was one hundred and forty four; and Khu-'gyur was one hundred and seventeen years of age.

Cho-kyi-khu-'gyur's chief disciple was the monk Myang Byang-chub-grags, a native of upper gYu-'brug, who received instructions from him at age forty-two. Later, he resided at bSam-yas mChims-phu where he met an elderly monk named Myang Shes-rab-'byung-gnas, to whom he also bestowed the lineage of teachings. While Myang Byang-chub-grags was residing on the great mountain of Phung-po in rGya-ma ne'u-kha in gTsang, his body appearing like a scattering cloud, was once seen disappearing above the slope of the mountain.

Myang Shes-rab-'byung-gnas's disciple was the Ācārya sBa-sgom who was a native of Lo-mo, and a member of the sBa clan. His parents had intrusted him to Myang- Shes-rab when he was sixteen to protect him from a civil war in his native country. While teacher and student were together, Myang Byang-chub visited them, leading a deer, and because of this he received the epithet, 'Myang with a deer'.

When Shes-rab-'byung-gnas and sBa-sgom came to Phug-po-che, Myang Byang-chub-grags disappeared and then transformed himself into a whirlwind which moved around and around, and then transformed itself into a fire. He then transformed himself into water and filled a brass bowl used in offerings. Continuing such exhibition of miraculous powers until dusk, he suddenly assumed his own form and explained that as long as the gross elements are not purified and the fine elements do not disappear, such phenomena cannot take place. But if one understands the object which cannot be meditated upon and is able to practice without distraction, such power as was demonstrated is not difficult to attain.

Once the Ācārya sBa-sgom had a lady disciple named Gang-mo. On one occasion he told her that he did not believe that visual objects had a true existence. Saying this, he struck a water stone with his hand, and his arm penetrated the stone up to his elbow. He then pulled his body backward and it entered a rock; the trace of his body could be clearly seen afterwards.

Late in his life, Shes-rab-'byung-gnas instructed sBa-sgom, "In my absence, gaze on the summit of Lha-ri." Later when Shes-rab-'byung-gnas did not return from a walk on the mountain, sBa-sgom discovered that the teacher had passed away without leaving a trace of his body behind. Only his garments, hat, and rosary made of peepul wood were found hanging on a Juniper tree.

When sBa-sgom was residing at the small cave of Zu-ra-ri, 'Dzeng Dharmabodhi (1052–1168) came to visit him and recognized him as a superior master. sBa-sgom told 'Dzeng that he possessed a secret precept called the *rDo-rje zam-pa*, the understanding of which, for only a single moment, results in enlightenment in this very life. He explained that the *rDo-rje zam-pa* had been transmitted through an uninterrupted lineage of teachers who attained the 'rainbow body'. sBa-sgom, who had until then kept these teachings as his most precious secret, bestowed on 'Dzeng Dharmabodhi the four complete initiations of the Path of Liberation, as well as the complete secret precepts.

Thereafter, 'Dzeng Dharmabodhi learned many teachings as he wandered in the company of prominent yogins; he also attracted numerous students, both male and female Siddhas. He attained the power of transforming his body into a spherical rainbow, and could cover great distances within a single moment. After receiving the secret instructions from sBas-gom, his mind had become merged with the sky, and all objects perceived by his mind were no longer beset with an apparent dualism. He practiced the 'Six Doctrines of Nāropa' imparted by the Ḍākinī Ni-gu-ma, especially the method of dreams (*rmi-lam*) and the methods of the Mahāmudrā. Later in his life, he had a vision of Amitābha Buddha and came to understand many highly guarded precepts.

On one occasion, having reached the great town of Mon-'gar, which stood on a freshly frozen river, 'Dzeng thought that it would be safe to cross the ice, but the ice broke under him and he fell into the water. His body entered the freezing water, sizzling like a red-hot iron, and then a column of vapor ascended into the sky. The onlookers could not understand how anyone could stand in the ice-cold water. His only response to this was, "I felt cold, of course."

'Dzeng was known especially for his many miraculous deeds and austere practices, and lived until the age of one hundred and seventeen. From the time of 'Dzeng Dharmabodhi on, the Oral-instructions of *rDo-rje zam-pa* have been practiced widely. His chief disciple was 'Dzeng Jo-sras, who, early in life, sought the teachings from many masters. Three times he sought the *rDo-rje zam-pa* instructions from 'Dzeng and was finally granted them. After this, whenever other disciples asked for the teachings, Jo-sras taught from the teacher's seat. 'Dzeng and Jo-sras worked together for eighteen years. The Ācārya Kun-bzang was a disciple of both 'Dzeng Dharmabodhi and 'Dzeng Jo-sras, and heard the

Sangs-rgyas bSang-ba

text of the *rDo-rje zam-pa* a total of thirty-five times. The Ācārya was known for his ceaseless meditation, and he set forth detailed interpretations of the basic texts to numerous disciples, including the teacher So-ston, who composed a commentary on the *rDo-rje zam-pa*. Thus, the precepts of the *rDo-rje zam-pa*, which originated with Vairocana, have been transmitted through a continuous series of enlightened teachers of the rNying-ma lineage.

The Transmission of the Guidance Section (Man-ngag-sde) of the Atiyoga

The transmission of the Guidance Section (Man-ngag-sde) was first received by dGa'-rab rDo-rje, the Nirmāṇakāya emanation of Vajra-

Padmasambhava

sattva (rDo-rje-sems-dpa') and the first of the Human-tradition of Vidyādhāras (Rig-'dzin). The successor to dGa'-rab rDo-rje was 'Jam-dpal bShes-gnyen, who in turn transmitted the teachings to Śrī Siṃha. Śrī Siṃha also received the transmission directly from dGa'-rab rDo-rje in the form of meditative visions. He was the teacher of Ye-shes-mdo (Jñānasūtra), Buddhaguhya (Sangs-rgyas bSang-ba), Vimalamitra, and Vairocana.

In this line of transmission, Padmasambhava is the first lama, as he is the living exemplar of the profound meaning of Buddhahood, and is coincident with its three manifestation patterns—the Dharmakāya (Chos-sku), Sambhōgakāya (Longs-sku), and Nirmāṇakāya (sPrul-sku). Guru Rinpoche's principal disciples in this line of mystical instruction—known more specifically as the mKha'-gro sNying-thig—were Śrī Siṃha and 'Jam-dpal bShes-gnyen.

Padmasambhava demonstrated these teachings at the court of King Khri-srong-lde'u-btsan by bringing back to life his daughter lHa-lcan Padma-gsal, belonging to one of the wives of the king, 'Brog-bza' Byang-chub-sgron. Padmasambhava went to the dead child and wrote the syllables N-R-I on the girl's chest with red chalk dust. With intense meditative concentration, Guru Rinpoche brought the girl back to life. He then imparted to her an empowerment (*dbang-bskur*) for the 'guidance of spiritual afflatus in the sNying-thig' (Man-ngag-mkha'-'gro'i sNying-thig). The Guru then concealed the precious sNying-thig teachings in a secret place, establishing their existence as gTer-ma or 'buried treasure'. This transmission ends in the spacio-temporal world with Padmasambhava, but continues in the transworldly sphere through Bodhisattvas and enlightened beings. These teachings are thus preserved for future times by beings endowed with spiritual inspiration (*mkha'-'gro-ma*), such as Ḍākinīs and masters of gTer-ma.

Śrī Siṃha Imparts the Transmission of the Central Doctrine of the Guidance Section to Vimalamitra

At a time well before his journey to Tibet, Vimalamitra, accompanied by Ye-shes-mdo (Jñānasūtra), received a vision of Vajrasattva. In this vision, the Bodhisattva instructed him to go to the temple near Byang-chub-zhing in China and study with Śrī Siṃha, if he wished to attain Buddhahood in this very-life.

Vimalamitra studied with Śrī Siṃha for a period of twenty years, during which time he learned the Transmission of the Central Doctrine of the Guidance Section (rDzogs-chen Man-ngag sNying-thig), and other highly treasured instructions. Upon his return to India, Vimalamitra met Ye-shes-mdo and related to him what he had learned during his long stay with the teacher of the Vidyādhara Tantras. Upon Vimalamitra's suggestion, Ye-shes-mdo proceeded to the temple in China where Śrī Siṃha was residing. Due to his knowledge of meditative speed running (*rkang-mgyogs*), he covered the nine month's journey in a single day. He then studied the Guidance Section with Śrī Siṃha for sixteen years.

One day, on hearing a peculiar sound, Ye-shes-mdo looked up and saw Śrī Siṃha sitting in the sky, encircled by a halo of light. The master was passing away, but before he did so he gave Ye-shes-mdo the book *gZer-bu bDun-pa*, which contained instructions for the attainment of non-duality and directed him to seek out the fourth division of the Guidance Section, which would be found in a pillar of the bKra-shis-khrigs-sgo Temple.

Ye-shes-mdo then took up residence in the Bha-shing cemetery, where he imparted to Vimalamitra the Atiyoga, its relevant texts and oral instructions. Vimalamitra proceeded to the city of Bhir-ya-la in western India, where King Dharmapāla welcomed him with a religious festival. He then traveled to a burial ground north of this city called Rab-tu-snang-byed, where he practiced the 'Quintessential Instructions' (*sNying-thig-gi gdam-pa*), the absolutely subtle doctrinal precepts leading to perfect attainment. Vimalamitra stayed there for thirteen years; as a result he attained an immutable body and displayed numerous miraculous deeds. Following this, he traveled to Kapilavāstu where he taught King Indrabodhi, and where he stayed until he reached the age of two hundred.

Upon invitation by King Khri-strong-lde'u-btsan, the highly respected master and comprehensive scholar, Vimalamitra traveled to Tibet. After his acceptance by the nobility, he took the seat of honor in the Translation Hall at bSam-yas Monastery and proceeded to translate the exoteric and esoteric treatises from Sanskrit into Tibetan.

Vimalamitra resided in Tibet for thirteen years, during which time he worked in close collaboration with Padmasambhava and Vairocana. These three distinguished masters were prime translators of the rDzogs-pa-chen-po texts and were central to their associated lineages of Oral-transmission. Vimalamitra went to a mountain retreat, Ri-bo-rtse-nga (Wu-tai-shan) near the borders of China, where he passed away, with his body vanishing into a rainbow (*'ja'-lus*). Numerous Tibetan masters, after pursuing the practices detailed in the works of Padmasambhava and Vimalamitra, attained many unusual powers and left behind no physical remains at their death.

Before he proceeded to Ri-bo-rtse-nag (Wu-tai-shan), Vimalamitra imparted the precepts of the sNying-thig to King Khri-srong-lde'u-btsan and Nyang Ting-nge-'dzin bzang-po who had been the king's playmate. Nyang founded the monastic settlement of Zhva'i lha-khang and built the temple of dbUs-ru-zwa, in which he hid the precepts of the sNying-thig. Nyang Ting-nge-'dzin became an important figure during the king's reign (755–797) and a prominent sup-

Nyang Ting-nge-'dzin bzang-po

porter of the growing Buddhist Saṅgha. At the age of fifty-five (c. 836) he was executed by Glang Dar-ma because he would not discontinue his Buddhist practices. On the day after his execution, rainbows appeared in the sky and natural miracles were observed to the amazement of all.

Nyang Tin-nge-'dzin bzang-po taught the 'Lineage of Words' (*tshig-brgyud*) to 'Brom Rin-chen-bar, who in turn taught them to sBas Blo-gros dBang-phyug. Sometime later, Nyang's hidden precepts were discovered and practiced by lDang-ma Lhun-rgyal, who transmitted the instructions to the noted rJe-btsun Seng-ge-dbang-phyung from upper Nyang, and bestowed on him the seven degrees of these mystic precepts. rJe-btsun, in turn, bestowed the precepts on Nyang bKa'-gdams-pa, who then meditated on the rock of Ti-sgro of gZo ('Little Lake'), and passed away, vanishing like a rainbow. rJe-btsun resided in the mountain range between Sangs and U-yug, practiced meditation, and obtained miraculous powers. He hid the precepts in three secret locations: U-yug, Lang-gro'i 'chad-pa-ltag, and Jal-gyi-phu.

Thirty years later, rJe-sgom Nag-po discovered and practiced these hidden precepts. Sangs-pa Ras-pa also discovered these hidden treasures, and taught them to others. Still later, when Zang bKra-shis rDo-rje (rGyal-ba-zhang-ston, 1097–1167) was residing at Upper Nyang, the Bodhisattva Vajrasādhu appeared to him and guided him to the summit of a high rock in the western mountains of U-yug. There, in a cave facing north, he discovered teachings hidden by rJe-btsun. He also discovered the teachings hidden at Jal-gyi-phu, and the treasures hidden by Vimalamitra himself in the rock of mChims-phu. These he taught extensively to all who requested his private instructions. He also obtained the secret precepts directly from rJe-sgom himself.

Zang bKra-shis rDo-rje's son, mKhas-pa Nyi-'bum (1158–1213) studied with his father for eleven years, as well as with several other teachers, most notably Sa-skya Grags-pa rGyal-mtshan. Having completed the study of the sNying-thig he composed a Śāstra named *Tshig-don chen-mo* ('The Great Meaning of Words').

mKhas-pa Nyi-'bum's son, Gu-ru Jo-'ber (1196–1231), as a youth listened to the complete precepts of the sNying-thig. At age eighteen he received instructions from the Sa-skya Pang-chen, the Saṃvara Cycle, and the precepts of the Mahāmudrā. Shortly after completing his studies at the age of thirty-six, he had visions of Vajrapāṇi and Avalokiteśvara surrounded by a halo of light; later he had a vision of Amitāyus, and shortly thereafter, he passed away.

Khrul-zhig Seng-ge-rgyal-pa received the complete secret precepts of the sNying-thig from Gu-ru Jo-'ber. He also obtained many precepts of the 'Old' and 'New' Tantras, in Mahāmudrā and the Zhi-byed systems, and for many years earnestly practiced meditation in hermitages and uninhabited valleys. He led many worthy disciples on the path of empowerment and guidance.

Khrul-zhig's principal disciple was sGrub-chen Me-long rDo-rje (1243–1303) who obtained the faculty of prescience at an early age. During his youth he received teachings from a number of well-known masters. When he was eighteen, Seng-ge-dbon-po transmitted the sNying-thig doctrine to him at Seng-ge-rgyab; thereafter, he had a continuous vision of Vajrasattva for six days and nights. During the initiation ceremony, he received the blessing of the preceptors of his Spiritual Lineage in the form of a dream. A few years later he became the

sGrub-chen Me-long rDo-rje

recipient of many hidden treatises (*gter-chos*), such as the *Vajravārahī* (*rDo-rje Phag-mo*), from Sangs-rgyas-ras-pa. He was blessed by numerous illuminating visions, including those of Vajravārahī, Hayagrīva, Tārā, Avalokiteśvara, Samantrabhadra (Bodhisattva), Vajrasattva, Vimalamitra, Padmasambhava, Za-lung-pa, Sangs-rgyas-ras-pa, and 'Gro-mgon Rinpoche, all enveloped within a sphere of multi-hued light.

Me-long rDo-rje's principal disciple was Rig-'dzin-chen-po Ku-ma-rā-dza (Kumarāja, 1266–1343), who was the teacher of Klong-chen-pa and the young incarnate lama, Rang-'byung rDo-rje. From childhood, Rig-'dzin-pa showed great wisdom, naturally understanding how to read and write. At the age of seven, he was initiated into the Hevajra and Saṃvaracakra systems, and at nine, into the Cycle of Avalokiteśvara according to the rNying-ma-pa system. He later received the ordination name of gZhon-nu rGyal-po, studied the Vinaya, the Six Doctrines of Nāropa, and other systems with the teacher Grags-se-ba. He also studied painting and became a famous artist, and later obtained many precepts, instructions, and Tantras of the rNying-ma-pa from Khyung-ma Sak-dar.

Rig-'dzin Chen-po Ku-ma-rā-dza obtained from Me-long rDo-rje an exposition of the Mahāmudrā and attained yogic insight through identifying his mind with the teaching. In a dream Ku-ma-rā-dza conversed with Padmasambhava who instructed him secretly; he then proceeded to mTshur-phu Monastery and studied the Kar-ma-pa doctrines with Lama gNyan-ras and Dar-ma-mgon-po. Afterwards, he met the Mahāsiddhi U-rgyan-pa and Rang-'byung-rDo-rje, who was already a monk at the age of seven. From the Mahāsiddha he obtained many precepts, and from gNyan-ras he received complete instruction in the sNying-thig doctrine, along with many teachings of the rDzogs-chen, including the "Mirror of the Hidden Main Point" (gSang-ba gnad-kyi me-long). Then at mKar-chu, he obtained a full empowerment of the sNying-thig, together with the expositions and oral instructions from Me-long rDo-rje. Later, at mTshur-phu, he offered the precepts of sNying-thig to Rang-'byung rDo-rje. From the Ācārya sGom-pa, of the lineage of rJe-sgom Nag-po, he obtained the *gSang-skor* and the *bSam-gtan Mig-gi sgron-me* ("The Lamp of the Eye of Meditation). Rig-'dzin Chen-po Ku-ma-rā-dza taught skillfully the theory of sNying-thig with the help of terminology unique to that system, meditated in distant hermitages and mountain retreats, and passed away at the age of seventy-eight.

Klong-chen-pa. Kun-mkhyen Klong-chen-rab-'byams-pa (Dri-med-'od-zer) is one of the most important figures in the entire rDzog-chen lineage, for he ordered the philosophical truths and psychological applications of the rDzogs-chen into a cohesive system. He was a descendent on his father's side of the spiritual lineage of Rog Shes-rab-'od, whose ancestry goes back to Ye-shes dBang-po-srung of the clan of Rog, one of the seven monks (*sad-mi-bdun*) ordained by Śāntarakṣita around the year 790. He is also related to the clan of rGyal-ba mChog-dbangs, one of Padmasambhava's twenty-five foremost disciples, who gained mastery in the Hayagrīva Sādhana (*Padma-gsung*) and who incarnated as Dus-gsum-mkhyen-pa, the greatest disciple of sGam-po-pa. From his mother, 'Brom-gza'-ma bSod-nams-

Klong-chen-pa

rgyan, he was of the ancestral lineage of 'Brom-ston-pa ('Brom-ston rGyal-ba'i-'byung-gnas, 1005–64), Atiśa's foremost Tibetan disciple.

Early in life, Klong-chen-pa studied many doctrines, including the 'Five Doctrines of Maitreya' and Dharmakīrti's 'Seven Treatises', and became noted for his complete comprehension and accurate explanation of these texts. Among his peers he became known as 'The One who knows many verses' because of his vast knowledge of the Sūtras.

In 1319, Klong-chen-pa received ordination at bSam-yas Monastery in the presence of the Abbot bSam-grub Rin-chen and the lama Kun-dga' 'Od-zer, at which time he was given the name Tshul-khrims Blo-gros. He spent the next several years studying intensively with the most renowned teachers of his day. In addition to completely mastering the rNying-ma tradition, he also studied with Rang-'byung rDo-rje (1284–1339) and with lama Dam-pa bSod-nams rGyal-mtshan (1312–1375), both of whom represented to him the 'New (gSar-ma) Tradition'. Due to his unbounded knowledge, he received the appellations Ngag-gi-dbang-po of bSam-yas and Klong-chen-rab-'byams-pa, which he used as signatures for some of his works.

Although he was Abbot of bSam-yas Monastery early in his life, he retired from monastic duties to live simply in the mountains of Tibet. Throughout his life, he had innumerable visions of Bodhisattvas and enlightened masters. In his late twenties Klong-chen-pa experienced a vision of Padmasambhava and his consort Ye-shes mTsho-rgyal, in which he received the name Dri-med-'od-zer from Padmasambhava and the name rDo-rje gZi-brjid from Ye-shes mTsho-rgyal. During this same period he began to study and practice the *mKha'-'gro snying-thig,* mystical teachings connected with Padmasambhava which had a profound effect on his spiritual development. Later he composed a work in a similar vein, the *mKha'-'gro yang-tig*.

After spending five months secluded in the dark chambers of a cave, he journeyed to bSam-yas and met the person who would become his chief teacher, Rig-'dzin-chen-po Ku-ma-rā-dza. Upon meeting Klong-chen-pa, Rig-'dzin told him: "Last night I dreamt that a wonderful heavenly bird had arrived, indicating your coming. You are the holder of the spiritual lineage of my Doctrine, and the complete secret precepts will be given to you." After this meeting, they stayed together for some time, changing residence nine times during one spring and traveling from one uninhabited valley to another. Klong-chen-pa endured many hardships and austerities, practicing meditation in caves and hermitages, such as mChims-phu, and receiving the secret instructions from Rig-'dzin-pa. When the snow fell, he covered himself only with a woolen bag which during the day he used for a mat. In the presence of his teacher, he unerringly revised and synthesized the precepts and exhibited an unsullied lucidity in the three disciplines of teaching, debating, and writing; he authored a number of translations, commentaries, and original treatises.

Me-long rDo-rje (1243–1303) had transmitted Vimalamitra's teachings to Ku-ma-rā-dza, which had been summed up in the *Bi-ma snying-thig* and rediscovered by lDang-ma lHun-rgyal. Ku-ma-rā-dza, who was himself an embodiment of Vimalamitra, passed these teachings to Klong-chen-rab-'byams-pa, who elaborated on them in his *Bla-ma yang-tig* and then synthesized the contents of both the *mKha'-'gro yang-*

tig and the *Bla-ma yang-tig* into his most profound *Zab-mo yang-tig*. Despite the depth and complexity of the subjects to which Klong-chen-pa addressed himself, his presentations were exceptionally clear and understandable.

In the years to follow, Klong-chen-pa composed thirty-five books on the system of the sNying-thig which he titled *Bla-ma snying-thig*. Throughout his life he authored a total of 263 works, only about twenty-five of which are still extant. These texts present a unified account of the entire range of Buddhist teaching and practice, for Klong-chen-pa had received teachings from gurus belonging to both the rNying-ma and bSar-ma traditions. His treatises on the rDzog-chen system are the most profound, enduring, and poetic ever written, and his works taken as a whole are the most brilliant and original treatises in all of Tibetan literature. Klong-chen-pa became a master of logical organization and clarity of expression.

Among his shorter works are the "Three Triple Cycles" (*Ngal-bso skor-gsum, Rang-grol skor-gsum*, and *Mun-sel skor-gsum*), which emphasize the intrinsic freedom underlying all spiritual growth and the release and relief discovered in the proper concentration of one's being through meditation. All of Klong-chen-pa's writings are inspired by the teachings revealed in his major works known as the "Seven Treasures" (*mDzod bdun*) and the *sNying-thig ya-bzhi*, which comprise the quintessence of rNying-ma philosophy and psychology. In addition to these works he composed several liturgical texts for the performance of important offering ceremonies (*pu-ja*), instructional texts for the practice of Atiyoga meditation, poetical accounts of experiences of esoteric realizations, devotional pieces for use in regular religious practice, literary texts outlining higher meditative practice, works illustrating the principles of Tibetan poetics, didactic stories in verse, poetical texts in praise of various Bodhisattvas, and a general history of Buddhism (*chos-'byung*) and its essential teachings and Sādhanas.

Due to his affiliation with the opponents of the ascendant ruling power, Klong-chen-pa was forced into a decade of wandering retreat in Bhutan. However, even this he turned into fortune, for during this sojourn, he founded the monasteries of Thar-pa-gling, near Bum-thang (Bhutan), and Shar-mkho-thing Rin-chen-gling and bSam-gtan-gling in Spa-gro. Thus, from Bhutan, the rNying-ma teachings later spread to Nepal.

In his travels he restored a number of other monasteries and retreat centers throughout Tibet and Bhutan. He was instrumental in found-

Ye-shes mTsho-rgyal

ing or restoring the monastic settlements of lHa-ring-brag, O-rgyan-rdzong, and Zhva'i lha-khang. His principal accomplishment, however, was the restoration of bSam-yas Monastery, the first teaching center in Tibet (est. 768) and the site of the extensive translation work completed during the early spread of the Dharma.

Klong-chen-pa was finally allowed to return to Tibet at the time the Phag-mo-gru Dynasty rose to power. But before his return he expounded the sNying-thig to many disciples who had assembled near the riverbanks of sKyi-chu in Upper dbU-ru. It was at this time that he was honored with the title of Kun-mkhyen, which means 'the Omniscient One'. He is also revered as one of the three incarnations of Mañjuśrī and as the direct emanation of Vimalamitra. Having taught and given initiation into the higher esoteric teachings to over forty thousand students at one time, he received the title 'The Mañjuśrī of

Mandāravā

Tibet'. Through his instruction, many of his disciples attained Enlightenment.

Klong-chen-pa spent his last years repairing the Stūpas near bSam-yas Monastery and meditating in the cave at mChims-phu, which was formerly used by Padmasambhava. When Klong-chen-rab-'byams-pa was fifty-six years old, he gave his students his final teachings and passed away at his beloved O-rgyan-rdzong in Gangs-ri-thod-kar. Many marvelous occurrences heralded that occasion, and the air was filled with music. People who were in their homes thought that the music was coming from outside, and people who were outdoors thought that the music was coming from inside the houses. When his students retrieved the relics from his ashes, they found substances of the five rainbow colors which were as hard as diamonds. Because it was the depth of winter, ice and snow covered the entire countryside, but at the place

Śākyadevī

where Klong-chen-rab-'byams-pa passed away, the snows melted and flowers blossomed.

The rDzogs-chen teachings gained greater clarity and impact through the poetic, philosophical, and deeply experiential language utilized by Klong-chen-pa. His oral teachings have been preserved to this day having passed through O-rgyan gTer-bdag-gling-pa (1646–1714) and 'Jigs-med-gling-pa (1730–98), two foremost rDzogs-chen masters. They were further transmitted to dPal-sprul Rinpoche (b. 1808), Lama Mi-pham (1848–1912), Ā-Dzom 'Brug-pa (Rig-'dzin Nag-tsho-rang-grol), the Second 'Jam-dbyangs mKhyen-brtse'i-dbang-po (Chos-kyi-blo-gros, b. 1896), 'Gyur-med rDo-rje (Ā-Dzom rGyal-sras 'Gyur-med rDo-rje, b. 1895), and mChog-sprul Rinpoche (Dar-thang mChog-sprul Chos-kyi-zla-ba, b. 1893).

Kālasiddhi

gTer-ma, the Concealed Treasures

In essence, a *gter* can be anything that, when rediscovered, induces an individual towards the highest aspiration for enlightenement. Padmasambhava formulated eighteen classes of gTer-ma, which include innumerable forms of *gter*. The contents of a single gTer-ma work summarizes the quintessence of the Buddha's teachings as they find their practical application in the Inner Tantras. Because they are particularly suited to the time and milieu at which they are discovered, gTer-ma are especially applicable to daily life.

The term *gter* refers to anything that is precious or worthy of preservation. In addition to texts or fragments of manuscripts, *gter* can take the form of religious figurines, reliquaries, or ritual objects, denot-

Tashi Khye-dren

ing anything that stands for spiritual value. *gTer* may also manifest as natural objects, such as trees, rocks, and signs in the earth; *gter* can also be gifts of silver, gold, or precious jewels which may be exchanged for materials needed to build a temple or other religious monument. Thus, *gter* may denote material values as well. Furthermore, gTer-ma may serve as a catalyst to aid in deciphering a text or fragment concealed by Padmasmabhava or one of his disciples.

After his transmission of the doctrines arising from the Eight Heruka Sādhanas, Padmasambhava hid these texts, so that they became known as concealed treasure (gTer-ma). In a similar manner, he hid another collection of special texts, known as the *Klong-chen snying-thig*. As the principal gTer-ma texts appearing at later times were originally concealed by Padmasambhava, he may be called the supreme master of

Nyang-ral Nyi-ma-'od-zer

the gTer-ma. The principle of the *gter* and its method of discovery is unique to the rNying-ma-pa, as most gTer-stons, or masters of the *gter*, are emanations of Padmasambhava or his disciples, the Eight Great Ācārya.

Ye-shes mTsho-rgyal, Padmasambhava's consort*, set into writing some of the bKa'-ma transmission, and then committed these teachings to her unfailing memory. She then placed written teachings in appropriate receptacles which she later helped Padmasambhava to conceal. These concealed treasures, or continuing revelation, were uncovered by individuals who, through the process of 'emanation',

*Ye-shes mTsho-rgyal, together with Mandāravā, Śākyadevī, Kālasiddhi, and Tashi Khye-dren, were Padmasambhava's great female disciples.

Guru Chos-kyi-dbang-phyug

were directed by Padmasambhava to make the discovery at a designated time and place. Upon discovery, buried or concealed texts are called gTer-ma. Because the gTer-ston is a Bodhisattva endowed with special enlightenment qualities, and because he is the emanation of Padmasambhava, he has the ability to perfectly reconstruct or decipher and explain the theory and practice described in the discovered gTer-ma texts or fragments. In Western terms, the gTer-ston may be called a 'prodigy' as he has the remarkable power of implementing the spiritual methods revealed in his particular find. From the work of the gTer-ston, in a certain sense, new or innovative forms of Dharma have been produced, for Dharma always takes on the form appropriate to our ever-changing world.

Lama Rig-'dzin

Because the human mind can interpret the Buddhadharma in a manner generally agreeable to the ego, the essence of the teachings can become confused, misinterpreted, or lose its potency. The gTer-ma masters have thus appeared at various times throughout history in order to clarify, reinterpret, or re-energize the meaning of the original teachings.

The gTer-ma master customarily serves as both the discoverer and editor or expositor of the concealed treasure, and the discovery itself is invariably announced in a prophecy. In his biography, Padmasambhava prophesied that there would emerge three 'Grand', eight 'Great', twenty-one 'Powerful', one hundred and eight 'Intermediate', and one thousand 'Subsidiary' gTer-stons. To these individuals, Padmasambha-

'Jam-dpal-sku (gshin-rje)

va or his disciples had given a hint or 'cipher key' (*kha-byang* or *lde-mig*) which, when instrumented, gives the precise locations or place descriptions to facilitate in the discovery of these teachings.

Much of the gTer-ma teachings were written in a highly symbolic and codified form called 'Ḍākinī Language', incipherable by those who were not specifically instructed by Padmasambhava through the process of 'emanation' (*dgongs-gter*). Often Ḍākinīs aid the gTer-ma masters by whispering from mouth to ear the essence of the text or artifact that has been unearthed. Very often auspicious ornaments and consorts assist the gTer-ston in his discovery. Furthermore, most gTer-stons are psychically endowed with an enlightened awareness which allows them to recall the teachings which they have received from Padmasambhava.

Although many *gter* have already been uncovered, there are nu-

Padma-gsung

merous other *gter* at various localities throughout the world that were concealed by Padmasambhava. They are completely protected from premature or spurious discovery by means of a 'time-lock' or formula (*gtsug-las-khan*) for deciphering the encoded message, which can only be opened by the individual stipulated in the prophecy.

The earliest form of gTer-ma were the Buddha's Sūtras hidden by the Nāgas and subsequently uncovered by Nāgārjuna in the second century A.D., as prophesied by the Blessed One. However, the principle of continuing revelation was not made manifest until its widespread application in Tibet.

The gTer-ma texts and masters of the gTer-ma as prophesied by Padmasambhava during the early spread (*snga-dar*) began to appear around the twelfth and thirteenth centuries during the period of the

Yang-dag-thugs

later spread of the Dharma (*phyi-dar*). The first gTer-stons to appear at this time were the two prominant figures, Nyang-ral Nyi-ma-'od-zer '(The Sun's Rays', 1124–92) and Guru Chos-kyi-dbang-phyug ('Dharma-wealth', 1212–70). These two are known as the Sun and Moon, and the results of their findings are called the Upper and Lower Treasures (*gter-kha-gong-'od*). These two Grand gTer-stons mark the beginning of the first period of gTer-ma discoverers. Thereafter, a number of gTer-stons became known, and their findings were compiled and edited by Ratna-gling-pa late in the fifteenth century. Along with Ratna-gling-pa's significant contributions, this collection of gTer-ma became known as the Southern Treasures (*lho-gter*).

In the mid-fifteenth century the master Rig-'dzin-rgod-ldem-'phyul-can (1337–1409) was born with auspicious marks to a ruling family in the north. This third of the 'Grand' gTer-stons made a num-

(rDo-rje) Pur-ba-'phrin-las

ber of important discoveries and later edited and compiled what are known as the Northern Treasures (*byang-gter*). The three 'Grand' gTer-ma masters, Nyi-ma-'od-zer, Guru Chos-kyi-dbang-phyug, and Rig-'dzin-rgod-ldem, were Padmasambhava's mind (heart), speech, and body incarnations.

The eight 'Great' gTer-stons or Gling-pas emerged from the fourteenth century onwards. They are: Ratna-gling-pa, Padma (-kun-skyong)-gling-pa, O-rgyan-gling-pa (c. 1360), Sangs-rgyas-gling-pa (1340–96), rDo-rje-gling-pa (1346–1405), Karma-gling-pa (14th cent.), O-rgyan rDo-rje-gling-pa (1403–79), and O-rgyan Padma-gling-pa (b. 1450).

The period between Klong-chen-rab-'byams-pa (1308–63) and O-rgyan gTer-bdag-gling-pa ('Gyur-med rDo-rje, 1646–1714) witnessed a great flourishing of the gTer-ma tradition; this was the time when most

bDud-rtsi-yon-tan

of the one hundred and eight Intermediate gTer-stons manifested. Other significant Gling-pas authorized by Padmasambhava's prophecy include Las-'phro-gling-pa (Ngag-dbang Chos-rgyal-dbang-po), bSam-gtan bDe-chen-gling-pa, Zhig-po-gling-pa (Nam-mkha' Tshe-dbang-rgyal-po), and bDud-'dul-gling-pa. Kun-mkhyen 'Jigs-med-gling-pa (1729–98), who had numerous visions of Klong-chen-rab-'byams-pa throughout his life, was a principal editor and compiler of the *Klong-chen snying-thig* cycle, as well as the *rNying-ma'i rgyud-'bum* in its final form.

Later gTer-stons of the nineteenth century include mChog-gyur bDe-chen-zig-po-gling-pa (1829–70), 'Jam-dbyangs mKhyen-brtse'i-dbang-po (Padma'od-gsal-mdo-sngags-gling-pa, 1820–92), and 'Jam-mgon sKong-sprul (Padma-gar-dbang Yon-tan-rgya-mtsho) Blo-gros-mtha'-yas (1811–99), a chief compiler of gTer-ma. Late in the nineteenth

Ma-mo-rbod-stong

century, he completed the sixty-two volume *Rin-chen gter-mdzog*, which contains the majority of gTer-ma works compiled in earlier centuries. However, innumerable other gTer-ma teachings exist which are not contained in this collection. In addition, further teachings are yet to be revealed by the one thousand 'Subsidiary' gTer-stons, who were prophesied by Padmasambhava but the majority of whom have not yet appeared.

While all the major rNying-ma monasteries maintained the teaching lineages of gTer-ma texts and practices, the gTer-ma tradition is much vaster than could be encompassed by either its voluminous literature or its monastic traditions. However, Kaḥ-thog, sMin-grol-gling, and dPal-yul in particular were central to the lives of a number of discoverers of gTer-ma. For instance, the gTer-ma master bDud-'dul-rdo-rje (1615–72) assisted in the restoration of Kaḥ-thog, and 'Jigs-med-

'Jig-rten-mchos-bstod

gling-pa's compilation of the *rNying-ma'i rgyud-'bum* comes principally from the books available at sMin-grol-gling, the residence of Chos-rgyal gTer-bdag-gling-pa, its founder. These time-honored treasure texts and their discoveries have provided, to those who have followed the Inner Teachings of the Vajrayāna, streamlined methods to intensify the enlightenment process.

The Eight rNying-ma Heruka Sādhanas

The origin of the Eight rNying-ma Heruka Sādhanas, like the origin of the Mahāyoga, is the primordial Ādi-buddha Kun-tu-bzang-po. It is said that the Buddha's disciple Ānanda preserved the Sūtras,

dMod-pa-drag-sngags

the Bodhisattva Vajrapāṇi preserved and protected the Outer Tantras, and rDo-rje Grags-po-rtsal compiled and preserved the Inner Tantras, which were transmitted to him from Kun-tu-bzang-po.

rDo-rje Grags-po-rtsal then gave the Inner Tantras to the Ḍākinī Las-kyi-dbang-mo-che for safe keeping. Seeing that the Human tradition was in need of spiritual nourishment, she concealed all the Tantras of the Developing Stage (*bskyed-rim*) and Fulfillment Stage (*rdzogs-rim*), constituting the Three Inner Tantras (*nang-rgyud-sde-gsum*: Mahā-, Anu-, and Atiyoga) in the Stūpa bDe-byed-brtsegs-pa, located in the cremation ground bSil-ba'i-tshal (Śitavana).

The Ḍākinī concealed the *sGyu-'phrul-sde-brgyud* in the base of the Stūpa; in the middle, the *bDe-gshegs-'dus-pa*; and where the Stūpa located the four cardinal directions at the entrance gates, she buried the special

Kaḥ-'dam-pa-bde-shegs

Tantras (*Bye-brag-sgos-rgyud*). In the flute of the Stūpa, she placed the *gSang-ba-yongs-rdzogs*, and in the rim of the spire she placed the *Rang-byung-rang-shar* Tantra. In the middle of the spire was hidden the *Sangs-rgyas-mnyam-sbyor*, and at the top of the spire was concealed the *Yang-gsang-bla-med-yang-ti-nag-po*, which originates from the primary transmission of the Atiyoga (rDzogs-chen). Prajñā Ḍākinī, Karma Ḍākinī, as well as other Dharma-protecting Ḍākinīs and Vīras (heroes) were appointed as guardians of the Stūpa. This is the "Tradition of the concealed texts which had been entrusted to the givers of spiritual afflatus" (*mkha'-'gro gtad-rgya'i brgyud-pa*).

During one of his journeys in India, Padmasambhava went to the Stūpa bDe-byed-btsal-pa located in the cremation ground bSil-ba'i-tshal, uncovered the *bDe-gshegs-'dus-pa*, and proceeded with it to Nepal. Entering the Asura Cave he vowed to all the Ḍākas, Ḍākinīs, and

Kaḥ-thog

Dharmapālas in his presence that he would not leave the cave until he reached supreme *siddhi*. The Lotus-born Guru then began the Che-mchog Sādhana by symbolically opening the 'basket' of the *bDe-gshegs-'dus-pa*. He then vigorously practiced the Yang-dag-thugs (Che-mchog) and 'Phrin-las Phur-pa Sādhanas until he attained supreme *siddhi*. During his extensive practice of the *bDe-gshegs-'dus-pa,* he found it to contain eight Sādhanas. Each of these appeared as a lotus petal arising from within the dome-shaped basket and each specialized in the propitation of a certain Heruka.

Padmasambhava then proceeded to Tibet and brought to bSam-yas Monastery these Eight Heruka Sādhanas. This precious family of esoteric Sādhanas contains the source for the realization of the enlightenment experience as contained in the *bDe-gshegs-'dus-pa*.

Each Sādhana is related to a specific text, *maṇḍala*, *mantra*, Bud-

Rig-'dzin Ngag-gi-dbang-po

dha-pattern, divine power (*lha*) in visualization, color, and quality of awareness. Although Padmasambhava was the principal propitiator (Vidhyādhāra) of the Eight Heruka Sādhanas, they were also propitiated by Khri-srong-lde'u-btsan (Che-mchog), Śāntigarbha (gShin-rje), Nāgārjuna (Hayagrīva), Vimalamitra (bDud-rtsi), gNyags Jñānakumāra (bDud-rtsi), and Huṃkara (Yang-dag). Eight of Padmasambhava's principal disciples were initiated by him at mChims-phu into the practice of one of these Sādhanas, and each of them became very successful in their mastery. These eight masters became known as the Eight Great Ācaryas (sLob-dpon Chen-po brGyad) or The Eight Vidhyādhāras (Rig-'dzin sLob-dpon brGyad).

The Eight rNying-ma Heruka Sādhanas, originally propagated

rDo-rje-brag

by Guru Padmasambhava and his disciples, were preserved by the Mahāyoga lineages of the So, Zur, gNubs, gNyags, rMa, and Rong–all leading exponents in the transmission of the Cycle of the sGyu-'phrul (Māyā). These Sādhanas are based upon root texts and extensive commentaries which serve as practical instructions leading to meditative and spiritual development. Their accompanying texts also comprise the basis for the compilation of the sixty-two volume *Rin-chen gter-mdzod*, and are a basis for Sādhanas practiced throughout all parts of Tibet. Two of the texts included in this listing are "The Serene and Wrathful in Transformation" (*sGyu-'phrul-zhi-khro*) and the "Nucleus of Mysticism–the King of Treatises" (*rGyud-rgyal-gsang-ba-snying-po*). In the rich symbolism which pervades these works there are contained fifty-

Rig-'dzin Kun-bzang-shes-rab

eight peaceful tutelary deities and forty-two tutelary deities of wrathful manifestation, making a total of "One hundred most supreme serene and wrathful tutelaries" (*Zhi-khro-dam-pa-rigs-brgya*).

The Later rNying-ma Monasteries

During the period between the tenth and fourteenth centuries the rNying-ma-pa built innumerable retreat centers and small lay communities where teachers and pupils could gather to interchange the Buddhadharma and execute the more advanced practices. These centers invariably had a temple, which was attended to by lamas, monks, nuns, and laypeople, and they were, in all due respects, monasteries. However,

dPal-yul

other than bSam-yas, the rNying-ma-pa did not establish major monastic institutions until very late in history.

Monasteries within the Tibetan framework were not merely religious institutions which housed celibate monks and nuns. They were major centers of culture and learning somewhat similar to the largest Western universities with their graduate schools and extensions. The major monasteries were actually cities unto themselves with complete facilities and personnel.

Most of the rNying-ma monasteries were located in the central provinces of dbUs and gTsang and in the eastern province of Khams, with smaller centers in the northerly province of A-mdo. During the energetic spread of rNying-ma teachings in the seventeenth century, five of the six major rNying-ma monasteries were established: Kaḥ-

Padma Rig-'dzin

thog, rDo-rje-brag, dPal-yul, sMin-grol-gling, and rDzogs-chen. The sixth major center, Zhe-chen, was founded a century later.

Each of these six major monasteries served as a 'mother monastery' for numerous smaller centers in the vicinity, and each was essentially an outgrowth of early study centers which had been most favored by the Saṅgha. Records show that over twelve hundred rNying-ma-pa monasteries were located throughout Tibet. In themselves, these branch monasteries were whole communities and related to each one of them were numerous smaller monasteries.

Kaḥ-thog was originally founded by Kaḥ-'dam-pa bDe-gshegs in 1159 in Khams, but fell into partial disrepair during the fifteenth and sixteenth centuries. The monastery was expanded in 1656 and became well-known for its scholastic achievements relating to the sNying-thig Atiyoga transmission, especially the Khams transmission. Though only

rDzogs-chen

eight hundred monks and seven incarnate lamas resided there at one time, from the twelfth century onwards over one hundred thousand persons, through their practice of the Inner Tantras of the lineage of Kaḥ-'dam-pa bDe-shegs, achieved the miraculous rainbow body (*'ja'-lus,* indicating total enlightenment).

rDo-rje-brag was founded in 1610 by Rig-'dzin Ngag-gi-dbang-po in the central region of Tibet. The monastery was destroyed in 1717, along with its neighbor sMin-grol-gling, but was rebuilt in the years that followed. It held a monastic population of two hundred monks and had three incarnate lamas.

dPal-yul was founded by Rig-'dzin Kun-bzang Shes-rab in 1665 in Khams and was best known for its strength in Sādhanas, meditation practice and gTer-ma of Ratna-gling-pa. Over six hundred monks and seven incarnate lamas resided there.

Zhe-chen Rab-byams

Of the many branch monasteries associated with dPal-yul, Dar-thang (Tarthang) Monastery is the largest. Actually, Dar-thang Monastery is much larger than its mother monastery and is widely attended by the rNying-ma community around the regions of A-mdo, 'Gu-log (Golok), and rGyal-rong. Dar-thang Monastery was founded around the middle of the nineteenth century by lHa-sprul Rinpoche (an incarnation of Avalokiteśvara), who was originally from dPal-yul. It became one of the primary centers of philosophical thought throughout Tibet. A very important lama at Dar-thang Monastery was Padma mDo-sdags-btan-'dzin who reincarnated as Dar-thang mChog-sprul Chos kyi-zla-ba (b. 1893), one of the seven principal teachers of Tarthang Tulku. Dar-thang Monastery had over one hundred branch monasteries throughout the regions of 'Gu-log, A-mdo, rGyal-rong, and generally all over East Tibet.

Zhe-chen

rDzogs-chen, founded in 1685 by Padma Rig-'dzin, was destined to become the largest rNying-ma monastery in Tibet, holding over eight hundred and fifty monks and eleven incarnate lamas. With the patronage of the sDe-dge royal family, it was an exceptionally active center of learning, associated especially with the Atiyoga doctrine and practices. rDzogs-chen, highly respected for the vastness of its philosophical studies, was a huge city with thirteen different retreat centers. Lama Mi-pham meditated there for seven years.

Zhe-chen, founded in 1735 by the Second Zhe-chen Rab-'byams, 'Gyur-med Kun-gzang-rnam-rgyal, was the last of the great monasteries. Modeled on sMin-grol-gling and rDzogs-chen, it held over two hundred monks and nine incarnate lamas. Even in the twentieth century, the Zhe-chen Monastery was well-known in Tibet for the profoundness of its doctrines and its strict monastic discipline.

O-rgyan gTer-bdag-gling-pa

sMin-grol-gling was founded in 1676 by O-rgyan gter-bdag-gling-pa and housed over four hundred monks, as well as three incarnate lamas. Its poetry and literary achievements made it one of the most esteemed centers of learning in Tibet.

Throughout the centuries, these monasteries and their associated branch monasteries and retreat centers have aided numerous followers of the Buddhadharma to achieve spiritual attainment through both philosophical and meditative development. Each monastery had its own departments of study and respective lineages of Oral-transmission of Vinaya, Sūtra, Mahā-, Anu-, and Atiyoga, bKa'-ma and gTer-ma teachings. Many of these monasteries were great respositories of texts and manuscripts associated with these teachings and practices.*

*See appendix for a list of Nying-ma monasteries.

sMin-grol-gling

Later Lamas of the rNying-ma Lineage

O-rgyan gTer-bdag-gling-pa. O-rgyan gTer-bdag-gling-pa (1617–1682) was one of the most essential links in the preservation of the entire rNying-ma lineage of bKa'-ma teachings of the Mahā-, Anu-, and Atiyoga. In his meditative training, he received a number of advanced empowerments and had potent visions of Padmasambhava. Both disciple and teacher to the Fifth Dalai Lama, Ngag-dbang Blo-bzang-rgya-mtsho, he was the holder of the entire corpus of bKa'-ma teachings and practices, as well as the Yang-dag and Phur-pa Heruka Sādhanas. Although gTer-bdag-gling-pa's accomplishments are too numerous to mention here, it can be said that he was one of the most ardent and devoted masters in the history of the rNying-ma-pa. 'Jam-dbyangs mKhyen-brtse'i-dbang-po's lineage also comes directly from this mas-

Dar-thang Monastery

ter. gTer-bdag-ling-pa's younger brother, Lo-chen Dharma Śrī, an incarnation of gYu-sgra sNying-po, was his spiritual son.

'Jigs-med-gling-pa. Kun-mkhyen 'Jigs-med-gling-pa (1730–1798) follows the tradition of Klong-chen-pa by continuing to inspire the intellectual renaissance initiated by the omniscient Master. In carrying forth the spirit of the master, 'Jigs-med-gling-pa represents a further stage of the bKa'-ma tradition of the Inner rNying-ma Tantras. Through visions of the Master on numerous occasions during his life, 'Jigs-med-gling-pa became a direct disciple of Klong-chen-rab-'byams-pa. These visions of Klong-chen-pa inspired him to compose the *Klong-chen-snying-thig* cycle, and in all, 'Jigs-med-gling-pa's collected works comprise nine volumes. The compilation of the *rNying-ma'i-rgyud-'bum*

Rig-'dzin rgod-ldem 'phyul

(*Hundred Thousand rNying-ma Tantras*) in its final form is chiefly the result of the efforts of this outstanding scholar.

In response to the sectarian rivalry and persecution that became prominant during the eighteenth century among certain factions of the bSar-ma-pa, 'Jigs-med-gling-pa initiated a spirit of religious tolerance, mutual understanding, and rich synthesis of philosophical tradition, which became known as the Eclectic (Ris-med) Movement. Although this movement was formally begun by 'Jigs-med-gling-pa, it directly followed the tradition set forth by Klong-chen-rab-'byams-pa (1308–1363), who was also eclectic in his approach, having studied with teachers of all the major lineages of his time. 'Jigs-med-gling-pa and his disciple rDo-ba Grub-chen became the two most outstanding teachers in sDe-dge (in Khams), the intellectual and cultural center of

Kun-mkhyen rGyal-mchog-lnga-pa

Eastern Tibet, which became the nucleus of the Ris-med Movement. Through a fresh and revitalizing approach, these masters and their spiritual successors in the nineteenth century scientifically and artistically systematized and synthesized Buddhist philosophy and practice into a coherent path.

'Jigs-med-gling-pa's root guru was Rigs-'dzin Thugs-mchog rDorje, and his four major disciples were known as the four " 'Jigs-meds." Of these, 'Jigs-med-rgyal-ba'i-myu-gu and 'Jigs-med-'phrin-las-'odzer were essential to the continuation of the sNying-thig lineage after the passing of 'Jigs-med-gling-pa.

There are three recognized incarnations of 'Jigs-med-gling-pa, each one echoing a particular aspect of the Master's body, speech, and

'Jigs-med-gling-pa

mind (heart). These three incarnations were: the great nineteenth century luminary, 'Jam-dbyangs mKhyen-brtse'i-dbang-po, the most compassionate dPal-sprul Rinpoche, and the accomplished Siddha mDo mKhyen-brtse'i Ye-shes rDo-rje.

rGyal-sras gZhan-phan-mtha'-yas. During the time of 'Jigs-med-gling-pa, rGyal-sras gZhan-phan-mtha'-yas (b. 1740) revitalized the study of Vinaya, encouraged the study of the Sūtras and Śāstras, and became a leading proponent in the scholastic tradition of the time. He served for a number of years as Abbot at rDzogs-chen Monastery, was well-versed in the Atiyoga teachings and was a holder of O-rgyan gTer-bdag-gling-pa's lineage. He was a teacher of sPal-sprul Rinpoche,

'Jigs-med-rgyal-ba'i-myu-gu

and his main lineage of teachings were received by 'Jam-dbyangs mKhyen-brtse'i-dbang-po.

dPal-sprul Rinpoche. dPal-sprul Rinpoche (b. 1808), an incarnation of Śāntideva, was a remarkable paragon of Bodhisattva action. An erudite scholar, he was highly respected by all the schools of Tibetan Buddhism. Faithfully displaying a nonsectarian approach to the Buddhadharma, he became a leader in the nineteenth century cultural renaissance (Ris-med Movement). A humble scholar, dPal-sprul Rinpoche's root guru was 'Jigs-med-rgyal-ba'i-myu-gu, a chief disciple of 'Jigs-med-gling-pa. Of his numerous works, the *Kun-bzang-bla-ma'i-zhal-lung* is an important introduction to the general subject of Vajrayāna and a summary of the rDzogs-chen sNying-thig teach-

rGyal-sras gZhan-phan-mtha'-yas

ings. dPal-sprul Rinpoche was the unique possessor of the Oral-explanation lineage of the sNying-thig, and especially the *Ye-shes bla-ma*. Written by 'Jigs-med-gling-pa, it is a summary of Klong-chen-pa's teachings, the essence of the sNying-thig. dPal-sprul Rinpoche was also the holder of the precious Oral-transmission lineage of the *rTsa-rlung*.

As dPal-sprul's mother was getting old, he asked Ā-Dzom 'Brug-pa to attend to her in his absence. In return for this favor, dPal-sprul wished to give Ā-Dzom a gift, but he had no possessions. So he gave Ā-Dzom 'Brug-pa the most precious gift he had, the Oral-explanation lineage of the *Ye-shes bla-ma* and *rTsa-rlung*.

'Jam-dbyangs mKhyen-brtse'i-dbang-po. 'Jam-dbyangs mKhyen-brtse'i-dbang-po (1820–1892) was born in sDe-dge (mDo-

dPal-sprul Rinpoche

Khams) and studied at sMin-grol-gling, as well as at a number of Sa-skya monasteries. As a comprehensive scholar, he studied all the branches of science, the teachings of the Ngor-lugs (inner Sa-skya-pa teachings), the Tantric cycles, the entire bKa'-'gyur and bsTan-'gyur, and the Hundred Thousand rNying-ma Tantras. He received all the major teachings lineages that were available during this time and was blessed by visions of Padmasambhava and Vimalamitra. A direct incarnation of Khri-stong-lde'u-btsan, he studied over seven hundred texts, while composing fifteen volumes himself. 'Jam-dbyangs mKhyen-brtse'i-dbang-po, a receiver of the sNying-thig lineage, was one of the leaders in the nineteenth century Eclectic Movement (Ris-med) and had several incarnations recognized by different schools. His principal teacher was rGyal-sras gZhan-phan-mtha'-yas.

'Jam-dbyangs mKhyen-brtse'i-dbang-po

Kong-sprul Rinpoche. 'Jam-mgon Kong-sprul Blo-gros-mtha'-yas (1811–1899) was a principal student of 'Jam-dbyangs mKhyen-brtse'i-dbang-po and a prominent leader of the Eclectic Movement. Author of over ninety volumes, he compiled many of the Sūtras, Śāstras, bKa'-ma, and gTer-ma. One of his 'Five Treasures' is the sixty-two volume *Rin-chen-gter-mdzod,* which contains the essence of the gTer-ma teachings. Because of his great knowledge he has been recognized as the direct incarnation of Vairocana, a chief disciple of Padmasambhava.

Lama Mi-pham. Mi-pham 'Jam-dbyangs rNam-rgyal-rgya-mtsho (1846–1912) was a major contributor to the nineteenth century scholastic and practice-oriented renaissance of the rNying-ma. Born in

Kong-sprul Rinpoche

Khams, many of his teachers were leaders of the Eclectic Movement. A most versatile and comprehensive scholar, Mi-pham systematized the Sūtras and Tantras and their voluminous Tibetan commentaries and wrote over thirty-two volumes on subjects ranging from painting, poetics, and sculpture, to engineering, chemistry, alchemy, medicine, logic, philosophy, and Tantra—as well as two volumes on Kālacakra cosmology. Lama Mi-pham compiled and practiced innumerable Sādhanas, and at one time he spent seven years in meditatative retreat. He was a leading disciple of 'Jam-dbyangs mKhyen-brtse'i-dbang-po, who considered Mi-pham as his spiritual son. Lama Mi-pham's three chief successors were Kaḥ-thog Siddha, Zhe-chen rGyal-tshab, and Kun-bzang-dpal-ldan, also known as Kun-dpal.

Ā-Dzom 'Brug-pa. Ā-Dzom 'Brug-pa (Rigs-'dzin sna-tshogs-

Lama Mi-pham

rang-grol) was the disciple of 'Jam-dbyangs mKhyen-brtse'i-dbang-po and a teacher of the Second 'Jam-dbyangs mKhyen-brtse'i-dbang-po. Lama Mi-pham was his trusted spiritual friend, and he received visions from 'Jigs-med-gling-pa when he was thirty. An essential link in the sNying-thig Oral-transmission, several of Ā-Dzom 'Brug-pa's disciples achieved the rainbow body. He was also one of the last gTer-ma masters, and he studied the *Ye-shes bla-ma* and *rTsa'-rlung* from dPal-sprul Rinpoche. Ā-Dzom 'Brug-pa received teaching transmission on thirty-seven occasions from 'Jam-dbyangs mKhyen-brtse'i-dbang-po, his principal guru.

Kaḥ-thog Siddha. Kaḥ-thog Siddha Chos-kyi-rgya-mtsho was also a direct disciple of the First 'Jam-dbyangs mKhyen-brtse'i-dbang-po and a teacher of the Second 'Jam-dbyangs mKhyen-brtse'i-dbang-

Ā-Dzom 'Brug-pa

po. A great preserver of Nying-ma teachings, he was one of the spiritual successors of Lama Mi-pham. He received sMin-grol-gling's Vinaya and Bodhisattva lineages, and as a lineage holder of gTer-ma teachings, he rediscovered many essential rNying-ma Tantric texts and had them republished. At Kaḥ-thog Monastery, he rebuilt "Padmasambhava's Palace," using generous quantities of copper and gold.

Zhe-chen rGyal-tshab. Zhe-chen rGyal-tshab was a principal student of Kong-sprul. Highly learned in the teachings of Lama Mi-pham, he was the spiritual successor of the Master. He was also very proficient in the practice of the Vajrakīla Sādhana and was a poetic author, writing over thirteen volumes. 'Jam-mgon Kong-sprul imparted his lineage of the mDo-sGyu-Sems to Zhe-chen rGyal-tshab, who in turn passed it on to Zhe-chen Kong-sprul, the Second 'Jam-mgon Kong-sprul.

Kaḥ-thog Siddha

mKhan-po Ngag-dga'. mKhan-po Ngag-dga', also known as Ngag-dbang-dpal-bzang, follows the lineage of dPal-sprul Rinpoche through mKhan-po Ngag-chen, who was the disciple of dPal-sprul. He wrote a number of commentaries in the traditional style of the Indian Sūtras and Śāstras, and during his time, was the principal teacher at Kaḥ-thog Monastery. His major disciple was the Abbot at Dar-thang Monastery, mChog-sprul Chos-kyi zla-ba, who received the teachings of the sNying-thig from him.

Kun-bzang-dpal-ldan. Kun-bzang-dpal-ldan, also known as Kun-dpal, was a spiritual son of Lama Mi-pham and philosophy teacher at Kaḥ-thog Monastery. He received Mi-pham's oral instructions and teachings on Śāntideva's commentary to the *Bodhicaryāvatāra* from

Zhe-chen rGyal-tshab

dPal-sprul Rinpoche, his root guru. He was the principal teacher of sPo-ba sPrul-sku.

Seven Mūlagurus of Tarthang Tulku

In his youth, Tarthang Tulku (Dar-thang sPrul-sku, Kun-dga' dGe-legs) underwent an intense period of instruction in traditional introductory areas of study from a number of learned teachers, including his own father. His more advanced studies began when he was fourteen and were completed at the age of twenty-seven. During his life, Tarthang Tulku has received instructions from twenty-five teachers, seven of whom were his Root Gurus. These masters imparted to him initiations, esoteric instructions, advanced philosophical doc-

mKhan-po Ngag-dga'

trines, inner Tantric explanations and practices, and a multitude of Oral-transmission lineages.

The entire corpus of Buddhist teachings, as reflected throughout the pages of this short history, were held by these seven gurus. Without the continuation of the lineage by such masters, the study of Buddhism would become an academic subject bearing no ultimate meaning and having no real value. Through the efforts of these masters, the vibrancy and dynamism of Lord Buddha's realization continues to be carried on today for the benefit of those fortunate enough to study and practice within their lineage.

The Second 'Jam-dbyangs mKhyen-brtse'i-dbang-po. The Second 'Jam-dbyangs mKhyen-brtse'i-dbang-po (Chos-kyi-blo-gros, b. 1896) was born in Golok ('Gu-log). Kaḥ-thog Siddha was his first

Kun-bzang-dpal-ldan

teacher. After living at Kaḥ-thog Monastery, he went to rDzong-gsar Monastery, which was the original monastery of the First 'Jam-dbyangs mKhyen-brtse'i-dbang-po. In his travels he founded a number of retreat centers and soon became known as the 'King of Teachers'. A comprehensive scholar and accomplished meditator, his wealth of knowledge was almost identical with that of the First 'Jam-dbyangs mKhyen-brtse'i-dbang-po. Respected by followers of all schools, he extensively practiced the teachings of all of Tibet's philosophical and experiential traditions. He was the holder of all the major rNying-ma and Sa-skya lineages and was a recipient of the complete sNying-thig teachings. This outstanding master, who lived into the late 1950's, was a living example of King Khri-srong-lde'u-btsan, and his disciples considered him omniscient.

Tarthang Tulku extensively studied under him at rDzong-gsar

'Jam-dbyangs mKhen-brtse'i Chos-kyi-blo-gros

Monastery, receiving the teachings of the Sa-skya-pa, as well as the rNying-ma-pa. Imparting to him precious teachings leading to inward realization, mKhyen-brtse'i Rinpoche's oral explanations to Tarthang Tulku included a wide range of experiential and meditation lineages. His teachings included Lama Mi-pham's lineage of Oral-explanation, Atiyoga Instructions, gTer-ma initiations, the 'Path-and-Fruit' instructions of the Sa-skya-pa, the collected writings of the First 'Jam-dbyangs mKhyen-brtse'i-dbang-po, 'Jigs-med-gling-pa's sNying-thig teachings, and the commentaries on the Vajrakīla Sādhana.

Zhe-chen Kong-sprul. A direct disciple of Zhe-chen rGyal-tshab, Zhe-chen Kong-sprul (b. 1901) was known as the Second 'Jam-mgon Kong-sprul. Upon the death of his teacher, he became Abbot of Zhe-chen Monastery. Tarthang Tulku received from him the complete

Zhe-chen Kong-sprul

mDo-sGyu-Sems Inner Tantric Yoga Teachings, the lineage of the entire thirty-two volumes of Lama Mi-pham, and instructions in the thirteen volumes of Zhe-chen rGyal-tshab.

Ā-'Gyur Rinpoche. 'Gyur-med rDo-rje (Ā-Dzom rGyal-sras 'Gyur-med rDo-rje, b. 1895), also known as Ā-'Gyur Rinpoche, was a principal carrier of the rDzogs-chen sNying-thig teachings. He was a master of both bKa'-ma and gTer-ma, and a holder of the Oral-transmissions of his father, Ā-Dzom 'Brug-pa. He was also the unique possessor of the teachings of all the commentaries on the *gSang-ba-snying-po*, and was a devoted follower of the three inner Tantric yoga practices (Mahā-, Anu-, Ati-yoga). Ā-'Gyur Rinpoche was the author of a large autocommentary to Sangs-rgyas gSang-ba's (Buddhaguhya) commen-

Ā-'Gyur Rinpoche

tary on the *gSang-ba snying-po* (Mahāyoga Tantric cycles). Recognized as the incarnation of O-rgyan gTer-bdag-gling-pa, he had innumerable students from parts of Khams and throughout Tibet.

Tarthang Tulku studied under him for two and one-half years, receiving from him the sNying-thig teachings and special Oral-explanations, Klong-chen-pa's "Seven Treasures," as well as some of his own stylistic commentaries on Mahāyoga.

mChog-sprul Rinpoche. mChog-sprul Rinpoche (Dar-thang mChog-sprul Chos-kyi-zla-ba, b. 1893) was born in gZi'-gag (gZigs-rag) in rGyal-rong and is an essential carrier of dPal-yul's three hundred year old lineage of gTer-ma, which he received from dPal-yul Padma Nor-bu (d. 1932). This lineage of gTer-ma is based principally

mChog-sprul Rinpoche

upon Padmasambhava's eight Heruka Sādhanas. As a monk, he received from Kaḥ-thog Siddha sMin-drol-gling's Vinaya and Bodhisattva lineages.

mChog-sprul Rinpoche imparted to Tarthang Tulku private instructions on being a lama and dPal-yul's lineage of gTer-ma and Padmasambhava's Heruka Sādhanas, as well as Klong-chen-pa's "Seven Treasures." He also imparted to Tarthang Tulku most of the teachings and practices of three great gTer-ma masters: Ratna-gling-pa, gNam-chos Mi-'gyur-rdo-rje, and Rigs-'dzin-'ja'-tshon-snying-po. After bestowing to him private meditation instructions, he offered Tarthang Tulku valuable advice on who his next teachers should be and what subject matter he should focus on.

sNang-mdzad-grub-pa'i-rdo-rje. sNang-mdzad-grub-pa'i-rdo-

sNang-mdzad-grub-pa'i-rdo-rje

rje (b. 1910), the sixth Zhe-chen Rab-'byams, was an essential lineage holder of the sixty-two volume *Rin-chen-gter-dzod*, which he received from Zhe-chen rGyal-tshab, who received it from the Second 'Jam-dbyangs mKhyen-brtse'i-dbang-po. He was one of the five most distinguished masters in the province of Khams and a principal lama to the kings of sDe-dge. Tarthang Tulku received from him the entire corpus of gTer-ma teachings, the *Rin-chen gter-mdzod* lineage and thousands of initiations and practices.

sPo-ba sPrul-sku. mDo-sngags-bstan-pa'i-nyi-ma (b. 1900), also known as sPo-ba sPrul-sku, was an incarnation of dPal-sprul Rinpoche. He was the disciple of Kung-bzang-dpal-ldan, with whom he studied for thirty-seven years. Spiritual successor Lama Mi-pham's lineage, he was highly learned in all the philosophical viewpoints put forth by the

sPo-ba Sprul-sku

Master. One of the very last scholars of the rNying-ma philosophical tradition, he was also the holder of a number of Sūtra and Śāstra lineages. sPo-ba sPrul-sku was versed in the teachings of Klong-chen-pa, the *gSang-ba snying-po* commentaries, and the rDzogs-chen sNying-thig. Like Mi-pham, he was a versatile scholar and wrote on a wide range of subjects, formulating insightful interpretations on the rNying-ma-pa view. He was the author of the popular work, *A Summary of Philosophical Viewpoints*, which is a clarification of difficult points that are often misunderstood.

Tarthang Tulku received from him a wide variety of philosophical instruction, including Klong-chen-pa's commentary on the *Guhya-mūla-garbha-tantra* and 'Jigs-med-gling-pa's sNying-thig teachings, as well as his own commentaries on the *Prajñāpāramitā-sūtra* and the *Abhisamāyalaṅkāra*.

Padma Siddhi

Padma Siddhi. Padma Siddhi's birth in 'Gu-log in 1888 had been predicted by thirteen gTer-ma masters. He was recognized as an incarnation of Srong-btsan-sgam-po, and his teachings were based to a great extent on the *Mani Padme* mantras. A most compassionate teacher, he was a living exemplar of Bodhisattva-action and one of the very last holders of the Bodhisattva lineage.

Tarthang Tulku received from him numerous childhood recognitions and meditation instructions. Through his blessings, Tarthang Tulku had the opportunity to study the Buddhadharma, and he received a number of special realizations from him. With the inspiration of Padma Siddhi, Tarthang Tulku continues to work on his behalf in service to the Dharma.

Appendices

rNying-ma Monasteries in Tibet

The following are the names of all the monasteries in Tibet that preserved the rNying-ma tradition until recent times. The figure in parenthesis indicates the number of resident monks.

bSam-yas-mi-'gyur-lhun-gyis-grub-pa'i-gtsug-lag-khang (100)
sKu'i-dben-gnas-sgrags-yang-rdzong (18)
gSung-gi-dben-gnas-mchim-phu (30)
Thugs-kyi-dben-gnas-lho-brag-mkhar-chu (80)
Yon-tan-dben-gnas-yar-klung-shel-brag (50)
Phrin-las-dben-gnas-mon-kha-ne-ring (8)
Guru'i-sgrub-gnas-rdzong-kham-phug (10)
sDrags-mda'-mthso-rgyal-bla-mtso (8)
Brag-dmar-mgrin-bzang-dgon (6)
sNe'u-gdong-bna-gtsang-gra-tshang (90)
Yum-bu-gla-sgang (5)
'On-phu-stag-tshang (20)
'On-lha-khang-dgon (25)
dPal-ri-theg-mchog-gling (150)
Cho-rgyal-srong-bstan-bang-so (25)
bYing-mda'-ao-dkar-brag (1)
Kun-bzang-theg-mchog-chos-gling (8)
Dar-rgyas-chos-gling (50)
sNying-mdo-dgon (70)
Kun-mkhyen-klong-chen-gzims-phug (1)
Yar-rje-lha-khang (5)
Sog-lha-khang-dgon (1)
Drod-sa-o-'rgyan-rdzong (9)
Byang-chub-gling (103)
gZhog-pa-lha-chu (20)
Ri-sni-dgon (30)
Bud-rde-sgom-chen-dgon (60)
'U-shang-rdo-yi-lha-khang (10)
Zang-yag-brag (65)
Gangs-ri-thod-dkar (8)
gNubs-chen-gdan-sa (12)
Lha-lung-theg-mchog-rab-rgyas-gling (110)
sMra-bo-lcog (60)
La-yag-gu-ru-lha-khang (8)
Lho-brag-byang-chub-gling (23)
gNas-gzhi-dgon (60)

Tshe-lam-dpal-ri-dgon (10)
Chog-pu-ri-khrod (10)
Lha-ri-bum-thang-dgon (12)
mKho-mthing-lha-khang (15)
Lho-brag-seng-ri-dgon (17)
Ngo-mtshar-rdo-yi-mchod-rten (8)
lChags-phur-dgon (20)
bSam-yas-gya'-ma-lung (30)
sTag-lung-gsang-chos-dgon (90)
Chos-rdzong-theg-mchog-rab-gling (10)
bSam-gtan-chos-gling (20)
Chos-rdzong-ri-khrod (10)
Brag-nag-ri-khrod (1)
gNas-ri-dgon (8)
Lha-lung-shar-dgon (10)
dGon-pa-byang (25)
Theg-mchog-rig-gling (22)
Chos-rdzong-tshe-bcu-lha-khang (5)
Chos-rdzong-sge'u-dgon (1)
'Brog-brag-ra-dgon (60)
Yon-rdo-dgon (52)
Phu-ma-sa-mtsams-dgon (10)
mDo-snags-chos-gling (30)
Yar-'brog-gling-gra-tshang (8)
Do-nang-padma-ri-khrod (10)
Do-nang-nyan-pa-ri-khrod (1)
Kha-lung-ri-khrod (15)
dBon-gzim-dgon (50)
Chos-sngon-dgon (60)
Yar-'brog-bla-brang-dgon (10)
Bla-brang-brag-dmar-dgon (1)
Do-nang-lu-gu-dgon (1)
Lho-rdzong-spang-legs-dgon (20)
rDza-yul-grub-dgon (50)
Mon-mkhar-dgon (33)
Theg-mchog-gling (53)
sMin-grol-rab-brtan-gling (60)
gTsang-dpal-ri-dgon (30)
Chos-sde-gling (45)
sGrub-gnas-mkhar-chen-brag (70)
sGe'u-lcag-phug-dgon (10)
gTsang-na-bza'-phug (8)
lCags-kha-lha-khang-tshogs-pa (1)
gTsang-gci-tsha-phug (8)
gTsang-rgyang-nam-snying-sgrub-phug (1)
gTsang-rgyang-bla-brang-dgon (15)
Lha-rtse-dgon-sbug (20)
gTsang-bla-gad-ser-dgon (8)
gra-phu-dgon-phug (60)
Mus-mdog-'ug-bya-lung-pa (12)
Bde-gling-ma-ni-tshog-pa (20)
gTsang-sgrol-lhas-dgon (15)
bsTar-brgyas-sgrub-tshogs (21)
rDze-lung-bla-brang-dgon (33)
sMon-'gro-sgrub-sde-dgon (102)
Nyin-khang-bla-brang-dgon (50)
mKhas-sngon-dgon (30)
Khrab-sgrub-sgrub-sde (12)
Man-khang-sgrub-sde (10)
gSang-sngags-chos-gling (123)
gTsang-bya-kar-dgon (30)
Brag-nag-bla-brang (20)
Ngam-ring-lha-bu-bla-brang (15)
bDe-phug-dgon (20)
rDzong-phu-sgrub-sde-dgon (10)
sBar-bug-rta-ze-dgon (12)
gTsang-rin-lding-sgrub-phug (1)
gCung-ri-che-dgon (30)
Ri-mo-dgon (25)
gCung-lha-lding-dgon (33)
dPal-ri-padma-chos-gling (20)
Lha-brag-srid-gsum-dgon (52)
gCung-gi-nya-ma-phug (8)
gZhung-'od-dkar-dgon (20)
La-rgyab-mthong-gling-dgon (25)
gTsang-la-byang-dgon (10)

'Ong-mgo-lha-khang (1)
bDe-chen-steng-dgon (33)
bDe-chen-chung-dgon (1)
Rong-khams-bu-lung (8)
gyu-ri-gzim-phug (9)
Brag-dkar-chos-sde (20)
gTsang-gling-phu-dgon (10)
Ṭa-phig-bkra-shis-sgang (20)
gTsang-bsam-sgang-dgon (25)
Khyung-bde-bcan (15)
gTsang-bde-chen-dgon (21)
Rab-brtan-nor-bu-chos-gling (30)
gTsang-rgya-mcho-bla-brang (40)
Gram-bu-dpal-chen-ldings (45)
'od-phug-rdza-ra-dgon (23)
gTsang-rja-thun-dgon (30)
gTsang-gya'-ri-dgon (31)
Khams-mdzes-dgon (20)
'O-bran-bla-brang (25)
mKhar-ka-na-min-dgon (33)
gSang-gling-bla-tshogs (50)
sred-padma-chos-gling (10)
sGrol-ma-ldings (10)
sred-mkhar-chen-dgon (9)
mNgon-mngal-chos-sde-dgon (30)
De'u-ri-khrod (31)
gTsang-sher-lung-dgon (20)
Ba-ri-lo-tsa-dgon (25)
dGon-pa-jo-khang (33)
mChod-rten-nyi-ma'i-dgon (50)
Lhun-grub-chos-rdzong-dgon (10)
Ri-khrod-dpal-'byor-gling (10)
dGa'-ldan-chos-sbub-dgon (18)
gTsang-sa'-og-dgon (20)
gYag-sde-drag-gzhong-ma-lak-gnyis (45)
O-rgyan-chos-lhun-chos-bcu-lha-khang (25)
gTsang-thar-gling-dgon (10)
Byang-lding-dgon (12)
Bu-dgon-sgrub-gra (8)
Chos-sde-rig-lding-gra-tsang (80)
Se-ra-sgrub-sde-dgon (15)
sKye-lung-ri-khrod (8)
rDza-rong-phu-dgon (25)
Phu-chung-sgrub-khang (1)
Phung-po-ri-bo-che (50)
Zang-zang-lha-brag (33)
Nyi-shar-khu-lung-sgrub-khang (1)
gTsang-lung-shar-dgon (12)
Pa-nam-chu-bzang-dgon (70)
Nya-mo-ha-'o-dgon (30)
Lha-ri-gzim-phug (22)
gTsang-byang-zab-mo-dgon (40)
Lha-gdong-gsang-sngags-chos-gling (10)
'O-yug-gos-sngon-dgon (30)
Zab-phu-lung-dgon (100)
sNye-mo-ru-dgon (50)
Rong-phu-rdza (1)
Pho-gang-rdo-mgo-dgon (20)
sGrub-sde-dgon (31)
bKhra-lung-dgon (35)
Sog-rtse-dgon (30)
sKye-lung-dgon (10)
bKra-shis-mthong-smon-dgon (20)
mDo-sngags-chos-gling (60)
Pad-ma-bde-gling (50)
Kha-rag-sgrub-sde (10)
bDe-skyid-chos-gling (30)
Shri-chos-'khor-sgang (10)
Yan-ched-nub-dgon (12)
sPo-rong-padma-chos-gling (35)
Zur-mtsho-na-khra-dgon (15)
Gangs-ri-nam-mkha'-khyung-rdzong (30)
La-stod-nub-dgon-che-ba (21)

Nub-dgon-chung-ba (10)
mTsho-sgo-se-ra-lhun-po (8)
Shri-bya-rog-rdzong (4)
Byang-do-skya-dgon (150)
Drag-po-rtse-le-dgon (30)
Khra-mo-byang (30)
rGya-tsha-ze-mo-dgon (25)
gNyal-dre'u-sles (140)
rDo-mkhar-dgon (70)
Long-po-bde-chen-dgon (83)
rDo-dung-dgon (120)
dGa'-ba-lung (10)
sBa-kha-gsang-sngags-gling (120)
Yid'-ong-gsang-sngags-gling (100)
gNas-chung-rdo-rje-sgra-dbyangs-gling (115)
Phur-cham-dgon (40)
Pre-ta-bu-ri-dgon (30)
Seng-'khor-sgrub-rgyud-dgon (30)
mDun-chung-dgon (50)
Ri-rdo-dgon (15)
sTong-rtse-ra-che-dgon (32)
mKhar-chen-dgon (40)
Phun-tshogs-chos-sde-gling (200)
Nag-tshang-bye-phug-dgon (30)
sGar-nam-mkha'-khyung-rjong (35)
Bud-bde-skyid-tshal-gdon (10)
lCags-zam-dgon (40)
Nam-mkha'-lding-dgon (55)
bSam-gtan-gling (75)
Rab-gling-chos-lung-dgon (15)
bDe-chen-dgon-pa-byang (33)
Si-shing-dgon (10)
Kha-reg-chos-ldings-dgon (50)
Brag-dmar-dgon (15)
bKa'-'gyur-lha-khang-dgon (20)
sTong-ra-ra-sde-dgon (8)
Brag-'go-dgon (8)
rLung-lung-dgon (6)
Shing-rtsa-dgon (20)
rNam-gling-sang-dgon (25)
sTag-lung-dbon-dgon (10)
Karma-lha-lding-dgon (12)
Shar-gling-dgon (70)
rGyal-ba-nub-dgon (9)
rTse'u-lha-khang (2)
Byams-pa-gling-dgon (3)
sGrub-sde-dgon (70)
Gra-ri-bo-rnam-rgyal (67)
bSam-gtan-dgon (15)
Gling-stod-dgon (17)
Nyin-mo-dgon (30)
Na-ring-dgon (35)
rTsag-sgrub-sde-dgon (9)
Cha-dkar-dga'-dlan-chos-gling (100)
Zur-mkhar-o-rgyan-nam-mkha'-gling (30)
mDo-sngags-gling (35)
gSang-sngags-dga'-tsal-dgon (25)
He-ru-ka'i-lha-khang (8)
Byang-'phrang-ri-khrod (6)
Brag-sne-dgon (300)
Shel-grong-gsang-sngags-gling (50)
'Jun-chos-ldan-dgon (50)
Srin-ri-dgon (25)
Byang-chub-lding-dgon (20)
Sgo-ra-chos-rdzong-dgon (30)
Lha-ru-sman-rgyal-lha-khang (35)
Pad-bkod-dgon (45)
sGrub-sde-dgon (30)
sNgags-ra-dgon (25)
Brag-dmar-steng-dgon (15)
kCung-tshang-dgon (10)
rGya'u-dgon (20)
'Byad-dgon (3)
Seng-sna-dgon (3)

Bye-ri-dgon (3)
Brag-'jla-dgon (8)
Ba-sha-ri-dgon (5)
dGon-spar-dgon (63)
Nam-steng-dgon (60)
Nyi-sde-dgon (50)
Phu-mo-dgon (8)
mKho-skyid-ri-khrod (22)
dKar-chen-dgon (8)
lCags-zhur-lha-khang (9)
dKyil-lkhor-sbug-ri-khrod (8)
'Bum-sde-lha-khang (20)
Khrangs-gnyer-tsang-dgon (15)
bSe-phug-dgon (6)
Ser-mig-dgon (12)
dGon-ngar-ri-khrod-steng (8)
'Od-zer-chos-gling (20)
Lha-brag-dgon (15)
O-rgyan-bde-chen-gling (60)
Rong-ri-sna-dgon (55)
Chos-sde-gling (103)
Rong-thog-spo-dgon (5)
Chos-rdzong-dgon (30)
Chu-tshan-dgon (20)
rTa-nag-rtsi'u-dgon (75)
Bya-tsa-dgon (35)
Gung-thang-dgon (15)
bsTan-'phel-chos-gling-dgon (20)
Pa-rnam-dga'-gdong-dgon (350)
Brang-chen-dgon (30)
Tsa-ri-ri-khrod (8)
Brag-skye-dgon (50)
Khra-mo-ri-khrod (4)
sKyid-sbug-dgon (100)
Theg-mchog-gling (205)
'Brag-sngon-dgon (20)
Brag-dmar-seng-gdong-dgon (30)
Sho-gla-dgon (31)
Tse-dpag-dgon (50)
sByang-bu-byams-dgon (8)
Thog-'brum-dgon (38)
bSangs-byon-lab-phye-dgon (60)
Dur-khrod-dgon (63)
Bu-ru-strin-bsam-dgon (35)
dGon-pa-gra-tshang (30)
Rin-chen-chos-gling (10)
Lha-ri-gzim-phug (50)
Shod-nang-dgon (3)
Ma-sbum-ri-khrod (8)
sGrub-phu-ri-khrod (9)
Khram-stod-thang-pu-dgon (20)
Nor-bu-dga'-ldan-dgon (22)
Ka-dgon-ri-khrod (2)
'Grel-ma-ri-khrod (6)
Gyo-rngam-chos-dgon (15)
Ba-ma-chos-dgon (30)
Lung-dgon-pa (8)
gNas-bbas-dgon (30)
'Jug-ri-khrod (25)
sKyel-dkar-rdzong-ri-khrod (8)
Thang-spe-ri-khrod (10)
Lha-khang-gra-tsang (28)
gYer-dbang-dgon (8)
Chos-lung-dgon (3)
sBub-chos-lung-ri-khrod (15)
Ri'u-che-ri-khrod (10)
dGu-thang-dgon (80)
Nya-pa-grub-dgon (30)
btSan-phug-dgon (90)
Khengs-khengs-dgon (70)
sPang-zhin-dgon (20)
gTam-bu-rig-chen-spungs (40)
bDe-chen-chos-gling (50)
Legs-spongs-dgon (30)
Ma-hā-ko-tra (55)
dGa'-ldan-chos-'pel-gling (50)
gTsang-chung-dgon (8)
Ser-kong-dgon (22)
Nyang-kha-bang-ri-bkra-shis-'od-'bar (10)

Bu-chu-bde-chen-steng (30)
Bu-chu-bla-ma-gling (70)
Ba-pa-rig-'dzin-gling (8)
Bang-'khor-bya-khung-dgon (9)
Shing-ki-dgon (10)
Kar-me-ba-dgon (50)
rDe-mo-dgon (50)
Shi-ba-dgon (20)
sTag-lung-tses-bchu-lha-khang (10)
Mang-dkar-gnas-gsar-dgon (50)
Myu-gu-lung-thugs-chen-tshogs-pa (20)
rKya-mkhar-bla (25)
Chu-bzang-dgon (15)
bKra-shis-sbug-sgrub-khang (20)
Gra-phyi-o-rgyan-smin-grol-gling (400)
Thub-bstan-rdo-rje-brag (200)
Ri-bo-dpal-'bar-dgon (50)
Dur-lha-dgon (5)
dGe-phu-mdo-bla-dgon (8)
Ko-jag-'gro-mgon-bla-brag (10)
sPel-legs-bde-chen-skyid-phug (20)
rDzong-'dun-sngags-pa-chos-bca (30)
gZhis-rtse-sngags-tshogs (100)
Nyi-shor-jo-bo-dgon (20)
Rong-pu-lha-khang (10)
bSos-snga-chos-ste-dgon (20)
dGon-pa-phug (10)
Gram-mtsho-dga-ldan-dgon (31)
Shel-dgar-ma-'dur-dgon (33)
mDo-chen-dgon (8)
Chu-'das-spe-lags-dgon (18)
gSang-gling-dgon (35)
Shang-ha'u-dgon (20)
Ser-brag-sgrub-sde (25)
Shang-zar-bu-dgon (155)
gNya'-nang-sngo-ra-dgon (300)
'Or-sbug-dgon (80)
Be-rtshe-dgon (70)
dKar-rkyan-dgon (90)
dGon-gsum-thar-pa-gling (120)
Brag-khed-ri-gong-dgon (40)
gZhung-rgyas-dgon (30)
Khram-gzigs-dgon (20)
E-'byod-dgon (30)
De-mo-rtshe-le-dgon (10)
Kong-po-gong-dgon (10)
rTa-thog-yungs-dkar-dgon (20)
Trag-po-sgrub-phug (10)
Lha-brag-ldam (80)
Sel-kyi-mchod-rten (20)
Har-shing-dgon (35)
Shel-khung-dgon (30)
dKyes-gling-dgon (2)
Ta-nag-dbyangs-chos (120)
Phu-chu-kha-rag-dgon (10)
mKhar-rkya'u-dgon (20)
bSam-yas-gya'-ma-lung (10)
'On-lha-khang-dgon (20)
tShe-ring-ljong (50)
Bē-ro-sgrub-dgon (20)
bSam-gtan-rtshe (70)
'Od-gsal-gling (35)
bSam-gtan-gling (25)
Trag-sgrub-dgon (8)
bDe-chen-gling (5)
Chu-bzang-dgon (10)
Gra-phyi-brag-po-che (15)
Chos-rdzong-ri-khrod (30)
O'rgyan-chos-lhun (20)
Yar-'brog-shugs-gseb-dgon (10)
Gangs-phug-dgon (10)
Brag-dmar-keh'u-tshang (15)
Sha-ri-dgon-gsar (60)
sMon-gling-dgon (30)
gYung-phu-rdza-lhud (20)
Lha-lung-dgon (40)

bSam-gtan-yang-rtse (31)
Sog-po-dgon (50)
Cha-lung-dgon (8)
sLe-pa-dgon (20)
Lhun-rtshe-dgon (25)
'Od-gsal-theg-gling (55)
Zangs-zangs-'od-gsal-gling (40)
Gangs-blon-chen-dgon (10)
Rin-chen-ldings (10)
Brag-gyag-dgon (10)
Chos-lung-dgon (20)
bDe-ldan-chos-gling (35)
Tha-ra-dgon (35)
Zha-lu-dgon (10)
dBen-tsa-dgon (15)
sByin-mdo-dgon (21)
mChong-rab-dgon (8)
Bar-thang-dgon (10)
Tha-gru-dgon (10)
Gong-khang-dgon (20)
dBen-phug-dgon (10)
dPal-ri-dgon (10)
'Od-gsal-yang-rtshe (20)
sKhyid-gzhong-dgon (10)
Bru-smug-dgon (20)
Bar-thang-skyed-phug-dgon (10)
Yul-lha-brag-dkar-dgon (20)
sPang-chen-nyi-dgon (10)
sGo-rab-gyar-sngo-dgon (25)
Chos-lung-dgon (40)
sKyog-po-mkar-rkya-dgon (20)
dPal-chen-dgon (20)
bYe-ma-lha-khang (25)
sTag-tshang-dgon (35)
bDe-chen-ri-khrod (30)
sGrol-ma-sbug (10)
Gu-ru-lha-khang (12)
rTa-phu-dgon (11)
Khang-stod-dgon (25)
Dung-skyong-dgon (13)
Sa-sgang-dgon (14)
sGrub-khang-dgon (35)
dByang-mo-dgon (22)
Pad-lung-dgon (15)
bKra-shis-gdong-dgon (10)
bKra-shis-gling (12)
Chos-gling-dgon (30)
bSam-gtan-chos-gling (15)
lDab-lung-dgon-gsar (15)
Gro-lung-dgon (35)
Phu-chung-dgon (10)
dPal-sde-dgon-gsar (22)
Phung Po-ri-bo-che (20)
Phu-mar-bsam-chos-dgon (40)
Brag-lung-bkra-shi-chos-dbings (10)
Chos-sbug-dgon (10)
bKras-'dzom-dgon (12)
sGrub-khang-dgon (15)
Phu-chung-'u-brag-dgon (18)
Bē-ro-dgon (13)
sMar-lam-dgon (35)
mDo-sngags-chos-gling (17)
Byang-chub-theg-gling (50)
Rong-chung-dgon (45)
Rong-phu-stod-dgon (38)
mTsho-sgo-dgon-'og (27)
mTsho-sgo-dgon-gsar (13)
dGon-ra-bzhi (17)
dGon-ra-dkar (20)
bDo-chen-dgon (11)
Chos-lung-dgon (4)
dGon-gsar-dgon (10)
dGon-pa-rtse (40)
bYang-gling-dgon (51)
Gram-mtsho-dgon (30)
Mu-stong-dgon (10)
Shī-khu-ba-dgon (20)
Mang-mkhar-chos-lding (50)
Padma-gling (18)

Bum-sgrub-dgon (12)
'Brong-phu-dgon (22)
Gzim-sbug-dgon (11)
Thar-rtshe-dgon (20)
Shugs-gseb-dgon (410)
'Od-zer-gling (40)
rTa-ra-mdo'i-dgon (13)
rNam-rab-bsam-gtan-dgon (33)
Chu-mig-dgon (17)
'Dre-stag-dgon (20)
Gong-dkar-dgon (12)
Lo'i-mo-dgon (15)
dPal-di-dgon (15)
Chos-phu-dgon (13)
sNa-dkar-dgon (15)
gLing-klung-dgon (30)
Zang-ri-khang-dmar (4)
bLo-dkar-dgon (20)
Brag-rtshe-dgon (15)
dKyil-chung-dgon (25)
Nyi-sde-dgon (15)
dGe-bcu-bkra-shi-lding (30)
Gur-tshur-dgon (17)
bSangs-'dzin-dgon (10)
Khra-phug-dgon (15)
bKra-shi-lha-lding-dgon (22)
Zhabs-brtan-dgon (12)
dByar-smug-dgon (10)
Gong-ra-dgon (15)
bSam-gtan-gling (25)
Chos-sding-dgon (35)
Stag-tsang-rtse-shod-dgon (27)
Zab-thu-dgon (33)
Yod-dkar-dgon (25)
Mo-lung-dgon (40)
Hrad-khang-dgon (45)
sMad-chung-dgon (25)
Gad-se-dgon (20)
Gra-lung-dgon (25)
rTa-rag-brag-dgon (23)
Gangs-pha-thang-'brog-dgon (40)
Gangs-ro-gla-chu-dgon (15)
bLa-brang-dgon (20)
Srab-mo-gya'-lung-dgon (20)
Gad-mo-shi-chen-dgon (25)
dBye-legs-dgon (5)
Khyim-'brog-dgon (25)
Ka-dag-dgon (15)
Khra-tsang-dgon (10)
gLang-rdo-bsam-'grub-dgon (7)
lDing-chen-dgon (22)
Nyi-smad-shi-khul-dgon (11)
'O-drag-dgon (17)
dGa'-ldan-lhun-po-dgon (45)
Lung-dmar-dgon (20)
Gnas-'khor-dgon (45)
Pho-lha-don-chos-dgon (5)
dGon-pa-byang (22)
bKra-shis-chos-gling (15)
bLa-brag-dgon (10)
sGang-dga'-dgon (5)
bSam-gtan-gling (17)
Chu-mig-dwangs-sang-dgon (50)
Rin-chen-sgang (70)
Brag-dkar-dgon (6)
'Dum-ra-dgon (15)
Phun-tsogs-chos-gling (37)
gLa-phyu-dgon (40)
gZhon-byang-dgon (50)
Og-chos-dgon (20)
Dzi-ma-dgon (15)
Du-ru-dgon-gsar (3)
Thus-mo-dgon-gsar (20)
Brang-ka-tog-dgon (25)
Chos-'khor-dgon (15)
Chos-rdzong-dgon (8)
Lha-lung-dgon (7)
Byams-pa-gling (40)
Spo-bu-ma-ni-dgon (30)
sMan-chung-dgon (35)

sGang-'go-dgon (90)
bDe-chen-dgon (20)
Long-po-ka-thog-dgon (30)
Len-ri-dgon (31)
'Bru-la-rin-chen-steng (25)
Be-la-ri-khrod (33)
mTsho-rdzong-dgon (27)
bSam-gtan-gling (7)
Chos-'khor-gling (60)
Rang-phu-dgon (22)
'Od-lkhor-dgon (30)
gSang-ba-ga-tshaḷ (40)
bDe-chen-gling (25)
Gu-ru-sgrub-phug (8)
rTa-mgrin-sgrub-phug (26)
mGo-gug-dgon (32)
dPa'-lung-dgon (8)
bDe-chen-dgon (9)
Phug-mo-che (32)
Nang-so-dgon (20)
rTa-mgrin-gnas (10)
rDo-rje-dbyings-dzong (20)
Gangg'i-ldem (35)
gTer-phu-dgon (26)
sPa-rogs-dgon (22)
Mar-spangs-dgon (80)
Nar-gtong-dgon (31)
Maṇḍal-ldem (27)
mChod-rten-mskor-ba (100)
Brgya-spyin-dgon (150)
Mel-tshe-dgon (100)
rTogs-'phel-ri-khrod (50)
Gnas-brtan-dgon (200)
dGe-legs-dgon (40)
lJon-steng-dgon (405)
rNgas-gzhung-dgon (141)
rNes-stod-dgon (133)
Chos-rdzong-dgon (40)
sTag-tsang-dgon (100)
sNgon-yag-dgon (100)
Chen-mo-dgon (50)
sPos-ni-ri-khrod (31)
'Bar-rdo-ri-khrod (45)
Ra-kho-bde-chen-dgon (30)
Ci-byed-dgon (203)
Nor-bu-ri-khrod (105)
Kho-tsa-ri-khrod (30)
gSal-steng-dgon (25)
Sog-chu-mdo-nyi-grags-dgon (705)
gChung-pa-chos-'khor-dgon (303)
sBa-sha-dgon (17)
Tha-mi-dgon (18)
lJongs-ljong-dgon (55)
Ga-gra-dgon (38)
sNgo-sne-dgon (11)
rGya-chen-dgon (7)
Ri-ba-dgon-bkra-shis-chos-gling (25)
La-ba-dgon (30)
bZo-ru-dgon (14)
sGo-chen-dgon (18)
mTsho-dkar-dgon (20)
'Brog-dgon (10)
Phag-mo-dgon (9)
Ba-reg-dgon (101)
Gu-ru-skal-ldan-dgon (30)
rNying-ma-gra-tsang (150)
Gru-ya-dgon (32)
gSang-chen-mthong-grol-dgon (115)
Chos-'khor-gling (51)
Ḍal-sad-dgon (89)
Zhi-khro-ri-khrod (95)
Kis-thog-can-byang-chub-gling (70)
dGes-la-dgon (60)
bDe-chen-gling (35)
Ra-ya-dgon (11)
Chos-gling-dgon (39)
Chos-srid-dar-rgyas-gling (50)
Su-zhug-dgon (75)

gSang-chen-dgon (125)
Ra-tsa-dgon (25)
dGe-rgyal-rdzogs-chen-dgon (137)
Ra-chen-dgon (87)
Nas-tsha-dgon (25)
rNying-ma-gra-tshang (450)
gNas-mgo-dgon (100)
rGyal-sras-dgon (350)
Sid-dhi-dgon (30)
Dpal-ri-dge-'dun-steng-dgon (150)
Lhun-grub-steng-dgon (157)
dGon-lung-ri-khrod (20)
Go-'jo-skyid-po-dgon (150)
rTse-rong-brag-nag-dgon (55)
mKho-khyim-dgon (150)
Dur-khrod-dgon (35)
sTag-mo-dgon (25)
Wa-ti-bde-chen-dgon (70)
'On-mtso-dgon (60)
Nyag-bla-dgon (135)
Ra-mgo-dgon (140)
dNgul-ra-dgon (150)
sKya-thang-dgon (80)
Ri-mgo-dgon (35)
rGya-ra-dgon (125)
Kha-legs-dgon (70)
Chos-rgyal-dgon (50)
'Thab-ra-dgon (75)
Lhu-chu-dgon (20)
bSam-'grub-dgon (42)
sBa-nag-dgon (30)
tSha-ru-dgon (80)
bLa-ma-ri-cog-dgon (8)
Lung-phu-dgon (55)
Yang-dgon-sgrub-sde (45)
'Jo-khe-ri-khrod (30)
Bo-nongs-la-khad-dgon (55)
Bang-na-ri-khod-dgon (7)
sTag-lung-dgon (70)
rDzogs-chen-shrī-sengha (55)
rDzogs-chen-sgrub-gra (60)
rDzogs-chen-ru-dam-bsam-gtan-chos-gling (850)
Zhe-chen-bstan-gnyis-dar-rgyas-gling (200)
Padma-thang (12)
Tshe-ring-ljongs (15)
gShin-rje-sgrub-phug (10)
Nag-chung-khar (10)
lCham-mo-'du-long-dgon (50)
rTse-gong-dgon (150)
Mangs-dgon-pa (70)
Nyi-lung-dgon (80)
rDza-rgyal-dgon (340)
Che-mo-dgon (105)
lCang-ma-ri-khrod (5)
Gu-lung-dgon (30)
Nor-gling-dgon (150)
Phyag-tsha-dgon (150)
Dril-dkar-dgon (80)
A-bse-dgon (30)
Ye-shes-dgon (41)
dBon-ru-stod-ma'i-dgon (135)
Bu-bgyud-dgon (127)
Nyi-zer-dgon (90)
sMan-legs-dgon (80)
sMad-stan-dgon (30)
Khro-shul-'gab-ma-dgon (105)
Ge-chag-dgon (50)
Khro-shul-gong-ma-dgon (100)
'Ju-mo-hor-dgon (225)
Phug-shung-dgon (125)
rDzi-mgo-dgon (202)
'Ju-mong-dgon (370)
Bar-sha-ri-khrod-nor-bu-bsam-'phel-gling (70)
rGyal-chen-ri-khrod-o-rgyan rnam-grol-gling (50)
Phug-sngon-ri-khrod-bstan-gnyis-dar-rgyas-gling (30)
rGyal-chen-ri-khrod (30)

gYang-khri-ri-khrod (30)
Seng-ge-ri-khrod (30)
Ra-ga-ri-khrod (30)
sTag-lam-ri-khrod (30)
kLong-rong-ri-khrod-bkra-shes-gling (25)
Pa-tam-dgon (100)
Chos-'khor-gling (70)
rNa-pad-dgon (40)
'Go-tsha-dgon (108)
bDe-chen-gling (25)
Ra-ya-dgon (37)
Tha-ma-dgon (20)
Su-ru-dgon (58)
gSang-chen-dgon (25)
Brag-gsar-dgon (40)
Ra-tsha-dgon (85)
dGe-rgyal-rdzogs-chen-dgon (27)
Ra-chen-dgon (105)
Nas-tsang-dgon (35)
dGe-'phel-dgon (41)
Kha-ri-bon-phrug-dgon (60)
bDe-chen-dgon (120)
dGe-rtse-'brug-grags-dgon (60)
Dzong-'go-dgon (331)
Rak-chab-sing-ri-dgon (437)
Rak-chab-dgon (437)
Seng-ri-rnam-brag-dgon (75)
Khram-dge-dgon (225)
A-'dzom-sgar (450)
sMyo-shul-dgon (170)
Yi-le-dgon (35)
sTag-mo-dgon (100)
Khang-sgar-dgon (355)
Tse-shul-dgon (205)
Gyag-ze-dgon (225)
dPe-war-e-wam-dgon (30)
rGya-bo-ri-khrod (8)
rNam-brag-dgon (45)
gNas-phu-ri-khrod (7)
dPe-war-rdo-brag-dgon (130)
brDa'-go-dgon (108)
Bro-brdung-dgon (185)
rMu-sang-dgon (225)
'Gu-re-dgon (70)
'Bo-ra-dgon (8)
Chos-nyid-dgon (21)
A-rab-dgon (8)
Chos-rgyal-dgon (75)
Drung-yig-dgon (55)
dPal-chen-dgon (25)
sGam-phug-dgon (108)
'Om-thang-dgon (80)
Gra-shing-dgon (22)
gLing-tsang-kaḥ-tog-dgon (105)
Legs-dgon-dgon (60)
mGo-tsha-dgon (405)
Khams-'ung-dgon (225)
bDe-chen-dgon (301)
rMog-rtsa-dgon (108)
lCim-stod-dgon (50)
sTag-rdzong-dgon (130)
Brag-dmar-dgon (250)
rDza-ka-dgon (245)
Tshang-rag-dgon (150)
rGyal-khri-dgon (90)
Gyag-rgyal-dgon (78)
gSer-chab-dgon (55)
Ga-ta-bsam-'grub-dgon (35)
Le-dge-chos-gling-dgon (50)
dPe-ri-dgon (155)
Nyi-dgon-steng (223)
'A-gnas-dgon (108)
Ko-mgo-dgon (55)
Stag-bla-dgon (51)
Ba-zer-dgon (47)
bKra-shis-chos-gling (500)
Gu-ru-dgon-gsar (55)
Zur-ba-dgon (40)
Go-'jo-dgon (35)

sNyu-'ong-dgon (70)
mTsho-kha-dgon (22)
Ye-shes-dgon (60)
A-'ung-dgon (87)
rTsa-rol-dgon (35)
Lhang-lhang-nor-bu-dgon (70)
Ge-sar-khyung-rdzong-dgon (75)
Brang-dkar-rdo-rje-yang-rdzong (110)
Gu-ru-dgon (170)
Zhi-ba-dgon (278)
'Byung-khungs-dgon (30)
'Ur-ba-dgon (70)
lCag-mdud-dgon (75)
mYa-gzi-dgon (90)
Tsha-ru-dgon (85)
A-ṇi-dgon (90)
gLag-brag-rdzong-dgon (75)
sKal-bzang-dgon (255)
Lha-'bum-dgon (100)
E-wam-dgon (95)
brDa'-dge-dgon (505)
Ngar-ngar-dgon (40)
'Od-phug-dgon (305)
dPe-ru-dgon (80)
Sa-nag-dgon (75)
'Jam-'Jam-dgon (250)
Bag-chags-dgon (60)
gLu-mo-ra (605)
Hor-dbyar-dgon (100)
'Dre-'tsal-dgon (260)
Gu-lus-dgon (35)
gNas-nang-dgon (321)
A-lcog-sgrub-sde-dgon (50)
'Brug-po-dgon (325)
sGo-chen-dgon (181)
Nyi-chen-dgon (60)
dGon-rnying-dgon (45)
Chos-'khor-gling (165)
sDis-lcam-dgon (60)
'Jang-sgang-dgon (83)
Cha-nang-dgon (90)
mKhar-gdong-dgon (200)
rGod-chen-dgon (250)
Shugs-khog-dgon (225)
mKar-nya-dgon (107)
mDo-mang-dgon (275)
sByi-mkhar-dgon (1125)
Kun-gling-dgon (308)
rBa-dag-ri-khrod (71)
gTsang-mda'-dgon (550)
Seng-ri-dgon (110)
rGya-khag-dgon (60)
Ra-sher-dgon (55)
Brag-mkhar-dgon (25)
Zu-nang-dgon (35)
gSer-kha-dgon (70)
gSer-phye-dgon (40)
dPal-ri-dgon (55)
rTa-drel-dgon (77)
sKyabs-gnang-dgon (30)
sKyer-gnang-dgon (45)
Ba-la-sgang (55)
Ba-la-sum-mdo-dgon (70)
Tse-nor-dgon (31)
Grangs-mkhar-dgon (75)
gRya'-nang-dgon (80)
mDo-sgar-gra-tsang (105)
Yig-chung-dgon (30)
sGrub-sde-dgon (28)
bKa'-babs-dgon (103)
La-khug-dgon (60)
sTag-tsang-dgon (32)
'Ba'-sgong-dgon (45)
Seng-ge-dgon (388)
rNam-kun-dgon (125)
Chos-ra-dgon (83)
bsTan-'dzin-dgon (102)
Sha-chen-dgon (20)
Nad-chags-dgon (15)

sDer-mo-dgon (150)
sTeng-chen-dgon (137)
lCags-mo-dgon (12)
Sa-dkar-ri-khrod (60)
dMar-mo-dgon (50)
Shugs-mgo-dgon (44)
dGon-mgod-dgon (55)
Khri-bcu-bsam-gtan-gling (1830)
Yan-rdo-dgon (165)
Pad-rdo-dgon (2580)
sTag-stag-dgon (790)
Sa-man-ta-ka-dgon (583)
So-nam-dgon (355)
lDi-li-dgon (380)
bDe-chen-gling (140)
Khri-bcu-bde-chen-dgon (1408)
Sa-stod-dgon (1800)
Sa-stod-stobs-chen-dgon (1250)
bLo-bzang-dgon (187)
Tsa-she-dgon (230)
Ku-ze-dgon (310)
Tsha-khang-dgon (175)
Ko-rog-dgon (255)
Dar-rgyas-dgon (158)
gLo-gyas-dgon (184)
Sing-so-dgon (40)
dKon-dbang-dgon (45)
sTag-tsang-dgon (159)
Mang-dskur-dgon (48)
mTsho-bdun-dgon (730)
Kun-khyab-gling (46)
sTobs-ldan-dgon (93)
'Bo-ka-gra-dgon (350)
Tsha-ba-dgon (35)
Pa-la-dgon (213)
bsTan-dar gling (37)
Khang-gsar-dgon (217)
Tsha-lung-dgon (80)
mDo-lung-dgon (258)
rGyab-dgon (40)
Brag-dkar-dgon (288)
Nor-lon-dgon (35)
bSam-gtan-chos-gling (338)
'Bar-mkhar-dgon (470)
dGon-gsar-dgon (75)
Tshad-pa-dgon (40)
Tsha-dos-dgon (35)
Tsha-khug-dgon (190)
lCe-dag-dgon (45)
So-yog-dgon (47)
'Ja'-thugs-dgon (80)
Yab-'di-dgon (81)
Sak-ra-dgon (40)
sKya-dgon-pa (60)
Shugs-pa-dgon (120)
sBas-gter-dgon (205)
Khams-ril-dgon (115)
sBa-gnyis-dgon (270)
Ya-yong-dgon (60)
Dza-ti-dgon (30)
Si-wi-dgon (35)
nYag-tshe-dgon (60)
Pha-ri-dgon (65)
Ta-ro-gyang-dgon (30)
Mi-ngor-dgon (35)
Tse-ri-dgon (50)
Cha-mi-dgon (60)
Lha-skyabs-dgon (70)
bKra-shis-sgang (170)
Tshang-song-dgon (275)
Ru-'byung-dgon (180)
Lhun-grub-dgon (1291)
Mi-rgyal-dgon (10)
Te-lo-dgon (150)
gSham-lding-dgon (40)
Ba-to-dgon (350)
Tsag-dgon-pa (50)
Khang-mga-dgon (10)
'Bo-to-stod-ma-dgon (151)
dGon-gsar-dgon (110)

A-ri-dgon (25)
Go-ri-dpal-dgon (350)
Bis-mgu-dgon (120)
sNa-'di-dgon (200)
Ze-sgro-dgon (250)
Wa-zo-dgon (156)
'Bo-to-'og-ma-dgon (130)
dPal-dgon-dgon (40)
rNam-gyal-dgon (500)
Gu-skyul-dgon (30)
Kha-la-dgon (50)
Shon-to-dgon (80)
rDi-wi-dgon (31)
dPon-skor-chos-sgar (351)
gSang-ru-chos-sgar (205)
Stag-thog-bar-ma'i-dgon (300)
Gangs-pa'i-dgon (135)
Ka-tog-dgon (135)
Tsa-mon-dgon (225)
Mo-sku-dgon (75)
Du-po-dgon (27)
Kho-pa-dgon (85)
bZhi-sde-dgon (77)
Si-ri-dgon (10)
Kyo-dag-dgon (75)
bZhag-dpal-dgon (55)
Mu-rtse-dgon (55)
rTa-thig-dgon (101)
nYo-khi-dgon (207)
dByar-dgon (100)
Dam-chos-dgon (201)
Bram-dgon (225)
Kin-tab-dgon (35)
Tsham-nag-dgon (78)
Ri-shi-dgon (19)
Dar-kyi-snyan-ri-dgon (405)
rDo-dgon (80)
Khra-gling-dgon (55)
Drug-shog-dgon (170)
'Bol-pa'i-dgon (250)
Zla-ba-dgon (125)
Dar-thang-mdo-sngags-bshad-sgrub-dar-rgyas-gling (1210)
Rung-dgon (150)
sGo-mang-dgon (70)
Ban-chen-dgon (90)
gDong-rdzong-dgon (50)
Khang-gsar-dgon (150)
Sta-thog-'og-ma'i-dgon (405)
'E-mda'-dgon (800)
Bon-yul-dgon (235)
mDo-thog-bkra-shis-bga'-'khyil-dgon (200)
dPal-'byor-dgon (37)
Ci-nang-dgon (100)
gSang-lung-dgon (200)
Ber-nag-dgon (47)
'Bar-'byug-dgon (78)
rDi-la-dgon (80)
dPal-ri-dgon (300)
Sog-tsa-dgon (125)
Chu-skya-dgon (10)
rMa-chen-go-mtshon-dgon (37)
Dga-ris-dgon (300)
rDa'o-gung-biug-dgon (308)
dGon-gung-kha (503)
Khri-skya-dgon (207)
Shrī-dgon (225)
Tha-thad-dgon (280)
Tho-thugs-dgon (195)
Tsha-gsum-dgon (408)
sMar-khams-dgon (260)
Ban-shul-dgon (300)
Rong-byi-skya-dgon (201)
dBon-bskor-dgon (205)
gTer-ston-dgon (508)
Sras-tsang-dgon (130)
Gyu-ngog-dgon (250)
Ra-dgon-pa (170)
Ya-'gro-dgon-pa (203)

mKhor-tse-rdo-ring-dgon (302)
mGon-shes-dgon (250)
dPe-shul-dgon (190)
Sog-gter-stong-dgon (180)
'Go-ram-'god-byang-dgon (50)
Bya-khung-ri-khrod (30)
Gu-ru-chos-lung-dgon (100)
rDzogs-pa-yar-long-dgon (705)
dKyil-longs-dgon (121)
Zis-dgon-pa (25)
Ra-ri-dgon-pa (60)
Kaḥ-thog-rdo-rje-gdan (800)
dPal-yul-rnam-rgyal-byang-chub-chos-gling (600)
Gu-ru-dgon-pa (205)
gShin-zog-dgon (808)
Hor-shes-dgon (300)
bStan-rkyas-dgon (550)
gTsang-mda'-dgon (790)
dKyil-sngon-dgon (302)
gSer-lha-tshe-ye-shes-sing-ge'i-dgon (1150)
Phya-nang-dgon (1875)
mTsho-kha-dgon (225)
gSer-stod-mdon-po-'brong-rir-gnas-'go'-dgon (220)
Sing-sing-dung-dkar-dgon (1208)
Lha-rtse-dgon (60)
gSer-thar-sbra-dgon (50)
'Jang-sgang-dgon (185)
bKra-shis-chos-gling (550)
rMig-rjes-dgon (90)
A-'u-se-ra-dgon (250)
Be-ru-dgon (50)
rBu-zur-dgon (330)
'U-brdung-dgon (90)
Sog-steng-dgon (40)
rTags-rgyal-dgon (100)
Khri-steng-dgon (1500)
Gru-rdza-dgon (50)
Sa-mgo-dgon (30)
'Un-'ja'-dgon (50)
Ra-khe-dgon (121)
Thugs-rje-chen-po'i-dgon (330)
'Od-zer-dgon (221)
Ba-la-dgon (70)
rGya-mtsho-dgon (55)
Gar-mchod-dgon (405)
Ses-khra-dgon (52)
Mu-mtsho-dgon (75)
Li-'bag-dgon (285)
Sa-stod-dgon (230)
Nor-shul-dgon (401)
Chu-dkyil-khrod (70)
rDzong-stod-dgon (81)
bSod-rgyal-chos-skar (50)
rGya-ru-dgon (55)
Shugs-sgang-dgon (151)
gSer-bgya-phyugs-dgon (110)
A-bong-dgon (90)
Pho-gdong-dgon (350)
gZhi-chen-mkhar-dmar-gsang-sngad-dgon (1100)
Rag-khrom-byams-pa-dgon (1300)
Stag-rtse-bsam-'grub-dgon (500)
rTa-shul-gong-mi'i-dgon (508)
Bo-chung-ru-gsal-ma'i-dgon (100)
rRag-thog-gong-ma'i-dgon (160)
'Dzi-ka-smad-a-skye'i-dgon (80)
'Go-log-a-bzod-dgon (280)
'Go-log-khang-gsar-ru-mang-dgon (300)
'Go-log-mi-ra-dgon (350)
'Go-log-phyag-chung-dgon (105)
Khang-gsar-ru-nyung-dgon (100)
gZhis-nang-dgon-pa (300)
Pho-chen-'bum-thang-dgon (200)
Stag-lung-dgon (700)
Wa-shul-rme-ba'i-dgon-chen (1010)

dGe-rtshe-gra-lag-dgon (1360)
Wa-shul-dpon-dgon-gsum (300)
dHo'i-ri-nang-dgon (50)
mKhan-leb-dgon (50)
Phug-pa-dgon (150)
rTa-shul-bar-ma'i-dgon (80)
rTa-shul-'og-ma'i-dgon (100)
Sang-sang-gra-gra-dgon (110)
gSer-zho-rog-dgon (300)
dKyil-lung-dgon (167)
gSer-rgong-rgon-mchod-rten-dgon (20)
gSer-gnub-zur-dgon (300)
Khang-dgongs-dgon-pa (380)
Ra-hor-dgon (1000)
Khro-skyabs-dbe-dgon (700)
Khro-smad-skya-pa'i-dgon (800)
Khro-skyabs-dbang-zu-dgon (200)
Mi-nyag-dpal-ri-dgon (250)
Brag-mkhar-dgon (340)
Seng-ge-dgon (990)
gSer-lha-tse-chu-byar-dgon (90)
gSer-kyi-reb-dgon (80)
gSer-brgya-dgon (110)
gSer-nyug-sgang-dgon (80)
rJe-dkar-lug-lha-dgon (450)
rDzong-smad-nyag-bla-dgon (87)
rDzong-stod-mtso-dkar-dgon (150)
Yar-stod-mtso-nag-dgon (55)
gSer-snyag-gi-shug-'bos dgon (105)
rTo-smad-dgon-gong-ma (951)
sMar-mdo-dgon-bar-ma (50)
sMar-mdo-gong-ma'i-dgon-pa (70)
'Bos-stod-nag-rgar-dgon (600)
dBang-chen-'brog-dgon (100)
rTse-mda'-dgon-chen (110)
rTses-mda'-dgon-chung (150)
mDe-nang-dgon (80)
Mug-yang-dgon (100)
Rab-cha-dgon (50)
Bong-nge-dgon (50)
Gyag-'go-dgon (200)
'Go-yongs-dgon (55)
Dzi-rung-dgon (60)
A-khyung-khang-sgar-dgon (208)
Ra-los-dgon (450)
rMa-stod-ser-shes-dgon (200)
'Go-log-gad-mar-dgon (50)
Ko-chen-nyi-lung-dgon (200)
rGya-skor-dgon (200)
'Go-log-sba-sar-dgon (160)
Tsang-skor-dgon (220)
Shar-'od-dgon (2100)
Smar-yul-bar-bzhi'-dgon (400)
Sbu-tsha-dgon (100)
Ban-nag-dgon (100)
Ban-nag-ri-khrod-dgon (103)
lCag-ri-'od-'bar-dgon (30)
'Brug-sgang-dgon (200)
Hor-skor-dgon (50)
Ri-zur-dgon (410)
sNyan-lung-dgon (100)
mKhar-sgang-chos-sgar (120)
Skyid-lung-dgon (200)
Sang-sang-ri-nang-dgon (105)
'Ja'-gur-ri-khrod (235)
bYa-bral-dgon (50)
mDa'-tsang-dgon (20)
Rag-chab-dgon (551)
rDo-shugs-chung-dgon (502)
rDo-gyu-thog-dgon (500)
Gyu-khog-dgon (552)
Gyu-khog-bya-bral-dgon (710)
Gyu-khog-bya-bral-dgon (105)
Yar-lung-dgon (141)
mKhar-nang-'gab-dgon (40)
'Dzam-thog-tsa-dkar-dgon (1005)

rDo-grub-chen-dgon (250)
sMar-dar-thang-dgon (1525)
Khri-dar-rgyas-dgon (130)
'Dzam-thang-gsang-lung-dgon (300)
Bla-brang-dkra-shes-'khyil (710)
A-khyung-gnam-rdzong (500)
Grubs-dgon-pa (300)
Brag-dkar-sna-ba-dgon (202)
Re-kong-nyin-dgon (1240)
Re-kong-srib-dgon (1760)
Gos-sde-dgon (300)
Zhabs-dkar-dgon (30)
lJang-skya-dgon (125)
Phyogs-ra-dgon (210)
Khra-gzhung-dgon (130)
Ke-ba-dgon (40)
Hor-brgya-dgon (45)
Kha-cig-dgon (305)
Dang-'gya-dgon (700)
sPre'u-rdzong-dgon (402)
sNgags-si-dgon (410)
Gra-pa-dgon (102)
Nya-nag-dgon (208)
Sa-twa'i-dgon (300)
bsTan-dar-dgon (130)

Transmission Lineages

The seven lines of transmission which follow name the principal holders of the lineage. There were also innumerable branches and minor lines.

Vinaya Lineage (Main Line of Transmission)

Śākyamuni Buddha
Śāriputra
Rāhula
Rāhulabhadra
Nāgārjuna
Bhāvaviveka
Śrīgupta
Jñānagarbha
Śāntarakṣita
sBa-rigs Ratna
gTsang-pa Rab-gsal
sMar Shakya-mu-ni
gYo dGe-'byung
Bla-chen dGongs-pa-rab-gsal
Klu-mes Tshul-khrims-shes-rab
rDo-rje rGyal-mtshan
gNe-po Grags-pa-rgyal-mtshan
'Bre chen-po Shes-rab-'bar
brTson-'brus-'bar
gZhon-nu-seng-ge
Gro-mo-che-ba bDud-rtsi-grags
mChims-chen Nam-mkha'-grags
Grags-pa-shes-rab
mChims-ston Blo-bzang-grags-pa
Kun-dga-rgyal-mtshan
Grub-pa-shes-rab
Pang-chen dGe-'dun-grub-pa
gNas-snying-pa Kun-dga'-gde-legs
dGe-'dun-rgya-mtsho

dGe-legs-dpal-bzang
dPal-'byor-rgya-mtsho
'Jam-dbyangs dKon-mchog-chos-'phel
dKon-mchog-bstan-'dzin
sMin-gling Lo-chen Dharma-śri

Bodhisattva Lineage (Main Line of Transmission)

Buddha Śākyamuni
Mañjuśrī
Nāgārjuna
Candrakīrti
Rig-pa'i-khu-bhyug
Kusala the Elder
Kusala the Younger
Atiśa
Thang-pa Dza
'Jigs-med-'byung-gnas
sGro-lung-pa
Byang-chub-'od
rMa-bya Śakya-seng-ge
mChims-chen
sMon-tshul-pa
Byang-chub-grub-pa
gZhon-nu rDo-rje
Kun-mkhyen rDo-rje
Khyab-brdal-lhun-grub-grags
'Od-sangs-rgyas-dbon-bo
Zla-grags
Kun-bzang rDo-rje-rgyal-mtshan
sNa-tshogs-rang-grol
bsTan-'dzin-grags-pa
mDo-snags-bstan-'dzin
'Phrin-las-lhun-grub
O-rgyan gTer-bdag-gling-pa

Mahāyoga Lineage (Main Line of Transmission)

Ādi-Buddha Kun-tu-bzang-po
rGyal-rshab-rig-lnga
Rig-gsum-drva-lnga
Indrabodhi
Ku-ku-rā-dza
Siṃha-rā-dza
Upa-rā-dza
Gom-ma devī
Lalitavajra
Nyi-'od sangs-rgyas
Buddhaguhya
Vimalamitra
rMa Rin-chen-mchog
gTsug-ru Rin-chen gzhon-nu
Gye-re mChog-skyong
Zhang rGyal-ba'i-yon-tan
gNubs-chen Sangs-rgyas-ye-shes
Yon-tan rgya-mtsho
Ye-shes rgya-mtsho
Nyang Shes-rab-mchog
Nyang Ye-shes 'byung-gnas
Zur-po-che Shākya 'byung-gnas
Zur-chung shes-rab grags-pa
sGro-sbug-pa
Tsag-tsha-shākya rDo-rje
Shākya-'byung-gnas

Glang-ston rDo-rje-'od
bSod-nams-rnam-par-rgyal-ba
Chos-kyi seng-ge
Sangs-rgyas-dpal
bSod-nams mGon-po
rGrol-chen-bsam-grub
Seng-ge dPal-bzang
Rigs-rgyal-lhun-grub
Sangs-rgyas rDo-rje
Tshe-dbang mGon-po
rDo-rje-tshe-dpal
Shākya dPal-'byor
Siddhaphala
'Phags-pa-rin-chen
Shākyaratna
Zur-ston-rgyal-sras
Padma bDud-'dul
Chos-rgyal rDo-rje
rGya-ston-'od-gsal-rang-drol
O-rgyan gTer-bdag-gling-pa

Anuyoga Lineage (*Main Line of Transmission*)

Ādi-Buddha Kun-tu bzang-po
rGyal-tshab-rig-lnga
Rig-gsum-drva-lnga
Indrabodhi
Upa-rā-dza
Indrabodhi
Na-ga-pu-tra
Ga-ya-su-tri
Ku-ku-rā-dza
dGa'-rab rDo-rje
rDo-rje-bzhad-pa
Prabhahasti
Shākya-'od the Younger
Shākya-bshes-gnyen
Shākya-seng-ge
Dhanarakṣita
Hūṃkara
Sthiramati
bDe-ba-gsal-mdzad
Bodhidharma
Vasudhara
Bal-po Nor-'dzin
Bru-sha Ru-che-btsan-skyes
gNubs-chen Sangs-rgyas Ye-shes
gNubs-chen Sangs-po-che
Yon-tan rGya-mtsho
Ye-shes rGya-mtsho
rGya Blo-gros Byang-chub
Tho-gar-nam-mkha'-sde
Zur-po-che Shākya 'byung-gnas
Zur-chung Shes-rab grags-pa
sGro-sbug-pa
gLang-ston rDo-rje-'od
brTson-'drus-seng-ge
bSod-nams-rnam-rgyal
Chos-kyi-seng-ge
Sangs-rgyas-dpal
bSod-nams mGon-po
sGrol-chen Yab-sras
Nam-mkha' rDo-rje
Sha-mi-la-dgu-pa
Blo-gros-rgyal-mtshan
gZhan-phan-'phrin-las-lhun-grub
O-rgyan gTer-bdag-gling-pa

*A Time Line of Western and Buddhist Civilizations**

Year		*Western*	*Buddhist*
BC	500		
			Śākyamuni Buddha
	450	Peloponnesian Wars	First Council at Rājagṛha
		Socrates	
	400		
		Aristotle	Second Council at Vaiśālī
	350		
		Alexander the Great	Second Council at Pāṭaliputra
	300		
		Archimedes	
	250	Punic Wars	Third Council at Pāṭṭaliputra
			Aśokan Empire
	200	Timon	
	150		Assembly at Puruṣapuna
			Sāñchī Stūpa built
	100	Cicero	
	50	Julius Caesar	
AD	0	Jesus Christ	
	50	Augustus Caesar	
			dGa'-rab rDo-rje
	100	Trajan	
			'Jam-dpal bShes-gnyen
	150	Marcus Aurelius	Nāgārjuna
			Āryadeva
	200		Amarāvatī Stūpa completed
	250	Diocletian	
	300	Constantine	Śrī Siṃha
			Lha-tho-tho-ri
	350		Asaṅga
			Vasubandu
	400	Anglos conquer Briton	Gupta Dynasty consolidated
		Goths sack Rome	Nālandā flourishing

*Tracing the development of the rNying-ma tradition in particular.

The bKa'-ma Transmission up to gTer-bdag-gling-pa

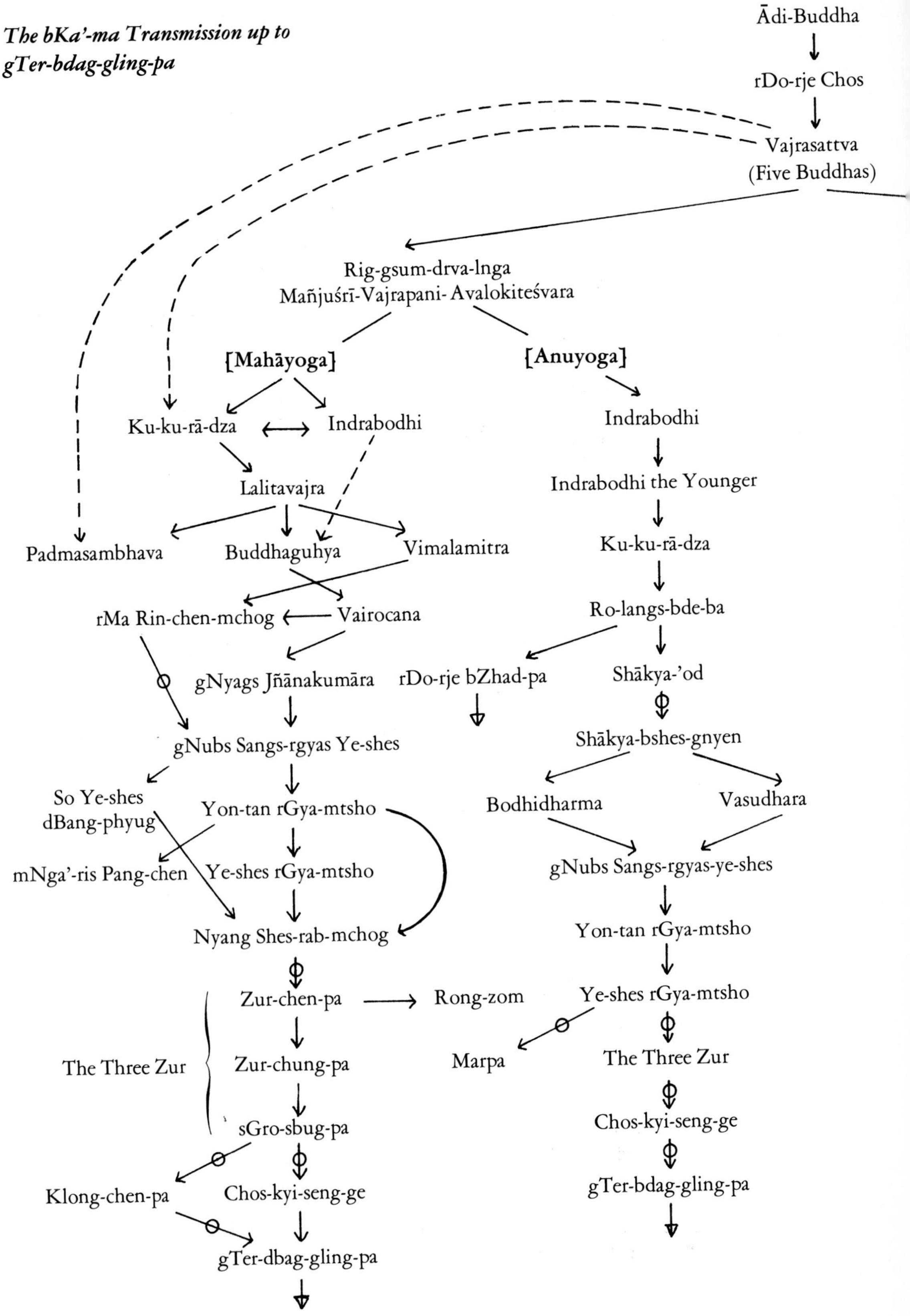

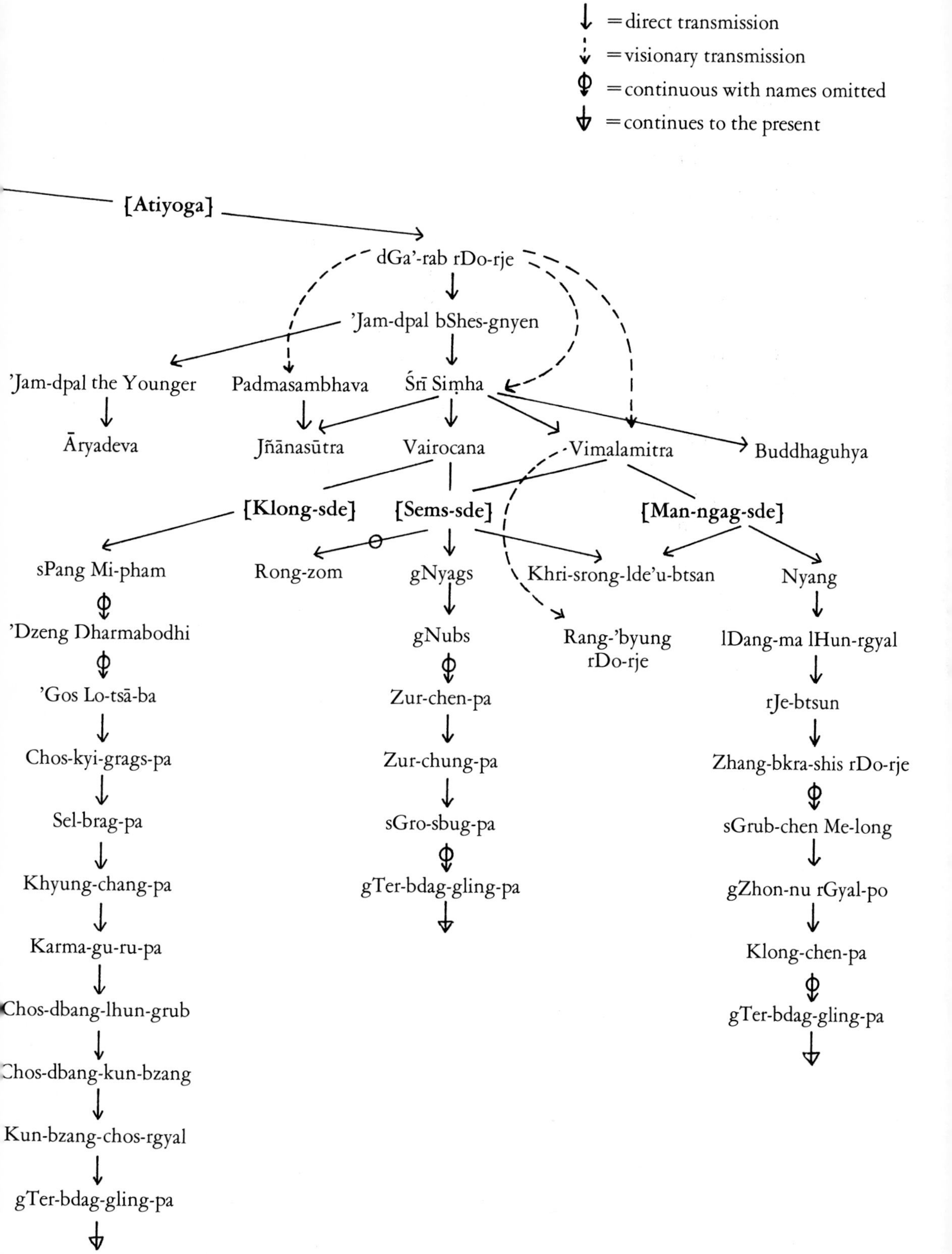
= direct transmission
= visionary transmission
= continuous with names omitted
= continues to the present
[Atiyoga]
dGa'-rab rDo-rje
'Jam-dpal bShes-gnyen
'Jam-dpal the Younger
Padmasambhava
Śrī Siṃha
Āryadeva
Jñānasūtra
Vairocana
Vimalamitra
Buddhaguhya
[Klong-sde]
[Sems-sde]
[Man-ngag-sde]
sPang Mi-pham
Rong-zom
gNyags
Khri-srong-lde'u-btsan
Nyang
'Dzeng Dharmabodhi
gNubs
Rang-'byung rDo-rje
lDang-ma lHun-rgyal
'Gos Lo-tsā-ba
Zur-chen-pa
rJe-btsun
Chos-kyi-grags-pa
Zur-chung-pa
Zhang-bkra-shis rDo-rje
Sel-brag-pa
sGro-sbug-pa
sGrub-chen Me-long
Khyung-chang-pa
gTer-bdag-gling-pa
gZhon-nu rGyal-po
Karma-gu-ru-pa
Klong-chen-pa
Chos-dbang-lhun-grub
gTer-bdag-gling-pa
Chos-dbang-kun-bzang
Kun-bzang-chos-rgyal
gTer-bdag-gling-pa

Atiyoga Lineage (*Main Line of Transmission: Man-ngag-gi-sde*)

Ādi-buddha Kun-tu-bzang-po
rDo-rje-'chang
rGyal-tshab-rig-lnga
Vajrasattva
Vajrapāṇi
dGa'-rab rDo-rje
'Jam-dpal bShes-gnyen
Śrī Siṃha
Jñānasūtra
Vimalamitra
Padmasambhava
Nyang Ting-nge-'dzin bZang-po
lDang-ma Lhun-rgyal
rJe-btsun Seng-ge bBang-phyug
Zhang-bkra-shis rDo-rje
mKhas-pa Nyi-'bum
Gu-ru Ju-'ber
'Khrul-zhig Seng-ge-rgyal-pa
sGrub-chen Me-long rDo-rje
Rig-'dzin-chen-po Ku-ma-rā-dza
Klong-chen-rab-'byams-pa
mKhas-grub Chen-po Khyab-brdal-lhun-grub
Grags-pa-'od-zer
Sangs-rgyas-dbon-po
gDung-'tshob Zla-ba-grags-pa
Grub-pa'i-dbang-phyug Kun-bzang rDo-rje
rGyal-mchan dPal-bzang
sNa-tshogs-rang-grol
bsTan-'dzin-grags-pa
mDo-sngags-bsTan-'dzin
'Phrin-las-lhun-grub
O-rgyan gTer-bdag-gling-pa

Year	*Western*	*Buddhist*
450	Atilla in Gaul	
		Dignāga
500		
550		
600	Mohammed	Srong-bstan-sgam-po
	Pope Gregory	Dharmakīrti
650		Guṇaprabha
		Chandrakīrti
700		Śāntideva
		Khri-srong-lde'u-btsan
750		Śāntarakṣita in Tibet
	Charlemagne	Padmasambhava and Vimalamitra in Tibet
800		
		Vairocana
850		gNubs-chen Sangs-rgyas Ye-shes
900		
950		Zur-po-che
		Rin-chen-bzang-po
1000	Norsemen reach N. America	Atiśa in Tibet
	Anselm	Zur-chung-pa
1050		Rong-zom Chos-kyi-bzang-po
1100	First Crusade	sGro-sbug-pa
		Marpa
1150		Milarepa
	Magna Carta	gTer-ston Nyi-ma-'od-zer
1200	Fourth Crusade	Nālandā destroyed
	St. Francis of Assisi	
1250	Thomas Aquinas	Chos-kyi-dbang-phyug
	Marco Polo	
1300	Dante	Ku-ma-rā-dza
		Klong-chen-pa
1350	Black Plague	
	Chaucer	
1400	Copernicus	Tsong-kha-pa
1450	Gutenburg	
	Columbus	
1500	Leonardo da Vinci	
	Magellan	Fifth Dalai Lama

Year	*Western*	*Buddhist*
1550	Martin Luther	
	John Calvin	
1600	Shakespeare	
	Jamestown	
1650	Galileo	
	Descartes	O-rgyan gTer-dbag-gling-pa
1700	Newton	
1750		
	American Revolution	'Jigs-med-gling-pa
1800	Louis XVI	
	Napoleon	dPal-sprul Rinpoche
1850	Queen Victoria	First 'Jam-dbyangs mKhyen-brtse'i
	Darwin	
1900	John Stuart Mill	Lama Mi-pham
	World War I	Second 'Jam-dbyangs mKhyen-brtse'i
1950	World War II	
1969	USA lands on moon	rNying-ma in America

Now That I Come to Die

Klong-chen rab-'byams-pa

Translated by Herbert V. Guenther

KLONG-CHEN RAB-'BYAMS-PA'S parting injunctions[1] present the essentials of Buddhism in a poetic form whose special appeal lies in the use of striking similes and a beseeching refrain. The tenor of these injunctions is the realization of Being, of which it cannot be said that it is or that it is not, but which as dynamic wholeness makes all differentiations and assertions, positive or negative, possible. In its experience, this wholeness is cognitively meaningful from deep within itself and spreads unlimited as the open sky in its felt immediacy. It is impossible to say that this wholeness has ever come into existence as a thing, but precisely because it is not a thing, it remains infinitely fertile.

The Translation

Homage to all noble persons endowed with great compassion.

Homage to Him who is the sun, shining in the wondrous
 brightness of what is good and pure,
In the primordial (sky-like) ground of Being:
Displaying various manifestations of His compassion
And looking after living beings by His charismatic actions.[2]

Homage to Him who, after completing
All that was to be done by him, went to
 Kuśīnagara,[3]
Truly the most wondrous city,
To teach a lesson to those who believe in everlastingness.

From former time I know the nature of Saṃsāra:
Therefore, from one about to leave behind this body which
    is transitory and deceptive
Listen to this admonition which is solely for your benefit–
In worldly things there is no abiding essence.

Although you may hold, in this your life, to it as true, it will most
    likely deceive you.
Once you have fully understood that you cannot rely
On that which is impermanent and without essence,
Attend to the real meaning of Being straight away.

Friends do not last forever, but are rather like guests:
They meet occasionally and quickly go their ways.
Dismiss attachment to your companions in this magic show,
And attend to the real meaning of Being, which alone is
    beneficial.

The wealth and possessions you have amassed must be
    left behind–
They are like honey–to be enjoyed by those who did not
    gather them.
Now, while you still can, make arrangements for your needs
    on the way hereafter–
The wealth that on you will confer excellent qualities.

The house you have built is going to collapse; it is only
    a temporary abode;
You cannot stay on, but must go.
Dismiss your attachment and craving for places of excitement–
Resort to solitary places straight away.

Friendship and hostility are like the play of children:
Love and hatred for that which has no value are a blazing fire.
Avoid squabbles and resentments–
Control your mind straight away.

Deeds, having no essence, resemble a magic show:
Although you involve yourself in them for a while,
    ultimately they are fruitless.
Cease troubling about this life, dismiss worldly concerns–
Look for the road to deliverance straight away.

Your bodily existence, a unique occasion and right juncture,
is like a precious boat:
While you still have the power to steer it across the ocean
of frustrations,
Shun laziness, indolence, and idleness–
Activate the power of strenuous exertion straight away.

The real Guru is like an escort on a dangerous road:
With great devotion, confident of body, speech, and mind,
Depend on this guide who protects against the enemy of
Saṃsāra–
Revere and rely on him, straight away.

Instruction in the profound is like the elixir of immortality:
Since it is the best cure for the disease of emotionality,
Depend on your inner being, discover precisely its quality–
Imbibe it and allow it to affect you straight away.

The three trainings,[4] when utterly pure, are like the Wish-
Fulfilling Gem:
They are the path itself, which here and hereafter offers
bliss, and ultimately leads to what is good and pure.
Through them you find real peace in limpid clearness and
consummate perspicacity[5] (your very Being)–
Let them develop straight away.

Learnedness is like a precious lamp:
Dispelling darkness and illuminating the path toward liberation,
Its beacon of prosperity and bliss opens the eye of pristine
cognitions–
Let it shine unrestricted straight away.

Proper thoughts are like a skilled goldsmith:
They remove all impositions and doubts about 'this' and 'that'
By exercising a discriminating awareness born from thinking
about what you have heard–
Absorb them within you straight away.

Cultivation (of what you have learned) is like the taste
of nectar:
Through the cultivation of what has been heard and thought
about, all emotional afflictions are remedied,

The ocean of propositions is crossed, and the other shore
of Being is reached–
In forest groves start contemplative cultivation straight away.

Vision is like the bright sky:
Free from all that is high or low, divided or partial,
Neither wide nor narrow, it is beyond attempts to verbalize it–
Apply the tool of understanding straight away.

Contemplation is like a mountain or a sea:
Neither moving nor changing, it is lucent and unsullied:
All labeling which erupts through the proliferation of
perturbations thus ceases–
Contemplate (things) as they really are straight away.

Conduct is like the wise person:
It acts in accordance with what is appropriate and beneficial.
This realm of magic with its attachments and clingings,
acceptances and rejections, denials and affirmations–
Free it from the object-subject division straight away.

Fruition is like a guide gathering riches:
Wealthy himself, he allows others' values spontaneously to
come forth.
Without expectations and apprehensions, the mind feels
naturally blissful–
Exert yourself to win this wealth straight away.

Mind, a continual source of meanings, is like the sky:
The sky is Mind,[6] genuine meaningfulness,
Without duality, complete and identical with itself–
Understand it thoroughly straight away.

All the variety of things and ideas are like images in
a mirror:
Void of appearances, there is yet no emptiness;
If (this paradox) is left unresolved as to being identical
or different, complacency prevails–
Know experience thoroughly for what it is straight away.

The subject dealing with its object is like a dream:
Although there is no duality (of subject and object),
ingrained tendencies cause duality to appear.

What is postulated by the intellect is nothing self-sufficient–
Know non-duality straight away.

Saṃsāra and Nirvāṇa are like a magic play:
Although good and evil seem to exist (independently), the
identity (of Being with itself) remains (unaffected by
these deformations).
All that is remains unborn, like the sky–
Know this thoroughly straight away.

Mistaken identities are like a parade of happiness and misery:
Once good and evil have individually arisen they perpetuate
themselves.
In actuality they remain unborn; in facticity they neither move
nor change–
Know this thoroughly and straight away.

Intellectual postulates are like the quarrels of foolish men:
There is nothing substantial about them.
Divisive notions have introduced a split and
Philosophical axioms will take good and evil to be separate–
Know identity straight away.

The bestowing of gifts is like a precious treasure:
Inexhaustible, increasing ever more, the cause of good fortune.
To the fields of merits,[7] whether they be inferior, mediocre,
or superior–
Give what is deserving straight away.

Self-discipline is like a fine, clean carriage:
The ladder for climbing up to heaven or to the citadel of
happiness.
Restraint, adherence to what is meaningful, and aiding all
beings–
Let these qualities abide in yourself straight away.

Patience is like the unruffled ocean:
It cannot be disturbed by injury; it is the best rigorous
training,
Accepting frustrations and developing a sense of compassion–
Accustom and familiarize yourself with patience straight away.

Effort is like a blazing bonfire:
Burning away the unsuitable, it rushes toward the good.
Neither idle, unconcerned, nor lazy–
Realize this path towards deliverance straight away.

Concentration, unswerving, is like the king of mountains:
Unshaken by objectifying tendencies, unperturbed in the presence of objects,
Wherever it is firmly settled, it cannot be upset by anything–
Familiarize yourself with it straight away.

Appreciation is like the sun's great orb:
Dispelling the darkness of your mind's murkiness and causing the real meaning to shine,
Raising up the sublime island of deliverance and drying up the ocean of evil–
Intensify it straight away.

Appropriate action is like a sea captain in charge of his precious cargo:
With it you cross the ocean of frustration, go to the island of utter bliss, and
Realize the three sublime strata whereby the twofold aim of life is spontaneously fulfilled[8]–
Benefit others by appropriate action straight away.

Strength is like a hero conquering his enemies:
It overcomes the army of emotions and proceeds toward enlightenment.
Since strength does not admit of hindrances, and by it wholesomeness will reach its ultimate quality–
Develop it in yourself straight away.

Supplication is like the Wish-Fulfilling Gem:
All desires are granted and bliss grows naturally.
It puts the mind at rest and fulfills one's expectations–
Give supplication its great chance straight away.

Pristine awareness is like clouds gathering in the sky:
From the nourishing clouds of holistic feelings, it lets fall the rain of prosperity and bliss,
And makes the crop of the wholesome prosper in all beings–
Make efforts to gain this awareness straight away.

Appropriate action and appreciation are like excellent steeds:
Never stumbling into worldliness or quiescence, one's own
 and others' values are realized.
The five paths are traversed to their end, and the three
 strata are spontaneously present–
Realize these two through your efforts straight away.

Qualities conducive to (the realization of) limpid clearness
 and consummate perspicacity are like a highway:
This road has been and will be traveled by noble people
 throughout all time,
Beginning with the four inspections, there are thirty-seven
 qualities in all[9]–
Make an effort to develop them straight away.

Kindness is like one's parents:
Caring ceaselessly for their children, the six kinds of beings.
Their love forever aids and enables (spiritual) success to be realized–
Familiarize yourself with kindness straight away.

Compassion is like the Bodhisattvas, the Buddha's spiritual sons:
Clothed in the armour of perseverance, they desire to free
Beings from suffering, as if it were their own–
Let compassion grow in yourself straight away.

Joy is like the considerate family elders:
Happy over the welfare of others,
They delight in providing for such welfare–
Attend intensively to joy straight away.

Equanimity is like the level earth:
Without attachment or aversion to those near or far, and
 free from afflictions,
Great bliss emerges from its everlasting evenness–
Familiarize yourself with equanimity straight away.

Aspiration and perseverance, needed for realizing limpid clearness
 and consummate perspicacity, are like a true leader:
The helmsman, guiding (you) to the island of deliverance where
 all wholesomeness is found,
Not deterred by worldliness, the value in others stands out–
Over and over again bring aspiration and perseverance to life
 straight away.

Devotion is like the great ocean and the high seas:
Full of what is wholesome, maintaining one flavor throughout,
Its waves of faith surge, never wavering–
Let devotion swell in your heart straight away.

Dedication is like the inexhaustible treasure of the sky:
By dedicating everything to the realm of reality, wealth will
not lessen but will grow even more.
(In) the one-flavored stratum of meaningfulness, the other two
strata are spontaneously present–
Purify the three aspects (of the situation) from their
concretization straight away.

Rejoicing is like the vault of the sky:
Its merits are unlimited; it is unobjectifiable and without pride,
Thoroughly transparent and unshakable–
Let rejoicing grow on and on straight away.

Furthermore, inspection is like an iron hook:
It keeps in check the untamed, drunken elephant of mind.
Turning it away from evil and tying it to what is wholesome–
Let inspection reside in you straight away.

Circumspect alertness is like an attentive sentinel:
It does not offer the thief, unwholesomeness, a chance;
It is there to guard the wealth of wholesomeness–
Have such alertness with you straight away.

Concern is like the world-encircling mountain:
It is safe from the thieving horde of emotions
And it commands the army that defeats karmic actions–
Make effort to guard the mind straight away.

Trust is like a fertile field:
It lets all desires grow into the harvest of limpid clearness and
consummate perspicacity;
The field of bliss here and hereafter, trust always yields
good fortune–
Let it increase straight away.

Generosity is like a lovely lotus pond:
What is genuine gathers there, delightful to behold.
It is true enjoyment; it is its own reward–
Let generosity bring joy to others straight away.

Pleasant speech is like the sound of thunder:
It captivates and pleases the minds of beings,
It reverberates around those to be taught and makes them
feel happy–
Gladden others by singing their praises straight away.

Calm behavior is like a true sage:
Unwholesomeness ceases, and people's trust increases.
Give up artificiality and make this natural discipline–
Your supreme conduct straight away.

Life's real meaning is like the Buddha's power:
In accord with everything, yet superior to all;
Similar to everything, yet dissimilar to all–
Let it reside in yourself straight away.

This body, a unique occasion and right juncture, is like a
phantom house:
For a while it is there, but the time of collapse is uncertain.
It will not linger, you must part with it–
Remember this again and again, straight away.

Opportunities are unstable, like autumn clouds:
Their occasion is certain to dissipate;
They have no solid core–
Thoroughly and from your heart understand this straight away.

All beings are transients, like past and future guests:
The old have gone; the young will also go.
This generation won't even last a hundred years–
Understand this thoroughly straight away.

The presence of this life is like a single day:
The presence of the intermediate state is like tonight's dream.
The presence of a future life will come as quickly as tomorrow–
Deal with life's real meaning straight away.

When all that is important has been illustrated by appropriate
examples,
To those who have firm trust, my exhortation is:
What has come together will have to separate.
Hence I shall not tarry, but will proceed to the island of
deliverance.

Since no reliance can be placed on the things of Saṃsāra,
Let me sit down firmly on Being's unborn throne.

The appearances in this world are like a trickster,
Mendacious, a wanton whore.
Since they turn the mind from the wholesome and cause the
crowd of emotions to increase,
Send them far away and practice what is right.

Without contentment, even 'wealth' is poverty.
The avaricious mind enjoys no satisfaction.
Contentment itself is the greatest wealth;
Even a little fills the mind with happiness.

Wine and women are the source of emotional turmoil.
Dismiss such thoughts which cause clinging, hankering,
and craving.
Set out to emulate the sages
And contemplate in sylvan solitudes the value of inner calm.

With mind focussed on the wholesome, day and night,
Renounce wrong doing and do what is beneficial, as the Buddha
has advised:
Unswervingly practice what is right.
Then you need not worry about death, for things will develop as
they should.

Through actions and supplications developed over a long
period of time,
Learning and commitment naturally reside in the disciples who
must eventually go their own ways.
So also teacher and disciple must part—
Know them to be like customers in a marketplace.

These words are spoken from the heart, for (your) sole
benefit:
Give up the distractions and diversions of this life
Which are provided by country, property, friends, and relatives,
And cultivate meditation in quiet places.

When nothing prevails anymore, and the time has come to pass on,
You need (to understand the) real meaning (of life), fearless
of death.

Familiarize yourself with the quintessence of the profoundness of the Guru's instruction.
Make effort (to comprehend it) straight away.

Strive to realize this ultimate bliss, good through and through,
The very light within,
This mystery of the within in the within,
The most supreme, the path towards Buddhahood within a single lifetime.

Seek the meaning which worthy men transmit
By possessing the immortality-giving essence, Being's profound value.
Experience their unique meaning through the power of your efforts
And quickly reach the citadel of the Victorious One.

Straight away bliss supreme is realized and
Even at a later time benefits accrue.
Strive from now on for the quintessence of Being
With its vast qualities both seen and unseen.

The stars, attendants of the full moon in a cloudless sky, have assembled,
The Lord of stars himself is about to appear.
The lotus-face of the Lord of Comassion, is made even more beautiful by the host of Ḍākas and Ḍākinīs,
With their canopies, umbrellas, royal standards, and courtly music.
Gently he breathes on me, intimating my acceptance.

The time has come to go; like a traveller, I must be on my way.
My joy in dying has been well earned: It is
Greater than all the wealth in the ocean a merchant may have won, or
The godlike power of having conquered armies, or
The bliss found in meditation.
So I, Padma-las-'brel-rtsal,[10] wait no longer,
But go to sit firmly on my seat in the bliss supreme that knows no death.

This life is finished, Karma is exhausted, what supplication could achieve has ended;
Worldliness is done with; this life's show is over.

Having realized, in one moment, the very nature of (Being's)
self-manifestation
Through the vast realms in the intermediate state,
I am close to taking up my seat at the beginning of all
and everything.

The riches found in myself have made the minds of others happy,
Through this magic existence the opulence of the island of
deliverance has been realized.
Having been with you, my excellent disciples, during this time,
I have been satiated with the joy of meaningfulness.

Now that the connection with this life has lost its karmic
power,
Do not lament about this beggar who died happily and unattached,
But constantly pray (that he be with you in spirit).

These words spoken for your benefit
Are like a multitude of lotus-flowers gladdening the bee(-like)
trusting beings.

Through the good of these words may the beings of the three
worlds
Go to the place of the origin of all and everything, Nirvāṇa.

Notes

1. The year of Klong-chen rab-'byams-pa's (1308–1364) death is often given as 1363, referring to the beginning of the Tibetan lunar year, not to the end which falls into early 1364, when Klong-chen rab-'byams-pa actually died (see my *Kindly Bent to Ease Us*, Part I, p. xv). Klong-chen rab-'byams-pa wrote three 'particular injunctions' (*zhal-chems*), of which this, the *Zhal-chems dri-ma med-pa'i 'od*, is the first. The last two, the *Zhal-chems gnad-kyi me-long* and the *Zhal-chems mthar thug gcig-ma*, are extremely technical, requiring a lengthy commentary for every word. The positive sentiment of this 'particular injunction' calls to mind a line by the British poet Robert Browning. It therefore has been chosen as the title.

2. This verse contains an allusion to the three 'existentials' (*sku*) as distinct from 'categories', which deal with an ontic inquiry, not with the problem of what it means to be. Being, which is not an entity, as rDzogs-chen philosophers knew long before Martin Heidegger exploded the ontic, substantive notion of it, is likened to the open sky and is experienced as intrinsic meaningfulness (*chos-sku*); this meaningfulness radiates like the sun, convey-

ing something of this intrinsic meaningfulness experienced empathically (*longs-sku*); and just as the sun is the source of life for the individual lifeforms, the charismatic activity gives meaning to each individual's life so that it is felt to have meaning (*sprul-sku*). For further philsophical implications of these terms, see *Kindly Bent to Ease Us*, Part I, pp. 223 ff.

3. Kuśīnagara, also spelled Kuśanagara, Kuśinagarī and, in Pāli, Kusinārā, is the name of a city in ancient India. Nearby, the Buddha passed away.

4. Self-discipline, without which nothing is possible; concentration, leading to the 'feeling' of wholeness as the basis for gaining a fresh vision of reality; and discriminative appreciation, which assists in removing the fictions about reality we ordinarily perpetuate.

5. On this concept see *Kindly Bent to Ease Us*, Part I, pp. 123 ff.

6. The capital letter attempts to indicate that we deal not with a 'thing' mind, with the intrinsic cognitiveness of 'intelligence' of Being.

7. Śrāvakas, Pratyekabuddhas, and Bodhisattvas.

8. The three sublime strata are *chos-sku, longs-sku*, and *sprul-sku*. See above note 2. The twofold aim is the unity of the 'in-itself' and the 'for-others'.

9. For a detailed account see *Kindly Bent to Ease Us*, Part I, pp. 241 ff.

10. One of the many names of Klong-chen rab-'byams-pa.

How the Saṃsāra is Fabricated from the Ground of Being

Klong-chen rab-'byams-pa

Translated by Kennard Lipman

THE YID-BZHIN RIN-PO-CHE'I MDZOD[1] is an early work of Klong-chen-pa, in which he used his monastic name, Tshul-khrims blo-gros. Dr. H. V. Guenther has already translated Mi-pham rgya-mtsho's summary of the chapter on philosophical systems (*grub-mtha'*) from this work, in his *Buddhist Philosophy in Theory and Practice*.[2] Characteristic of Klong-chen-pa's genius is the way in which he has integrated what goes under the name of Buddhist cosmology into his presentation, which covers the whole range of Buddhist experience. He begins with the chapter translated here, dealing with ontology (and epistemology), and then proceeds to give a detailed presentation of cosmology, incorporating both the conception of the *Hwa-Yen* (*Phal-po-che, Avataṃsaka*) *Sūtra*, and that of the third chapter of the *Abhidharma-kośa*. Thus the second chapter of the *Yid-bzhin mdzod* deals with a vision of the Buddha-fields (*zhing-khams*) according to the *Hwa-Yen*, of which our world, the Saha (*mi-mjed*) world-system (*'jig-rten-gyi khams*), with its well-known mountains, oceans, and continents, is only an infinitesimal part. This context is entirely lacking in the cosmological presentation of the *Abhidharma-kośa*; but interestingly enough, we find it in the presentation of cosmology by the *bKa' brgyud-pa* encyclopedist, 'Ba'-ra-ba rGyal-mtshan dPal-bzang, who was a contemporary of Klong-chen-pa.[3] After detailing the evolution of the environment (*gnod*) and inhabitants (*bcud*) of our world-system (which is an 'impure' Buddha-field) including a discussion on the origin of man,

Klong-chen-pa presents a chapter on the pleasures and frustrations of these beings and their 'worlds'. This serves as the basis for the second major portion of his work, dealing with the Path to Nirvāṇa, which begins with the reliance on a spiritual friend (*dge-ba'i bshes-gnyen*) who can point out to us the meaning of the situation we find ourselves in (Saṃsāra). Thus, cosmology provides us with a total perspective on the situation we find ourselves in; but cosmology cannot be properly understood without clarifying the ontological (and epistemological) question of the 'nature' of the world, *i.e.*, how has Saṃsāra come about?

This is what is provided in the first chapter. Here, Klong-chen-pa presents a skillful blending of the basic ideas of the Yogācāra and Mādhyamika philosophies, that is, he combines the Yogācāra theory of the potentialities of experience (*bag-chags, vāsanā*), with the Mādhyamika rejection of the concept of an essence (*rang-bzhin med, niḥsvabhāva*). The *bag-chags* are habitually developed 'schemata', 'invariants', or 'perceptual skills' built up in the course of experience by manipulating and experimenting with the environment, which begins as a potentially differentiable field in childhood and is gradually hardened into a world of stable objects (*yul-gyi bag-chags*), individual minds (*don-gyi bag-chags*), and bodies (*lus-kyi bag-chags* [as the focal point of experience]).[4] It is experience in terms of these *bag-chags* that is termed *'khrul-pa*, 'going astray', 'mistakenness', 'deceptiveness'.

These *bag-chags* are not inert 'traces' lying around in a container mind (the unconscious), but are process-product words for the protentional-retentional character of experience, which always operates within a certain horizon of meaning and understanding. This horizon is both an indeterminate awareness of being-in-our-world (*kun-gzhi rnam-shes, ālaya-vijñāna*), as well as the existential horizon of the world (*kun-gzhi*) "as that in which the human being always already finds himself as a 'thrown project'."[5] The *kun-gzhi* (*rnam-shes*) is not an unconscious; its development went hand in hand with the Cittamātra denial of the *belief* in an external world, a notion which is foreign to any Western psychological theory of the unconscious, to say the least. Such a denial is an attempt to bring us back from our hypotheses, our beliefs, our explanations, to the phenomena of world as horizon-of-meaning, rather than world 'out there'. Only then can we begin to untangle our involvement in our 'world-as-saṃsāra' and also begin to respond to the 'world-as-nirvāṇa', which is set forth in the second chapter of the *Yid-bzhin mdzod*.

The difference between the mentalistic and Mādhyamika systems is that the former locates this mistakenness in not recognizing a purely luminous (*gsal*) and cognitive (*rig*) noetic capacity (*shes-pa*) which is beyond the subject-object dichotomy (*gzung,'dzin*), as the source of experience; while the latter reject even this noetic capacity as as much a postualte as that of a corresponding external object. Thus, in the Mādhyamika, mistakenness is radicalized into a more general 'taking something to exist where there is nothing', for any ontological positing is seen as a limitation of the openness (*stong-pa-nyid*) of experience. The point is not to believe or explain, but to *know*, and to *be*. There is no universal mind standing outside our experiencing, which somehow remains 'above it all', a pure witness, and yet still accounts for going astray. This is nicely brought out in the ninth chapter of Śāntideva's *Bodhicaryāvatāra*. The mentalist attacks the Mādhyamika presentation that *all* entities, *both* internal and external, are like an apparition. He believes there must be a pure consciousness which is not taken in by this deceptive show; without it, he says, we would be just like the magician who *must* hopelessly fall in love with the beautiful māyā-woman/man of our own conjuring. There would be no-where out of our own deceptions if everything is such an apparition. Śāntideva says no, the only reason you fall in love with this māyā-woman/man is that your experience of *śūnyatā* is weak. If it were stronger you would never fall for this māyā-woman/man which you have taken to be a 'real woman/man'. In other words, *you didn't see her/him as an apparition* at all, but as some 'real', apprehendable object of your obsessed mind. Apparitionalness is not a lack, it is presence freed from the deceptiveness/obsessiveness of the *bag-chags* (a prominent *bag-chags* being the desirable body-presence of others).

The key to Klong-chen-pa's presentation is his rejection of any mentalistic conclusion to the theory of the *bag-chags*, i.e., that everything is one's mind. Although presencing (*snang-ba*), which is the presencing *of* the *bag-chags*, seeing 'this' *as* an object, a mind, etc., whether tacitly or explicitly, may be mental (*sems*), the apparent object (*snang-yul*) is not mental. Or to put it another way, the primary conditions for presencing may be mental, but it does not follow that the object presented is mental. Klong-chen-pa's conclusion, however, is not a reversion to some kind of realism, but rather the conclusion that such entities are "presencing although there has never been anything (to appear)" (*med-bzhin snang-ba*).[6] This distinction of *snang-ba* and *snang-yul* was an attempt to clear up the sloppy thinking of mentalistic trends in Tibet. Klong-chen-pa's unification of the Yogācāra (rNal-

'byor spyod-pa) and Mādhyamika (dbU-ma-pa) philosophies is also set forth in Mi-pham-rgya-mtsho's commentary on the *Dharma-dharmatā-vibhaṅga* (*Chos dang chos-nyid rnam-'byed*) of Maitreya-Asaṅga.[7] Mi-pham says that this text sets forth the unity (*zung-'jug*) of the 'two realities' (*bden-pa gnyis*) and equates the mentalistic system with the 'operational-conventional reality' (*kun-rdzob*) and the 'reflective-thematic' aspect of experiencing (*chos-can*), while he equates the Mādhyamika with the 'primary-absolute reality' (*don-dam*) and the 'prereflective-nonthematic' aspect of experiencing (*chos-nyid*).

What Mi-pham is saying is that the Yogācāra provides a good phenomenological description of our samsaric experiencing. However, the "phenomenon of phenomenology" must also be thoroughly put into question. In questioning directly *what gives* phenomena their presence, we are led into what we can only call the Open Dimension of Being (*stong-pa-nyid*). The rNying-ma-pa position in regard to the Mādhyamika in Tibet is complex. *Ris-med* masters such as Mi-pham clearly want to preserve valid aspects of both Śāntarakṣita's Svātantrika-Yogācāra approach which the rNying-ma-pa's inherited during the earlier spread of Buddhism in Tibet, as well as Candrakīrti's Prāsaṅgika approach which was taken up by the gSar-ma-pa schools.

It should also be noted that this 'mistaken mode of presencing', called Saṃsāra, is characterized by existence in functional correlation (*rten-'brel, pratītya-samutpāda*). The student should consider deeply Klong-chen-pa's beautiful words about this oft-misunderstood central principle of Buddhism:

> Although all these (entities) have no reality,
> By the power of the (duality of) the apprehendable and the
> apprehending there is presencing in functional
> correlation, like an apparition.
> As long as the (duality of) the apprehending and the
> apprehendable has not been completely exhausted,
> There will miraculously appear the cause and result
> of action.

Such breadth of vision and profundity of interpretation shines through in each topic Klong-chen-pa discusses. One can never be let down in trying to understand, experience, and fully realize the import of his words.

The following chapter of Klong-chen-pa's work is in the form of verses with an auto-commentary.[8]

The Translation

Now we shall explain the subject matter which makes up the body of the text: the explanation of that which is to be given up (Saṃsāra) and that which is to be taken up (Nirvāṇa). The presentation of these two is the important part (of the treatise). First we shall explain the ground of going astray, from which the Saṃsāra, characterized by mistakenness and lack of intrinsic perceptivity, (has come):

> Out of the motive force for well-being which is primordial
> sheer lucency,
> The unconditioned, pivotal pervasive stratum (of the
> world-horizon),[9]
> From the very beginning pure like the sun in the sky,

When the experientially-initiated potentialities for experience (*bag-chags*), which come in the wake of a loss of intrinsic perceptivity, stir, sentient beings go astray (from the ground of their Being). The ground of Being, in regard to its being the foundation for the site of Saṃsāra, is, like the sky, from the very beginning an open dimension without an essence. It is luminous like the sun and moon, and spontaneous (in its shining). Since beginningless time it remains what it is and does not change into something else. Since it is the reach and range which is beyond the limitations set by propositions, it is sheer lucency; and since it remains in the totality-field (*dbyings*) in which meaningful existence and pristine cognitiveness[10] cannot be added to or subtracted from one another, it is the motive force for well-being (*dbe-bar-gshegs-pa'i snying-po*). Since it is the existential presence (*gnas-lugs*) of the foundation of Saṃsāra and Nirvāṇa, it is called the pivotal pervasive stratum (of the world-horizon). Finally, it is unconditioned and has remained absolutely pure from the beginning.

Furthermore, conflicting emotions and unstable actions (that go with them) are founded (on this pervasive stratum), although they actually have no foundation, just like a mass of clouds (seems to) rest on the sun and sky. However, the ground of Being remains in its own reach and range–these (conflicting emotions and unstable actions) do not touch or join it. Since they are without any actuality, they appear as founded, although the founding and the founded cannot be established; they are mere ascriptions.[11] As the *Uttaratantra* says: "Earthsolidity rests on water-cohesion, water on wind-motility, and wind on space-spatility. Space does not rest on any of the elementary constituents of earth, water, or wind. In the same way, the psychophysical constituents, the elements of our experiential make-up, and the sense-field are founded on conflicting emotions and unstable actions; conflicting emotions and unstable actions rest on the improper use of the mind; the improper use of the mind rests on mind in its purity; and mind in its purity does not rest on anything."[12]

Nirvāṇa is also founded (on this pervasive stratum), but it is inseparable from it, like the sun and its rays, since from the very beginning it cannot be added to or subtracted from. Since we shall explain these things in detail below, we will not say any more here. From the reach and range of this ground of Being:

> The clouds of incidental obscurations, the proliferating
> postulations coming in the wake of a loss of
> intrinsic perceptivity,
> (Become) the potentialities for the experience of (intended)
> objects, (intending) consciousness, and one's body
> By the rising of the latent tendencies for going astray
> into (the duality) of apprehending acts and
> apprehendable projects.
> Thus, the motive force of sheer lucency, intrinsic
> perceptivity, has been obscured.

From the reach and range of the primordial existential presence of Being, which is naturally lucent, beginningless[13] loss of intrinsic perceptivity arises as observable qualities which are able to shine in their own light. This rising of the latent tendencies of the (split into) the apprehending and the apprehendable, which have now become a sustaining factor, is an incidental obscuration. The three potentialities for experience which make up (the intentive structure) of mind become sedimented on the pervasive stratum. They are: objects (*yul*), such as color-form, etc.; consciousness (*don*), the perceptive functions (*rnam-shes*) which apprehend these objects; and one's body (*lus*). Since these potentialities for experience, which make themselves felt although there has never been anything (to appear) (*med-bzhin snang-ba*), have obscured, like dust which settles on a mirror, the motive force of sheer lucency, pristine cognitiveness informed by intrinsic perceptivity, which is the primordial ground of Being, one wanders about in the

Saṃsāra. As the *gSang-ba snying-po*[14] states: "Listen! Out of the motive force for well-being, conceptual fictions and unstable actions miraculously appear." As an analogy for obscuration:

> Just as the continuum of the sky has become obscured
> by clouds,
> Buddha capacilities are no longer manifest and the mistaken mode
> of presencing,[15] (consisting of) happiness and frustration,
> makes itself felt.

From the reach and range of the totality-field (*dbyings*) of primordial sheer lucency, which is like the sky, incidental obscurations like clouds (appear), although pristine cognitiveness, which is like the sun, remains from the very beginning spontaneously co-existent with this reach and range. The limitless capabilities do not make themselves felt on account of this obscuring activity in the situation of an ordinary being, although they are manifest in meaningful existence (Rupakāya), as well as in meaningful existence in its absoluteness (Dharmakāya) – the inseparability of pristine cognitiveness and its continuum of experience. This is due to the presence of the many clouds of potentialities for the experience of various happinesses and frustrations (which make up) the mistaken mode of presencing. The actuality of mind is sheer lucency, therefore all obscurations are incidental and can be cleared up. As the *Pramāṇa-varttikā*[16] says: "The actuality of mind is sheer lucency, obscurations are incidental." If one asks how (the obscurations) are similar to clouds:

> Just as the crop grows when rain falls from the clouds,
> The rain of actions (leading to) happiness and frustration
> falls
> By the stirring of the cloud of intentive mind,[17] with its
> projects and acts of projection characterized by a loss
> of intrinsic perceptivity.
> The crop produced is the three realms of Saṃsāra.

Just like rain-clouds trembling in the sky and falling rain are necessary for the growth of the crop, out of the reach and range of Mind-as-such, naturally pure, involvement in the proliferating fictions (*kun-tu rtog-pa*) of one's projects and acts of projection begin to stir. By the accumulation of many actions, either positive or negative, which are the motivating force in the Saṃsāra, the six life-forms of the three realms appear with their corresponding modes of behavior. Since the crop of the variety of happiness and frustration multiplies, the Saṃsāra is just like a circle of fire (i.e., like a torch waved in a circular motion). As it says in the *Ratnamālā*:[18] "The circle of Saṃsāra has sustaining causes following one after another like a circle of fire. This is asserted to be 'running around in circles'." Now we shall explain extensively the division into the three potentialities for experience in the Saṃsāra:

> From among the three potentialities for experience, which
> comprise the mistaken mode of presencing
> The potentiality for experience of objects, the world-
> as-container
> Appears as the objects of the five senses, color-form, etc.

Because the beginningless potentialities for experience which have three different characteristics are implanted on the universal ground, presencing also manifests itself in three different ways. The potentiality for experience of objects, color-form, sound, odor, flavor, and tangibility, which are summed up by the external world and its inhabitants, appear as if they existed externally although there is no such thing as internal or external. Having appeared before the mind, one becomes completely taken in by (the belief in) them as real objects; one makes them into objects of judgments, either affirming or denying (their reality). The object that one is involved with is called color-form; considered as external it is the postulate of the apprehendable. The same holds for sound and the others. As for oneself, the internal, appearance as mind:

> The potentiality for experience of consciousness appears as
> the eight perceptive functions
> And the healthy and destructive actions based on them.

The foundational-horizonal perceptive function (*kun-gzhi rnam-shes*) has founded itself on the pervasive stratum (*kun-gzhi*) (of the world-horizon) as the variety of potentialities for experience, and from this spread the five perceptions, seeing and the others; the conceptualizing perceptive function (*yid-shes*), which follows a cognition of a sense object; and the emotively-toned ego-act (*nyon-yid*). These eight functions are called the apprehending mind. The split into these (eight) constitutes the concept of apprehending.

If one asks why it is (called) apprehending, the answer is as follows: since, on the level of the potentialities for experience implanted on the pervasive stratum, existentially it is a loss of intrinsic perceptivity and functionally it remains without conceptualizations connected with any apparent object, it is (called) apprehending as the potentiality for experience of the realm of formlessness (*gzugs-med khams*). Based on this is a cognition which is only partially clear and lucent and which is not connected with an object; this is the foundational-horizontal perceptive function, called apprehending as the potentiality for experience of the realm of form (*gzugs-khams*). The five sense perceptions, which have spread from this and which are without conceptualization, are (called) apprehending as the potentiality for the experience of wholeness (*ting-nge-'dzin*) on the level of form. The conceptualizing perceptive function and the emotively-toned ego-act are (called) apprehending as the potentiality for the experience of the realm of sensuousness (*'dod-khams*). These eight perceptive functions, since they apprehend their respective objects, both with and without conceptualization, are known as the apprehending mind. Unhealthy actions and merits accruing to healthy actions, which are founded on apprehending and rise as a whole by virtue of it, become sedimented in the mind, since they remain like tarnish on gold. Pacification of this involvement in mind and mental events is the intent of the Middle Way. These perceptive functions are founded on (the body):

> The potentiality for the experience of the body appears as the individual forms of the six kinds of beings
> And the major and minor characteristics based on them.

Because of a presencing as the various bodies of gods, men, and so forth, one becomes taken in by (the idea) my body. Even in a dream when one sees water or fire or an abyss or an enemy or dogs, or other things, one sees them as a danger to one's own body and runs away; thus the experience of frustration makes itself felt. Furthermore, the word 'body' is ascribed to the assemblage made up of the many major and minor divisions (of the body), and even the corpse is called a body. Even though the gods leave no corpse, that which is free from this (perishable form) is called their body.

Why is there presencing as body, consciousness, and objects? If one thinks that either everything presencing as object is a sufficient explanation, or that presencing as only body and consciousness is sufficient, this is not so. (One must) take into account each mode of appearing:

Thus the three potentialities for experience which have been
implanted on the pervasive stratum since beginningless time,
By habituation manifest themselves throughout one's span
of life.

By the power of the three potentialities for experience which rest on the pervasive stratum, arise the three modes of presencing as presences, just as from various seeds various shoots arise. No matter where one is born, as long as the potentialities for experience are not exhausted, presencing will make itself felt like a body, mind, and objects in a dream. The variety of former potentialities, since they have existed since beginningless time, have produced former spans of life, and by continuous habituation[19] this life is produced. Activity during the day forms dream (at night), and from the continuity of the potentialities for experience in this life, arises the body, consciousness, and objects of the next. As the *Mahāyāna-sūtra-laṅkāra*[20] describes this process. "The three types of potentialities for experience have three modes of presencing." And the Lord Maitreya[21] has taught: "Since the three types of potentialities have been implanted on the pervasive stratum, appearance has three different modes of presentation."

Now,[22] the refutation of the errors of those proud people who have for a long time been separated from the excellent path (of the Mahāyāna) and are far from the sight of the Buddha:

Ignorant people say that everything is mental.
About the meaning of the three modes of presencing they
are very confused.
One must protect oneself and eliminate these incorrect ways
of speaking
That contain many errors, and commit various contradictions,
and lead to extreme conclusions.

Those people who do not understand the Mahāyāna say that presencing and projective existence,[23] Saṃsāra and Nirvāṇa, the inner and the outer, beings and their world, everything, is one's mind; and speaking out of evident pride they deceive many people. They do not understand the meaning in the Mahāyāna of the three modes of presencing. Although the potentialities for experience sedimented as intentive mind may be mental, how can that which is sedimented as body and objects be mental? Now, as to their many errors: like the body and its appearance which exist as seen by the eye, will also the mind be established as a tangible form? Or will the body and objects which are mind-like be unable to be seen and heard? Or will the mind have color and shape, and also seeing and hearing? And if one person becomes a Buddha or goes to the lower realms, then will all become like this? And if the many presenced objects become one (in mind), then will the cognitive capacities (of people) also become one? When a presence disappears, then will the mind also disappear? And since the evolutive phases of earth, fire, water, and wind have mental abilities, hasn't one joined the ranks of the heretical Mīmāṁsakas?[24]

As to their various contradictions: just as a cognition has its own object, they are led to the conclusion that even an inert object has its own cognition. Then one's mind becomes something external on account of presence being external, and presencing becomes something internal because the cognitive and illuminative capacity of mind is internal. But then the presenced object which exists externally and one's cognitiveness which exists internally will not be able to appear as different, because they are non-dual, both being aspects of one fact.

As to their extreme conclusions: at the time one is not born, they are led to the conclusion that one's mind exists, since there is presencing at this time; but then at the time of one's death presencing would cease to exist here. When an object that is before one goes somewhere else, they are led to the conclusion that, since presencing is one's mind, it comes and goes following one's own mind. But at the same time it goes somewhere else, they are also led to assert that one's mind is left here, in order for presencing to (continue to) be here.

On account of these and many other errors, one must protect oneself and get rid of these stupid people's incorrect ways of speaking who, like cowherds, have never heard anything (of the Mahāyāna). One asks whether presencing is mind or not because of such statements as, "What appears is itself presencing," "O Buddha-sons, the three realms are mind-only," "Because of the potentialities for experience, the mind which is stirred up gives rise to presencing as (external) objects." One must understand that the statement, "Presencing is mind," which is made in the light of the distinction between presencing (*snang-ba*) and presenced object (*snang-yul*) is made because apprehending (something) as present or not is (the activity) of one's mind. Although the statement, "Presencing is mind," is intended to refute the Śrāvakas and others, who hold things to exist in truth, and to destroy the erroneous belief in an independently-existing world, mountains, etc., are not thereby shown to be mental. One should recognize as mental presencing in which one becomes obsessed with the split into (a world of) objects (*don*), where one thinks, "Oh, this is a mountain," etc.[25] Therefore, presenced objects, such as mountains and so forth, are not mental, because one finds that their cause, effects, functioning, origin, and cessation are different from that of the mind.

If one asks, then, do they (presenced objects) exist as independent objects—the answer is no. Although the realists take macroscopic, external presences as something which is other, made up of atoms, etc., because we maintain that this presencing is without a root or ground, occasioned by the intoxicant of the deceptive potentialities for experience making themselves felt before the mind, we are those who say that there is no actuality (to presenced objects).

Now we shall explain the activity which produces the duality of the apprehending and the apprehendable from the three modes of presencing:

> The fiction of the apprehendable arises from the object
> potentiality,
> And the fiction of the apprehending from the consciousness
> potentiality.
> The basis and peg of emotionality comes from the body
> potentiality.
> Because ignorant people take (these) as veridical, they
> continually go round in Saṃsāra.

Because one has apprehended presencing in the object mode as present, the fiction of the apprehendable arises; if the eight perceptive functions remain focused internally and then come outward (to meet their respective objects), the fiction of the apprehending, called mind, arises. The body is the basis of the arising of the apprehendable and the apprehending, and provides the locus for the manifest evils due to pleasures and frustrations. By taking the three modes of appearing as veridical, one wanders continuously in projective existences, and this is frustration. As the *Ārya-rāṣṭrapala-paripṛcchā-nāma-sūtra*[26] states: "All the entities of reality have no actuality at all, like an illusion, a mirage, and the moon reflected in water. Because ignorant people take (these entities) as veridical, they become bound, they go round continuously like a potter's wheel."

Now, although the Saṃsāra has nothing to it, like a reflection, as long as the fictions of the apprehending and the apprehendable have not been completely exhausted, instruction in action and its results is very important:

> Although all these (entities) have no reality,
> By the power of the (duality of) the apprehendable and the apprehending there is presencing in functional correlation, like an apparition.
> As long as the (duality of) the apprehendable and the apprehending has not been completely exhausted,
> There will miraculously appear the cause and result of karmic action.

Although, from the point of view of the primary reality of pre-reflective, non-thematic experience (*chos-nyid don-dam-pa'i bden-pa*), there is neither running around in circles, nor the unstable actions produced by it. However, operationally (*kun-rdzob-tu*), Saṃsāra makes itself felt like an apparition arising in functional correlation according to its corresponding causes and conditions. For this reason it is necessary to deal with Saṃsāra's causes and results. If one has completely exhausted all the pervasive fictions of the apprehendable and the apprehending, there is no karmic action since there is no loss in intrinsic perceptivity together with the potentialities for experience which make up the cause of Saṃsāra. There will be karmic action as long as one has not directly experienced this. Since loss of intrinsic perceptivity and all the conflicting emotions produced by this are not destroyed, it is important to take up (a stance of) acceptance and rejection in regard to the motivating cause of karmic action and its results. The karmic action produced by the mistaken mode of presencing which is Saṃsāra, is like a poisonous snake, since it always makes for frustration.

If one asks who produces and accumulates this karmic action:

> The mind is all-creative of motivations and karmic actions.
> Since (mistaken presences produced by these) make themselves felt before the mind and are examined by the mind,
> Exert oneself in order to discipline the errant mind.

Karmic action, the cause, is the origin (of frustration): unstable actions and conflicting emotions, the result, can only be frustration. The root of these has been produced (as follows): on account of having come from motivations based on the (intentive structure of) mind, the mind accumulates good, bad, and neutral karmic actions, and by the power of various karmic actions there appears the variety of the mistaken mode of presencing, which is present before one's mind like what is observed in a dream. Because the mind takes (this) as the apprehendable and the apprehending, error arises continually. As the *Ratnacūḍa*[27] states: "From mind arise motivations; from motivations come (further) healthy, unhealthy, and neutral motivations. From motivatedness the happiness, frustration, and all that lies in between, of sentient beings makes itself felt." On account of this it makes sense to exert oneself in refining and disciplining one's mind. For an analogy to the arising of the mistaken mode of presencing:

> As long as one is intoxicated by datura,[28]
> Although a variety of presences come about which seem to
> be like men,
> All of them are deceptive forms; there is not anything
> there.

Although those who have taken a decoction of datura see all the earth and sky full of men and women, at the time of seeing them, these presences are non-existent. Presences, due to this substance and by the power of the mistaken mind, arise as the variety of the external world; this is only the mistaken mode of presencing. To set forth an analogy for presencing, although there has never been anything (to appear):

> All the six life-forms that make up the mistaken mode
> of presencing, without exception,
> Have been produced by the erring mind and its
> involvements–
> Know that there is nothing which is not (like) a reflection,
> there, yet nothing.

All the entities of reality–summed up by presencing and projective existence, beings and their world, i.e., objects, which appear externally as other, which may be even broken up into a hundred fine particles; and the apprehending mind, which is internal, the self, (apart from this there is no other entity whatsoever to be found)–are incidental (contingent), since they are presencing although there has never been anything (to appear). For example, when a person is drunk on beer, although the world appears to turn round and round, there really is no turning. From the *Samādhirāja-sūtra*:[29] "When people are drunk on beer; although the earth seems to move, there is actually no moving or shaking. Know that all the entities of reality (are present) in this way."

Now, in summary, the exhortation to know what is the primordial ground for going astray into presencing although there has never been anything (to appear):

> Actually, Saṃsāra is like a reflection;
> Investigate from what it arises originally.
> By this one knows Nirvāṇa.
> Thus one will become a Buddha, free from projective existence.

One knows what Saṃsāra is by properly investigating the motive force of primordial sheer lucency, the totality-field from which Saṃsāra, which is without actuality like a reflection in a mirror, arises. (And when one knows this), by entering into a non-dual pristine cognitiveness, one is free from the partiality of the mistaken mode of presencing which makes up projective existence. In order to manifest complete clarity (*mngon-par byang-chub*), investigate the primordial actuality (from which Saṃsāra arises). From the *Samādhirāja-sūtra*: "Once the world arises, then it is destroyed; it has no abiding essence. What is before and after it remains the same. Investigate that from which the world originally arose."

Notes

1. The full title of the auto-commentary is *Theg-pa chen-po man-ngag-gi bstan-bcos Yid-bzhin rin-po-che'i mdzod-kyi 'grel-pa padma-dkar-po*, pub. by Dodrup Chen Rinpoche, Gangtok, Sikkim. Chapter One is from pp. 8–23.

2. The twelfth chapter of the *Yid-bzhin mdzod* is on the philosophical systems.

3. See *A Tibetan Encyclopedia of Buddhist Scholasticism*, vol. 7: "Byang-chub sems-dpa'i bslab-pa rin-po-che'i gter-mdzod-las nges-'byung-gi dad-pa 'jig-rten-gyi khams bstan-pa'i bskor," pub. by Ngawang Gyalsten & Ngawang Lungtok, Dehradun: 1970, esp. pp. 247–270. Note here that the title indicates that the study of cosmology produces a confident determination to "get out" of Saṃsāra (*nges-'byung-gi dad-pa skyed-pa*).

4. Indian texts speak of *grāhaka-*, *grāhya-*, and *karma-vāsanā*. *Grāhaka* (*'dzin-pa*) corresponds to *don*, the apprehending mind, and *grāhya* (*gzung-ba*) to *yul*, the apprehendable object. Karma (*las*) corresponds to *lus*, bodily subjectivity, because, as Klong-chen-pa states, *karma-vāsanā* indicates the gathering of one's karma "in" the body as the focal point of experience. See *Vijñaptimātratāsiddhi*, Poussin, L., trans., (Paris, Paul Geuthner, 1929), pp. 473ff.

5. Heidegger, M., *The Piety of Thinking*, Indiana Univ. Press, 1976, p. 84.

6. See pp. 356–358, where these ideas are presented.

7. The title of Mi-pham's commentary is *Chos dang chos-nyid rnam-par byed-pa'i tshig-le'ur byas-pa'i grel-pa ye-shes snang-ba rnam-'byed*, pub. by Tarthang Tulku, Varanasi, India, 1967. The statements made above are to be found on pp. 4–5 of this text.

8. Indian philosophic-religious treatises were usually written in this way. The verses are extremely terse nmemonic devices memorized by the student and usually quite unintelligible without the commentary, usually written by the teacher himself or a disciple. Thus, after you had mastered the text, you could later have the whole teaching "at your fingertips" in the form of the memorized verses, whose meaning had now become a part of you.

9. *don-gyi kun-gzhi*: "*don* is the value of Being residing in the experiencer as the pivot (*don*)of experiences which he tends to externalize and project into a fictitious realm." (H. V. Guenther, tr., *Kindly Bent to Ease Us, Part One: Mind*, Dharma, Emeryville, Ca.: 1975, p. 291). We must distinguish between the ground (*gzhi*) and the pervasive stratum (*kun-gzhi*). Going astray (*'khrul-pa*) into the subject-object dichotomy (*gzhung-'dzin*), which we call mind, is the result of not understanding that everything proceeds from the Ground, not as an emanation of some sort, but as its active presentifying or functioning (*gzhi-snang*). As an on-going act or possibility, this understanding (Nirvāṇa) or lack of understanding (Saṃsāra) is referred to as the *kun-gzhi*. In other words, we are already on our way whenever we make a start (*gzhi*)–there are always latent tendencies, there is no pure beginning within the mistaken mode of presencing that we call mind. Not to succumb to these tendencies is to move on the path to Nirvana. The Ground of Being, however, is *rang-byung-gi rig-pa*, the cognitive intrinsicality of Being, which is not mixed up with these habitual potentialities for experiencing. When it is mixed up with these we then speak of the *kun-gzhi* as potential for Saṃsāra and Nirvāṇa. Klong-chen-pa states, in elucidating the first three members of the principle of functional correlation (*rten-'brel*):

> Because one does not understand self-presentational immediacy, when facticity (*ngo-bo*), actuality (*rang-bzhin*), and cognitive responsiveness (*thugs-rje*), which (come) out of the primordial Ground of Being, a presence tending in the direction of objectness, (there is) loss of intrinsic perceptivity (*ma-rig-pa*). From this, since one makes an object-like apprehension by virtue of the proliferating postulations which come in the wake of a loss of intrinsic perceptivity, (there is) motivatedness (*'du-byed*) in the Saṃsāra. From this, because intrinsic perceptivity has been contaminated by the potentialities for experiencing, it is transformed into the pervasive stratum (of the world-horizon) (*kun-gzhi*). (*mKha-'gro yang-tig*, Part Two, Tulku Tsewang, Jamyang and L. Tashi, Pubs., New Delhi, 1971, f.88a)

Ground is thus a short-hand term for the unitary functioning (*ngo-bo, rang-bzhin, thugs-rje*) that is Being.

10. *sku dang ye-shes*. Being, as founding, and Knowing, as founded, are

inseparable. The subordination of Knowing to Being leads to the limitations of Realism; the subordination of Being to Knowing leads to the limitations of Idealism. *sku* has many affinities with the existential-phenomenological concept of *Existenz*, which should be distinguished from the traditional concept of existence. It "is neither a simple designation of a *quid est* nor a designation of finite existents in general. It has to do with the emerging of experience in the contextualism of its embodiment, speech, and sociality, whence organizing and interpretive notions arise and whither they return for their justification," and it involves "the world-fact of the emerging of experience in its varied intentionalities." (C. O. Schrag, *Experience and Being*, Northwestern Univ. Press, Evanston, Ill.: 1969, pp. 268–9.

11. We have translated *gzhi* as Ground of Being (literally it means ground). However, this should not be taken as the metaphysical Ground of Western philosophy, the logos, the reason which grounds the existence of particular beings: "Nothing exists without a ground." Heidegger calls Western metaphysics "Onto-theo-logical" because such a Ground, in the course of Western thinking, comes to be taken as the highest or most perfect Being. Our text states that the mistaken presencing (*'khrul-snang*) that makes up Saṃsāra is *groundless* and exhorts us, at the end of the chapter, to investigate the "primordial actuality" from which the whole relation of founded and founding, that we call the world, arises. Heidegger states: "All founding and every appearance of something being able to be grounded would degrade Being to a being" (Heidegger, M., *The Piety of Thinking*, p. 100). *gZhi* is not *a* being. The admonition of our text is also stated by a translator of Heidegger: "The task is to presence that which is nearer than all that is present and which is prior to all measures, reasons, and grounds. . . . In the Why of metaphysical inquiry, and thereby in the Why of all other inquiries, there is concealed an original determination which always thinks of Being as foundation or ground. 'Why?' never ceases to mean For what reason? On what basis? Thinking which attempts to undo itself from this initial presupposition will then think without the Why. In searching for the measure with which one thinks without the Why, one comes upon a groundlessness wherein the human being is not at all at home" (*The Piety of Thinking*, p. 101). Thus, in the Buddhist context, the question "Why is there this loss of intrinsic awareness (*ma-rig-pa*)?" or "Why is there Saṃsāra?" must be "undone" for it is part of *ma-rig-pa* itself. That is, one's whole questioning, always begins in a *finding-oneself in an already on-going* situation. We tend to forget this in searching for *reasons* within this now discovered state of affairs, whether we locate these reasons in the present or our past. What really calls for our thinking, in the first place, according to Heidegger and Klong-chen-pa, is this phenomenon of "always already finding ourselves," which first "gives" us reflective, thematizing experience. The basic point is that, in the Mahāyāna, "going astray" is a process of self-deception *intrinsic* to experiencing; one cannot appeal to any causal principles operating on the process from without.

12. That is, the analogy is made between Earth and the psycho-physical

constituents (*phung-po*), sense-fields (*skye-mched*), and elements of our experiential make-up (*khams*), which constitute our 'world' of frustration; between water and conflicting emotions (*nyon-mongs*) and unstable actions (*las*); between wind and the improper use of the mind (*tshul-min yid-la byed-pa*); and between space and mind in its purity (*dag-pa'i sems*). The *Uttaratantra* (*rGyud bla-ma*) is one of the Five Treatises of Maitreya-Asanga. Its subject matter is the Tathāgathagarbha.

Two things should be noted in regard to the practice of quoting "scripture" in Buddhist commentarial literature. First, unlike the Hinduist philosophical traditions, the Buddhists did not accept scripture (*āgama*) as a valid means of knowing (*pramāṇa*); they only accepted perceptual encounter (*pratyakṣa*) and its explication, including the formal procedures of inference, (*anumāna*). Why then are Sūtras and Śāstras so frequently quoted? Simply because they often make the point as well as it could be made; it could not have been said better. Of course, an author will also cite older texts to lend credence to his particular interpretation, but this in itself would never be recognized as a valid argument. It must also be remembered that the Sūtras themselves were subjected to an evaluation as to whether their meaning was explicit or required interpretation. So even claims of orthodoxy for a certain position based on scripture, although accepted, would still be subject to this evaluation. For example, in Tibet, the issue regarding the evaluation of the Sūtras and Śāstras of the Second and Third Dharmacakras has never been settled. Some say that the *Prajñāpāramitā-sūtras* and their Mādhyamika interpretation represents the explicit, definitive meaning of the Buddha's teaching, while texts belonging to the Third Dharmacakra, which teach such subjects as *ālaya-vijñāna* and Tathāgatagarbha, require further interpretation because they are not the definitive meaning. Others, such as the rNying-ma-pa, hold the reverse: the Third Dharmacakra is definitive (see, for example, Klong-chen-pa, *Grub-mtha' mdzod*, Dodrup Chen Rinpoche, pub., Gangtok, Sikkim, n.d., p. 33).

Second, Western philosophy, particularly of the Anglo-American variety, has degenerated into the program of resolving all philosophical problems through clearing up confusions said to be caused by the unwitting use of words in ways not sanctioned by ordinary usage. Furthermore, any thinking which does not simply proceed through the cut and dry method of proving one's premises and consistently deducing one's conclusions from them, is not considered worthy of the name philosophy. Now, Buddhist philosophy, particularly of the Indian variety, was also particularly fond of the argumentative style of philosophizing. But they also clearly recognized that certain philosophical problems, and indeed the most important, were not subject to such a procedure. That is, philosophizing may enter a realm where nothing can be proven, although a good deal may be pointed out (Heidegger). This "pointing out" is accomplished, in Buddhist texts, through a skillful building up of images intending to guide the reader towards fuller comprehension. An example would be the ten similes for the Tathāgatagarbha in the *Uttaratantra*. Quotations are also used in this way; each quotation presents a further facet of the 'gem' one is trying to point out. They are not arguments from analogy to prove certain propositions.

13. Why are the Saṃsāra, the potentialities for experience, and the lack of intrinsic perceptivity often said to be 'beginningless'? One might suggest the following: although there is a 'dimming' of intrinsic perceptivity by virtue of the operation of the potentialities for experience, since Being-as-such cannot decrease (or increase), this 'dimming' still represents a total response to Being, albeit in the 'defected form' of objectivizing experience and 'creating' all sorts of 'things'. This limitation, with its attending feeling of incompleteness, leads to the constant search for 'something more'. There is an 'end' to the Saṃsāra in the sense that there is 'nothing more' to search for once the initial limitation has gone.

14. The *gSang-ba snying-po* (*Guhya-garbha-tantra*) is the main text of the Mahāyoga class of "Old Tantras" (rNying-rgyud) which were excluded from the later compilations of the Tibetan Buddhist canon.

15. *'khrul-snang*. This involves the creation of fictitious duplicates to what is presented to us (*snang-ba*), taking this presence to be the presence of something existing in-itself. See below note 24.

16. The *Pramāṇa-varttikā* (*Tshad-ma rnam-'grel*) is the greatest work of Indian Buddhist epistemology and logic, written by Dharmakīrti (seventh c.). It reflects the Indian predilection for inquiry into the "valid means of knowing" (*tshad-ma, pramāṇa*).

17. *sems*. This is a term for the intentive structure of mind, analyzed into acts of consciousness (*noeses*), and their intended meanings (*noemata*).

18. *Ratnamālā* (*Rin-chen 'phreng-ba*) is a work by Nāgārjuna giving advice to a King on the realization of the Dharma.

19. *goms-pa*. In Western psychology, habituation can refer to the tendency for the subject's level of attention to drop off after repeated contacts with the same object.

20. *Mahāyāna-sūtra-laṅkāra* (*mDo-sde rgyan*) is Maitreya-Asaṅga's encyclopedic treatise on the Mahāyāna path from the standpoint of the Cittamātra (Sems-tsam) trend of thought, which held that objects do not exist apart from mind.

21. Maitreya, the future Buddha of this Aeon, is the reputed author of the five Treatises which he transmitted to Asaṅga, i.e., *Abhisamayālaṅkāra, Mahāyāna-sūtra-laṅkāra, Dharma-dharmatā-vibhaṅga, Madhyānta-vibhāga,* and *Uttaratantra*. The question of Maitreya's historicity and the authorship of these five texts and their commentaries is actively debated among specialists. It is *most likely* that Asaṅga put together *most* of these works from previous materials and his own ideas under the "inspiration" (*byin-rlabs*) of Maitreya, which enabled him to actualize (*mngon-du-gyur, adiṣṭhāna*) them in his mind. Cf. Ruegg, D. S., *La Théorie du Tathāgatagarbha et du Gotra*, Paris, École Française D'Extreme Orient, 1969, pp. 54–5.

22. The following arguments point out the absurdities in claiming that all appearances are mental. Certainly everything must be presented to an experiencing subject; how we experience (*snang-ba*), the either implicit or explicit "seeing as," is a mental process (*sems*). This does not mean, however, that what is presented is one's own mind, or that there is some universal Mind. The Cittamātra position is a corrective to earlier common-sense notions that the commonality of presences before several individuals is due to a single, public external object. This is a mere belief. The basis for this belief is precisely the commonality of presences before different individuals. The realist confuses perceptions (presences) with beliefs or hypotheses (themselves presences of another type, which, of course, have their relative practical validity). The issue here is not one of "practical validity" (*kun-rdzob*), i.e., what is commonly accepted, but of man's obsession with his beliefs and their emotional underpinnings, which bring him so much misery. In regard to this level of questioning (*don-dam*) regarding what is primary in our existence, we are not very practical at all.

Our habitual ways of perceiving (*bag-chags*) are built up through *intersubjective* experience, so that we all have our typical human ways of experiencing. The Cittamātra texts are fond of pointing out that what is water to us is the elixir of longevity to the gods. The *bag-chags* lead to the split (*rtog-pa*) into a world of apprehendable objects and apprehending subjects. But, we must emphasize again, in denying that these apprehendable objects are not one's mind, Klong-chen-pa is not retreating to a realist position. Rather, he states that they are a presence without any actuality (*rang-bzhin-med*), like a reflection in a mirror or a mirage. These presences are not what we take them to be (*bden-med*). Their fact of being, which the realist likes to explain in terms of atoms or whatever, is simply no-thing (*stong-pa*), yet a wondrous, and all too easily deceptive, presence.

These apprehendable objects, since they have no actuality, cannot even be *grounded* as being mental, for mind, as we understand it, makes no sense without anything to apprehend. Mind is a symptom of the disease called mistaken presencing; it will, however, let itself be cured of its incidental sickness, for mind, too, is not what it is taken to be. Try to locate the symptom to see if you can surgically remove it!

23. *snang-srid*: *snang-ba* denotes presence, thereness, and *srid-pa*, 'what you do with it'. *Srid-pa*, 'becoming', is the tenth member of the wheel of functional correlation, coming before *skye-ba*, 'birth'. It indicates that individual existence is pro-jective, in which one is always 'ahead of oneself', 'sketching out' possible ways to be. To put it simply: we are constantly being born into a world which we have already created for ourselves.

24. The Mīmāṁsakas were one of the six major schools (*darśana*) of Hinduist philosophy. The Buddhist rejected both the notions that consciousness could arise from the 'contact' of inert 'elements' (materialist), and that these 'elements' themselves had consciousness (objective idealist).

25. What is crucial here is the obsessiveness (*zhen-pa*) of the mistaken mode of presencing, the obsession for objects which are held to exist 'in truth' (*bden-grub*), i.e., exist as we take them to be. P. Ricoeur states beautifully, "In experience we are already on the level of a perception shot through with a 'thesis', that is to say with a believeing that posits its object as being. *We live through perception in giving credit to the vehemence of presence, if I may use such language, to the point of forgetting ourselves or losing ourselves in it.*" (P. Ricoeur, *Husserl, An Analysis of His Phenomenology*, Northwestern Univ. Press, Evanston, Ill.: 1967, p. 40, emphasis added.) *'Khrul-snang* applies to both valid and invalid perceptions in our everyday world; both can be equally obsessive. On *zhen-yul* and *snag-yul* see Mi-pham, *mKhas-'jug*, f.16a.

26. This is one of the *Ratnacūḍa* group of Sūtras (see next note).

27. The *Ratnacāḍa* (*dKon-brtsegs*) is a collection of about two dozen early Mahāyāna Sūtras.

28. Datura is known in the Western United States as Jimson or "Loco" weed; and was made famous by Carlos Casteneda in his *Teachings of Don Juan*.

29. This is one of the greatest Mahāyāna Sūtras, which is said to represent the Mādhyamika point of view.

Bibliography

This bibliography will give the reader an introduction to some of the texts which have been translated into Western languages. The groupings generally follow the historical development of the teachings.

The Early Tripiṭaka

Sutra Piṭaka

Dīrgha Āgama. Translated by T. W. Rhys Davids as *Dialogues of the Buddha*. 3 vols. 4th ed. Sacred Books of the Buddhists, vols. 2–4. London: Luzac and Co., Ltd., 1899–1921.

Collection of thirty of the longest discourses of the Buddha on the theoretical and practical aspects of the Dharma.

Madhyama Āgama. Translated by I. B. Horner as *The Middle Length Sayings*. 3 vols. London: Luzac and Co., Ltd., 1954–59.

A collection of 150 Sūtras of intermediate length discussing the topics important to early Buddhism.

Saṃyukta Āgama. Translated by C. A. F. Rhys Davids and F. L. Woodward as *The Book of the Kindred Sayings*. 5 vols. London: Luzac and Co., Ltd., 1917–30.

A collection of short Sūtras arranged by topic: the truths, mindfulness, sense, dependent origination, etc.

Ekotarra Āgama. Translated by E. M. Hare and F. L. Woodward as *The Book of the Gradual Sayings*. 5 vols. London: Luzac and Co., Ltd., 1932–36.

The second of the collections of short Sūtras of the Pali canon.

Khaḍgaviṣāṇagāthā. Translated by R. Chalmers in *Buddha's Teaching, Being the Sutta-Nipata or Discourse-Collection*. Harvard Oriental Series, vol. 37. Cambridge: Harvard University Press, 1932.

A poem by a sage living alone in the forest.

Munigāthā. Translated by R. Chalmers in *Buddha's Teaching, Being the Sutta-Nipata or Discourse-Collection.* Harvard Oriental Series, vol. 37. Cambridge: Harvard University Press, 1932.

Śailagāthā. Translated by R. Chalmers in *Buddha's Teachings, Being the Sutta-Nipata or Discourse-Collection.* Harvard Oriental Series, vol. 37. Cambridge: Harvard University Press, 1932.

A dialogue in verse between the Buddha and a Brahman named Śaila.

Arthavargīyāṇi Sūtrāṇi. Translated by R. Chalmers in *Buddha's Teachings, the Sutta-Nipata or Discourse-Collection.* Harvard Oriental Series, vol. 37. Cambridge: Harvard University Press, 1932.

Sixteen short poems on the Dharma which are largely ethical in content.

Pārāyaṇa. Translated by R. Chalmers in *Buddha's Teaching, Being the Sutta-Nipata or Discourse-Collection.* Harvard Oriental Series, vol. 37. Cambridge: Harvard University Press, 1932.

Sixteen brief verse dialogues between the Buddha and Brahmans concerning the Dharma.

Theragāthā and *Therigāthā.* Translated by K. R. Norman as *Elder's Verses.* 2 vols. Pali Text Society Translation Series, vols. 38 and 40. London: Luzac and Co., Ltd., 1969–71.

Autobiographical lyrics of Theravāda monks and nuns, showing the living spirit of early Buddhism.

Itivuttaka and *Udāna.* Translated by F. L. Woodward as *Minor Anthologies,* II. Sacred Books of the Buddhists, vol. 8. London: Geoffrey Cumberlege, 1948.

Collections of short discourses in prose and verse.

Dharmapada. Translated by Irving Babbitt. New York and London: Oxford University Press, 1936; translated by Max Müller, Sacred Books of the East, vol. 10. Oxford: Clarendon Press, 1881; reproduced in Lin Yutang, *The Wisdom of China and India.* (New York: Random House, 1942), pp. 321–56, and in Clarence Hamilton, *Buddhism.* (New York: Liberal Arts Press, 1952), pp. 64–67; translated by S. Radhakrishnan, Oxford: The University Press, 1950; translated by P. S. Dhammarama, "Dhammapada, Texte et Traduction." *Bulletin de l'Ecole française d'Extrême-Orient* 61 (2): 238–319; translated by T. Byron. New York: Vintage, 1976.

A popular and non-technical presentation of the Dharma, known as the "Verses on the Doctrine."

Jātaka. Translated by Chalmers, Francis, Rouse and Neil as *The Jātaka or Stories of the Buddha's Former Births*. 6 vols. London: Luzac and Co., Ltd., 1969.

Vinaya Piṭaka

Vinaya Piṭaka. Translated by I. B. Horner as *The Book of the Discipline*. 6 vols. Sacred Books of the Buddhists, vols. 10, 11, 13, 14, 20, 25. London: Luzac and Co., Ltd., 1938–1966.

The rules of conduct and discipline which form the foundation of Theravāda monastic life. Presented as discourses of the Buddha.

Abhidharma Piṭaka

Vibhaṅga. Translated by U Thiṭṭila as *The Book of Analysis*. London: Luzac and Co., Ltd., 1969.

Analyses of the aggregates, elements, dependent origination, foundations of mindfulness, etc.

Dhātukathā. Translated by U Narada as *Discourse on Elements*. Pali Text Society Translation Series, vol. 34. London: Luzac and Co., Ltd., 1962.

A manual for Theravāda students. Concerns itself, among other things, with the classification and conjunction of phenomena.

Paṭṭhāna. Translated by U Narada as *Conditional Relations*. Pali Text Society Translation Series, vol. 37. London: Luzac and Co., Ltd., 1969.

Undertakes to give a full account of conditioned origination, concentrating on the conditional relation itself.

Works of the Schools

Sthaviravāda

Sūtra Piṭaka Additions

Khuddakapāṭha. Translated by Ñānamoli as *The Minor Readings*. Pali Text Society Translation Series, vol. 32. London: Luzac and Co., Ltd., 1960.

Shortest of the Theravāda texts. Published with Buddhaghosa's commentary.

Paṭisambhidāmagga. Translated by Ñānamoli, London: Pali Text Society, 1970.

Buddhavaṁsa. Translated by I. B. Horner in *The Minor Anthologies of the Pali Canon*, Part III. London: Pali Text Society, 1975.

An account, narrated by the Buddha Gotama, of certain features in the lives of the twenty-four past Buddhas who made declarations to him, in his past lives, that his aspiration to Buddhahood would succeed. Contains a development of the Bodhisattva ideal.

Cariyāpiṭaka. Translated by I. B. Horner as "The Basket of Conduct" in *Minor Anthologies of the Pali Canon*, Part III. London: Pali Text Society, 1975.

A collection of stories illustrating the resolution of Bodhisattvas to accomplish the Ten Perfections.

Dasabodhisattuppattikathā. Translated by H. Saddhatissa as *The Birth-Stories of the Ten Bodhisattvas.* London: Pali Text Society, 1975.

Stories of the Buddha extolling the Bodhisattvas who will be Buddhas in future ages.

Abhidharma Piṭaka Additions

Dhammasangaṇi. Translated by C. A. F. Rhys Davids as *A Buddhist Manual of Psychological Ethics.* 2d ed. London: Royal Asiatic Society, 1923.

Deals with elements of existence considered as 'real', classified under the five groups (*skandhas*).

Puggalapaññatti. Translated by B. C. Law. Pali Text Society Translation Series, vol. 12, London: Oxford University Press, 1924.

A treatise on the concept of 'person', defined as a sequence of conditions.

Kathāvatthu. Translated by S. Z. Aung and C. A. F. Rhys Davids as *Points of Controversy, or Subjects of Discourse.* Pali Text Society Translation Series, vol. 5, London: Humphry Milford, 1915.

An important text consisting of refutations in strict logical form of more than two hundred propositions held by various schools of Buddhism.

Other Sūtra Works

Milindapañhā. Translated by I. B. Horner as *Milinda's Questions.* 2 vols. Sacred Books of the Buddhists, vols. 22 and 23, London: Luzac and Co., Ltd., 1969; translated by T. W. Rhys Davids as *The Questions of King Milinda.* 2 vols., Sacred Books of the East, vols. 35–6, New York: Dover, 1963.

A dialogue between King Milinda (Menander) and the monk Nāgasena on the Dharma. One of the most important non-canonical works of Theravada Buddhism.

Peṭakopadesa. Translated by Ñānamoli as *The Piṭaka Disclosure*. London: Luzac and Co., Ltd., 1964.

A text concerned with scholastic methodology, including all aspects of interpretation of the Dharma.

Nettippakaraṇa. Translated by Ñānamoli as *The Guide*. London: Pali Text Society, 1962.

Considered to be a re-writing of the *Peṭakopadesa*.

Commentaries

Buddhaghosa. *Paramatthajotikā*. Translated by Ñānamoli as *The Illustrator of Ultimate Meaning*. Pali Text Society Translation Series, vol. 32. London: Luzac and Co., Ltd., 1960.

Commentary on the *Khuddakapāṭha*. Discusses the refuge, contemplation, and most of the topics important to early Buddhism.

———. *Samantapāsādika*. Translated by N. A. Jayawickrama as *The Inception of Discipline*. Sacred Books of the Buddhists, vol. 21. London: Luzac and Co., Ltd., 1962.

Translation of the introduction of Buddhaghosa's commentary on the Vinaya.

———. *Atthasālini*. Translated by Maung Tin as *The Expositor*. 2 vols. Pali Text Translation Series, vols. 8 and 9. London: Oxford University Press, 1920–1921.

Commentary on the *Dhammasaṅgaṇi*, the first book of the Abhidharma Piṭaka.

———. *Pañcappakaraṇaṭṭhakathā*. Part III translated by B. C. Law as *The Debates Commentary*. London: Luzac and Co., Ltd., 1940.

Commentary on the *Kathāvatthu*.

Dhammapadaṭṭakathā. Translated by E. W. Burlingame as *Buddhist Legends*. 3 vols. Harvard Oriental Series, vols. 28–30. Cambridge: Harvard University Press, 1921.

Commentary on the *Dharmapada*.

Manuals

Thera Upatissa. *Vimuttimagga.* Translated by Ehara, Soma and Keminda as *The Path of Freedom.* Colombo: Balcombe House, 1961.

Collection of practical instructions. Divided into the Three Trainings: Virtue, Concentration and Understanding.

Buddhaghosa. *Visuddhimagga.* Translated by Bhikkhu N̄yāṇamoli as *The Path of Purification.* Berkeley: Shambhala, 1976; translated by Pe Maung Tin as *The Path of Purity.* 3 vols. Pali Text Society Translation Series, vols. 11, 17, and 21. London: Luzac and Co., Ltd., 1923–31.

The principal non-canonical authority of the Theravāda, which systematically summarizes and interprets the teachings of the Buddha. A textbook of Buddhist psychology, a work of reference, and a detailed manual for meditation.

Anuruddha. *Abhidhammattha-Sangaha.* Translated by S. Z. Aung as *Compendium of Philosophy.* Pali Text Society Translation Series, vol. 2. London: Oxford University Press, 1910.

Abhidharma manual discussing consciousness, dreams, karma, liberation, etc.

Sarvāstivāda

Saṃgharakṣa. *Yogācāra-bhūmi.* Translated by Demieville in *Bulletin de l'École française d'Extrême-Orient* 44 (1954): 339–436.

A treatise on meditation.

Mūlasarvāstivāda

Dharma-samuccaya. Translated by Lin Li-kouang. *Dharma-Samuccaya: Compendium de la Loi.* Publications de Musée Guimet, Bibliothèque d'études, vol. 53, Paris: A. Maisonneuve, 1946.

Collection of verses from a Mūlasarvāstivāda Sūtra. Contains much of the theory and practice of Buddhism. Detailed descriptions of the Six Realms.

Patimokkha. Translated by Charles S. Prebish as *Buddhist Monastic Discipline: the Sanskrit Pratimokṣa Sūtras of the Mahāsāṃghikas and Mūlasarvāstivādins.* University Park: Pennsylvania State University Press, 1975.

The texts are placed face to face for purposes of comparison.

Sautrāntika

Vasubandhu. *Abhidharma-kośa*. Translated by L. de La Vallée Poussin as *L'Abhidharmakośa de Vasubandhu*. 6 vols. Paris: Paul Geuthner, 1923–31.

Vasubandhu. *Karmasiddhi-prakaraṇa*. Translated by E. Lamotte in "Le traite de l'acte de Vasubandhu, Karmasiddhi-prakarana." *Mélanges Chinois et bouddhiques* 4 (1936): 151–288.

A treatise on action, deals with memory, the causes of apparent fixivity, etc.

The Mahayana Tripiṭaka

The Early Mahāyāna

Mahāvastu. Translated by J. J. Jones. 3 vols. Sacred Books of the Buddhists, vols. 16, 18, 19. London: Pali Text Society, 1949–1956.

An early Mahāyāna work which contains discussions which foreshadow important Mahāyāna themes. A collection of practically all the history and legends relating to the Buddha which were current at the time of its compilation.

Rāṣṭrapālaparipṛcchā. Translated by J. Ensink as *The Question of Rāṣṭrapāla*. Zwolle: N. V. Drukkerij & Vitgerverij van de Erven J. J. Tijl, 1952.

One of the earliest Mahāyāna Sūtras, illustrating the Bodhisattva ideal with fifty Jātaka tales of the former lives of the Buddha.

Aṣṭasāhasrikā-prajñāpāramitā-sūtra. Translated by E. Conze in *The Perfection of Wisdom in Eight Thousand Lines and its Verse Summary*. Bolinas: Four Seasons Foundation, 1973.

Oldest of the *Prajñāpāramitā-sūtras*, the central theme of which is the Open Dimension of Being.

Prajñāpāramitā Ratna-guṇa-saṃcayagāthā. Translated by E. Conze in *The Perfection of Wisdom in Eight Thousand Lines and its Verse Summary*. Bolinas: Four Seasons Foundation, 1973.

A collection of 302 verses summarizing the *Aṣṭasāhasrikā-prajñāpāramitā-sūtra*.

Prajñāpāramitā-sūtra (25,000 lines). Translated by E. Conze in *The Large*

Sutra on Perfect Wisdom. Berkeley, Los Angeles and London: University of California Press, 1975.

Covers topics like training, nonduality, purity of *dharmas* and the foundationlessness of all phenomena.

Aṣṭadaśasāhasrikā-prajñāpāramitā-sūtra (18,000 lines). Translated by E. Conze in *The Large Sutra on Perfect Wisdom*. Berkeley, Los Angeles and London: University of California Press, 1975.

Discusses traits of enlightened mind, the signless nature of *dharmas*, etc.

Suvikrāntavikrāmiparipṛccha-prajñāpāramitā-sūtra (2,500 lines). Translated by E. Conze in *The Short Prajñāpāramitā Texts*. London: Luzac and Co., 1973.

The latest in time of the full scale Prajñāpāramitā texts. Discusses doctrine at a high level of ratiocination.

Prajñāpāramitā-sūtra (500 lines). Translated by E. Conze in *The Short Prajñāpāramitā Texts*. London: Luzac and Co., 1973.

Prajñāpāramitā-sūtra (700 lines). Translated by E. Conze in *The Short Prajñāpāramitā Texts*. London: Luzac and Co., 1973.

A dialogue between Mañjuśrī and the Buddha on emptiness, non-apprehension of *dharmas*, non-discrimination, Suchness, etc.

Prajñāpāramitā-sūtra (300 lines) or *Vajracchedikā*. Translated by Max Müller in *Buddhist Mahāyāna Texts*. Sacred Books of the East, vol. 49. New York: Dover, 1969; translated by A. F. Price in *The Diamond Sūtra and the Sūtra of Hui Neng*. Berkeley: Shambhala, 1969; translated by E. Conze in *Buddhist Wisdom Books*. New York: Harper and Row, 1972; translated by N. Poppe in *The Diamond Sūtra. Three Mongolian Versions of the Vajracchedikā Prajñāpāramitā*. Wiesbaden: Otto Harrassowitz, 1971.

The "Diamond Sūtra," or the 'Perfection of Wisdom which cuts like a thunderbolt', is one of the most popular of the Prajñāpāramitā texts.

Naya-prajñāpāramitā-sūtra (150 lines). Translated by E. Conze in *The Short Prajñāpāramitā Texts*. London: Luzac and Co., 1973.

A tantric text, which briefly describes the transmission of the Perfect Wisdom to Vajrapaṇi by a number of Tathāgatas and Bodhisattvas.

Prajñāpāramitā-hṛdaya-sutra. The longer and shorter versions are both translated by Max Müller in *Buddhist Mahāyāna Texts*. Sacred Books of the

East. vol. 49, New York: Dover, 1969; both translated in *The Short Prajñā-pāramitā Texts*, by E. Conze. London: Luzac and Co., 1973.

The "Heart Sūtra," which sets forth the very essence of the Prajñā-pāramitā literature.

Prajñāpāramitā-sūtra (50 lines). Translated by E. Conze in *The Short Prajñā-pāramitā Texts*. London: Luzac and Co., 1973.

Consists primarily of lists of topics to which the Bodhisattva should turn his attention.

The Later Mahāyāna

Saddharmapuṇḍarīka-sūtra. Translated by H. Kern in *Saddharma-puṇḍarīka* or *The Lotus of the True Law*. Sacred Books of the East, vol. 21. New York: Dover, 1963; translated by Bunnō Katō in *The Threefold Lotus Sūtra*. New York: Weatherhill, 1975; translated by Leon Hurvitz as *Scripture of Fine Dharma* (*The Lotus Sūtra*). New York: Columbia University Press, 1976.

The Lotus Sūtra is one of the most popular and influential of Mahāyāna texts, known for its parables and its warmth and directness of style.

Vimalakīrtinirdeśa-sūtra. Translated by E. Lamotte as *L'enseignement de Vimalakīrti* (*Vimalakīrtinirdeśa*). Biblioteque du Muséon, vol. 51. Louvain: Publ. Univ. Inst. Orientaliste, 1962; translated by Charles Luk, Berkeley and London: Shambhala, 1972; and translated by Robt. A. F. Thurman as *The Holy Teaching of Vimalakīrti*. University Park and London, 1976.

An influential text dealing primarily with teachings on emptiness.

Suvarṇabhāsa-sūtra. Translated by Nobel. Leiden: 1958; translated by R. E. Emmeric as *The Sutra of Golden Light*. Sacred Books of the East, vol. 27. London: Luzac and Co., Ltd., 1970.

A Jātaka tale provides the framework for expounding the doctrine of dependent origination which, later in the Sūtra, is explained to be without content.

Śrīmāladevisimhanāda-sūtra. Translated by Alex and Hideko Wayman as *The Lion's Roar of Queen Śrīmala*. New York: Columbia University Press, 1973.

Elaborates the theory of the Tathāgatagarbha, the essence or potentiality of the Buddha-nature. Explains that the cessation of suffering does not imply the destruction of phenomena.

Avataṃsaka-sūtra. Small portions translated by Garma C. C. Chang in *The Buddhist Teaching of Totality*. University Park and London: Pennsylvania State University Press, 1971.

The fundamental text of the Hwa Yen School. Teaches of a Totality in which infinitely many realms interpenetrate.

Gaṇḍavyūha-sūtra. Excerpts translated by Herbert V. Guenther in *Tibetan Buddhism in Western Perspective*. Emeryville: Dharma Publishing, 1977.

Principal text of the Avataṃsaka school. It describes Sudhana's quest for enlightenment.

Sūrangamasamādhi-sūtra. Translated by Wei-Tao and D. Goddard. Published as *Surangama Sutra* in *A Buddhist Bible* (ed. D. Goddard). Boston: Beacon Press, 1966; translated in *The Wisdom of China and India* (ed. Lin Yutang). New York: Modern Library, 1942.

While harmonious with Mādhyamika and Yogācāra ideas, this Sūtra seems to be moving in the direction of Tantrism.

Saṁdhinirmocana-sūtra. Translated by E. Lamotte in *Saṁdhinirmocana Sūtra. L'explication des mysteres*. Louvain: Beureaux du Recueil, 1935.

Lankavatara-sūtra. Translated by D. T. Suzuki, London: Routledge & Kegan Paul, 1956.

A major work of importance, in particular, to the Yogācāra and the Mādhyamika.

Bhadramāvāravyākarana. Translated by Konstantin Regamey. Warsaw: 1938.

The Mahāyāna Schools

Mādhyamika

Nāgārjuna. *Mūla-madhyamaka-kārikā*. Translated by F. J. Streng in *Emptiness: A Study in Religious Meaning*. Nashville & New York: Abingdon Press, 1967; translated by Kenneth Inada, Tokyo: The Hokuseido Press, 1970; [*kārikās* 1 and 25] translated by Th. Stcherbatsky in *The Conception of Buddhist Nirvana*. London, The Hague & Paris: Mouton & Co., 1965; [*kārikās* 5, 12–16] translated by Schayer in *Ausgewählte Kapitel aus der Prasannapada*. Krakow: Polska Akadmeja Umiejetnosci, 1931 and [*kārikā* 10] in *Rocznik Orjentalistyczny* (1931; [*kārikā* 17] translated by E. Lamotte in *Melanges Chinois et Bouddhiques* 4 (1936); [*kārikās* 2–4, 6–9, 11, 23–4 and 26–7] translated by J. May in *Prasannapada Madhyamakavṛtti, douze chapitres traduits du sanscrit et du tibetain*. Paris: A. Maisonneuve, 1959.

The major work of Nāgārjuna, which became the fundamental text of the Mādhyamika school.

———. *Vigraha-vyāvarttani* and *Vṛtti*. Translated by Schaeffer. Materialen zür Kunde des Buddhismus, vol. 3. Heidelberg: 1923, translated by G. Tucci in *Pre-Diṅnāga Buddhist Texts on Logic*. Gaekwad Oriental Series, vol. 49. Baroda: 1929; translated by S. Yamaguchi. *Journal Asiatique* 215 (1959): 1–86.

Refutation of possible objections that might be raised against his negative method of Śūnyatā.

———. *Yuktiṣaṣṭika*. Translated by Schaeffer in Materialen zür Kunde des Buddhismus. Heidelberg: 1923.

One of the main treatises by the founder of Mādhyamika, summarizing his doctrine in sixty stanzas.

———. *Suhṛllekha*. Translated by L. Kawamura in *Golden Zephyr*. Emeryville: Dharma Publishing, 1975.

This "Letter to a Friend" provides a concise and thorough introduction to the entire Buddhist path. Published with a commentary by Lama Mipham (19th c.).

———. *Lugs kyi bstan-bcos shes-rab sdong-po*. Translated in *Elegant Sayings* as "*The Staff of Wisdom*." Emeryville: Dharma Publishing, 1977.

———. *Ratnāvalī*. Translated by G. Tucci. "Ratnāvalī of Nāgārjuna." *Journal of the Royal Asiatic Society*. (1934) pp. 307–25 and (1936) pp. 237–52, 423–35.

A popular work, addressed to a king, in which Nāgārjuna expounds ethics and philosophy and a poetic manner.

———. *Rājaparikathā-ratnamālā*. Translated by Jeffrey Hopkins and Lati Rinpoche in *The Precious Garland and The Song of the Four Mindfulnesses*. New York, Evanston, San Francisco, and London: Harper and Row,1975.

Advice to the king, explaining emptiness, compassion, and techniques for social welfare.

———. *Mahāyānaviṃśaka*. Translated by V. Bhattacharya in *Viśvabharati Quarterly*, vol. 8, (1930-31) pp. 107–50; translated by G. Tucci in *Minor Buddhist Texts*, Pt. I, Serie Orientale Roma, vol. 9. Rome: 1956.

______. *Catuḥstava*. Translated by G. Tucci in *Journal of the Royal Asiatic Society* (1932) pp. 309–25.

Two devotional poems by the founder of the Mādhyamika school.

______. *Iśvarakartṛtvanirākaraṇaviṣṇoḥ ekakartṛtvanirakaraṇa*. Translated by H. C. Gupta from Stcherbatsky's Russian translation. *Indian Studies Past and Present* 10 (1968): 57–66.

Āryadeva. *Śataśāstra*. Translated by G. Tucci in *Pre-Diṅnāga Buddhist Texts on Logic*. Gaekwad Oriental Series, vol. 59, Baroda: 1929.

A refutation of the doctrines of other Buddhist schools from the Madhyamika position.

______. *Akṣara-catakam*. Translated by V. Gokhale. Materialen zür Kunde des Buddhismus, vol. 14. Heidelberg: 1930.

______. *Cathuśataka*. Chapters 8–16 translated into French by P. L. Vaidya, Vaidya. Paris: 1923; chapter 7 translated by V. Battacharya in *Proceedings of the All-India Oriental Conference* 4 (1928): 831–71.

The major work of Āryadeva, which presents the Mahāyāna, and particularly the Mādhyamika lines of thought.

Nāgabodhi. *Mahā-prajñāpāramitā-śāstra*. Translated by E. Lamotte as *Le Traité de la Grande Vertu de Sagesse*. 2 vols. Bibliothèque du Muséon, vol. 18. Louvain Bureaux de Muséon, 1944 & 1949.

An enormous commentary on the *Prajñāpāramitā-sūtra* in 25,000 lines by a student of Nāgārjuna, showing the connection between Mādhyamika and the Mahāyāna Sūtras.

Sthiramati. *Ratnagotravibhāga Mahāyāna Uttaratantra-Śāstra*. Translated by Obermiller. "The Sublime Science." *Acta Orientalia* 9 (1931); translated by J. Takesaki in *A Study on the Ratnotravibhāga* (*Uttaratantra*), *Being a Treatise on the Tathāgatagarbha Theory of Mahāyāna Buddhism*. Serie Orientale Roma, vol. 33. Rome: 1966.

A basically Mādhyamika position, but quite different from Nāgārjuna's. Sets up an absolute, which is eternal and has various characteristics.

Maitreya-Asaṅga. *Abhisamayālaṃkāra*. Translated by E. Conze in Serie Orientale Roma, vol. 6. Rome: 1954.

An important commentary on the Prajñāpāramitā-sūtras studied by both the Mādhyamikas and the Yogācārins.

Candrakīrti. *Madhyamakāvatāra.* Translated by Louis de la Vallée Poussin. *Madya makā vatāra, introduction au traité du milieu l'Ācarya Candrakīrti, avec le commentaire de l'auteur traduit d'apres la version tibetain. Muséon*, vols. 8, 11, 12 (1907–1911).

An independent working out of the Mādhyamika position by a chief exponent of the Prāsaṅgika school.

Candrakīrti. *Prasannapadā Madyamakavṛtti.* Portions translated by J. W. de Jong. *Cinq Chapitres de la Prasannapadā.* Paris: Paul Geuthner, 1959; other portions translated by J. May, Th. Stcherbatsky, and Schayer with Nāgārjuna's *Karikas* (see above).

Commentary on the *Mūla-madhyamaka-kārikā*; a major work of Candrakīrti.

Śāntideva. *Śikṣāsammuccaya.* Translated by C. Bendall and W. H. D. Rouse as *Çikshā-Samuccaya. A compendium of Buddhist doctrine. Compiled by Çāntideva, chiefly from earlier Mahāyāna Sūtras (sic).* Indian Texts Series, London: John Murray, 1922.

One of Śāntideva's ethical studies on the way of the Bodhisattva.

———. *Bodhicaryāvatāra.* Translated by L. D. Barnett as *The Path of Light.* 2d. ed., New York: Grove Press, 1948; translated by L. Finot as *La Marche à la Lumière.* Les Classiques de l'Orient, vol. 2. Paris: Editions Bossard, 1920; translated by L. de la Vallée Poussin in *Introduction a la pratique des futurs Bouddas, poème de Çāntideva.* Paris: Bloud, 1907; translated by M. L. Matics as *Entering the Path of Enlightenment: The Bodhicaryāvatāra of the Buddhist Poet Śāntideva.* New York: Macmillan, 1970; translated by R. Schmidt as *Der Entritt in den Wandel in Erleuchtung.* Paderborn: Ferdinance Schoningle, 1923.

A basic poetical text outlining the path of the Bodhisattvas; studied by all schools in India and Tibet.

Yogācāra

Maitreya-Asaṅga. *Mahāyāna-sūtralaṅkāra.* Translated by S. Levi. *Mahāyāna-Sūtralaṃkāra Exposé de la doctrine du Grand Vehicule selon le système Yogācāra.* 2 vols. Paris: Champion, 1907–11.

A detailed presentation of the Bodhisattva Path and an interpretation of the *Prajñāpāramitā-sūtra.*

———. *Madhyānta-vibhaṅga.* Translated by Th. Stcherbatshy as *Madhyānta-*

vibhaṅga. Discourse on Discrimination between Middle and Extremes, ascribed to Maitreya and commented by Vasubandhu and Sthiramati. Bibliotecha Buddhica, vol. 30. Moscow-Leningrad: 1938.

Presents the Yogācāra view according to the teachings of the Middle Way and elucidates the Three Natures.

Asaṅga. *Mahāyāna-saṃgraha.* Translated by E. Lamotte, *La Somme du Grand Vehicule d'Asanga (Mahāyānasaṃgraha)* 1 vols. Louvain: 1938–39.

A full treatment of *alāya-vijñāna.*

———. *Triśatikāyah Prajñāpāramitāyāh Kārikāsaptatih.* Translated by G. Tucci in *Minor Buddhist Texts.* Serie Orientale Roma, vol. 9. Rome: 1956.

A commentary on the "Diamond Sutra," emphasizing that nothing including the Dharma, the practice, and the practitioner, has existence.

———. *Bodhisattva-bhūmi.* Translated by C. Bendall and L. de la Vallée Poussin in *La Muséon* (n.s.) 4 (1905): 38–52, 7 (1906): 213–30, 11 (1911): 155–91.

A basic text of the Yogācāra school.

Vasubandhu. *Viṃśatikā (Viṃśikākārikāprakarana)* and *Vṛtti* and *Triṃśikā (Triṃśikākārikāprakarana).* Translated by L. de la Vallée Poussin in *La Siddhi de Hsuan-tsang.* 3 vols. Paris: 1928–48; translated by S. Levi as *Vijñaptimatratāsiddhi. Deux traites de Vasubandhu.* Paris: Champion, 1925; *Triṃśikā* translated by H. Jacobi as *Triṃśikāvijñapti des Vasubandhu. Beitrage zur indischen Sprachwissenschaft und Religionsgeschichte,* vol. 7. Stuttgart, 1932; *Viṃśatkā* translated by C. Hamilton as *Wei Shih Er Shih Lun or The Treatise in Twenty Stanzas on Representation-Only.* New Haven: American Orienal Society, 1938; *Viṃśatikā* translated by S. S. Bogchi. Nava-Nalanda-Mahavira Research Publications, I.

The *Triṃśikā,* a treatise of thirty verses, was a very popular text of the Yogācārins. The *Viṃśatikā,* a treatise of twenty verses, has a prose explication by Vasubandhu and is a polemic refuting views of other schools.

———. *Trisvabhāvanirdesa.* Translated by S. Mukhopadhyaya. Visvabharati Series, vol. 4. Calcutta: Visvabharati, 1939.

Stresses that what appears is real but not the manner of its appearance.

———. *Vādavidhi.* Fragments translated by E. Frauwallner in *Wiener Zeitschrift für die Kunde Sud- und Ostasien* 1 (1957): 104–34; inference section translated by H. Kitagawa in *Tohogaku* (1959): 143ff.

Tract on proof and refutation.

Sthiramati. Commentary on *Triṃśikā*. Translated by Levi and Jacobi and published with their translations of Vasubandhu's *Triṃśikā* (see above).

A commentary of Maitreya-Asaṅga's *Madhyānta-vibhaṅga*.

Dharmapala. Commentary on *Triṃśikā* and *Vimśatikā*. Translated by L. de la Vallée Poussin in *La Siddhi de Hsüan-tsang*. 3 vols. Paris: 1928–48.

Logic

Dignāga. *Prajñāpāramitā-piṇḍartha-saṃgraha*. Translated by G. Tucci in *Journal of the Royal Asiatic Society* (1947): 53–57.

Summarizes the 8,000 line *Prajñāpāramitā-sūtra* from the Yogācāra standpoint.

———. *Hastavālaprakaṇa*. Translated by F. W. Thomas and H. Vi in *Journal of the Royal Asiatic Society* (1918): 267–374.

Considers the nature of entities.

———. *Ālambanaparīkṣā*. Translated by Yamaguchi as "Examen de l'objet de la connaissance" in *Journal Asiatique* 214 (1929): 1–66; translated by Frauwallner in *Wiener Zeitschrift für die Kunde des Morgenlandes* 37 (1930): 174–94; translated by N. Aiyaswami Sastri in The Adyar Library, 1942; summarized by Th. Stcherbatsky in *Buddhist Logic*. vol. I, pp. 518ff.

———. *Hetucakraḍamaru*. Translated by D. Catterji in *Indian Historical Quarterly* 9 (1933): 511–14.

A basic contribution to the doctrine of proof.

———. *Nyāyamukha*. Translated by G. Tucci in Materialen zur Kunde des Buddhismus, vol. 15, Heidelburg: 1930.

A comprehensive introduction to logic.

———. *Pramāṇa-samuccaya*. First chapter translated by M. Hattori as *Dignāga on Perception*. Harvard Oriental Series, vol. 47, Cambridge, Mass.: Harvard University Press, 1968; passages translated by H. N. Randle in his *Fragments from Dignāga*. London: 1926.

A translation of the first chapter and autocommentary, dealing with perception. Includes refutations of false views.

———. *Trikālaparīkṣā*. Translated by M. Hattori in "The Date of Dignāga and his Milieu," *Essays on the History of Buddhism Presented to Prof. Zenryu Tsukamoto*. Kyoto: 1961.

Dharmakīrti. *Pramāṇavārttikam*. [*kārikās* 42–187] Translated by E. Frauwallner in "Beitrage zur Apohalehre," *Wiener Zeitschrift für die Kunde des Morgenlandes* 39 (1932): 247–285, 40 (1933): 51–94, 37 (1930): 259sq., 42 (1935): 93–102); [*kārikās* 1–6] translated by S. Mookerjee and Hojun Nagasaki in *The Pramāṇa-vārttikam of Dharmakīrti.* Nalanda: Nava Nalanda Mahavira, 1964.

Sets out to meet all the refutations which had arisen since Dignāga's pioneering work.

———. *Nyāyabindu.* Translated by Th. Stcherbatsky in *Buddhist Logic*, vol. 2, New York: Dover, 1962.

A brief but comprehensive manual of the Pramāṇa school.

———. *Hetuhbindu.* Translated by E. Steinkellner. 2 vols. Wien: Böhlaus Nachf., 1967.

A short classification of logical reasons.

———. *Sambandhaparīkṣa.* Translated by Frauwallner in *Wiener Zeitschrift für die Kunde des Morgenlandes* 41 (1934): 261–300.

An examination of the problem of relations.

———. *Santānāntara-siddhi.* Translated freely by Th. Stcherbatsky in *Papers of Th. Stcherbatsky.* Calcutta: Indian Studies Past and Present, 1969, pp. 81–121; summary in Stcherbatsky's *Buddhist Logic*, vol. 1, 521ff.; translated by H. Kitagawa in *Journal of the Greater India Society* 14 (1955)

A debate between philosophical idealism and realism.

Vinītadeva. *Nyāyabindu-tikā.* Translated by M. Gangopadhyaya, Calcutta: Indian Studies Past and Present, 1971.

Commentary on Dharmakirti's *Nyāyabindu.*

Śāntarakṣīta. *Tattvasaṃgraha.* Translated by G. Jha. Gaekwad Oriental Series, Baroda: Oriental Institute, 1937.

Critique of twenty-six 'principles', i.e., ultimate realities, first causes, categories, etc., thus establishing the truth of pratītya-samutpāda.

Kamalaśīla. *Tattvasaṃgraha-pañjika.* Translated by G. Jha with the *Tattvasaṃgraha of* Śāntarakṣīta (see above).

Commentary on the *Tattvasaṃgraha.*

Dharmottara. *Nyāyabindu-tīkā.* Translated by Th. Stcherbatsky in *Buddhist Logic*, vol. 2, New York: Dover, 1962.

Commentary on the *Nyāyabindu* of Dharmakīrti.

———. *Apohaprakarana*. Translated by Frauwallner in *Wiener Zeitschrift für die Kunde des Morgenlandes* 44 (1936): 233ff.

Deals with the relationship between concepts and reality.

———. *Kṣaṇabhaṅgasiddhi*. Translated by Frauwallner in *Wiener Zeitschrift für die Kunde des Morgenlandes* 42 (1935): 217–258.

Dharmapāla. Commentary on *Ālambanaparīkṣā*. Translated by M. Schott in *Sein als Bewusstsein*. Materialen zur Kunde Buddhismus, vol. 20, Heidelberg: 1935; also included in the translations by Frauwallner and Yamaguchi of the *Ālambanaparīkṣā* (see above).

Ratnakīrti. *Apohasiddhi*. Translated by D. Sharma in *The Differentiation Theory of Meaning in Indian Logic*. The Hague, Paris: 1969.

———. *Kṣaṇabhaṅgasiddhi*. Translated by A. C. S. McDermott as *An Eleventh-Century Buddhist Logic of 'Exists'*. Foundations of Language, Supplementary Series, vol. 11, Dordrecht: D. Reidel, 1969.

A explanation of the realm of relative truth.

Svātantrika

Bhāvaviveka. *Prajñāpradīpa*. Chapter 1. Translated by Yuichi Kajiyama in *Wiener Zeitschrift für die Kunde Sud- und Ostasiens* 7 (1963): 37–62, 8 (1964): 100–130.

Commentary on Nāgārjuna's *Mūla-mādhyamaka-kārikā*.

———. *Madhyamaka-hṛdaya*. Chapter 5 partly translated by V. V. Gokhale in *Indo-Iranian Journal* 5 (1962): 271–75.

Sets out the Mādhyamika doctrine of ultimate reality and critiques other schools.

———. *Madhyamaka-kārthasaṃgraha*. Translated by N. Aiyasvami Sastri in *Journal of Oriental Research* 5 (1931): 41–9.

A study of the two truths.

———. *Karatalaratna*. Translated by Aiysvami Sastri in *Viśvabhāratī Studies* 9 (1949); translated by L. de la Vallée Poussin in *Mélanges Chinois et Bouddhiques* 2 (1933): 68–146.

An independent argument for the Mādhyamika doctrine.

Kamaśīla. *Bhāvanākrama*. (I). English summary by G. Tucci in *Minor Buddhist Texts*, Pt. II, Serie Orientale Roma, vol. 9. Rome: 1958.

The first of a series of manuals summarizing the Mādhyamika Pāramitā course of training.

Mantrayāna

Mahāvairocana-sūtra. Translated by R. Tajima in *Étude sur le Mahāvairocana Sūtra.* Paris: Adrien Maisonneuve, 1936.

A Caryā-tantra text.

Hevajra Tantra (Muktikāvili) Translated by D. L. Snellgrove, 2 vols, London Oriental Series, vol. 6, London: Oxford University Press, 1959.

While primarily a set of instructions for the practitioner, there are brief philosophical passages.

Saṁvarodaya-tantra. Selected chapters translated by S. Tsuda, Tokyo: Hokuseido Press, 1974.

Discusses ultimate reality, individual existence, and their relationship.

Anthologies of Buddhist Texts in English Translation

A Buddhist Bible. Edited by D. Goddard, Boston: Beacon Press, 1966.

Contains an edited selection of Theravāda texts together with the Heart, Diamond, Surangama, Lankavatara and Platform Sūtras, and others.

Buddhist Mahāyāna Texts. Edited by E. B. Cowell, New York: Dover, 1969.

Includes the Heart and Diamond Sūtras and three Pure Land Sūtras.

Buddhist Scriptures. Selected and translated by E. Conze, Baltimore, Md.: Penguin, 1959.

Fairly short selections from Theravāda and Mahāyāna texts organized by subject.

Buddhist Suttas. Translated by T. W. Rhys Davids, Sacred Books of the East, vol. 11. New York: Dover, 1969.

Translations of seven basic Sūtras of the Theravāda.

Buddhist Texts Through the Ages. Edited by E. Conze, New York, Evanston and London: Harper and Row, 1964.

Includes Theravāda and Indian, Tibetan, Chinese and Japanese Mahāyāna selections.

Buddhism in Translation. Edited by H. C Warren, Harvard Oriental Series, vol. 3. New York: Athenaeum, 1963.

A fine anthology of Theravāda materials.

The Teachings of the Compassionate Buddha. Edited by E. A. Burtt, New York: New American Library (Mentor), 1955.

An edited selection of short excerpts from both of the major segments of Buddhism.

World of the Buddha. Edited by Lucien Stryk, Garden City and New York: Anchor-Doubleday, 1969.

Mostly Theravāda materials, but a wide variety of Mahāyāna positions are represented with short selections.

Tibetan Buddhist Works

rNying-ma-pa

Padmasambhava/mKha'gro Ye-shes mTsho-rgyal (Yeshe Tsogyal). *Padma Thang Yid.* Translation by G. C. Toussaint, Kenneth Douglas, and Gwendolyn Bays as *The Life and Liberation of Padmasambhava.* Emeryville: Dharma Publishing, 1978; a shortened version translated in *The Tibetan Book of the Great Liberation.* ed., W. Y. Evans-Wentz, London, Oxford and New York: Oxford University Press, 1954; short versions may also be found in *The Legend of the Great Stupa* and *Crystal Mirror* 4 (1975) both published by Dharma Publishing, Emeryville, California.

A complete biography of the master Padmasambhava, the founder of Tibetan Buddhism.

———. *The Legend of the Great Stupa.* Translated by Tarthang Tulku and K. Dowman. Berkeley: Tibetan Nyingma Meditation Center, 1973.

The story centers on Padmasambhava and events surrounding the Great Stupa. Contains a prophecy of the dispersal of the Tibetan people and the migration of the Dharma to the land of the red man.

———. *Zab-chos zhi-khro dgongo-pa rang-grol las rig-pa ngo-spröd gcer-mthong rang-grol shes.* Translated by Lama Karma Sumdhon Paul and Lama Lobzang Mingyur Dorje in *The Tibetan Book of the Great Liberation,* ed. W. Y. Evans-Wentz. London, Oxford and New York: Oxford University Press, 1954.

Yogic text on "the method of realizing *nirvāṇa* through knowing the mind."

———. *Bar-do Thos-grol* (*Bardo Thödol*). Translated by Lama Kazi Dawa-Samdup as *The Tibetan Book of the Dead.* ed., W. Y. Evans-Wentz. 2d. ed. London, Oxford and New York: Oxford University Press, 1957; also translated by Trungpa and Fremantle as *Tibetan Book of the Dead.* Berkeley: Shambhala, 1975.

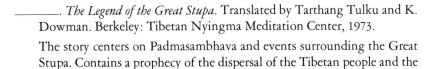

A guide to the realm of consciousness encountered between death and re-birth.

Pha-dham-pa Sangs-rgyas. *Pha-dham-pa Sangs-rgyas kyis Zhal-dgams dhing-ri brgya-rtsa-ma*. Translated by Lama Kazi Dawa-Samdup in *The Tibetan Book of the Great Liberation*. ed., W. Y. Evans-Wentz, London, Oxford and New York: Oxford University Press, 1954.

The final teachings of the rNying-ma Lama Phadampa Sangay (11th century).

Klong-chen-rab-'byams-pa (Longchenpa). *Ngal-gso skor-gsum*. Translated by H. V. Guenther as *Kindly Bent to Ease Us*. 3 vols. Emeryville: Dharma Publishing, 1975–77.

A thorough presentation of the Buddhist path and the nature of experience from the rDzogs-chen view of the rNying-ma school, by the foremost lama of the tradition.

———. *Sems-nyid rang-grol*. Translated by H. V. Guenther as "The Natural Freedom of Mind," *Crystal Mirror* 4 (1975): 113–146.

The first work in a trilogy by Longchenpa which presents the rDzogs-chen teaching on the nature of Mind-as-such.

Mi-pham 'Jam-dbyangs rNam-gyal rgya-mtsho (Lama Mipham). *Sems-kyi dpyod-pa rnam-par sbyong-ba so-sor brtag-pa'i dpyad sgom 'khor-lo-ma zhes*. Translated by Tarthang Tulku as "The Wheel of Analytic Meditation" in *Calm and Clear*. Emeryville, Dharma Publishing, 1973.

A practical introduction to meditation by an outstanding nineteenth century rNying-ma lama. Begins with a systematic analysis of an object of desire.

———. *Yid-bzhin-mdzod-kyi grub-mtha' bsdus-pa*. Translated by H. V. Guenther in *Buddhist Philosophy in Theory and Practice*. Boulder and London: Shambhala, 1976.

Mipham's summary of the Buddhist philosophical systems according to the four major traditions: Vaibhāṣika, Sautrāntika, Yogācāra, and Mādhyamika.

———. *dbU-ma'i lta khrid zab-mo bzhugs-so*. Translated by Tarthang Tulku as "Instructions on Vision in the Middle Way," in *Calm and Clear*. Emeryville: Dharma Publishing, 1973.

A guide to the later stages of meditation.

———. *bShes-spring-gi mchan-'grel padma-dkar-po'i phreng-ba*. Translated by L. Kawamura in *Golden Zephyr*. Emeryville: Dharma Publishing, 1975.

Mipham's commentary on Nāgārjuna's "Letter to a Friend."

———. *Mind is the Root.* Translated by H. V. Guenther in *Crystal Mirror* 3 (1974): 3–6.

A short account of mind, pristine awareness, and the world of objects.

———. *A Look into the Sky-like Mirror.* Translated by H. V. Guenther in *Crystal Mirror* 3 (1974): 41–44.

A short but precise summary of the rDzogs-chen philosophy.

bKa'-brgyud-pa

lHa'i-btsun-pa Rin-chen-rnam-rgyal. *The Life and Teaching of Nāropa.* Translated by H. V. Guenther, London, Oxford and New York: Oxford University Press, 1963.

An account of the inner development of an important scholar-saint of this lineage. Includes a philosophical commentary by the translator.

Mi-la-ras-pa/gTsan sMyon Heruka. *Mi-la-ras-pa'i mgur-hbum.* Translated by Garma C. C. Chang. *The Hundred Thousand Songs of Milarepa.* 2 vols. New Hyde Park, N.Y.: University Books, 1962; an abridged edition of Chang's translation published under the same title, New York, Evanston and London: Harper and Row, 1970; some of the songs are also translated by Lama Kazi Dawa-Samdup in *Tibet's Great Yogi Milarepa.* ed. W. Y. Evans-Wentz. London, Oxford and New York: Oxford University Press, 1951 (2d. ed.)

Songs by one of the world's great poet-saints.

gTsang sMyong Heruka. *Mi-la bka'-'bum (or Nam thar).* Translated by J. Bacot. *Milarepa, ses méfaits, ses épreuves, son illumination.* Documents Spirituels, vol. 5, Paris: Fayard, 1971; translated by Lama Kazi Dawa-Samdup in *Tibet's Great Yogi Milarepa.* ed., W. Y. Evans-Wentz, London, Oxford and New York: Oxford University Press, 1951 (2d ed.); translated by Lobsang Lhallungpa as *The Life of Milarepa.* New York: E. P. Dutton, 1977.

The fascinating biography of a central figure of the bKa'-brgyud-pa lineage.

———. *La Vie de Marpa.* Excerpts translated by J. Bacot, Paris: Librairie Orientaliste, Paul Geuthner, 1937.

Biography of Marpa, the disciple of Nāropa and the guru of Milarepa.

Dvags-po lHa-rje (sGam-po-pa). *Jewel Ornament of Liberation.* Translated by H. V. Guenther. Berkeley: Shambhala, 1971.

A work by one of Milarepa's foremost disciples aimed at guiding students from the elementary tenets of Buddhism to the realization of Buddhahood.

Tibetan Yoga and the Secret Doctrines. Edited by W. Y. Evans-Wentz, London, Oxford and New York: Oxford University Press, 1958 (2d. ed.)

A collection of seven yogic texts translated by Lama Kazi Dawa-Samdup. Contains works by sGampopa, mPadma dKarpo and other bKa'-brgyud-pa teachers on Mahāmudrā, the Six Yogas of Nāropa, the Yoga of Consciousness Transference, etc.

Geshe Rabten. *The Preliminary Practices.* Translated by Consar Tulku, Burton, Wash.: Tusum Ling Publications, 1974.

An oral teaching based on a text by Padma Karpo. Discusses human birth, impermanence, karma, and preliminary practices.

'Jam-mgon Kong-sprul Blo-gro-mtha'-yas (Jamgon Kongtrul). *Nges-don sgron-me.* Translated as *The Torch of Certainty* by Judith Hanson. Boulder: Shambhala, 1977.

A practice-oriented text which explains the "Four Foundations" according to the bKa'-brgyud view.

Sa-skya-pa

Kun-dga' rGyal-mtshan dPal-bzang-po (Sa-skya Paṇḍita). *Legs-bsad rin-po-che'i gter.* Translated in *Elegant Sayings* as "A Precious Treasury of Elegant Sayings," Emeryville: Dharma Publishing, 1977; also translated by J. E. Bosson as *A Treasury of Aphoristic Jewels.* Indiana University Publications, Uralic and Altaic Series, vol. 92, Bloomington: Indiana University, 1969.

A collection of practical instructions for pursuing the Buddhist path.

dGe-lugs-pa

mKhas-grub-rje. *rGyud sde spyi'rnam-par gzhag-pa rgyas-par brjod.* Translated by F. Lessing and A. Wayman as *Fundamentals of the Buddhist Tantras.* Indo-Iranian monographs, vol. 3, The Hague, Paris: Mouton, 1968.

Discusses the four division of the Tantras and the subjects to be mastered in preparation for them.

Konchog Tänpa Dönmé. *Nor-bu'i gling-du-ba sgrod-pa'i lam-yig.* Translated by Olschak and Wangyal as *Guide to the Jewel Island.* Zürich: Buddhist Publications, 1973.

Advice on meditation, concentration, and the study of tantric texts. English and German.

Ye-shes rGyal-mtshan. *Sems dang sems-byung-gi tshul gsal-par ston-pa blo-gsal-mgul-rgyan.* Translated by H. V. Guenther and L. Kawamura in *Mind in Buddhist Psychology.* Emeryville: Dharma Publishing, 1975.

An Abhidharma text, this work systematically studies mind and mental events as a foundation for self-understanding.

dKon-mchog 'Jigs-med-dbang-po. *Grub-pa'i mtha'i rnam-par bzhag-pa rin-po-che'i phreng-ba.* Translated by H. V. Guenther as 'The Jewel Garland' in *Buddhist Philosophy in Theory and Practice.* Boulder and London: Shambhala, 1976; translated by L. Sopa and J. Hopkins as "Precious Garland of Tenets" in *Practice and Theory of Tibetan Buddhism.* New York: Grove Press, 1976.

A systematic presentation of the schools of Buddhist philosophy and a summary of their tenets.

Blo-bzang-dpal-ldan-bstan-pa'i-nyi-ma. *gSung-rab kun-gyi sning-po lam-gyi gtso-bo rnam-pa gsum-gyi khrid-yig gzhan phan sning-po.* Translated by L. Sopa and J. Hopkins as "Instructions on the Three Principal Aspects of the Path to Highest Enlightenment, Essence of All the Scriptures, Quintessence of Helping Others" in *Practice and Theory of Tibetan Buddhism.* New York: Grove Press, 1976.

A practical meditiation manual by the Fourth Panchen Lama.

Guenther, H. V. *Treasures on the Tibetan Middle Way.* Berkeley: Shambhala, 1969.

A long philosophical introduction to Tibetan Buddhism by Prof. Guenther, followed by the translations of four concise but comprehensive dGe-lugs-pa texts.

Index

Tarthang Tulku Rinpoche, founder
of Nyingma in the West.